The Afterlives of the *Bhagavad Gītā*

The Afterlives of the *Bhagavad Gītā*

Readings in Translation

DOROTHY M. FIGUEIRA

OXFORD
UNIVERSITY PRESS

OXFORD
UNIVERSITY PRESS

Great Clarendon Street, Oxford, ox2 6dp,
United Kingdom

Oxford University Press is a department of the University of Oxford.
It furthers the University's objective of excellence in research, scholarship,
and education by publishing worldwide. Oxford is a registered trade mark of
Oxford University Press in the UK and in certain other countries

First Edition published in 2023

Published in the United States of America by Oxford University Press
198 Madison Avenue, New York, NY 10016, United States of America

British Library Cataloguing in Publication Data

Data available

Library of Congress Control Number: 2022951836

ISBN 978–0–19–887348–8

DOI: 10.1093/oso/9780198873488.001.0001

Contents

Introduction 1

PART I THE [IM]POSSIBILITY OF TRANSLATION: CAN WE TRANSLATE THE OTHER?

1. Translation Theories 13
2. Translation and Mystification: Wilkins 31
3. European Linguists, Philosophers, and Intellectual Rabble-Rousers 48
   A.W. Schlegel and W. von Humboldt 51
   Hegel 58
   Cousin 69
   Conclusion 75

PART II TRANSLATING COMMENSURABILITY, CLASS, AND CASTE

4. *Brahman* as the Cosmic Translator and the *Gītā*'s Potentiality in American Transcendentalism 85
   Introduction 85
   Emerson 87
   Thoreau 95
   Whitman 103
   Conclusion 110
5. Nationalism, Sedition, and Mysticism 113
   Vivekananda 114
   Tilak 120
   Sri Aurobindo 137

PART III THE DEFEAT OF TRANSLATION AND THE END OF CRITICISM

6. Gandhi's Convenient Text 149
Introduction 149
Allegory and Experience 155
Gandhi as an Interpreter and his Theory of Translation 158

7. Ambedkar's Counter-Revolutionary *Gītā*: Historical and Political Context 174
Ambedkar on the *Gītā* 183
The Annihilation of Caste (1936) 191

PART IV THE WESTERN WARTIME, COUNTERCULTURAL, AND NEO-LIBERAL *GĪTĀ*

8. The Nazi *Kṣatriya* Ethos 203
Introduction 203
Indologists 206
Hauer 211
Himmler 222
Conclusion 228

9. Is This What Krishna Meant? 230
T.S. Eliot 231
J. Robert Oppenheimer 246

10. What Becomes of *Dharma* in a Conquered Country? 259
Simone Weil 260
Savitri Devi 286

11. The Beats, the Monk, and Multicultural Artists 301
Introduction 301
The Countercultural *Gītā* 303
Operatic Gītās 312
Conclusion 333

Epilogue 337
Bibliography 345
Author Biography 369
Index 371

Introduction

In recent years, scholars have speculated on the degree to which Asian religions are modern creations of the West.[1] The construction of Hinduism, in particular, has garnered considerable attention, in part due to the popularity of postcolonial studies. Many of the arguments purporting to show that Hinduism was a product of colonial discursive strategies dovetail nicely with anti-essentialist visions of historiography. A number of scholars have specifically examined the reception of the *Bhagavad Gītā* with a view to how it 'defined' Hinduism, acknowledging how its translations and interpretations coloured the understanding of Indian religion in given periods and among different populations. Indeed, the *Gītā* was a 'politically useful text' (Sawhney 88). British imperialism's role in the construction of Hinduism (Halbfass 1989; Ludden 1993; Israel 2014), the classification of Hinduism as a coherent system of practices (Staal 1989, Jackson 1996), and the missionary activities all figure in the reception of the *Gītā* (Sharpe 1985; Davis 2015).[2] This present volume does not seek to replicate this valuable research. It also parts company from postcolonial theory's one-sided influence stream in that it investigates the reception of the *Gītā* by Indians and Westerners alike, a topic that has also been extensively analysed (Minor 1986; Robinson 2006; Gowda 2011, to name but a few), primarily from an historical perspective. This study, in contrast, focuses on how translation, as a site of textual analysis, along with

[1] See, for example, studies of Confucianism as a Jesuit construction (Jenson 1995).

[2] For a summary of this discussion, see Robinson (5–9). Given this wealth of scholarship, I will not in this study examine the issue of authorship (Feuerstein 1983: 41; Edgerton 1972: 107), dating (Radhakrishnan 1989a: 14; van Buitenen 1981: 5; Zaehner 1976: 7), or its place with respect to or relationship with the *Mahābhārata* (Edgerton 1972: 105–6; van Buitenen 1981: 5; Zaehner 1976: 7). I also do not look at its syncretism (Feuerstein 1983: 39; Johnson 1937: 6–7); its association with *śruti* literature (Coburn 1984:448–9); or its role in effacing the distinction between *śruti* and *smṛti* (Bharati 1971: 84–5). It is of note that, when I was reading the *Mahābhārata* as a student in Paris under Madeleine Biardeau, in her many year-long readings of the epic in her seminars at École Pratique des Hautes Études, she skipped the *Gītā* as not an originary part of the epic.

The Afterlives of the Bhagavad Gītā. Dorothy M. Figueira, Oxford University Press.
DOI: 10.1093/oso/9780198873488.003.0001

its theories and methodologies has informed the initial renditions and subsequent interpretations of the *Gītā*. Given the *Gītā's* status as the most translated religious text after the Bible, an analysis of its reception in light of translation theory is, perhaps, overdue.[3] Translations are not neutral, nor is their utilization; they present issues that are largely overlooked in historiographical analyses of the *Gītā*'s reception.

The work of Kees Bolle (1979) and J.A.B. van Buitenen (1981) first acknowledged the important role translation played in the general reception of the *Gītā*. Bolle and van Buitenen recognized the tendency to disregard earlier meanings of terms in translations from Sanskrit. These Indologists pointed out how, for example, the focus of *karma* as action, in both Western and Indian nationalist translations alike, moved meaning away from the understanding of *karma* as rites or rituals to the individual translator's predilection for an anti-ritualistic and devotional reading (Eder 38). They also acknowledged the importance of examining translational aims as well as the methods and theories underlying their practice. This present volume begins with this recognition and examines in greater depth and comparatively how the translations of the *Gītā* did not seek the same aims in all places and at all times nor were translation theories and methodologies uniform across nations and eras.[4] In a number of instances, translation entails a flattening out of the vocabulary. It also can involve a false continuity between pre-modern commentaries and modern discussions of the text.[5] Van Buitenen highlighted the fixed-equivalent translation strategy—words and the varied meanings of single words. He looked at the breakdown between the host and the guest language (van Buitenen 1973: xxxv–xliii), a translation concern emphasized also by translation theorists outlined in Chapter 1 and appearing throughout the *Gītā*'s reception. At one pole we find that consistency with fixed equivalents in the guest language allows one to build on philological analysis and textual specificity. At the other pole of translation practice, we discover the translation's intent (dynamic equivalence) to give the appearance of

[3] The issue of translation, its practices, justifications, and ethics are fascinating concerns, perhaps even more pressing in our present era when we are increasingly moving toward the reading of the world in translation as a preferred mode of understanding. I am thinking here of the recent trend in literary studies, World Literature.

[4] For an earlier study of national translation traditions, see Figueira 1991.

[5] See Eder 88, cited in Palshikar 10.

modern relevance (Eder 33). These two poles of translation, their contrast and tension delimit the sinewy paths of the *Gītā*'s reception. Our analysis grapples with these very issues of translational non-neutrality, distortion, and the afterlife of distortion, the text's shadow book.

'Transnational' (what we comparatists simply call 'comparative')[6] surveys and histories of the *Gītā*'s translations and reception reflect how a range of *Gītā* interpretations in modern times deviates from this text's historical commentatorial readings (Sinha 297). In nineteenth-century India, discussions of the *Gītā* by literary figures and political leaders often manipulated or systematically disregarded the earlier commentaries found in the tradition of darshanic (philosophical) commentaries on the text in order to present it as an authentic source of statecraft. Whether by stealth or openly, this 'management' of the text often resulted in neutralizing the intellectual hiatus between the ancient and the modern (Palshikar 18). By breaking with the Indian exegetical tradition, such translations enabled Indians to rethink politics in a new language of action. In this manner, the *Gītā* 'gave rise to a sort of nationalist seminar, providing a frame for wide-ranging debates about violence, resistance, duty, caste and indeed the very activity of approaching traditional religious texts' (Sawhney 87). The recuperation of nationality under colonialism invariably entailed a process of ego deformation (Nandy 85–100), and the translations of the *Gītā* played a significant role in this process. Once it was read outside the exegetical context, the *Gītā* could more easily travel beyond its geographical home.

There are some traits specific to the *Gītā* that impact on its reception, such as the heterogeneity of its narrative, suggesting the degree to which it combines older sections with later interpolations (Larson 659) and the text's attempt to reconcile philosophies (Sāṃkhya[7] and Yoga[8]) with the

[6] Sinha's (2010) notion of this reception as a transnational process of intercultural dialogue reveals nothing more than what I would just call a comparative approach that examines the cleavage between textual and contextual studies. Such a format is interdisciplinary; Indology connects to the humanities, and anthropology connects to religious communities, and hence to the social sciences. Comparative literature in the past has been the locus of such intercultural and interdisciplinary analyses.

[7] Sāṃkhya, one of the six schools of Indian philosophy, is dualistic in nature, with the universe consisting of two independent realities, *puruṣa* (consciousness) and *prakṛti* (matter). It promotes a theory of the *guṇas*, three modes of matter—*sattva* (harmony), *rajas* (chaos), and *tamas* (dullness).

[8] Yoga, one of the six schools of Indian philosophy, differs from Sāṃkhya, its views on ontology of *puruṣa*, and its soteriology.

devotional practices associated with the rise of the *bhakti* (devotional) tradition (Sinha 298). Throughout its commentary history, the *Gītā* has been treated as semi-doctrinal (van Buitenen 1962: 7–8)[9] but not necessarily as orthodox, since it presented anti-Vedic sarcasm (2.42–4) and suggested some very subversive theories, such as the possibility that *mokṣa* (liberation) was attainable by women, *vaiśyas* (merchant caste) and *śūdras* (labourers) (9.32). Although the *Gītā* never presented traditional orthopraxis (Larson 661), it was nevertheless prized as Vedāntic[10] (the end of the Veda), and subject to commentaries by philosophers such as the Advaitan (non-dualist) Śaṅkara (700 AD), the Viśiṣṭādvaitan (qualified non-dualist) Rāmānuja (1017–1137), and the Dvaitan (dualist) Madhva (1238–1317). It was also subject to a Śaivite reading by Abhinavagupta (950–1016) (*Bhagavadgītārthasaṃgraha*) (Robinson 10, 21–7, 57–9, 129–30, 213–15). These ancient commentators generally acknowledged that the *Gītā* presents an exposition of three paths to salvation: the *karma marg* (action or alternately ritual action), the *jñāna marg* (the path of knowledge), and *bhakti* (devotion).

What is particularly fascinating about the *Gītā* is that, given its promulgation of a rather clear (albeit perhaps contradictory) message, it nevertheless invited the variety of interpretations that it has received throughout its reception history. D.D. Kosambi's observation that the *Gītā* had a superb inconsistency of lending itself to any ideological slant[11] gains credence time and again in the readings examined in this volume. Some modern commentators focused on the *Gītā*'s metaphysics, its literary history, or its role as epic. Others read specific themes into the text. M.K. Gandhi, for example, read the *Gītā* in the 1920s as promoting nonviolence (*ahiṃsā*). Bal Gangadhar Tilak urged a reading of the *Gītā* to promote immediate political action in the world. Then, there were those in the extremist nationalist camp, such as V.D. Savarkar, who sought in their reading of the *Gītā* justification not just for action, but for the use

[9] The *Gītā* is deemed *smarta* (remembered/traditional) rather than *śrauta* (heard/revealed), although it has been treated as distinct from *smṛti* by commentaries as early as the ninth century.

[10] Vedānta, one of the six schools of Indian philosophy, refers to ideas that can be found in the *Upanishads*, the *Brahma Sūtra*, and the *Bhagavad Gītā*.

[11] See D.D. Kosambi (1965: 114–5) about the synthetic quality of the *Gītā*.

of violent means in order to gain self-rule.[12] The logic here entailed an understanding of an economy of violence. In the case of the extremists, it was thought that the wise investment of violence in the present could diminish the need for violence in the future.[13]

It was in this vein that one of the assassins of the British civil servant, W.C. Reed,[14] Damodar Chapekar,[15] took a copy of the *Gītā* with him to his execution, as would others (Varma 247). In fact, during the fight for self-rule, if you were found to have more than one copy of the *Gītā* in your possession, the British authorities took you for a revolutionary (Minor 223) and dealt with you accordingly.[16] For two generations before Independence, the *Gītā* was read to condone and even command action against what was seen by Indians as the illegitimacy of the British occupation (Klausen 184). In the 1920s the *Gītā* thus grew in stature, playing a significant role in Indian social and political activism. It became a requisite touchpoint for any Hindu leader, political or religious.

Both moderate and extremist Indian nationalists equated their understanding of political action with the *karma yoga* of the *Gītā*. In fact, the *yoga* of action was seen as the primary teaching of the *Gītā* in the modern period. The text could then be recast as promoting social change, as opposed to the equally viable perception that it taught the removal from worldly concerns in a quest for personal liberation. Nathuram Godse, the Hindu fundamentalist assassin of Gandhi, also took a copy of the *Gītā* with him to the gallows. In his case, the *Gītā* did not legitimize the murder of British colonial rulers, but rather his execution of the 'Mahātma' who was felt to have betrayed his fellow Hindus by his 'favoritism' toward the

[12] Gandhi held that Savarkar read the *Gītā* for spiritual justification for violent political action in the past (i.e. justifying Śivāji's killing of Afzal Khan) and the future (against the British colonizers) (Gandhi 1984: 37.82).

[13] This logic was not too different from that found in Communism under Stalin, as Arthur Koestler would subsequently describe it in *Darkness at Noon* (1940).

[14] W.C. Reed was a member of the Indian Civil Service Office who was charged as the Plague Commissioner in Maharashtra and who during Queen Victoria's Jubilee celebration was shot to death by the Chapekar brothers in retaliation for his insensitivity and polluting acts toward Hindus, and particularly Hindu women who under his orders had their honor and purity abused by searches made of their homes during the implementation of precautions to stem the plague's spread in Poona.

[15] Damodar Hari Chapekar (1870–98), along with his brothers Bal Krishna Hari (1873–99) and Vasudeo Hari (1878–99), planned the attack that also led to the death of another official.

[16] It is worth noting that the size of the *Gītā* contributed to this use. It was small enough to manage, could be sold cheaply and disseminated to a new reading class of Indians (Sharpe 76).

Muslims. We can see in Godse's act, perhaps, the most forceful rejection of Gandhi's reading of the *Gītā* as a text promoting non-violence, until, perhaps, December 1992, when prior to the razing of the Babri Mosque, there was a recitation of the *Gītā* by the militants assembled in Ayodhyā. When this recitation was completed, the leaders of the assembled nationalist groups who had gathered at the site announced that the Battle of Kurukshetra[17] was truly about to begin. They then razed the mosque and, in the days following the demolition, there ensued large-scale violence.[18]

In a collective volume of modern intellectual history that deals with the *Gītā* as an ethical text both in South Asian society as well as in its cultural outward journey into Western politics, the authors cite Slavoj Žižek (who seems to have an opinion about everything) and his claim that the *Gītā* represented the perfect philosophy for post-capitalist society (Kapila and Faisal 2010: 269). This contention is certainly open to debate. But one can support the belief that the *Gītā* played and continues to play a pivotal role in Indian nationalist fantasies, whether they are dreams of imperialism's violent overthrow or of redefining Indian secular democracy. It is significant that a number of the narratives presented in this volume explore Arjuna's dilemma of whether to fight and present the enemy as always a brother, friend, or teacher. Modern commentaries of the *Gītā* are often directed toward a future beyond the colonial state, to enemies other than the British—other brothers, friends. and teachers.

I approach the *Gītā* in this volume not from the vantage of history of religion or Indology, but rather as a comparatist whose literary analysis focuses on how translators and commentators choose to distance the text from its traditional interpretation and interpretive paradigms. Any text at a great remove from its traditional constituency engenders novel interpretations. An inquiry into the patterns and dynamics of unconventional readings might be foreign to religion scholars (Robinson 2006 and Sharpe 1985), but not so to the literary scholar versed in reception aesthetics. I am particularly interested in what we might term the *insolites* (out of the way) readings of the *Gītā* and how they seek to fill the hermeneutical gap between commentaries tied to its canonical and scriptural status and those interpretations distant from the text's tradition. We look

[17] The battle immortalized in the *Mahābhārata*.
[18] http://www.sabrang.com/cc/archive/2001/jan01/docu.htm/.

at the reception within a cross-cultural context, not merely as a linguistic problem nor just errors in the act of translation, but as having dimensions that are conceptual and cultural (Dhareshwar 257) as well as ethical.

The *Gītā* happens to be ambiguous enough to justify good, bad, and dangerous actions. Past and present readers, translators, and interpreters seek to reconcile these possible meanings.[19] But no such reconciliation is necessary if we accept (as we do here) that the *Gītā*'s seemingly ambiguous or contradictory messages concurrently serve different purposes. They can be used to reflect social imperatives, philosophy, and the interests of the masses as well as serve (more often than not) the concerns of some elite group. Throughout the history of its reception and at various stages of the evolution of this reception, we discover how select themes (Buddhism, violence, detachment, caste justification) become central to a given reading of the text. Yet, the text's ambiguity[20] continually introduces new venues for creative interpretation. Neither the content of the text nor its various interpretations ever hew together as a coherent body of ideas. The question ultimately becomes the following: What is the nature of its truth? Is it textual (even in translation) or religious?[21]

The contours of the initial reception of the *Gītā* open it to multiple and disparate readings. Perhaps the idea of interpretation (rather than reading) is useful here in addressing the theoretical and philosophical premises of this volume. What we might term an 'existential' condition of translation metaphorically speaks of exile, penetration, or fidelity. These views do not help us elucidate translation as a form of reception including a literary transaction. We may be better served by not viewing translation as limited to a linguistic act making some gesture towards culture, but rather interpret the activity of translation as a relation with alterity. My use of the term 'translation' borrows from André Lefevere's (1945–96) idea of

[19] B.R. Ambedkar summarizes the judgements of the *Gītā*. He cites Böhtlingk who saw it as contradictory, repetitious, and absurd; Hopkins who viewed it as illogical and ill-assorted; Telang who found it hard to reconcile its themes and harmonize them; and Műller who saw no original philosophy in it, just half-truths. Ambedkar himself found the *Gītā* bewildering (all cited in Ambedkar 2013: 357). Of modern Indologists, van Buitenen sees it as bringing together irreconcilable traditions (1981: 16) and A. Hiltebeitel sought to bridge the difference by delimiting the different periods of its production. David Gitomer sees the text as coming to terms with institutions like *kṣatriya*hood (Ambedkar 2013: 223).

[20] This ambiguity, while perhaps abetted by the text of the *Gītā*, can be found in any text and certainly in any translation that is contingent upon the movement from one culture to another. It is not a situation that is unique to the *Gītā*.

[21] Kumar (2015: 151) poses a similar question.

translation as a refraction or rewriting, since not all the texts examined in these pages are translations in the literal sense. Some are 'translations' in the metaphorical sense, what the field of Translation Studies terms 'cultural translation'.

To paraphrase Vivekananda, who once reportedly said that if you lost your cow, you could probably find it in the *Vedas*, so too it appears that many ideas can be found in the *Gītā*. It lends itself to such a variety of interpretations. None of these interpretations are misreadings, since flaws in translations are not necessarily linguistic, but also cultural. Moreover, I do not assume any idea of some pregiven, correct reading of the *Gītā*, since there are no fixed, given, or clear readings of any text. I wish merely to show the variety of interpretations available. The *Gītā* could be used to proselytize a reformed or Christianized Hinduism. It served Western questers as a propitious exotic model, an *imaginaire* created in order to work through the convoluted tension between the familiar and the fanciful. Like the exotic in general, the *Gītā* provides an alibi (an 'elsewhere') to reject the Other, reify the Self, promote false constructs, and explore darker purlieus of being.[22] It provided a good reading for Americans like Ralph Waldo Emerson in their rebellion against the confines of evangelical Christianity. It could also be enlisted to support racialist arguments as well as offer a mystical worldview. It became, to cite William Douglas Hill in his 1928 translation 'the playground of Western pseudo-mystics' who in the 1880s–90s produced 'theosophical versions' of the text (cited in Eder 33). In the period of the two World Wars, the *Gītā*'s setting on the battlefield elicited considerable commentary. Certain European Christian readers saw in it a platform for an 'aryanizing' anti-clericism (Sharpe 39–46). For other Westerners, particularly those caught up in the Second World War, the *Gītā* provided inspiration in its call to duty or its justification for violence. In the late twentieth century, it was adopted by Western ecumenical thinkers as well as counter-cultural poets and artists. Throughout this reception history, the *Gītā* consistently provided fertile ground for developing philosophical ideas and formulating theories on language, literature, and revolution. Finally, countercultural America with its Indomania, nurtured by touristic forays eastward and

[22] For a discussion of the exotic, see Figueira 1991, 1994, 2002.

often paralleling nineteenth-century Orientalist imaginings, reinterpreted the *Gītā* for self-consciously 'alternative' audiences.

To guide us in our understanding of the significant role the *Gītā* played in the development of both Indian and Western thought, we begin with an analysis of some of the key issues involved in translation theory. With the Charles Wilkins translation (1785), the *Gītā* leaves the orbit that it had occupied for centuries. Wilkins's translation would have tremendous bearing on how Orientalist and subsequent scholars would 'rewrite' the *Gītā*, particularly in the context of the secularization of knowledge from colonial times onward. The *Gītā*'s discovery in the West at the hands of European philosophers, bureaucrats, and Sanskritists called into question the very possibilities of translation and cultural commensurability. Theories of translation and the issue of translatability directly impacted on the *Gītā's* initial reception. They reflected the differing relationships between the source and the target cultures which are never uniform. After examining the initial translations of the *Gītā*, we quickly move onto interpretations of the text as its translations expand imaginatively. Both translation and interpretation are textual processes sharing some common aspirations, such as purity, possibility, ambiguity, and fidelity. Both depend on linguistic activity centred on the location of their creator. Both involve a dialectic of self-reflection derived from a specific concept of the Self, involving the self-estrangement of the subject in the object, a movement that culminates, according to G.W.F. Hegel (1770–1831), in the folding back into the subject. Hegel's phenomenology here is the source not only of this hermeneutical model, but also of imperialist historiography that colonizes the Other. By projecting oneself through some perceived Other, one rethinks the Self in order to expand one's cultural boundaries (Figueira 1994: 12–13). As Hans-Georg Gadamer (1900–2002) would claim in *Truth and Method* (1960), one recognizes one's own in what one considers Other, becomes at home in it in order to return to oneself from being otherwise (Gadamer 1960: 11). I approach the translations and interpretations examined in these pages through this optic, what Paul Ricoeur (1913–2005) refers to as the circular structure of hermeneutical understanding (Ricoeur 1969: 16–17), where the spirit of our translators, commentators, and interpreters moves to the unfamiliar in the *Gītā* and makes it their own. This process is often an autobiographical exercise, an interested and intentional interpretation that is both historical and contextual. The following analyses seek to chart the various journeys that the *Gītā* has inspired.

Part I deals with translation theory and the initial Western translations of the *Gītā*. Part II visits the issue of commensurability introduced in Part I. It also examines how the themes of class and caste are imbricated in the next generation of the *Gītā's* reception. With the exception of Tilak, the authors examined in Part II engage in interpretations rather than translations per se. But many of the issues raised by various translation theorists introduced in Chapter 1 will have bearing on these interpretations. The *Gītā*'s reception among the American Transcendentalists and Indian nationalists establishes elitist and mystical exoticism that resurfaces throughout subsequent Indian and Western readings. Part III returns to the issue of translation. In the case of Gandhi, we look at translation over and against interpretation. If the truth is known within us, then there is no need to follow the letter of the text. With Gandhi's commentaries on the *Gītā*, we encounter the defeat of translation and, as B.R. Ambedkar would put it, the end of criticism. Part IV examines the emplotment of the *Gītā* within nineteenth- and twentieth-century German Indology and the cooptation of this scholarship by National Socialism. We then look at the appropriation of the *Gītā* in the reformulation of wartime behaviour in French and American literary, political, and artistic production. After serving the aims of modernist exotic mysticism and wartime propaganda, the *Gītā* reaches a figurative extension on the postmodern operatic stage where, in the case of Philip Glass's *Satyagraha*, translation concerns are no longer at issue, and interpretation is ultimately a form of performance, at times more hysterical and histrionic than others.

PART I

THE [IM]POSSIBILITY OF TRANSLATION

Can We Translate the Other?

Part I announces the scope of the project as an examination of the reception of this Sanskrit text in both India and in the West. It will investigate how theories and methodologies of translation inform readings. It investigates the centrality of translation in the reception of this particular text.

1
Translation Theories

> Translation is readily seen as investing the foreign language text within domestic significance [. . .] Translation never communicates in an untroubled fashion because the translator negotiates the linguistic and cultural differences of the foreign text by reducing them and supplying another set of differences basically domestic, drawn from the receiving language and culture to enable the foreign to be received here. The foreign text, then, is not so much communicated as inscribed with domestic intelligibilities and interests. (Venuti 2000: 468–87)

Translation involves a reading of otherness in the Self and serves as a means for highlighting the otherness of the Other.[1] There are significant issues that are raised when we look at translation in general and particularly when we investigate the translations of the *Bhagavad Gītā* specifically. The *Gītā*, although often translated, is rarely considered in studies of translation. Its aesthetic or practical relevance within transnational commentarial exegesis has received little, if any, attention. The fact that the interpretation of the *Gītā* significantly relies on commentaries to interpret the text is troublesome for the translator and has invited misinterpretation (Eder 24–6). This chapter examines some of the theories and methodologies that inform Western translations and asks a more general question regarding translation in general: How much transformation can a text undergo in translation before it is no longer itself? This question strikes at the very heart of translation theory, articulated

[1] In this study of the *Gītā* translations and interpretations, this Other moves about, representing such varied entities as the Aryan, the Untouchable, and the Jew. For the purposes of this study, the Other is a site of alterity distinct from the translator's or the interpreter's own positionality.

The Afterlives of the Bhagavad Gītā. Dorothy M. Figueira, Oxford University Press. © Dorothy M. Figueira 2023.
DOI: 10.1093/oso/9780198873488.003.0002

initially in J.W. von Goethe's (1749–1832) vision of translation as metempsychosis and more recently by Walter Benjamin's (1892–1940) concept of translation as an afterlife, and Paul Ricoeur's conceptualization of it as transmigration.

Translation always brings a text into confrontation with what inspired it. There are several points we want to review in this initial discussion of the parameters of translation. They include loss and gain, national traditions in translation, translation as a creative and generative endeavour, and the relationship between interpretation and translation, as well as the status of supplemental materials to a translation. The ethics of translation are also an issue. Are translations possible or impossible endeavours? Can we talk of translating a text without knowing its source language? These issues and questions are not new to discussions on translation, and we raise them here primarily to offer a template and a vocabulary for our subsequent discussion of the *Gītā*'s translations and reception.

Lawrence Venuti, a prominent recent theorist on translation, envisioned the history of translation as a set of changing relationships between a translated text's relative autonomy and two other categories: equivalence (accuracy, adequacy, correctness, correspondence, fidelity, identity) and function (potentiality to release diverse effects, beginning with the communication of information and the production of a response comparable to that produced by the source in its own culture) (5). This issue of equivalence was first introduced by Jerome (345–420), the translator of the Hebrew Bible,[2] in his letter 'To Pammachius on the Best Method of Translating', where he made the case for aiming in translation for 'sense by sense, oneness of spirit'. Jerome was alluding to what would become a major concern in translation: Does one run the risk of being accused of falsification, if one does not produce a word-for-word translation? Jerome wanted us to 'render sense for sense and not word for word'. It is only in this manner that the reader can attain 'oneness of spirit' with the translated text and its culture (Jerome 21–30). The translator's language must adapt to the author's language, thus rendering the translation different from mere interpretation. Jerome maintained that when a translation ceases to give a word-for-word rendition, it becomes more of

[2] Jerome is the patron saint of translators.

an interpretation and, in the case of scripture, this process entails changing God's word. Such a rendition is not only problematic, but, according to Jerome, criminal. So, when the Bible was subsequently translated into German in 1522, Martin Luther (1483–1546) held to fidelity:

> Ah, translating is not everyman's skill as medieval saints imagine. It requires a right, honest, God-fearing, Christian, trained, informed, and experienced heart. Therefore, I hold that no false Christian or factitious spirit can be a decent translator. (Luther, cited in Berman 1992: 31)

Luther introduced here the important concept of good faith. By translating the Bible into German (and not Latin), Luther sought to bring the Word to the community of believers. In the process, his translation became the catalyst for the formulation and development of a national culture by crystalizing what would become the German language. Translation now became a tool for democratization, as it would many years later in India. Through the act of translation, one initiated an intensive relationship to the Other because the very thought of what is one's own is directly connected to the Other and the foreign. The relations one has to others thus have a quasi-ontological implication. The strangeness of the world becomes reflected in our mirror (Berman 1992: 32–45). We are as much a mystery to ourselves as the world without appears to us.

Between the initially hostile polarities of the Self and the Other, translation raised the issue that perhaps efforts must be made to reconcile the two and make them one, whether through the dialectical process of reconciling opposites formulated by G.W.F. Hegel or through the concept of thesis and synthesis found in J.G. Fichte (1762–1814). The Romantics, inspired by the Enlightenment experience of inner alterity, developed the hermeneutic understanding that it is through the Other that the spirit can and needs to remember itself and return to itself (Berman 1992: 45–46). Translation becomes, therefore, a dignified task. It not only contributes to the contours of the nation and its literature, but also to our understanding of the Self. German literature, particularly its poetry, was tremendously indebted to the foreign for its forms and models (Figueira 1990). Goethe, who believed that translation belongs authentically to the formation of a national literature, defined translation as threefold:

1. The prose translation neutralizes the formal characteristics of any sort of poetic art. It is simplistic, offering a word-by-word rendition that uplifts and acquaints us with the foreign in our own terms.
2. The parodistic appropriates the foreign by adaption and substitution ('grown in their own soil').
3. The third kind of translation, the highest, attempts to achieve perfect identity with the original, by replacing it with an identical translated text. With such a translation, the source text is no longer even needed.

For Goethe, translation becomes a metempsychosis. It enables the encounter with the foreign. Through this confrontation, translation makes us understand our Self: 'The captivation of oneself no longer passes merely through the captivation of the foreign, but through the captivation by the foreign of oneself' (Goethe 1819, cited in Berman 1992: 64–5).

This understanding of translation was intimately connected to the German concept of *Bildung* (formation), conceived as the development of the mind effected through a movement toward the Other. *Bildung* consists of the gradual passage of the individual from an infertile closure upon itself to a living interaction. Translation exemplifies this encounter. It allows us to move away from closed circles toward the universal. In fact, it seeks a unification of all cultural circles (Berman 1992: 58–62). *Bildung* also demands a movement toward the Other that is significantly not German. It recognizes that there is something within this Other from which the Self can gain, grow, and be edified.

For the Germans (and they did a lot of theorizing about translation and translating), translation completes the work of the text. It 'accomplishes the work, pushes it beyond itself' (Berman 1992: 127). *Bildung* is, therefore, a return to the Self through the Other. As Wilhelm von Humboldt (1767–1835) would put it, one must feel the foreignness of the Other, but not its strangeness. The process of translation makes the foreign near, but also makes the near, foreign and distant. *Bildung* represents the interaction between the Self and the foreign that enables the potential of the Self to develop, and this process primarily takes place through translation. Translating effects an *Erweiterung*, an expansion, and a mode of unfolding. *Bildung* functions as self-formation through the experience of alterity, with its culmination in reunion and identity.

The foreign thus has a mediating function when translation works as an agent of *Bildung* (Humboldt, cited in Berman 1992: 43–7). The process is structured in a threefold manner: there is the *Urbild* (original, archetype), then the *Vorbild* (model as the exemplification of the *Urbild*), and finally the *Nachbild* (reproduction).[3] Because *Bildung* as intimately connected to translation goes toward the foreign Other so that it might eventually return to its point of departure, it stands in opposition to the law of appropriation. One can never have the experience of the foreign simply by an annexation or reduction of the Other to the Same. This is not an encounter with the Other, although it often pretends to be. Reading in the language of the hegemon, does not necessarily dehegemonize; quite often the contrary occurs. Similarly attempts at decolonizing at times result in colonization (Humboldt 1841).[4]

It was the Jena Romantics and their efforts with the *Athenaeum* who spearheaded a revolution in translation theory and literary criticism. Friedrich Schlegel (1772–1829) developed the concept of translation as the reflection of some absent, desired, or potential work. He likened translation to dialogue, literary letter, or fragment, in that they all make constant reference to some absent Other embedded in the translation's relationship to the original. According to F. Schlegel, a translation has a profound and nostalgic relation to its original. It shares an intimacy of form and belongs to the space of the work, although it is equally outside it. The translation grasps the essence of the work (F. Schlegel, cited in Berman 1992: 72). In fact, F. Schlegel believed that everything is a translation, either as a conflation or as an 'infinitisation'. What could be interpreted as a negative aspect of translation became, for the *Athenaeum*, its poetic positivity (F. Schlegel 1965: 64, cited in Berman 100). As F. Schlegel would put it: 'The essence of spirit is to determine itself and, in a perpetual alternation, to go outside of itself and return to itself' (Schlegel 83, cited in Berman 47). F. Schlegel also noted that '[w]ithout delimitation, no *Bildung* is possible' (F. Schlegel 77, cited in Berman

[3] Such a vision of inevitable imitation was developed particularly by J.J. Winckelmann (1717–58), the Hellenist and art historian for whom the Greek *Urbild* became the *Vorbild* for Germans (Berman 49). We might compare this tripartite system to that formulated by Paul Ricoeur in *Time and Narrative* (1983).

[4] This is the very issue that the present author has with the democratizing claims of World Literature as it is practised in the US and postcolonial criticism in general.

1992: 48). For Enlightenment Germans, classical antiquity had been the first delimitation with Greece as the *Urbild* of culture. Beginning with the Romantics, however, the Orient and particularly India became another model (Figueira 1989; Berman 51), as F. Schlegel was prescient enough to announce in the *Athenaeum*. In *The Experience of the Foreign* (1992), Antoine Berman made the similar assessment regarding translation that I drew with reference to the exotic (Figueira 1994: 13) and to the reception of the *Gītā* that I propose in these pages: One's own seeks itself on its eccentric journeys (Berman 136).

The aggression and appropriation by translators of the German tradition were limited primarily because they saw translation as a creation, transmission, and expansion of their own language (Berman 27). Translation is no longer just a means to an end, but an end in itself; it was seen as doubled poetry, an ultra-literature. At this stage of the theorizing, there was no sense that translation entailed any loss. Quite the contrary. For the Germans, translation brought about an increase in the genius of a work, as one finds in the assessment by Novalis (Georg Philipp Friedrich Freiherr von Hardenberg) (1772–1801) that the German Shakespeare was better than the original precisely because it was a translation (Berman 106).

Novalis was not making a vain judgement here. According to German views on translation, the Schlegel–Tieck translation of Shakespeare[5] was better because it sought to mime (voluntarily vivify) and thus go beyond the original. In a letter to August Wilhelm Schlegel (1767–1845), Novalis wrote about how the Germans had a special *Trieb* (drive, urge) to translate. In this respect, they were like the Romans. This urge grew out of their concept of *Bildung*, their cosmopolitanism and individualism. It was only for the Germans that translation had become a form of expansion,[6] effected out of their love for the beautiful. According to Novalis, translation is literally *Bildung* and *Erweiterung* (Berman 105–8). He equated translation to the *Blüthenstaub* (the pollen of flowers) and, once again, it was threefold. There was the grammatical translation (equivalent to Goethe's prose translation) which rendered content. There was also mythical

[5] These famous translations by August Wilhelm Schlegel and Ludwig Tieck (1825) were considered by many Germans to be the original texts of the plays.

[6] For the difference between French and German translation traditions, see Figueira 1990.

translation, the highest form for which Novalis raises the original to the level of a symbol (as artistic representations of the Madonna) and finally transforming (*verändernd*) translations, which were potentiating and reproduced foreign individuality (113).[7] As J.G. von Herder (1744–1803) had expressed this sentiment, 'I walk through foreign gardens to pick flowers for my language' (Herder, cited in Berman 1992: 38). With the Schlegel brothers, the philological and the critical became closely entwined and were raised to the level of philosophy. One could no longer distinguish reading literature from translating literature and criticizing literature. But translation was seen as an *Über*-version of a work, its mystical or perfect realization (Berman 1992: 124). In contrast, for Friedrich Schleiermacher (1768–1834), translation could only produce an 'image' of a text.

Schleiermacher felt that translations incorporate the knowledge and taste of 'an amateur and connoisseur, a man who is well acquainted with the foreign language, yet to whom it remains nonetheless foreign' (Schleiermacher, cited in Venuti 44). In 'On the Different Methods of Translation', Schleiermacher maintained that the translator ends up either paraphrasing the text by adding restrictive and amplifying modifiers or imitating it to show its foreignness, but with different underpinnings (Venuti 48). The translator either moves the reader towards him (in an act of domestication) or leaves him in peace (foreignization). Schleiermacher opted for the latter goal, since for him translation functioned primarily as a cultural ambassador, expanding the readers' hearts and minds so they can experience as much 'pleasure in the writer as possible' (Venuti 49). The duty of the translator is to stay close to the original, so that the reader can connect 'with foreignness itself'. Schleiermacher envisioned this goal achieved through a word-by-word translation. For the reader to gain the desired knowledge of otherness, Schleiermacher believed that the text must still sound foreign. The two languages involved in a translation should not be made to appear as though they were equals, since that would be presumptuous. It would also be inauthentic, given that one cannot inhabit another language in the same spirit that one does one's

[7] Following in this tradition of threefold definitions, Berman also sees three types: grammatical, transforming (which reproduces and has potential to come close to the other and mythical), and the highest form, that raises the original to the state of a symbol.

own. Schleiermacher felt that the process of translation necessarily entails loss, and that this loss is rectified by making sacrifices in the process of rendering the foreign familiar to an audience. The task of the translator is, as Schleiermacher so felicitously put it, 'to unite all the jewels' (Venuti 62).

We are moving away from the understanding of translation as a uniquely fructifying endeavour, where a text reached its completion through translation, to concerns that there may be loss or even harm in the act of translating. The idea of the deleterious effects of translation, first voiced by Jerome, was foremost in the mind of Friedrich Nietzsche (1844–1900) who, as a classicist, understood just how the appropriation of things from the past through translation transforms them into conveying something relatable in the present. Nietzsche fully recognized how often translation is but a foreign conquest, where the translator omits what was historical, and makes it ahistorical to the original language. This process was exemplified in the custom of the translator's name even replacing that of the poet. Not only was the historicity and culture of a text lost, but the author's ownership was even erased.

Nietzsche's model for translation was that of the Romans towards the Greeks. They took from the Greeks what they wanted and then made it Roman for Roman purposes. According to Nietzsche, it was only with the modern moment that there even began the conscious recognition of the legitimacy of a culture and the emergence of a historical sense. Thus translation, while a noble endeavour, initially offered nations a chance to expand the boundaries of their empires, not only by conquering physically, but also by adapting foreign cultural artefacts to better fit their own national image (Nietzsche, in Venuti 67). While Nietzsche envisioned translation's paving over cultural markers of the original as a symptom of national expansion, he did not see this trait in a totally negative light.

As we move into the twentieth century, translation theory's concerns with loss, harm, and authenticity abound. In his oft-cited essay on translation, Walter Benjamin focused on the target language's effects on the source language. In translation, he claimed, one is foreignizing ideas and highlighting the issue of commensurability as opposed to incommensurability. Moving beyond Goethe's assessment of a translation as metempsychosis, Benjamin spoke about a text's afterlife, which involved its linguistic harmony being activated by first acknowledging 'mutually exclusive differences'. The pure language that is spellbound in the foreign language should be set free in the target language. The source language imprisoned in a work is thus liberated by rewriting it. This is the translator's task (Benjamin, cited in Venuti 82).

A real translation is transparent: it does not cover the original, does not block its light, but allows the pure language, as though reinforced by its own medium to shine upon the original all the more fully (Venuti 81).

Benjamin saw translation as a provisional way of coming to terms with the foreignness of languages. All such translations assume that there is the possibility of mutual translatability (that there is cultural commensurability), as A.W. Schlegel assumed existed when he translated the *Gītā* from Sanskrit into Latin in 1823. Translatability, the flexibility of the source language to accommodate change and the flexibility of the target language to accept change, is predicated on the acceptance that the two languages can be compared, that two words can be equal in both languages. In our analysis of the *Gītā* translations, we will see that this issue of commensurability was not always a given. The issue of loss remains a consistent theme in discussions on translation.

Ezra Pound (1885–1972) discussed how attempts to deal with loss were glossed over when translators sought some stylistic analogy in the receiving culture for their translations. Pound did not attribute particularly lofty goals to translators or their products. He saw the task of the translator as making up for the loss experienced by the 'linguistically lazy reader'. The translator thus shows where treasure is to be found, guides the reader to what languages need to be studied, and helps the student who has a smattering of language and energy to read alongside the 'metrical glaze' (Pound, in Venuti 91). There is a certain logic in Pound's assigning to translation such modest aims.

Vladimir Nabokov (1899–1977) also lamented what is lost in translation. For the obvious reasons of his forced exile, Nabokov was nostalgic for the lost language, culture, and aesthetics of the source context. He also saw the resultant harm. An avid lepidopterist, Nabokov drew the analogy between translation and the dead butterfly; both can be dissected and mounted (Nabokov, cited in Venuti 119). Like other theorists, he also viewed translation as an impossible task. However, for Nabokov, the impossibility could be partially remedied by the addition of 'copious footnotes', as in his own translation of Pushkin's *Eugene Onegin* (1964). He felt that the concept of a free translation, devoid of such scholarly apparatus, smacked of knavery and tyranny (Venuti 125):

> I want translations with copious footnotes, footnotes reaching up like skyscrapers to the top of this or that page as to leave only the gleam of one textual line between commentary and eternity. (Venuti 127)

Roughly contemporaneously with Nabokov's musings, Roman Jakobson (1896–1982) also brought up the issue of loss in translation when he compared it with the circular series of unfavourable currency transactions (Venuti 129). Jakobson distinguished between intra-lingual translation, the rewording from one poetic shape into another, and the interlingual, a translation from one language to another. He termed the latter 'translation' proper. There was also a third type of translation (translations always seem to have three types), the inter-semiotic, from one system of signs into another, a transmutation from the written to music, dance, cinema, or painting (Jakobson, in Venuti 127). As we shall see, the *Gītā* in recent years has experienced inter-semiotic transmutation into opera. In the wake of Jakobson, translation theory underwent a linguistic turn focusing more on various system analyses than on an engagement with the foreignness of the text.

The materialist analogy of translation as a transaction characterized by loss and gain was also echoed by the biblical scholar and linguist, Eugene Nida (1914–2011) in a 1964 essay, entitled 'Principles of Correspondence'. Nida noted that whoever takes on a translation in effect contracts a debt (Nida, in Venuti 141) that must be paid, not with the same money, but with the same sum. Often, a translator needs to circumnavigate a difficult word, by describing it rather than finding a perfect correspondent word. Nida posited two objectives that appear in tension in all translation work, the formal component (i.e. the message itself) and the dynamic equivalence (that which provokes an equivalent effect on the reader). Nida also believed that a debt needed to be paid by the translator who is enjoined to accommodate a given audience (child, individual, generalist, adult) in his translation. Nida set up a schema for these two types of translation. The formal focused on the message in both form and content. It sought to match this message as closely as possible to elements in the source (Venuti 144) and was able to achieve this goal partially by using footnotes.

The dynamic form of translation aimed for naturalness of expression. It tried to relate to the modes of behaviour in the target language. But the status of the translated text mattered. As Nida correctly claimed, when the translation of scripture was involved, issues of fidelity, equivalence, culture, and compatibility come into sharp focus. The translator of scripture engages in a high-stakes game, where fidelity and equivalence are tantamount to dogma and creed.

Following developments in structural anthropology, Kwame Anthony Appiah (1954–) speaks of 'thick translation' that creates a relationship between 'source text and its originary culture'. The notion of 'thick' translation borrows from the anthropologist Clifford Geertz's (1926–2006) concept of 'thick description'. Appiah's application of Geertz to translation posits that the translator has to take the time to learn the culture and linguistic practices of the source texts (Appiah, in Venuti 336). It is rather naïve that this philosopher, although a fine reader of Geertz, was clearly not knowledgeable about the vast literature on translation that preceded him and the fact that translators are rarely ignorant of the source text's culture. The ability to translate would be quite difficult without some modicum of such knowledge. We are now in the realm where the theories of translation are no longer in the hands of linguists and translators, but the purview of literary critics, national literature scholars, and cultural critics. Translation theory from the 1980s onward enters other fields of study, not necessarily tied to experience in translating.

This is the realm where discussions of translation extend to the notions of translation as a relational system that includes editing, history, and criticism as ways of 'rewriting'. In Lefevere's understanding of 'refraction' or Itamar Even-Zohar's (1932–) conception of translation functioning as a polysystem, where translations are an integral part of innovative forces, new literary models emerge, and new repertoires are elaborated. For Even-Zohar, texts choose to be translated and show themselves to be either compatible through new approaches or play an innovative role in the target language (Even-Zohar, in Venuti 163–4). So, translations can either be used conservatively, by adhering to the older norms, where the translation becomes a means of preserving traditional taste, or they can become an activity for change. Even-Zohar calls for translation to have this socio-literary status, depending on its place in a polysystem (Venuti 165), performing functions (innovative or conservatory), and its positionality (central or peripheral).

Translation is no longer a phenomenon whose nature and borders are fixed, but an activity dependent on the relations within a certain cultural system. The position that a text inhabits becomes an important factor in translating, particularly in pedagogies concerned with multiculturalism and the margins and peripheries of World Literature. This phase in translation studies will engender the platitudinous pronouncements of a Susan Sontag (1933–2004), Gayatri Spivak (1942–), Slavoj Žižek (1949–), or a David Damrosch (1953–). As in so many cases, Jacques Derrida (1930–2004) sets the standard, explaining, as if this question had never been previously asked, the following:

> A relevant translation would therefore be quite simply, a 'good' translation that does what one expects, of it, in short, a version that performs its mission, honors its debt and does its job while inscribing in the receiving language the most relevant equivalent for the original. The language that is the most right, appropriate, pertinent, adequate, opportune, univocal, idiomatic, or so on. (Derrida, in Venuti 368)

This insight appeared in 1998, after the 1993 De Man debacle.[8] Derrida is showing greater caution with regards to the implications of his theory of deconstruction with its inscrutable discourse calling into question the nature of truth and reality as not tied to real-world ramifications which he had been promoting (and which made him a *vedette* in the US) and for which he subsequently needed to recalibrate. The stakes had changed. For the remainder of his life, Derrida would subject his readers to a series of ethical engagements, one of them included his thoughts on translation.[9] Hermeneutic readings of translation, while eclipsed by what I will call (for the sake of convenience) various systems' approaches, could still

[8] Paul DeMan, the Yale professor and theorist of Deconstruction, was found to have written anti-Semitic articles for Belgian Nazi publications. This discovery called into question some of the underlying premises of this critical school of thought and its relation to truth claims and textual meaning. After this revelation about DeMan's past, the subsequent attempt to deconstruct his Nazi past by certain deconstructionist colleagues brought further negative attention to the entire affair.

[9] For an examination of Spivak's and Derrida's pronouncements on translation as forms of mystical speech, see Figueira 2020.

be found. They developed, however, to address the legitimate concerns raised by what can be termed the hermeneutics of suspicion. This return to the hermeneutic tradition as it relates to translation was revived and appeared with renewed vigour in the work of Ricoeur and George Steiner (1929–2020).

We now speak of acts of penetration, of embodiment, and of restitution. But Steiner views translation primarily as a hermeneutics of trust (*lancement*). The hermeneutic motion begins with initiating trust and seriousness; it is an adventure and a leap. There is something there to be understood. The translator is generous. He/she trusts in the Other, although it is yet unmapped and untried. Yet Steiner acknowledges, in contradistinction to a hermeneutics of engagement, the post-structural translation theory that sees in translation also an aggression which is incursive and entails an extraction (Steiner, in Venuti 157). One must appropriate another entity. We translate into something, and the result can be hostile as well as seductive. In these instances, the otherness is dissipated in the process of translating, where light appears through loose fibres and can be incorporated, assimilated, and naturalized. The translator invades, extracts, and brings home. But we come home laden (even off-balance) by adding our own prejudices with ambiguous consequences. The system is off kilter. So, to compensate (i.e. to be authentic), the translator needs to restore parity by creating a condition of significant exchange (Venuti 158–9). There is, of necessity, some loss, but the order of the source and the receptor is preserved. Steiner's elaboration here was influenced by Claude Lévi-Strauss's (1908–2009) model of equilibrium as delineated in *Anthropologie structurale*. By enlarging the parameters of translation, Steiner aims at overcoming its sterile classical model as literal, paraphrase, or free, as well as its depiction as an aggression of extraction, imposition, and hegemonic incursion. He questioned both the ethics of fidelity to the source in the translation but also, as noted by Jakobson and Nida, its economic component. Steiner claims that the act of translation creates a surplus of value: '[T]here is, ideally, exchange without loss' (Venuti 160).

Translation can be seen as a leap toward the Other or an identification with this Other in order to strategically borrow models. There is the possibility that translation leads to a change of Self, as part of a larger hermeneutic understanding. There is also concern with fidelity versus infidelity (Schleiermacher's 'word for word' and Jerome's 'sense of spirit') and commensurability (possible for Schleiermacher, impossible for Jakobson). If our understanding of translation is too flexible, then (according to Nietzsche) we lose the historicity of the text and (according to Schleiermacher) we no longer learn from the Other but filter it through the language of the hegemon. Can we be, as Jorge Luis Borges (1899–1986) demands in his study of Edward Lane's translation of *The Thousand and One Nights*, loyal to the source text (Borges, in Venuti 92–106)? Even before Michel Foucault (1926–1984), even before the insights gleaned from postcolonial theory, logic taught us that the centre dictates the margin and moves the Other farther from the Self. It is this reality that seems to haunt translation theories and practices and is addressed in the late work of Ricoeur, whose hermeneutic model I find particularly useful here since, as in much else of his work, Ricoeur seeks a viable mediation[10] between conflicting priorities. In *Sur la traduction* (2004), Ricoeur looks at the philosophical role of the translator from a phenomenological perspective. He challenges Martin Heidegger (1889–1976) and the pretentions of the *Cogito* as self-knowing. Being is always mediated through endless interpretations of all kinds, where symbols have double meanings as well as surplus meanings, as Ricoeur first investigated in *Le symbolisme du mal* (1960).[11]

In Ricoeur, there are also three paradigms for translation: the linguistic, the ontological (how it occurs between two beings), and the transmigratory. But Ricoeur primarily envisions translation as an encounter with the Other and holds all reading as just such an encounter. Reading and translation are companion processes (Ricoeur 2007: 4). What distinguished translation as a hermeneutic event is that the Other it seeks to encounter resides outside one's language. The translator functions as a middleman on two levels: between the reader and the author and between the reader and this Other. Reading and translating are twin actions; each facilitates a reflection on oneself through an encounter with others (4). Ricoeur viewed translation also as a *Durcharbeitung*, a

[10] For Ricoeur on mediation, see Figueira 2015: 5–6.

[11] I have been inspired by the work of Ricoeur since my early student days in the history of religion and throughout my graduate work when I had the opportunity to work with him. Likewise, I am greatly indebted to the work of Gadamer with whom I also had the opportunity to study.

Freudian working through.[12] In translation, as in Freudian analysis, work is advanced with some salvaging and with some acceptance of loss (3). Translators should continue to translate despite loss. They should accept, mourn, and move beyond. As the Ricoeur scholar Richard Kearney noted in the introduction to the English translation of *Sur la traduction*, for Ricoeur 'the best path to selfhood is through otherness' (Ricoeur 2007: xviii) and the experience of the foreign is crucial to self-knowledge and self-development. The translator meets with resistance at numerous stages of his enterprise. He encounters it, at a very early stage, as the presumption of non-translatability which inhibits him even before he tackles the work. Everything then transpires as though in initial fright, in what is sometimes experienced as the anguish of beginning. The foreign text towers up like a lifeless block of resistance to translation (5). But since translation mourns what cannot be articulated into another language it mourns the perfect non-existent 'third text' to which translators compare their own rendering. This third text becomes the model toward which the source and translation must aspire, their amalgam (8–9). It is always possible, according to Ricoeur, to say the same thing in another way (25).

So, each translation practises a movement towards the Other. Translation seeks to accommodate and assimilate itself to the object being translated. To elaborate what he means here, Ricoeur introduced the concept of linguistic hospitality, welcoming the Other into the domain of the Self, so that the Self can understand itself through the Other. Linguistic hospitality entails inhabiting the world of the Other and receiving the word of the Other in one's own home. Hospitality calls us to forego the lure of omnipotence, that is, the illusion of a total translation, and to respect that the two languages involved are not the same. Linguistic hospitality consists then of the pleasure one experiences when dwelling in the Other's language and when this pleasure is balanced by the pleasure of receiving the foreign word at home, in one's own welcoming house (Ricoeur 2007: 10).

Ricoeur abandons other theorists' notions of a good translation for the pleasure of linguistic hospitality supplanting other concerns.

[12] For Ricoeur's understanding of Sigmund Freud, see *Freud and Philosophy: An Essay on Interpretation*, translated by Denis Savage (1970).

> The faithfulness/betrayal dilemma claims to be practical because there is no absolute criterion of what would count as good translation. This absolute criterion would be the same meaning, written somewhere, on top of and between the original text and the target text. The third text would be the bearer of the identical meaning, supposed to move from the first to the second. Hence, the paradox, concealed behind the practical dilemma between faithfulness and betrayal: a good translation can aim only at a supposed equivalence, not founded on a demonstrable identity of meaning, equivalence without identity. (Ricoeur 2007: 34)

The third text is caught in the betweenness of 'faithfulness and betrayal' between two masters, the author and the reader. The translator tries to please both. So now, linguistic hospitality becomes a solution. Ricoeur asks us to abandon the quest for absolute translation for the happiness of linguistic hospitality:

> Bringing the reader to the author, bringing the author to the reader, at the risk of serving and of betraying two masters: this is to practice what I like to call linguistic hospitality. It is this which serves as a model for other forms of hospitality that I think resembles it: confessions, religions, are they not like languages that are foreign to one another, with their lexicon, their grammar, their rhetoric, their stylistics which we must learn to make our way into them? And is eucharistic hospitality not to be taken up with the same risks of translation-betrayal, but also the same renunciation of the perfect translation? I retain these analogies and these question marks . . . (Ricoeur 2007: 34)

What Goethe identified as a perfect translation, Ricoeur envisions as the third text, existing beyond and between the source and translated text. It is only good, not perfect. In fact, Ricoeur advises us to abandon the notion of the perfect translation, since translation is an ongoing process and not, as in Goethe, completed with the creation of the third text.

Translation is a dialogue between the Self and the Stranger, a model of hermeneutics, and an exposure to strangeness. Both hermeneutics and translation are paths to Selfhood through otherness rather than the Romantic notion of translation as a Platonic dialogue. The Romantic Self presented itself as a sovereign master. In Ricoeur, the Self becomes an engaged Self. One understands oneself as another, one that discovers the Other within the Self. Self-identity is thus the equivalent of translation between the Self and the Other within and outside the Self. Translation is also conceived as a wager, an *épreuve* (test) as in the sense of an ordeal.[13] It permits us to engage in resistance (Ricoeur 2007: 5) by its prescription of non-translatability. It offers the possibility of finding meaning when we move towards learning of the Self through the learning of the Other. Translation then presents the possibility of an encounter with the Other that brings change to the Self. Ricoeur, perhaps more than any other translation theorist, supports the vision of literary translation as pre-eminently an ethical task. It seeks to circulate, transport, disseminate, explain, and make more accessible. Translation has an evangelical goal of enlarging readership. It performs primarily an ethical task that mirrors the role of literature itself to extend our sympathies, educate the heart and mind, create inwardness, and secure and deepen the awareness that other, different people exist.

In the following pages, we will examine to what extent the various translations and interpretations of the *Gītā* give us a vision of the Indian Other that we can welcome into our own house. To what degree do they provide a creative force, as in Wilhelm von Humboldt's *energeia*, Steiner's notion of trust, or Ricoeur's belief in some seductive possibility of dialogue between the Self and a previously uncharted and unexplored Other? There are some analyses included here that engage in the 'painstaking comparisons' (Bassnett and Lefevere 1990: 4) between the Sanskrit text and its translation. The historical theories of translation enumerated in the preceding pages are meant to help us navigate these works. They do not, however, help elucidate those cases where the *Gītā* is not linguistically translated. For those chapters dealing with interpretation rather than translation, I consider the text in its cultural environment, what Bassnett and Lefevere see as the interaction between translation and culture, and what Lefevere identifies as refraction or rewriting. In these interpretations, I focus on issues of context, history, and convention (11). What recent Translation Studies identifies as the 'cultural turn' in translation has

[13] In this regard, Ricoeur is indebted to Franz Rosenzweig (1886–1929) who believed that to translate is to serve two masters, the first being the foreigner and his work and the other being the reader and his desire for appropriation.

particular relevance here, particularly in its de-emphasis on the idea of 'equivalence'. It serves as a metaphor that binds together the translations and the interpretations studied in these pages. In the following chapters, I examine both professionals within the literary system as well as patronage outside the literary system, consisting of influential individuals from a given historical period and institutions regulating the distribution of literature and literary ideas. Whether we are discussing linguistic or cultural translation, the central concern is this: How often in the *Gītā*'s various afterlives does the translator or the interpreter allow the Other, but insist on maintaining control over it?

2

Translation and Mystification: Wilkins

In 1785, Charles Wilkins (1749–1836), a senior merchant in the East India Company, produced the first direct translation of the *Bhagavad Gītā* from Sanskrit into English and declared it to be the supreme book of Hinduism (Gowda 3).[1] In the 'Preface' to his translation, Wilkins noted that brahmins[2] esteemed the *Gītā* as containing all the great mysteries of their tradition (Wilkins 23). While, indeed, the *Gītā* may unlock the mysteries of the Hindu tradition, the act of translating it sought to unravel its mysteries. The more exotic the translation, the more exotic the mystery. The more 'mysterious' or 'mystical' the text, the more translation is needed to explain this mystery. Theories of translation are inextricably bound to the mysteries of the text under translation. As we shall see in the course of this volume, exotic methods of translating mystical texts are devised to justify mystical translations of exotic texts.

For decades, Wilkins's translation was the only version of the *Gītā* available outside the original Sanskrit. Regarding Wilkins's translation, Sir William Jones wrote in 1786:

> If they wish to form a correct idea of Indian religion and literature, let them begin with forgetting all that has been written on the subject by ancients and moderns, before the publication of the *Gītā*.[3]

Wilkins's translation exerted considerable influence in both the East and the West. It was retranslated from English into other European languages long before these languages had independent translations of their

[1] There have been 887 translations of the *Gītā* published between 1785 and 1979 (Robinson 35).
[2] Priests. There are four major *varṇas* (castes), the *brahmins*, *vaishya*, *kṣatriyas*, and *śūdras*.
[3] Cited in E. Windisch, *Geschichte des Sanskrit-Philologie und indische Alterthumskunde*, 2 vols. Strasbourg: K.J. Truebner 1917–20, 1.24.

The Afterlives of the Bhagavad Gītā. Dorothy M. Figueira, Oxford University Press. © Dorothy M. Figueira 2023.
DOI: 10.1093/oso/9780198873488.003.0003

own.[4] Some of these initial translations merely reworked versions of Wilkins's translation, rather than offering independent efforts (Sharpe 10). They tended to be derivative of Wilkins, since his translation had been judged faithful and adequate.[5] The Governor General of Bengal,[6] Warren Hastings (1732–1818), had vouched for Wilkins's translation in the *Advertisement* which appeared after its title page and in a 'Letter to Nathaniel Smith', the Chairman of the East India Company, introducing the translation, outlining the motives for its publication, and vouchsafing for the fidelity, accuracy, and merit of the translator (Wilkins A2). Hastings, under whose patronage Wilkins's translation had been undertaken, commented to Wilkins on his skills in translating:

> I know that your extensive acquaintance with the customs and religious tenets of the Hindoos would elucidate every passage that was obscure. (Hastings 20)

Hastings thereby affirms Wilkins's knowledge of both the source and the target cultures. He also recognizes one of the major concerns with the limitations of translations in general: their level of cultural literacy. He acknowledges that knowing the letter of the language is not enough. Cultural and linguistic knowledge are interdependent: what Appiah would centuries later 'discover' and designate as a 'thick' translation. Such limitations to understanding a text can only be shrunk by the translator's grasp of a text's cultural background.

Of course, at this early stage, conceptualizations and contextualizations were sketchy, as evidenced in Hasting's 'Letter', where we are told that the *Gītā*, as part of the *Mahābhārata*, was written by the same author who composed the Vedas 4,000 years earlier (Hastings 7). Hastings believed that translating the Hindu epics was important because they could be mined for the philosophical essence of Indian thought, and such knowledge was worthwhile since it provided ethical and aesthetic benefits for the European reader. Hastings maintained that since India

[4] See in particular the 1787 French translation of Wilkins by Abbé J.P. Parraud and the translation into German by Friedrich von Majer in 1802 appearing in Julius Klaproth's *Asiatisches Magazin*.
[5] For a study of general translation traditions, see Figueira 1990.
[6] He served in that capacity from 1773–81.

provides a vision of antiquity that precedes the first efforts of civilization in the Western quarter of the globe (Hastings 7) and offers a key source of ancient wisdom in general, it was important to make its seminal texts, of which the *Gītā* was an exemplar, widely available. Hastings claimed that the English admiration for India is comparable to the German admiration for the Greeks. Europe should, therefore, seek cultural inspiration from India through the work of translating its masterpieces. Here we find a cogent expression of the idea that the Other and this Other's past (in this case India) should be studied as a means for improving Europe's cultural present and national identity. But, as in much discourse, so here too, Hastings and Wilkins would speak with a 'forked tongue' (Bhabha 85).[7]

Hastings admits to being unlettered (presumably signifying not being a linguist or a scholar) and asks the readers of the *Gītā* (who may, in fact, be like him) to allow for the text's obscurity, absurdity, barbarous habits, and perverted morality (Hastings 7). A postcolonial reading would rightfully view this directive as a standard colonialist denigration of Indian culture; it might even cite Macaulay[8] to show a racist and dismissive pattern. But beyond this legitimate assessment, we might also want to interrogate the political aims and the hermeneutics involved. Both Wilkins and Hastings voice curiosity regarding the *Gītā* as a cultural object. In interpreting the text, they ask readers to allow themselves to 'change their expectations', to engage ideas that are 'counter' to their tastes (however sublime, shocking, or metaphysical they may be) and to enter into these unknown realms (Hastings 8). They may not be competent to understand certain words rendered in English, such as 'action', 'application', and 'practice', since they are novel 'to us' in their use here (Hastings 9). But the original is 'not lacking in perspicuity' (Hastings 10). If the reader does not find something to be profound or intelligent in the *Gītā*, Hastings suggests that it may be the reader's limitations and not those of the text. He thus valorizes the text over the reader's capacities. He calls for a receptivity to the text; he

[7] I use Homi Bhabha's terminology here, although I do not believe such double speak is unique to colonialism, but common to discourse in general.

[8] Macaulay's 1835 *Minute on Education* is often cited as proof of the racist contempt in which the British held the Indians. It is worthwhile to note how there could be found, among the initial Orientalists, such as Jones and Wilkins (and certainly among the Germans of the time) a counter discourse. Not all discourse is uniquely "colonial" in nature as I have tried to show in various publications (Figueira 1991, 1994, etc.). There are often other agendas at work, such as religious and aesthetic.

asks the reader to try and enter into it on its own terms. Hastings's recognition that the words of the translation might not necessarily match the intent of the original, was a rather sophisticated hermeneutical consideration for its time, as was his advice on how his reader might approach the religion and the philosophy expounded in the text. It acknowledged the otherness of what the reader encounters in the *Gītā* and the need for the Self to engage this otherness, even though the translated word may signify some meaning different from what the reader can expect or even understand.

To further explain his point, Hastings begins by noting that Indians engage in a form of spiritual discipline that is very different from 'our' own. In a telling comparison, Hastings comments that it is not unlike what Catholics (the 'Romish Church') achieve when they too deny sensual desire through their attention to abstract thought. In fact, he has seen Indians also 'fingering their rosary beads', deep in repetitive chanting of the names of God. They are concentrating with 'convulsive movements' of their features (Hastings 8). Although perhaps as indicative of English attitudes toward Rome as toward India, Hastings's comment shows an early instance of an attempt to use another (and perhaps equally 'fanatic') faith (at least from the British Protestant perspective) as the point of comparison and measurement of the British Self and the Indian Other. But Hastings quickly points out that the *Gītā* is truly original, even if he faults it for giving a corporeal form to spiritual existences. Regardless of its 'faulty' perception of the Divine, the *Gītā* is stylistically excellent, sublime in its conception, reasoning, and diction. It is simply unequalled (Hastings 10). In fact, he avers that Wilkins's translation reads as well as any French translation of Homer! Hastings is at great pains here to valorize the *Gītā* as a work of faith (albeit a 'different' faith and as odd as Catholicism) as well as a work of supreme literary worth.

He also seeks to valorize the task of translation itself. Hastings projects the image of the translator as a self-sacrificing civil servant, noting how Wilkins suffered physically trying to translate not just the *Gītā*, but the entire *Mahābhārata*,[9] of which Hastings believes he had already translated

[9] In 1783, Wilkins began translating this entire epic and requested a leave of absence from his job on health grounds to go to Benares and work with pandits. On Hastings's recommendation the leave was granted. He worked with Pandit Kashinatha Bhatacharya (Davis 78). Wilkins did not finish the translation of the epic and decided to devote his energies instead to the *Gītā* (D. Singh 32).

a good portion.[10] The work was so taxing that Wilkins needed a new posting. His efforts show the degree to which, as Hastings claims, the employees of the East India Company are dedicated, suffer in the fulfilment of their jobs, and are diligent in their scientific endeavours (Hastings 12), especially in those cases where they are charged with translating Sanskrit. But here we have the double speak. Yes, this text is marvellous: it can open a world for the Western reader, but there are other concerns beyond the purely intellectual and aesthetic to consider. Translations from the Sanskrit such as Wilkins's *Gītā* are useful to the State.[11] It is necessary to be able to communicate with people over whom one 'exercises a dominion founded on the right of conquest' (Hastings 13). So, language training and cultural knowledge were deemed necessary because such understanding between peoples 'lessens the burden of the chain' by which the natives are held in subjection (Hastings 13). Moreover, Hastings avers that the *Gītā* is so valuable a cultural product that rendering it into English benefits humanity as a whole and it imprints on the colonizers' hearts the sense and obligation of benevolence (Hastings 13). The *Gītā* has the capability of expanding global sensibilities and relationships by conciliating distant affections. Lest we wax too enthusiastic of the worldview articulated here, we should note that Hastings quickly devolves back into unequivocal imperial thinking in the next phrase. He notes that 'we', the English, used to think the Indians were just savages. With increased interaction, that prejudice has abated a bit. Such attitudes will only continue to lessen once the English understand the Indians' real character and feel more for their natural rights and learn to estimate them. Translation plays a key role in this evolutionary process.

The bottom line is that this wonderful book is the product of a land that Britain has conquered because it requires and merits colonization. Translating this book should help the English better understand their subjects so they can more effectively rule their dominion. The more we learn about the Indian people, Hastings says, the more we will see that

[10] In this respect, he is not unlike the twentieth-century individual translators, such as Madeleine Biardeau and J.A.B. van Buitenen who each undertook the vast project of single-handedly translating the *Mahābhārata* and both died before the task could be completed. The recent successful translations of the Sanskrit epics have been the work of teams.

[11] This comment calls to mind how, even in America in the 1970s, the study of Sanskrit could be subsidized by Defense Department funds because Sanskrit was seen as crucial to American security.

they 'approach the stature that we enjoy'; the more we learn, the more we see in them the natural rights we know that we possess already. In fact, Hastings hazards to claim that the knowledge of Indians that is obtained through their writings is not only significant now but will continue to be important and will even survive long after the British have left the subcontinent (Hastings 13). So, Hastings is calling for a wider knowledge of this unexplored field. Sanskrit should be colonized by the colonialist English (D. Singh 35). The Company should encourage the 'adventurer' to study the field of Sanskrit, although it is not as valuable for the official exercise of profit as the Persian language (Hastings 14). In the past, brahmins had been reluctant to share the mysteries of their learning because their religion had been derided by previous subjugators in order to support intolerance.[12] The English, however, are different in that they are eager to receive Indian knowledge (Hastings 15).

In the case of the Wilkins translation, one might even be able to conscience such exaggerated claims as part and parcel of empire building, especially since Wilkins did, more or less, replicate the text as faithfully as possible within the bounds of the target language, without concessions or provisions for lost information or sentiments through his judicious use of footnotes. In his 'Translator's Preface', Wilkins acknowledged the need for supplemental materials, having arrived as the same conclusion that other translators would draw in his wake. Here one is reminded of Nida's and Nabokov's pertinent insistence on the necessity of copious notes, when languages and cultures are very different (and even perceived as lost). In the case of the Wilkins translation, these notes are not perfect or even copious, but they account for gaps in cultural understanding where translation alone proves insufficient. Wilkins chooses to provide marginal notes, as well as a pronunciation guide at the end of the 'Preface' to offer another philological artefact to guide readers through the *Gītā*. On this subject, Hasting informs us:

> This he hath attempted in his Note, but as he is conscious, they are still insufficient to remove the veil of mystery, he begs leave to remark, in

[12] One can here only surmise that he is talking about the Muslims and Catholic missionaries, clearly discounting (or ignorant of) their efforts to disseminate ancient texts of the populations they encountered.

> his own justification, that the text is but imperfectly understood by the most learned Brahmans [sic] of the present times. (Hastings 25)

Although they are 'insufficient to remove the veil of mystery', the notes do succeed (to evoke Ricoeur's aim for translation) in bringing the reader closer to the Other. Interestingly, Wilkins's remonstrances also seem to demonstrate the limitations attributable to reading in general, rather than simply applicable to certain translations. He accepts that the text, as any other, may be imperfectly understood. Hastings already had called attention to how even the 'most learned' brahmins participate in an act of translation when they read the *Gītā*, since they too must 'translate' an ancient text into a modern context. Wilkins chooses, therefore, to sacrifice the source language for the sake of clarity in the target language, in this sense prefiguring an approach similar to what Nabokov achieved two centuries later in his translation of *Onegin*. The *Gītā* offers an expression of mystery that, as Wilkins notes, one must simply accept, just as one must simply accept the intangibility of its foreignness.

This concern with fidelity is in the forefront of the early Western discussions on how best to decipher the Sanskrit language. When Sir William Jones spoke about the kinship between Sanskrit, Latin, Greek, and Germanic languages, he fully recognized that the need for an accurate knowledge of Sanskrit depended on a 'confidential intercourse' with learned brahmins as the only means of separating truth from fable.[13] Just as Wilkins had set out to achieve clarity, so too had Jones also sought an informed balance of linguistic and cultural knowledge in his own translations (Figueira 1994: 8–9, 23–5). These two Orientalists in the service of the British colonial administration set very high standards for subsequent translators of the *Gītā*.

Wilkins appealed to a pre-formed sense of his readership's European sensibility as well as its ethnic and religious homogeneity. As strange a work as the *Gītā* may appear, it must be seen as valuable since the learned brahmins esteem it as containing 'all the grand mysteries of their religion' (Wilkins 23). They valued it so much that they kept it not only from foreigners of different religious persuasions but also from 'the vulgar of their

[13] See the *Tenth Anniversary Discourse I: On Asiatick History* in his *Collected Works* (London 1793) cited in Majeed 1992: 309.

own'—a point made also by many Hindu reformers of the nineteenth century. They would have continued to keep it secret, had they not experienced 'the mildness' of the British government and 'the tolerating principles' of the Englishman's faith as well as the flattering personal attention that had been shown to Indian learned men by the British government and under which Indians at that time enjoyed such peace and encouragement!

Wilkins was as committed to clarity as he was to the source text but, quite simply, he found the *Gītā* hard to understand (Wilkins 25). He left several Sanskrit terms and proper names 'untranslated, and unexplained' because he felt that his skills as a translator were not up to the task and choices would only 'nearly approach the sense of the original' (Wilkins 25). Seemingly humble, he recognized his limitations. He also acknowledged that knowing a given culture beyond an individual text is crucial for any act of translation. He understood how his incomplete knowledge of the philosophy, theology, and 'the mythology of this ancient people' impacted upon his translation.[14] He even mentioned how little he knew of other important Sanskrit texts. He lamented that he did not possess any adequate knowledge of the larger literary canon and that he could not more fully grasp the larger philosophical context.

Wilkins was clearly concerned with his renderings of the obscure passages, fearing that he had failed to deal with them effectively, acknowledging that it 'was the translator's business to remove as much of this obscurity and confusion as his knowledge and abilities would permit' (Wilkins 24–5). He repeatedly excused 'the obscurity of many passages and the confusion of sentiments which runs through the whole' (Wilkins 24). To what degree did his sense of inadequacy inform his methodology? Evidently, Wilkins accepted that there would be passages that resist attempts to be rendered into clearer language. Yet, he eschewed excessive explanatory notes because, in the end, he felt they added more confusion than clarity.

Proper translation requires more than a minimal grasp of a language, since language is always infused and imbued with the values, worldviews,

[14] For example, he even questions if there are four *Vedas* and speculates about their dating, given the evidence found in the *Gītā*. He admits, however, to never having read a word of these *Vedas* (Wilkins 24–6).

sentiments, and tendencies of the larger culture. Since Wilkins, to a certain degree, anticipated the explicit concern that later theorists of translation would have with the cultural dimensions of translation (something akin to Nida's notion of formal and dynamic translations), he still hoped, despite such limitations, to convey to his readers some intimate knowledge of the mindset they might encounter in reading his translation. In this projected goal, Wilkins also anticipated Nida's conception of equivalence: the translator must be concerned with the effect a text has on the audience. What is different in Wilkins's translation is that the effect on the reader does not entirely dictate the manner in which he translated the *Gītā*. Rather, Wilkins was far more interested in achieving formal equivalence with the original language to such a degree that he did not even translate terms for which he felt he could not find sufficient equivalents. He recognized how his notes to the text were still insufficient to 'remove the veil of mystery from it'. But Wilkins concurs with Hastings in admitting how the text itself resisted translation, even 'by the most learned Brahmans of the present times' (Wilkins 25).

In Hastings's and Wilkins's comments, there is an interesting projection of the Judaeo-Christian tradition onto India. 'Unity of Godhead' is taught in the *Gītā* (Wilkins 24), rather than 'idolatrous' sacrifices and the worship of images. The monotheism that Hastings and Wilkins transpose onto the *Gītā* provides further proof of its worth as a text as well as the value of the culture which produced it. Wilkins saw the *Gītā* as a text designed to 'bring about the downfall of Polytheism' (Wilkins 24) and indirectly undermine the *Vedas*. We even learn that brahmins 'are Unitarians according to the doctrine of Kreeshna' (Wilkins 24). There is throughout the reception of the *Gītā* reception this anti-clerical discussion. Just as Voltaire 'used' the Chinese, and Montesquieu had his fictional Persians, several of the Western commentaries we will encounter in these pages fashioned their portraits of brahmins in order to talk about Catholic priests.

Outwardly, Hindus might comply with the ceremonies of the *Vedas*, such as sacrifice, ablutions, etc., but they do so because their economic livelihood depends on these remunerative rites. Wilkins admitted that performing actions for economic gain is standard behaviour of priests, it seems, in every tradition and in every country (Wilkins 25). Priests cannot be trusted anywhere.[15] One can certainly detect a Protestant discourse here that reflected one of the motivations inspiring the translation itself. It was the same motivation that led Martin Luther's translation of the Bible and Rammohun Roy's translations of the *Upanishads*: to put scripture in the hands of the people and to wrest it from priestly control and abuse.[16]

Both Indians and Westerners alike would subsequently agree that the *Gītā* needed to be saved from the machinations of pandits. This 'Protestant' approach to scripture takes as its presupposition the self-evident nature of scriptural truth in translation as easily grasped by the reader. In this vein, Wilkins could claim to leave the decipherment of the most difficult passages for the exercise of the reader's own judgement, if no adequate commentary existed or was forthcoming (Majeed 1992: 313). Just as this logic had worked for Martin Luther against the Church, so too could it work to undermine the brahmin custodianship of Hindu scripture. Wilkins and Hastings surely shared Sir William Jones's belief that translation provided a resource for empire building. Jones's translation of the *Laws of Manu* (*Mānavadharmaśāstra*) had been undertaken for this very purpose, so that Indians could best be ruled in accordance with their own laws (Figueira 2002: 25–7). Wilkins and Hastings both hoped that the *Gītā*'s translation would make the text transparent and contribute to the process of securing the foundations of British rule. In this respect, translation becomes a key strategy of containment.[17] Wilkins's translation of the *Gītā* also raises yet another significant issue, one that continues to resonate in literary studies today, the problem of translation itself. Hastings was the first to acknowledge that there were no ready-made criteria for assessing any Sanskrit text, since the rules of ancient and modern European literature could not apply nor could all 'our' references to 'standards of propriety for opinion and action' and 'tenets of religion and moral duty.'[18] At this stage, the issue of translatability, the

[15] Priesthoods, no matter their affiliation, came under criticism in the nineteenth century (see Figueira 2002: 50–63).

[16] For a discussion of Indian and Western efforts to wrest control of scriptures from the control of their brahmin custodians, see Figueira 2002, chapters 3, 5 and 8.

[17] Whether the translation 'fails ultimately to discipline the text of the *Gītā*,' as Majeed (1992: 314) claims, is open to speculation and may align far more with the theorizing of recent postcolonial criticism than with the text's actual reception theory.

[18] Hastings, 'Letter to Nathaniel Smith', 7, cited in Majeed (1992: 314).

incommensurability of worldviews, and the ethics of translation all enter into the theoretical discussion.[19]

Wilkins claimed that the philosophic abstruseness of the text makes it 'impossible to render by any of the known terms of science in our language, or even to make them intelligible by definition' (Wilkins 25). Wilkins realized and highlighted the gap between his understanding and the source text. It was not his intention to rewrite or interpret the text by following his insights. Instead, he invited his readers to join the journey no matter where it led. This too is a rather progressive hermeneutical approach for its time. Wilkins envisioned the obscure and difficult passages as the 'exercise of the reader's own judgement' (Wilkins 25). However, Wilkins recognized that, as the translator, he was inevitably required to 'bring the author back home' by accurately delivering the text's message. In this sense, his dependence on comments and footnotes brings into relief the tendency in translation to domesticate. To mitigate this problem, Wilkins decided to leave some terms with 'the same sounds in which he found them' (Wilkins 9). The Sanskrit terms, *om* and *yoga*, for example, were untranslated and unexplained (25), since they bear so many interpretations. Hastings had given Wilkins an out: if the *Gītā*'s meaning was still obscure, one can ascribe it to the 'incompetency of our own perceptions, or so novel an application of them rather than to less probable want of perspicacity in the original' (Hastings 12, cited in Majeed 1992: 315). This notion of incommensurability of terminology and cultures comes up repeatedly in the translations and commentary on the *Gītā*, particularly in Hegel. It is what Benjamin referred to as letting one's own language be affected by a foreign language (Benjamin 75–81). Such incommensurability would necessitate the use of certain strategies, not only on Wilkins's part, but also on the part of subsequent translators.

Wilkins claimed to rely on his collaboration with pandits to authenticate the translation. By 1823, however, August Wilhelm Schlegel would eschew such input and mould the Sanskrit of the *Gītā* to conform to the

[19] The ethics of translation is a central concern of literary criticism, particularly as it pertains to Comparative Literature, its relationship to dealing with original languages, the role of translation in literary studies in general and, particularly, with respect to the current reformulation in World Literature. Even the ways different cultures define 'literature' is often ignored in the 'worlding' of World Literature. It is indeed ironic that eighteenth-century colonial administrators appear to be more conscious of this ethical dimension of translation than we are today in our attempts to open global perspectives.

Western context, specifically as it was defined by the Latin language and cultural milieu.[20] Then, in 1855, J.C. Thomson[21] sought an alternative solution to the challenges of the Sanskrit text and perceptions of its untranslatability by adding to his translation long explanations, an index for proper names, and other commentary-like features. Thomson's scholarly apparatus proved to be an innovation on the barely sufficient notes Wilkins had appended to his translation. However, the inclusion of such an extensive scholarly apparatus initiated the subsequent blurring of the lines between translation and interpretation that would characterize subsequent translation efforts. Edwin Arnold, the author of the 1885 translation, *The Song Celestial*, brought the original close to the reader, but it was a reinvention of the text, something akin to Goethe's third option for translation, certainly not the *Gītā* 'as it is', the effort to which Gandhi and the Hare Krishna Movement would aspire. It is noteworthy that Arnold's version viewed the translator's authority as paramount. There was no longer any mention of receiving help from Hindu pandits. Very quickly, the role of the Western translator took prominence over other brahmin authorities. It was also no longer a question of fretting over the relationship between Sanskrit literature and European literatures or explaining any foreign philosophical nuances (Majeed 1992: 48). We no longer find discussions of the complex relationships between the *Gītā*, Greek, and Latin literatures, as one had found with the initial Orientalists. A translator such as Arnold 'owned' the text. By the end of its first century in translation, the *Gītā* was unmoored from its Sanskrit context. This decoupling of the text from its context would lead to subsequent appropriations rooted in grave distortions. However, that time was not yet upon us. With Wilkins, we were still just beginning the process and still very much caught up with the political purpose of containment that translating Indian texts had for the British colonizers.

This containment coexisted with a discussion on cultural commensurability and the religious agenda that would inform the *Gītā*'s initial translations, where its purpose was seen to uphold pure monotheism and

[20] In 1846, A.W. Schlegel's student, Christian Lassen, sought to improve on his teacher's work by including a large index. Between 1880 and 1885, there were three new English translations, the foremost being by Kashinath Trimbak Telang (1882) in the *Sacred Books of the East*, edited by F. Max Müller.

[21] Thomson was a student of H.H. Wilson, the first Boden Professor of Sanskrit at Oxford.

the notions of divine unity, as opposed to the idolatrous ritualism of the *Vedas* (Wilkins 24). Already, it was felt that the *Gītā* was composed to subvert Hindu polytheism and undermine the *Veda*'s authority (24). In fact, by the early nineteenth century, Christian missionaries and Hindu reformers were well at work questioning the *Vedas*, Hindu polytheism, and idolatry. Wilkins's and Hastings's claim that the *Gītā* subverted the baneful idolatrous practices of Hinduism and promoted monotheism would only support this reform effort. Wilkins could thus champion the *Gītā* and advocate its superiority to the little-known *Vedas* (24–6). His positive presentation of the *Gītā* would have the effect of undermining Vedic authority without actually challenging it (Robinson 37). The brahmins could still be seen as culprits, since they kept sacrifice alive and diluted the *Gītā*'s teaching. Priestcraft could thus be viewed as having weakened India. This tactic worked well for those segments of society, Indian or Western, who wanted to limit priestly hegemony. It certainly was a successful strategy for reformers such as Rammohun Roy and Dayānand Saraswatī (Figueira 2002: 90–117). Both Western Christians and Indian reformers had, therefore, a vested interest in distinguishing between Indian philosophical thought and the superstitious practices of the people. As noted, Hastings maintained that Wilkins translated the *Gītā* in order to support the colonial administration and to prove that the Indians were not primitive barbarians (Hastings 13). Hastings also claimed that Wilkins's translation was intended to promote mutual respect between the ruler and the ruled (Hastings 10–13). In fact, the appearance of the *Gītā* in book form, its translations, dissemination, reception history, and the 'endorsement' of a workable construct of Hinduism by Western commentators would undercut the brahmins' role as custodians of scripture as much as any of the works of nineteenth-century Hindu reformers.

Certainly, the Western concept of religion is alien to India and has no counterpart in Asian cultures and Asian religions, which should not be expected to conform to Western models. Nevertheless, beginning in the early nineteenth century, the translations of the *Gītā* which were motivated by various goals (to consolidate colonial power, to neutralize brahmin hegemony, to reform Hinduism, or to fight conversion by missionaries), contributed to simplifying the multiformity of Hindu practices, transforming the 'polymorphous paganism' of the text into an orderly monism (D. Singh 29), rewriting it in the image of the Bible (D.

Singh 36), reducing it to an image of Christianity, or maybe even calming Christian anxiety (D. Singh 37). These broader events may indeed be colonialist in nature. But the problem with an exclusively postcolonial reading is that it all too often limits the possibilities for discussion. There is more to be said that is often ignored because labelling something hegemonic or colonialist far too often suffices.[22]

One point worth noting is that the *Gītā* enabled Hinduism to become a book religion. This transformation cannot simply and uniformly be attributed to colonialism. In response to other religious groups operating in India, there was a need among believers to make sense of Hindu practices by focusing on a single text. There was also a need among pundits to 'lay claim' to truth by designating a specific text as expressing and vouchsafing religious practice.[23] With the gradual dissemination of Indian scriptures, it quickly became apparent that texts such as the *Vedas* and the *Upanishads* were simply less applicable than the *Gītā* as representative works for a book religion. It was at this juncture that the *Gītā* became particularly important. For the Westerner, it offered familiar themes: the notion of an incarnation, faith in a personal deity, and salvation. These were all themes that could resonate with Christians. In fact, in his 'Translator's Preface', Wilkins anticipates how the work of translation would be motivated by a kind of evangelical zeal that would subsequently fuel translation efforts well into the next century, especially in the work of Monier Monier-Williams[24] (1819–99), a staunch Evangelical Sanskritist (Sharpe 96), who particularly appreciated the *Gītā*'s teaching on devotion.[25] For

[22] In theoretical discussions, there is a continuing rehashing of Said's monolithic categorizations as well as the 'surprised' discovery that Said was not always correct (Israel 2014).

[23] In this regard, see the book disputations of Dayānand Saraswatī (Figueira 2002: 105–19).

[24] The second Boden Professor of Sanskrit at Oxford and author of the authoritative Sanskrit–English dictionary. In *Indian Wisdom* (1876), Monier-Williams focused on the concept of devotion in the *Gītā*.

[25] Both Hinduism and Christianity recognized human fallibility, the need for sacrifice, the importance of revelation, a common prayer, the futility of worldly existence, belief in a supreme deity, the trinity, and the incarnation (Monier Williams 1878: 100–1). Monier-Williams wanted to harness the similarities he saw between Hinduism and Christianity in order to foster and to build the mission. Although he referenced the *Gītā* along with the Bible (Robinson 214–15), he noted that Hindus were not that different from Christians. Monier-Williams would draw the line, however, on Hinduism holding its own vis-à-vis Christianity (Monier-Williams 1878: 211–17), which after all offered a personal God who had been made man, died, and was resurrected. Monier-Williams had a problem with the impersonal Absolute of Hinduism. He felt it could not engender the same level of devotion as could a personal deity. It could not challenge Christianity because devotion to Krishna could only be metaphorical and not literal. He saw commonality with Christianity, but Hinduism was certainly not commensurate with it.

Indian commentators also, the *Gītā* offered a faith that could be seen as propagating a definite improvement on the strictures of brahminical ritualism. It proved useful as a hedge against idolatry and proof of an initial form of monotheism in India. Seemingly offering an activist ethic (Minor 1986), the *Gītā* would remain the touchstone for understanding Hindu spirituality. It was simply a more manageable book for a book religion and easier to interpret than the enigmatic *Rig Veda* (with its limited availability) and the more speculative *Upanishads*, let alone the many other philosophical texts that over the next century would be translated.

In Hastings's long 'Letter' introducing the translation, we learn that the *Mahābhārata* and the *Gītā* were both written by one single reformer who tried to construct positive scriptural teachings that moved away from Vedic sacrifice (Robinson 38). Since the *Gītā* did, in fact, move closer to a Christian disposition, Hastings felt it justified and promoted a more humane and respectful treatment of Indians on the part of the British. He urged his readers to judge the *Gītā* as a prime example of the literature, myths, and religion of the ancient Hindus. Although replete with 'obscurity, absurdity, and barbarous habits and perverted morality', the *Gītā* possessed higher and nobler aspects. Although inferior to the *Vedas* and the *Purāṇas*, it nevertheless promoted the yogic separation of the mind and senses. The fact that Hindus did use those prayer beads, so reminiscent of 'the Church of Rome' made them not so foreign 'to us'. Their rituals were perhaps even easier to understand than what Catholics appeared (at least to non-Catholics) to practise.

It is significant to note here that it was primarily through Wilkins's translation and subsequent English renderings of the *Gītā* that 'utterly Westernized' Indian intellectuals sought to become orthodox Hindus overnight by projecting an untraditional political content onto its age-old rituals and symbols (Sarkar et al. 83). This Indian political appropriation of the *Gītā* in the form of translation would subsequently evolve into a debate as to whether the poem advocated an injunction to violence (as in the case of nationalist readings) or non-violence (as in Gandhi's unique interpretation). The *Gītā* would also be used by various readers to provide a public answer to their individual ideological and political positions. The *Gītā* could be read either as an allegorical construction, where its metaphors and symbols were used to express specific spiritual truths, or as a text of universal relevance.[26] In both instances, it is seen to provide some mystical and mysterious knowledge that could only to be revealed either by a translator or interpreter, who alone could recover its hidden truths through intense intellectual labour (Sinha, 2010: 303). This too was an element of the *Gītā's* exoticism for both Indians and Westerners alike.

Wilkins exhibited an awareness of the cultural distance between his native England and far-away India. Such an awareness is laudable for its time in that he allowed this sense of cultural distance to inform his role and purpose as a translator. While he recognized an ethical obligation to the text and Indian culture at large, his primary obligation was, of course, to his imperial benefactors. His responsibility to his English readership was limited, given the relative unfamiliarity of his reading public with Indian culture.[27] Since the distance was great between Sanskrit and English, his readers had to rely on good faith, his integrity as a scholar, and the fidelity of his translation. It is for this reason, perhaps, that Wilkins made the efforts that he did to address the effect his translation might have on his readers. Despite his concerns with formal equivalence, Wilkins sought to prepare his readers for the 'strangeness' of the *Gītā*. He did not exoticize or mystify it. He did, however, try to augment the expectations of his readers so that his translation might have a more dynamic effect, anticipating what Nida would seek to achieve almost 200 years later with Bible translations. In this respect, Wilkins is all the more noteworthy, especially since (as we shall see) subsequent translators and readers often foresaw so few of these issues and remained firmly planted in their own particular orbits.

Hastings fully recognized that the *Gītā* taught moral duty. He could praise its notion of *karma*, a concept he presented in a positive light as devoid of emotions. Hastings also liked the *Gītā*'s idea of a supreme deity. Morality and monotheism would always be selling points for Westerners viewing Hindu texts.[28] But, ultimately, the purpose of British Orientalist translation efforts, as Hastings readily acknowledged, was to rule the Indians more effectively by learning about them through their values and laws (as in the case of Sir William Jones) in order to better colonize and

[26] See Aldous Huxley's introduction to the Prabhavananda-Isherwood translation (1944).

[27] An interesting parallel can be drawn here between Wilkins and Simone Weil (see Chapter 10).

[28] Monotheism was also found in the reception of the *Upanishads* (see Figueira 2002: 96–100).

subjugate them. As Hastings very perspicaciously noted, the *Gītā* was so significant a text that it would outlive such political designs and even the British presence in India. When Hastings talks about the *Gītā* surviving long after the British had left India (Hastings 13), he foreshadows Benjamin's thoughts on a great work's potential afterlife through translation (Benjamin 2012: 76). It is curious that the initial endeavour of translating the *Gītā* from Sanskrit into English engendered this discussion on the temporality of British rule. Wilkins and Hastings both addressed in their introductory comments how the tactical use of translation can fail (Majeed 1992: 316), when the text or its commentary overwhelms various strategies of containment. Such a 'failure' will, in fact, occur in subsequent readings of the *Gītā*. But, at this juncture, the text succeeds in imposing its translatability on Wilkins. With Wilkins, the text leaves the orbit it had occupied for centuries. This point has bearing on how Orientalist and subsequent scholars and interpreters would 'rewrite' the *Gītā*, and it reflects the secularization of knowledge as it progresses from colonial times to the present.[29]It is a question of how the subsequent translators, commentators and interpreters either submit to the text or wield hegemonic power over it through their various interpretive strategies.

[29] I am grateful to an anonymous reader for this insight.

3

European Linguists, Philosophers, and Intellectual Rabble-Rousers

A.W. Schlegel, W. von Humboldt, Hegel, and Cousin

The latter decades of the eighteenth century witnessed a concerted effort to gather diverse material on unknown or little-known languages.[1] General theories of a purely abstract nature concerning the origins and development of language were also promulgated at this time (Figueira 1990: 1–3) without the necessary linguistic knowledge to support them. The discoveries of explorers and missionaries regarding languages and the efforts of linguistic theorists developed separately and in a parallel fashion in the years just prior to the discovery of the relationship between Sanskrit and the major languages of Europe. These efforts coalesced in the first two decades of the nineteenth century under favourable academic circumstances that allowed for the integration of language theory with linguistic and literary data. Such propitious circumstances contributed to the burgeoning historical study of Indo-European languages. In fact, linguistics in the first half of the nineteenth century was largely limited to Indo-European studies.

Since the advent of colonial discourse analysis, Indological scholarly productions have been almost exclusively seen as aiding and abetting Western political trends.[2] Postcolonial theory asserts that the European discovery of Indian philosophies, in addition to marking the beginning of modern Indology, paralleled the establishment of European hegemonic designs. It interprets Europe's reception of Indian philosophy as supporting the belief that India had nothing worthwhile to teach the West. Its tradition, deemed inimical to historical progress, was believed never

[1] An earlier version of this chapter appeared in Figueira 1994.
[2] See, for instance, the French Hellenist Jean-Pierre Vernant's introduction to Olender, xi.

The Afterlives of the Bhagavad Gītā. Dorothy M. Figueira, Oxford University Press. © Dorothy M. Figueira 2023.
DOI: 10.1093/oso/9780198873488.003.0004

to have reached the levels of philosophy and science that were thought to be uniquely European achievements (Halbfass). If one bases this analysis on Hegel (as is often the case), it is largely valid. The European scholarly reception of the *Gītā*, in particular, is singled out as contributing to the Western institutional philosophical and political refusal to take India seriously.[3] Wilkins's *Gītā* translation, as the then most important Sanskrit philosophical translation, would initially influence whatever understanding of Indian philosophy European intellectuals with no knowledge of Sanskrit would possess, as Sir William Jones noted (Windisch 20: 1.24).

After Wilkins's translation, 40 years would elapse before the next Western scholarly engagement with the *Gītā* would appear in the West. In 1823, August Wilhelm Schlegel, the first chair of Sanskrit at the University of Bonn, published the original Sanskrit text of the *Gītā* along with a Latin translation. Then, in the following year, H.T. Colebrooke wrote an extensive essay on Indian philosophy that would set the standard for the European exploration of the field.[4] Colebrooke's essays present a clear and non-judgemental exposition of the major Indian philosophical systems. He relied on the Sanskrit sources that he cited at the beginning of each part of his essay. He did not seek to draw any larger theoretical argument on the nature of Indian philosophy from this material. He equally eschewed speculation regarding the relationship between art, religion, and philosophy. On the whole, Colebrooke approached the classical schools of Indian thought in a straightforward, if somewhat simplistic fashion. His exposition was surprisingly non-polemical.

In the same year that Colebrooke wrote his essay, the French Sanskritist A.S. Langlois wrote a scathing review of A.W. Schlegel's translation.[5] Then, between 1825 and 1827, three thinkers who were to have a significant influence upon the pedagogical projects of their respective countries entered the fray. First, Wilhelm von Humboldt[6] reacted in detail to

[3] In addition to Halbfass, see Roger-Pol Droit 1989: 175–96 and Hulin 1979 for specific discussions of Hegel's essay.

[4] Henry Thomas Colebrooke, "On the Religion and Philosophy of the Hindus," Parts 1 and 2, *Transactions of the Royal Asiatic Society* 1 (1824): 19–43, 93–118. Part 1 was first read on 21 June 1823, and Part 2 on 21 February 1824.

[5] A. S. Langlois, "Bhagavad Gītā id est thespesion melos … traduit par M.A.G. de Schlegel," *Journal Asiatique* 4 (1824): 105–16, 236–52. Langlois criticized Schlegel's translation up to the twelfth canto.

[6] W. von Humboldt, "Über die unter dem Namen Bhagavad-Gītā bekannte Episode des Mahâ-Bhârata," in *Gesammelte Werke*, 1: 26–109.

Langlois's attack on Schlegel's translation (Humboldt 1841: I.110–84).[7] Humboldt subsequently followed this response with an essay on the *Gītā* (I.26–109), to which G.W.F. Hegel responded in an extensive review article in 1827 (Hegel 1910: 131–204).[8] Hegel commented specifically on Schlegel's view, seconded by Humboldt, that the *Gītā* was the only classical Sanskrit poem with philosophical content. Victor Cousin then made the *Gītā* the subject of his philosophical lectures of 1828.[9]

It is misleading to see this flurry of commentary as a purely philosophical debate centred on the presentation of the philosophical concepts promulgated in the *Gītā*. Rather, the discussion revolved in large part around issues of translation, artistic commensurability, and value. That these Europeans may have erred in their translations and interpretations of the *Gītā* is not of overriding significance here, especially given the tools and the multilevelled distortion necessarily imbricated in this initial European reception of India. Rather it is the way in which this reception involved issues of translation theory and practices that elicits our interest. A fundamental problem that Schlegel's translation of the *Gītā* raised centred on the translation of two principal terms, Sāṃkhya[10] and Yoga,[11] that designated the schools of philosophy expounded in the text. The Sāṃkhya doctrine designates the path to perfection reached

[7] W. von Humboldt, "Über die Bhagavad Gītā. Mit Bezug auf die Beurtheilung der Schlegelschen Ausgabe im Pariser Asiatischen Journal."

[8] G.W.F. Hegel, "Über die unter dem Namen Bhagavad-Gītā bekannte Episode des Mahabhatrata von Wilhelm von Humboldt," in the *Berliner Schriften*. With the exception of the *Berliner Schriften*, in all other citations the edition used is the *Sämtliche Werke, Neue kritische Ausgabe*, ed G. Lasson and D. Hoffmeister, 2nd ed. (Leipzig: F. Meiner, 1944).

[9] Victor Cousin, *Cours de l'histoire de la philosophie* (Paris: Pichon & Didier 1829), vol. 1, lessons 5 and 6.

[10] Sāṃkhya can be described as "dualistic realism." Its doctrine identifies two ultimate realities, *prakṛti* (matter) and *puruṣa* (self or spirit). The *puruṣa* denoted pure consciousness and pure subject. It differs completely from the ego, senses, and intellect. The *puruṣa* is passive and unchanging. The manifold objects constituting the universe arise from *prakṛti*. Before this evolution occurs, *prakṛti* is in a state of constant transformation, with the *guṇas* (nature's components) constantly balancing each other. Evolution occurs from a disequilibrium of *guṇas*. *Prakṛti* transforms into gross elements, which further disintegrate into subtle elements, which in turn disintegrate, resulting in the undifferentiated and homogenous *prakṛti* in dynamic equilibrium. *Prakṛti* develops with a purpose. It evolves for the sake of the *puruṣa* and required contact with the *puruṣa* for evolution. The distinction *puruṣa/prakṛti* is essentially that of subject and object; they are radically different from each other yet are required to interact.

[11] Yoga is based on the same dualist foundation as Sāṃkhya. It differs from Sāṃkhya by incorporating the concept of a personal god, different ontology for the *puruṣa*, and a different soteriology. When the term is in italics and not capitalized, it refers to the Sanskrit term rather than the philosophical school.

with the reasoning intellect. The path of Yoga is described in the *Gītā* as self-concentration through non-intellectual meditation. Principally at issue in the initial Western reception of the *Gītā* was the understanding of the term *yoga* itself. In his translation of 1785, Wilkins defined *yoga* as 'junction, devotion, bodily or mental application of the mind in spiritual things'. In his 1824 essay, Colebrooke obliquely referred to *yoga* as the 'meditation on special topics'. Schlegel had primarily chosen the Latin '*devotio*' as the primary 'equivalent' for the term *yoga*. As these three renditions suggest, the *Gītā*'s initial reception significantly involved what would appear to be conflicting approaches to the translation of this specific term (Gipper 109–28).

A.W. Schlegel and W. von Humboldt

Wilhelm von Humboldt, the Minister of State for Prussia, was an important Sanskrit scholar and philologist and pedagogical authority of his time. Provoked by Langlois's virulent criticism of A.W. Schlegel's Latin translation, Humboldt responded on 17 June 1825 in a letter to Schlegel commenting on Langlois's critique (Humboldt 1841: 84–110). Humboldt's letter to Schlegel investigates the specific issues of translation that Langlois's review had raised. Langlois's main dissatisfaction stemmed from Schlegel's translation methodology. To avoid the issue of loss, a topic first theorized by Jerome, Schlegel opted to translate difficult terms by a variety of words in order to grasp their plenitude. In contrast, Langlois felt that each word in the source language should have been rendered by a single term in the target language. So rather than the many renderings that Schlegel offered for the term '*yoga*'—*destinatio, exercitatio, applicatio, devotio, disciplina activa, mysterium, facultas mystica, maiestas*, and *contemplatio*—Langlois preferred the single French equivalent of '*dévotion*'. For the *yogi*, he favoured the term '*dévot*', disregarding its pejorative connotations in the French language.

Humboldt initiated his response to Langlois with the assertion that translating is, in principle, an impossible undertaking, because different languages do not offer synonyms of identically structured concepts. Humboldt maintained that a good translation was only an approximation in terms of replicating the beauty and the sense of the original. Ideally, a reader would have knowledge of both the source and the target language and could recognize the original term from its correspondent in translation. Humboldt felt that such recognition was possible in Schlegel's translation. Moreover, Humboldt felt that Schlegel had captured other important qualities of the original, such as its syntactical simplicity, brevity, emphasis, lightness, and elegance—all important issues from a literary point of view. Humboldt also raised the point that philosophical terms are often multifaceted and defy translation into one word. For this reason, Humboldt felt that Schlegel's decision to render a term with representations of its different aspects as appropriate to each occasion of its use provided the only reasonable solution for his translations. Humboldt then addressed the specific problem raised by Langlois (and subsequently reiterated by Hegel and Cousin) concerning the translation of the term *yoga*. He reiterated that he found it impossible to find in any language a single translation suitable for this term. While he readily admitted having problems with certain choices that Schlegel had made, Humboldt noted that 'anyone who knows the Sanskrit word *yoga* through translation cannot grasp its true meaning'. A non-linguist such as Schopenhauer noted that the translation of Indian philosophical terms was imprecise and weak, only expressing the contours of the original. The tone was strange, modern, empty, pale, flat, poor in meaning, and Western (Schopenhauer 174). Schleiermacher held that in translation we only have an 'image' of the text, since languages are not equivalent. Humboldt echoes these thoughts, noting that it is impossible to eliminate every blemish in a translation (Humboldt 1841: 1.137).

According to Humboldt, there was only one possible method in translation. Either the translator did what Langlois demanded and sought in the target language one word corresponding to the original concept with comprehension aided by appending a commentary, or the translator could do what Schlegel attempted—render an original term by different words in the target language that approximate the different uses of the original term. Humboldt recognized that the latter method might be detrimental to philosophical depth because the common link between the various applied meanings and the original concept is lost, as is the nuance of each word originating from the same source. But Humboldt here was addressing not only pertinent issues concerning translation conventions of nineteenth-century Germany,[12] he was also raising a larger issue: Beyond the very problem of translation itself and the particular difficulties involved in translating Sanskrit, Schlegel's translation of the *Gītā* prompted a more fundamental discussion of nineteenth-century philosophies of language.

Just as Herder had earlier theorized on the parallel development of a *Volk* and its language, Humboldt drew this connection from a linguistic point of view. In 'Über die Verschiedenheiten des Menschlichen Sprachbaues und ihren Einfluss auf die geistige Entwicklung des Menschengeschlechts', Humboldt maintained that 'a people's speech is their spirit, and this spirit is their speech' (Humboldt 1841: 6.2). In other words, Humboldt saw language as the outgrowth of a nation's spiritual strength (6.6). The national character of a language rested on its disposition (*Naturanlage*). With this claim, Humboldt detoured away from any suggestion that racial differences influenced language formation or even that such a determination was possible. He did not divide languages according to race or nations. Rather, Humboldt's theory of language stressed the creative linguistic ability inherent in the speaker's mind. He identified language, not with products of acts of speaking, but with the living capability with which speakers produced and understood utterances. Humboldt qualified language as *energeia* (activity). In German, he referred to it as *Tätigkeit* (activity) and *Erzeugung* (production, generation). Following Herder, Humboldt maintained that the individuality of each language represents the peculiar property of a given speaking group. While later nationalists' arguments would misuse such linguistic identifications, Humboldt should not be personally charged with initiating this trend. He himself was less interested in German, than in other languages. He viewed German as merely one language among many. Each and every language contained a specific and exclusive worldview. The extralinguistic world is transformed into language in a particular way, when extralinguistic realities become linguistic structures. Thus, for Humboldt, the act of translation becomes a continuous transposition from one worldview to another. Following the Romantic's vision of translation, as articulated by Friedrich Schlegel, Humboldt saw translation as a potentiality, not as

[12] For an examination of how early German translations of Sanskrit differed from the European language translation conventions of the nineteenth century, see Figueira 1991.

an end in itself but an ultra-literature marked by gain. Certainly, a philosophical poem such as the *Gītā* would demand additional contextual values. So, Humboldt viewed Langlois's demand for one-to-one correspondence in translation to be a totally inadequate method.

Humboldt's philosophy of language postulated that all languages can be understood as separate organisms that differ from one another both in unique grammatical forms and in specific semantic structures. Language was not an object (Humboldt 1841: 6.42) since linguistic diversity was not as much a matter of sounds and signs but an issue of worldview (3.241–68).[13] Its inner form consisted of structures articulating specific thought principles or strategies, *Sprachstilen*, that could be replicated by anyone who had practice in translating. Thus, when Humboldt spoke about translation techniques, he primarily addressed the nature of language, its origins and development, and its relationship to national identity. Such discussions on the philosophy of language and its relation to the formation of national identity reflected concerns that were not unique to his thought. They echoed conventional discourse regarding language at the time, as seen in Schlegel's response to Humboldt's letter.[14]

A.W. Schlegel had translated the *Gītā* into Latin because he considered it a particularly suitable language for translating the subtlety of meaning found in the Sanskrit language.[15] His foremost concern in the translation had been to retain context-dependent semantic variance, as in the case of translating the term *yoga*. Schlegel was an experienced translator, whose renditions of Dante, Calderon, Shakespeare, Ariosto, Petrarch, Camões, and the Classics had set the standards of nineteenth-century European translations. He was well aware of the pitfalls of translation. He felt that sublimity could not be translated, because the translator would have to recreate what the first author had achieved and would have to use the same tools and materials that the author had used. In his response to Langlois's review, Schlegel himself questioned where, even if those tasks were possible, the translator would find the fullness of sound and the flow

[13] Humboldt, 'Über das vergleichende Sprachstudium in Beziehung auf die verschiedenen Epochen der Sprachentwicklung'.

[14] Humboldt's letter first appeared in the *Indische Bibliotek*, where Schlegel followed it with his own response to Langlois's review. See A. W. Schlegel, *Indische Bibliotek*, vol. 2, part 2 (1826): 218–58; Part 3 (1828), 328–72. Reprinted in Humboldt's *Gesammelte Werke*, vol 1. Citations are from this reprint.

[15] He had initially considered translating the Sanskrit into Greek.

or 'happy succession' of consonants and vowels that originated together with the original idea and formed part of its essence. In India, particularly, he noted, the development of language and the formation of ideas were measurably different from anything with which Europeans were familiar. If language mirrored the soul of a nation and the national *Geist* was embodied in a nation's literature, Schlegel wondered whether they could ever be perfectly communicated. He responded to Langlois's demand for word-to-word correspondence by stating that such a method best suits the process of translating geometry textbooks. In poetry and philosophy, one cannot treat the 'poetic representation of the mind's innermost conceptions of itself and the eternal' like a collection of algebraic signs.

As a more than competent practising translator, Schlegel had explored all options he felt were available to him, given the literary conventions of his day. He compared their shortcomings and weaknesses and selected what seemed to him to be the most acceptable course of action. Given the choice of retaining a Sanskrit term because it was untranslatable—a method used by Wilkins and the Persian translators of the *Upanishads*—he found this option unprofitable. Such indirect translations require contextual assistance that he felt burdened the narrative flow. He deemed Langlois's demand for convergent translation unfeasible, because often no equivalences presented themselves in the target language, and when equivalents were employed, the richness of the original was lost.[16] Schlegel chose, therefore, the third option, a refractive translation, whereby complex expressions in the source language are rendered, according to context, by various expressions in the target language. He was not blind to the disadvantage of this method in terms of its inadmissible arbitrariness. However, he felt that it allowed the many-sidedness of a term to be grasped quite well. Schlegel admitted that, of all the terms to be translated, *yoga* had presented him with the most difficulty; he admitted struggling with it and forcing the term *yoga* to reveal its secrets. As they were formulated, both Humboldt's letter and Schlegel's response clearly reframed Langlois's individual criticisms of the *Gītā* translation into the larger debate on the transferability of meaning from one worldview to another. Humboldt would further develop this theme in his subsequent

[16] This reservation is particularly relevant in translating from Sanskrit, given the importance and role in Sanskrit poetry of *dhvani*, the suggestion or reverberation of words.

essay, 'On the Episode of the *Mahābhārata* known by the name *Bhagavad Gītā*',[17] and it was from this subsequent essay that Hegel would be inspired to re-examine the *Gītā* more closely and write his own critical assessment.

In 'On the Episode', Humboldt addressed the ways of thinking that he found unique to India and drew attention to what might, to Western non-specialist readers, appear as the text's apparent contradictions. He posited the doctrine of emanation as the main doctrine of Indian philosophy (Humboldt 1841: 1.138).[18] By the term 'emanation', Humboldt specifically referred to the Sāṃkhya school of philosophy. His interpretation of Sāṃkhya as the spiritual begetting upon nature, a definition based partially on Colebrooke, is lucid in its major contours (1.58–9). He correctly described the workings of *prakṛti* (nature), *puruṣa* (being), and the *guṇas* (natural qualities) (1.57–63). He noted that the *Gītā* presented human nature as an imitation and the particularization of the divine model, which creates bodies and permits them to be destroyed by entering or leaving them (1.47). God then joins the Self to mortal bodies that perform actions (*Gītā* 15.7–9). This involvement, however, in no way taints the divine (*Gītā* 9.8; 9.9). In discussing the philosophies of Sāṃkhya and Yoga, Humboldt primarily addressed their moral and intellectual implications. He cited the *Gītā* to the effect that Sāṃkhya calls for the application of rational understanding (1.66–7). He correctly distinguished Sāṃkhya from Yoga, which he claimed places God in his independent infinitude at the summit of all things and offers a means for reaching bliss through the concentration on God's Being.

According to Humboldt, the system of Yoga, as formulated by Patañjali,[19] agrees with the doctrine expressed (with less sophistry and mysticism) by Krishna (*Gītā* 2.25; 8.20; 13.27). Humboldt maintained that the poem's philosophical system pivots around two main dicta: (1) that the spirit is simple, imperishable by nature, and separate from the body which is complex and perishable (*Gītā* 2.14,18) and (2) that anyone

[17] This essay appeared in two parts. The first part was read on 30 June 1825, and the second part on 15 June 1826, at the Royal Academy of Sciences, Berlin. The entire article was first printed in the *Abhandlungen der historisch -philologischen Klasse der preussischen königlichen Akademie der Wissenschaften* (Berlin, 1827).

[18] This understanding of Indian philosophy had earlier been expressed by F. Schlegel in *Über die Sprache und Weisheit der Indier*.

[19] Patañjali (205 BC–150 BC) was the author of the *Yoga Sūtras*, the foremost text on Yoga.

who strives for consummation must perform any and all acts 'without regard for their consequences and with perfect equanimity' (*Gītā* 2.26–30).[20] From these key themes, Humboldt concluded that the *Gītā* teaches the inconsequentiality of death and action. Although death concerns only the perishable body, actions in and of themselves are not without weight. Humboldt correctly maintained that actions, once freed from passion and intuition, function as mere products of nature or precepts of duty. However, he did not perceive the whole system of Indian thought as resting on pure intellectuality. Rather, he cited the *Gītā* 3.3 to support the view that there are two operative systems, one of action and the other of insight. Humboldt recognized well that the *Gītā* warned about the bonds of action rather than actions themselves. He fully acknowledged the weight given to action as preferable to non-action and reaffirmed that the poem does not suggest anything as vain as the suppression of action (Humboldt 1841: 1.48).[21]

As in the earlier letter to Schlegel, Humboldt defines *yoga* as a process whereby spirituality can be controlled through immersion in the godhead or the personalized God (Humboldt 1841: 1.77). By choosing to translate *yoga* as *Vertiefung* (immersion), Humboldt hoped to convey the mystic mood characteristic of the *yogi*. Humboldt felt that A.W. Schlegel's translation of *yoga* as *devotio*, while adequate, lost too much of the original meaning of 'connecting' (1.68).[22] Moreover, he felt that the Latin term was too narrow and inapplicable in those instances where *yoga* should be understood as active energy. Explicating how the term *yoga* derived from the root *YUJ*, which means to connect or tie, Humboldt focused on how this term expresses a link between one thing and another. So, he glossed that *yoga* must involve a constant orientation of the mind toward the deity, since the mind has withdrawn from all other objects, thoughts, movement, or bodily functions (1.70).

Humboldt emphasized the importance that the *Gītā* always places upon action and reminds his reader that the setting of the poem is, after

[20] Humboldt 1841: 1.28: '... und dass von dem nach Vollendung strebenden jede Handlung ohne alle Rücksicht auf ihre Folgen, und mit völligem Gleichmuth über dieselben, vorgenommen warden muss.'

[21] Humboldt cites the *Gītā* 3.22–4; 4.13–14; 9.10; 12.31–2 to this effect.

[22] What is attained through *yoga* is *nirvāṇa*, understood by Humboldt as non-thinking or a wafting away of the earth spirit. Humboldt did not want it interpreted as the suppression of all earthly thoughts or as a permanent state defining man's entire contemplative life.

all, a battlefield. He elucidated how Krishna's message proceeds from the principle that truth cannot be found by means of discursive or rationalizing reason. To find truth, one must prepare the mind, purifying it of taint, call upon insight in order to control it, animate an inner feeling for truth, and direct the spirit to the point in which the Self connects with things as part of them. Such a doctrine—which teaches direct insight through perception—demands firmness, exertion, and steadfastness of spirit. Humboldt therefore recognized two paths as presenting themselves in the *Gītā*: one can proceed in accordance with reason or one can proceed through action (Humboldt 1841: 1.73–4). Both paths, however, ultimately aim at the transformation of human nature into godly nature and Humboldt reiterated that this goal cannot be obtained merely through intellectual exercise (1.79).

Thus, Humboldt maintained that the *Gītā* defended Indian philosophy against any accusation of fatalism and predestination independent of the will (Humboldt 1841: 1.82). Ethical freedom remains safe in the *Gītā*: the godhead participates causally in no human action, good or evil. All action originates in the character that performs it. Humboldt views *yoga* as founded on the necessity of ethical freedom, since perseverance and steadfastness of will function as its final aim and can spring only from absolute freedom, which, in turn, opposes itself to all stirrings of finite nature. He clearly denied the theme of quietism that Hegel would subsequently impute to Indian philosophical thought. In no way did Humboldt posit insight (*Erkenntnis*) as Hegel would, as the foremost of all human efforts promulgated in the *Gītā* (1.29–30). In his response to Humboldt, however, Hegel would discount his subtle reading. Hegel would seek to cut the *Gītā* and Indian philosophy to fit his own schema.

Hegel

Whereas Humboldt, knowing Sanskrit, worked from the *Gītā* itself, with reference to Colebrooke's exposition of the Indian philosophical schools, Hegel worked almost exclusively from Colebrooke's 1824 essay. So, his thoughts were rather removed from what was articulated in the *Gītā* in any language, whether it be the Sanskrit or in translation (Latin, English, French, German). Moreover, Hegel's judgements on Indian thought evolved considerably during the process of rewriting his lectures on the history of philosophy and they became more detailed in later versions. In the 1825–6 version, he first added a section on India, after having read the initial instalments of Colebrooke's essay dealing with the philosophies of Sāṃkhya and Nyāya-Vaiśeṣika.[23] Although this section was ostensibly a response to Humboldt, Hegel dealt less with his colleague's interpretation of the *Gītā* and more with the very acceptability of the Indian philosophy purportedly promulgated in the poem. The *Gītā* provided Hegel with an opportunity to prove the deficiency of Indian morality (Sawhney 96).

Hegel's analysis of India was also intimately bound up with his criticism of the Romantics. He responded negatively to their infatuation with the Orient (Halbfass 85) and sought to demythologize India's prestige in nineteenth-century Europe. His critique of German Romantic Indomania was initially directed against Friedrich Schlegel whom he saw as the major culprit in this valorization of and fascination with India. Hegel rejected Schlegel's ideas on revelation, primitive peoples, or an original unified state of humankind (Hegel 1955: 158ff.). Although Schlegel eventually had become disenchanted with Indian philosophy (Figueira 1990: 425–33), he continued to adhere to the view that India remained a source of spiritual force and orientation. Hegel simply could not accept this position. What rankled him most was that the fascination the Romantics had for India articulated what he perceived as both a sentimental nostalgia for and theology of origins (Olender 19) as well as a blatant disregard for the present (Hegel 1955: 1.138ff). According to Hegel, the Orient represented merely vestiges of the past. It was of no use in deciphering the present. Thus, Hegel's assessment of Indian philosophy is embedded within his more general critique of the Romantic notion of an *Urvolk*, the belief in the Asian origin of European mythology,[24] and the neo-Catholic belief, defended by Friedrich Schlegel, of continuous revelation.[25] Humboldt's essay on Indian philosophy offered Hegel the

[23] Nyāya-Vaiśeṣika, one of the six schools of Indian philosophy, focused on two means to knowledge: perception and inference.

[24] The *Symbolik* of Creuzer and Görres's *Mythengeschichte der asiatischen Welt* (1810) promulgated the origins of Greek and Latin mythology in India. Myths were superior in India and became poorer and degraded in the West, just as Sanskrit was closer to a more primitive language.

[25] In fact, one cannot disregard the connection between Hegel's reception of Indian metaphysics and his more general attack upon Christianity. According to F. Schlegel, humans who are led by primitive revelation, lived in direct contact with nature presented through sentiment and interiority. After original sin, they were left to themselves, guided by their memory of primitive

long-awaited opportunity to attack Romantic enthusiasts of antiquity, modern pietists, and the Romantic ego-centred concept of faith (Hegel 1966: I.2: 168).

The study of the history of philosophy thus parallels the study of philosophy itself (Hegel 1944: 1.34). Hegel viewed philosophy as occurring within a process of unfolding, with his system as the complete realization of this movement. In the dynamic movement of history, earlier developments are taken up (*aufgehoben*) into what succeeds them (1.14). In Hegel's estimation, the Orient represents merely the first stage in this development, so any investigation of India would just be viewed as an examination of the roots of the Western tradition. The significant problem India posed for Hegel was what he saw as its lack of dynamism. According to Hegel, Indian history lacked Europe's dynamic of progress, epitomized in the then European present. Since Indian thought was static, Hegel felt that it could play no role in the European past, present, or future. Hegel constructed his interpretation of the *Gītā* to support this thesis of India as a static entity.

He maintained that the acme of Indian speculative thought consisted of a sinking into *brahman* (the universal soul) (Hegel 1966: I.3.118ff), the annihilation of the subject and unconsciousness (Hegel 1944: 1.227). Before *brahman*, everything else is accidental and nothing (Hegel 1970: 67). Therefore, religious action is contentless and inessential (Hegel 1944: 1.379). Since *brahman* as substance is abstract, Hegel claimed that the Hindu renounces everything pertaining to life and the world in order to be united with it (1.370). For Hegel, the Hindu union with God consists in destroying and benumbing all self-consciousness. Rather than

revelation. Vestiges of the time immediately after the Fall appear in the system of emanation. Left to himself, man creates philosophical systems that are more and more barbaric, dualistic, pantheistic, and polytheistic, eventually culminating in the *Old Testament*. Hegel took umbrage not so much with the particular issues in F. Schlegel's thought as with his entire approach to the philosophy of history. Schlegel held that the task of the philosopher of history was 'to reestablish the divine image in man, the image which is lost' (Schlegel 9. 5). His starting point is fallen man, who is believed to have had in the beginning of history very high powers but, by misusing them, gradually lost them (Schlegel 31ff; 43f). Hegel cannot help but disparage Schlegel (Hegel 1944: 1: 264). He made a snide remark about F. Schlegel's conversion in a letter to F.P.I. Niethammer (7 May 1809, in *Briefe*, 1: 283) and maintained that neither Schlegel brother was capable of laying claim to speculative thinking. They 'admire matters of mediocre value' and 'give universal honor to what is only relatively important' and are 'enthusiastic even with cheekiness' about things that are 'cheap and secondary' as though they were the most important (Schlegel 10: 81–2).

understanding union as liberation, Hegel sees it as a process of emptying. The individual escapes into nothing and has no freedom (1.229, 235). Since there is no freedom for the subject, Indian philosophy cannot, according to Hegel, even present a true philosophy.

Hegel had previously taken for granted India's exclusion from the history of philosophy (Hegel 1944: 1.232), and his reading of Colebrooke did not radically transform this assessment.[26] But, with the appearance of Schlegel's *Gītā* translation, Hegel realized that he now had to address the existence of Indian philosophy (1.293ff).[27] So, in responding to Humboldt, Hegel had a specific purpose in mind: He needed to present the *Gītā* in such a way that he could impose on Indian philosophy what his own vision of philosophy and history demanded: a vision of fatalism that implied moral failure.

It is clear from even the most uninformed reading of the *Gītā* that this text calls for the recognition of the identity of the individual soul (*ātman*) with the Universal (*brahman*) as the path to salvation. Unbelievably (because it is so often reiterated in the text), Hegel disregarded this pivotal identification of *brahman* with *ātman* (Halbfass 1988: 91), and in doing so he simply ignored the single most affirmative aspect of Indian theology. Instead, Hegel described the union with *brahman* as a permanent state of abstraction, a union where the self 'plunges into itself',[28] and an intuition of nothing (*das Anschauung des Nichts*) (Hegel 1970: 183). To reach union with *brahman*, Hegel maintained the Indian extinguished all awareness of content in order to attain abstract unity through utter stupefaction and insensibility (Hegel 1970: 151).[29] Hegel read into the *Gītā* a constant call to immobility and inaction (157–8). 'The Indian soul's

[26] The only insights that Hegel took from Colebrooke's essay were that philosophy existed in India and he and Europe were largely ignorant of this fact. After Colebrooke's essay appeared in 1824, Hegel integrated 'Oriental' philosophy into his history of philosophy in the Winter semester of 1825–6. But Hegel had already begun to study India in 1822 and had kept abreast of the Orientalist scholarship of the time.

[27] Hegel found in Colebrooke the most reliable and authoritative of all scholars of his time dealing with Indian materials (Hegel 1944: 1. 293). Colebrooke's method differed radically from that of Hegel. He did not proceed from the definition of what is or what ought to be philosophy; nor did he question the relationship between religion and philosophy; nor were art, religion, and philosophy of interest to Colebrooke.

[28] Hegel 1970: 142: '... das Handeln wird im Erkennen oder vielmehr in der *abstrakten Vertiefung* des Bewusstsein in sich absorbiert.' See also Hegel 1970: 182.

[29] Hegel 1970: 151. See also *Philosophie der Weltgeschichte* 2:407: 'Die Erhebung zum Brahm wird durch höchste Abgestumpftheit und Bewusstlosigkeit bewirkt,' cited in Halbfass 91.

union in emptiness is rather deadening.'[30] It leads to no truth, since it is without content.

It was to prioritize this reading of Indian philosophy that Hegel gave primacy to the *Gītā* and posited *yoga* as its central theme,[31] attributing to it an abstract character (Hegel 1970: 146). Correcting Schlegel's translation of *yoga* as *devotio* and Humboldt's translation as *Vertiefung*, Hegel defined *yoga* as a fusion of subject and object leading to a loss of consciousness (100–1). He argued that the term *devotio* could not be used because it implied divine orientation, content, and meaning—all of which *yoga* did not possess. Similarly, *yoga* could not be *Vertiefung*, as in art or science, because it lacked image, idea, and definite thought (101). Moreover, *yoga* could not adequately be rendered by the term *Vertiefung* because, according to Hegel, *yoga* involves absorption into nothingness. It consists of emptying the mind and renouncing thought. For Hegel, the *yoga* described in the *Gītā* falls into the contentlessness of subject and object. At best, it encourages one to perform work senselessly and stupidly (152). It exemplified for Hegel the negative attitude of the Indian mind (157, 152, 165; 1966: 2.1.166) as well as the negative nature of Indian religion (163).[32] Hegel diametrically opposed *yoga*, interpreted as a quietistic exercise, to his own vision of historical orientation.

After his initial dismissal of Indian philosophy, Hegel could then concede that India, with its concept of *brahman* as pure substance, had indeed developed an idea of the Universal and could grudgingly be said to have a religion and philosophy. However, he noted that the Indian concept of *brahman*[33] was in no way comparable to the Christian idea of God. Moreover, he did not recognize in Indian speculative thought (as he understood it in the *Gītā*) any return to the concrete particularity of the world. Hegel found that Hinduism lacked the essential mediation (*Vermittlung*) of the abstract Universal with the particular and therefore

[30] Hegel 1970: 161: 'Das indische Vereinsamen der Seele in die Leerheit ist vielmehr eine Verstumpfung.'

[31] Hegel 1970: 145, 148, 151. Hegel perceived that the union with *brahman* was achieved by birth and *yoga* (145) with *yoga* as the designated path for non-brahmins (Hegel 1970: 146) and the real focus of Indian philosophy and religion (148).

[32] Hegel defines *yoga* alternately as the absence of thought, vacuity (Hegel 1966: 2.1:166), and a *Verdumpfung* of self-consciousness (185). See also Hegel 1968: 2:378).

[33] Hegel 1970: 185–190. Hegel defines Brahm (*sic*) as the 'abstrakte Einheit ohne Bestimmung', 'die Einheit nur als die abstrakte Allgemeinheit, als bestimmungslose Substanz', 'Substanz ohne Subjektivität', 'das reine Sein, ohne alle konkrete Bestimmung in sich'.

it negated the dialectic of subject and object necessary for the creative development of humankind within history.[34] The finite becomes lost in the infinite; the world becomes absorbed in *brahman*—which Hegel identified with pure nothingness, '*das Nichts alles Endlichen*' (Hegel 1970: 190). If God contains all finite and particular beings as non-essential modifications, then humanity must, of necessity, possess neither identity nor dignity (Hegel 1966: I.1:95ff.). By precluding mediation (Hegel 1968: 2.334), Hindu abstraction also abolished freedom (Hegel 1966: I.1:232, 334). Hence, Hegel's definition of a Hindu Absolute precluded the possibility of a free individuality ever manifesting itself in India (Hegel 1968: 2.399).

For Hegel, therefore, Indian substantiality presented the opposite of European reflection and the vanity of the subject (Hegel 1968: 2.333). As onerous as this vanity was, Hegel found it to be of far greater value[35] than what he claimed was an Indian alternative vision (2.334), where the subject is obliterated and humiliated, where individuality disappears, and where eternal happiness is understood as the loss of Self (Hegel 1944: 1.227). With the absolute void as the substructure of the Indian worldview, the Hindu vision of humanity appeared to Hegel as a large anthill closed to historic existence, with *nirvāṇa* giving life its only value.[36] Hegel concluded, therefore, that Hindus can empower themselves only in a negative sense (Hegel 1970: 163, 181): knowledge, happiness, and human value are all equally impossible for them (Hegel 1968: 2.334).

Although Hegel felt that with A.W. Schlegel's translation of the *Gītā*[37] he had the necessary information to take on Indian philosophy, he evidently did not, or rather he chose only what suited his preconceived

[34] Hegel 1970: 181ff. Nor does Hegel conceive of the undivided unity of *brahman* and the multiplicity of the world as permeating each other (158, 175, 184f, 190ff). Rather, he maintains that they relate to each other in unreconciled negation and exclusion.

[35] He valued European vanity of the subject because of its permanent element of the subjective power of unity.

[36] Hegel expresses these thoughts elsewhere in his writings. *Nirvāṇa*, which Hegel uses in the sense of 'nothingness', is perceived as the ultimate goal (1966: I.2: 124–34). Through meditation, one should produce emptiness within oneself (1968: 2:334ff.). Hegel sees liberation (*mokṣa*) as only something negative.

[37] Although contemptuous of A. W. Schlegel, Hegel made good use of his translation of the *Gītā* in the *Encyclopädie*, the lectures in *Philosophy of Art*, and the review of Humboldt's essay. Hegel recognized Schlegel's possession of a 'cultivated, poetical and spirited gift' for translation (1970: 150), although he had utter disdain for his supposed lack of depth (Hegel 1954: 3.165, 171). He compared Schlegel's translation to that of Wilkins. Hegel knew Charles Wilkins as 'the first translator of the *Bhagavad Gītā* (1970: 134). It is clear from Hegel's review of Humboldt's article on the *Gītā* that he had consulted Wilkins' translation (1970: 135, 150, 153, 155, 157).

argument. Hegel presented Sāṃkhya as the primary school of the Indian philosophical thought (Hegel 1970: 143–4) because it wonderfully supported his thesis of quietude. Michel Hulin has speculated that Hegel based his reading largely on the *Sāṃkhya Kārikā* 21 (Hulin 119). What is important to note here is how Hegel read the passage in question.[38] He seems to have based his entire interpretation upon a partial translation of the verses involved.[39] Hulin claims that Hegel omits the two significant passages upon which his entire analysis rests (Hulin 121). First, he disregards *kārikās* 19 and 20, translated adequately by Colebrooke in this manner:

> From the contrast between soul and the other principles, it follows ... that soul is witness, bystander, spectator, solitary, and passive ... by reason of union with it, insensible body seems sensible and though the qualities be active, the stranger (soul) appears as the agent. (Colebrooke 42)

Both knowledge and action have value in this system. Knowledge allows one to recognize one's bondage. It is by actively subduing the senses and suppressing the emotions that knowledge of one's true nature is gained. Thus, *yoga* provides the method and the techniques to break through the veil of *māyā* (illusion). This very significant point is lost in Hegel's editing. Furthermore, as Hulin reveals, Hegel misread *kārikā* 21. Colebrooke translated this strophe as follows:

[38] As Cousin subsequently would do, Hegel altered Colebrooke's order. This change might be explained by Colebrooke's having emphasized the affinity of the two doctrines by treating Yoga separately only when it manifests a divergence in reference to Sāṃkhya. Hegel subordinates Yoga to Sāṃkhya, associating it with religious cults (Hegel 1970: 148) and reduces Sāṃkhya more or less to a systematic inventory of phenomenal categories.

[39] As Hulin notes (121) the fundamental idea of this *kārikā* is that the frontier between nature and spirit passes at the interior of concrete psychological experience. The passive *puruṣa* possesses will and knowledge, although, in its ignorance, it identifies with the products of *prakṛti*. By falling victim to this false identification, the self comes to feel that it experiences pain and suffering. It then develops attachments and becomes entangled in *saṃsāra*. Deliverance consists in breaking these bonds of ignorance and illusion and realizing one's true being as the *puruṣa* rather than some product of *prakṛti*. Thus, in Sāṃkhya, salvation comes from knowledge of the total independence of the self from the non-self as it manifests itself in activity, sensation, or volition.

> It is for contemplation of nature and for abstraction from it, that union of the soul with nature takes place, as the lame and the blind join for conveyance and for guidance: (one bearing and directed, the other borne and directing). By that union of soul and nature, creation, consisting in the development of intellect, is affected. (Colebrooke 32)

Hegel, however, renders it:

> It is by contemplation and by abstraction ... that the union of soul and nature is affected.... by this union of nature and soul, creation is affected. (Hegel 1944: 1.321)

As Hulin notes, Hegel thus identifies contemplation with abstraction and with the union of nature and soul (Hulin 120). Through what Colebrooke correctly identified as 'proximity' (Colebrooke 37), (*puruṣa* enables *prakṛti* to surge forth and create the world), the liberating knowledge of what belongs to *prakṛti* and what constitutes the *puruṣa* is made clear. This knowledge, in turn, terminates their proximity. Hegel, however, omits the passage referring to proximity (121).

Through such emendations and omissions, Hegel effectively presents Sāṃkhya as masking monism (Hegel 1944: 1.321). Furthermore, he is able to attribute to Sāṃkhya the same fatal binary of blind practice over and against abstract reflection that dominated all of his pronouncements on Indian thought. Hegel's treatment of *kārikā* 21 is thus illustrative of the way in which he supported his interpretation of the *Gītā* through partial translation. His truncated reading of Colebrooke allowed him to impose upon the *Gītā* a despairing quietism that tallied with his initial negative assessment of Indian thought.[40] Hegel then posited this nothingness as the single principle from which all diverse individual persons and things

[40] This interpretation paralleled his totally idiosyncratic (and false) interpretation of Buddhism and supported his judgement of Hindu religious observances. Hegel claimed the absolute of Buddhism was also *Brahm* (sic), cut off from deployment in the multitude of differences, a calm unity, not differentiated, the pure retreat into Self or the void. The Buddhist draws his mind into himself and comes to bliss (1968: 2: 335). 'The Mongolian Principle' deals mainly with the concept of *nirvāṇa*. Of course, there is no concept of 'Brahm' in Buddhism. The appendix entitled, 'The Mongolian Principle' in the Lasson edition (2: 332–42), after the chapter on China, deals with the religions of China, Burma, and Sri Lanka. Hegel defines the Mongolian Principle as the principle of 'Nichts' (334).

proceed and to which they return. Completely subtle, absolutely simple, and pure, this void consists of nothing other than the substantial which is identical to itself (1.321). It does not produce the world by generation, but by auto-division; it lets the self *distractedly* emanate from itself like an evanescent appearance (Hegel 1968: 2.339).

Hegel also imposed this same negative characterization that he saw in Hindu philosophy onto Indian cultic practices, which he described as the physical destruction of concrete vitality through long ascetic training and mortifications of the flesh. Everything in India is petrified into distinctions, and caprice holds sway. There is no ethical life or human dignity. The spirit wanders in the world of dreams and the highest value is annihilation (Hegel 1968: 2.378). Hegel consistently viewed Indian ascetics as placing themselves beyond good and evil (2.393). They tear themselves from nature through a process of depersonalizing ascesis, instead of using their intellect to situate themselves as individuals within the world (Hegel 1944: 1.333). Through the paths of cult and ascesis, Indians raise themselves above the finite only to lose themselves without return 'in the night of *Brahm* (sic)' (1.336).

A number of scholars have addressed Hegel's distorted interpretation of Indian philosophy and have theorized about his motivations for developing his arguments. As I have tried to show, the manner in which Hegel went about his critique of India is of more than a passing interest because his method of manipulating the translation of this text can also be seen in the subsequent reception history of the *Gītā* in both India and the West, where distortions appear not only in the themes chosen for emphasis, but also in the manner in which interpretations are legitimated through translation.[41] The issue of translation played a pivotal role in Hegel's interpretation of the text, both on the level of the problems originating in the *Gītā* as a translated text and also on the level of translation theory in general. Hegel's ability to draw the conclusions that he did depended to a large extent, on the misuse he made of translation and his justification for such usage.

[41] His dismissal of Indian philosophy was largely adopted by the discipline. While a complex philosophical system, Indian philosophy is never taught in philosophy departments in the US: it is relegated to the discipline of 'religion.' Hegel was instrumental in this dismissal of Indian philosophical schools as a worthy philosophical object of study.

As we have noted, Hegel's understanding of the *Gītā* was to a large extent shaped by the problem of adequately translating the term *yoga*. He felt that Humboldt's reservations about translating it with the French *dévotion* or the Latin *devotio* were misplaced. Humboldt had asserted that these terms failed to denote the concept's particularity. The terminology was too narrow to represent the overall concept; it expressed only a derivation not contained in the actual meaning of the term. Hegel preferred *Vertiefung* (in the sense of 'absorption'). He found it more appropriate but felt that it did not go far enough in defining *yoga*, since the Sanskrit term possesses a specific meaning beyond 'absorption'. Wilkins's elaboration—'that junction and bodily or mental application'—could be generally used as a theological gloss to express the application of the mind in spiritual things and the performance of religious ceremonies. However, Hegel felt that, as a translation, Wilkins's gloss proved unwieldly. Hegel's difficulty in finding an adequate translation for the term *yoga* was not due to mere semantic quibbling. It stemmed from far deeper theoretical concerns having to do with the (im)possibility of translation itself.

Hegel cites J.D. Guignault, the French translator of Friedrich Creuzer (1771–1858), as his authority on translation. Guignault held that A.W. Schlegel's general method of translation altogether failed to convey the originality, exactness, and local colour of a text. In this judgement, Guignault articulated a theory of translation that Hegel fully espoused, namely, that translation does grave injustice to terms that are sacrosanct in their own context. For Hegel, it comes down to meaning being non-transferable; original theological and mythological sense is, of necessity, lost (Hegel 1970: 188). For translation in general, Hegel posed a fundamental epistemological problem: A translation cannot articulate specific meaning. If such is the case, how then can one possibly translate in any precise manner a term such as *yoga*, which denotes a concept so essential to the understanding of Indian religion? One simply cannot. Hegel maintained that it was impossible, for example, to render *yoga* into the German language, since the concept did not exist in German culture and religion (150–1). Hegel noted that one cannot demand that an expression in a source language, with its specific mentality and culture, be rendered by a corresponding expression in a target language. A word in our language is given our specific conceptions and not those of other people with their own conceptions (149).

When Humboldt spoke of the impossibility of translation, his reasons were different from those of Hegel. Humboldt was making an aesthetic judgement rather than positing a philosophical pronouncement. Humboldt focused on the loss of philosophical depth and exactitude, as well as on the aesthetic parameters in terms of 'blemishes', associated links, contextual values, and the non-translatability of worldviews. Humboldt also eschewed any temptation to compare; his universalism rejected arguments of commensurability. Hegel's theory of translation, however, was predicated upon the need to judge incommensurability. It corresponded well with his need, expressed throughout his discussion of the *Gītā*, to impose value judgements on Indian philosophy in light of his own philosophy. The discussion concerning the inadequacy of translating the term *yoga* led Hegel to postulate a theory concerning the impossibility of translation in general, due to the incommensurability of source and target languages (Gipper 117). Hegel constructed his reading of the *Gītā* as well as the conclusions he drew from it concerning the value of Indian philosophy, to highlight this incommensurability.

The impossibility of exact translation changes everything. A text retains little value when subject to such a translation methodology. With this theory on the impossibility of translation, Hegel opens up the possibility of alternative and creative translations. The hermeneutical process breaks down, since the reader's prejudices are never called into question, and the text functions as a mould into which these prejudices are poured. Hegel could thus act unconstrained in offering imprecise and fragmentary renditions that also happened to support a judgement on Indian philosophy that was grounded in a defence of his own philosophical system, a vision of fatalism, and a denial of Indian morality.

It is, indeed, ironic that Hegel, the virulent critic of the Romantic emplotment of India, produced a reading that was no less a contrivance than that of the Romantics he sought to debunk. India will be no less a conscious fiction for Hegel than it is for any of the interpreters we study in this volume, even though the motivations for their various translation projects differ radically. Whereas general unfamiliarity and linguistic indecipherability had hampered initial Romantic interpretations of India (Figueira 1991), it was Hegel's abuse of translation that provided him with a potent weapon to distort an already distorted picture even further. This misuse of translation would continue throughout the *Gītā's* reception history. It was immediately implemented by Hegel's disciple Victor Cousin, who would follow his lead in his popularization of the *Gītā* in French academic circles.

Cousin

Victor Cousin excelled as a persecuted liberal hero. Due to his political activism, his course at the École Normale Supérieure had been suspended in 1818–19. In 1824, he was arrested in Berlin by order of the French police, only to be released upon Hegel's intervention with the Prussian Minister of the Interior. Cousin resumed lecturing in Paris in April–July 1828 and was incredibly popular with the students. Viewed as a cult figure, Cousin issued pronouncements in his lectures that were hailed as acts of insurrection to the unpopular regime of the restored monarchy. Cousin's set goal was to open up philosophy, especially German philosophy, and Hegel's work in particular, to the French. His lectures drew many auditors. The content of those lectures alluded to contemporary political issues and were fully publicized. In newspapers, the appearance of their *comptes rendus* received the same attention as parliamentary debates (Droit 175). By defending a form of spirituality autonomous from revelation and faith, Cousin's message found a ready audience in troubled times.

Between 1818 and 1825, Cousin devised a schema for the history of philosophy that he later published in the *Histoire générale de la philosophie* (1863). Cousin presented philosophy as the history of the human spirit, which could be broken down into four distinct categories: sensualism, idealism, scepticism, and mysticism (Cousin 177–8). In the fifth and sixth lessons of the *Cours de l'histoire de la philosophie* (1829), Cousin applied this schema to Indian speculative thought. In fact, the primary purpose of the *Cours* was to prove the universality of his system. If Cousin could discover elements of his schema operant in ancient India, how could his method be contested? Similarly, he reasoned, one cannot reject a universal system of philosophy, if it has been discovered nascent in India (212–14), the cradle of civilization[42] and philosophy (175). It was

[42] Droit (175–96) judges Cousin's positioning of the origin of civilization in the Orient, and his identification of the Orient with India, as reductive. As far as Cousin is concerned, India

in this context that the fifth and sixth lessons of Cousin's *Cours* (taught in 1828) contributed to the diffusion of Indian philosophy in Europe. Goethe's mention of these lectures to Eckermann[43] is indicative of their popularity and circulation abroad.

Cousin followed Hegel and prioritized Sāṃkhya. He dropped the *Vedas* from consideration, omitted the Mīmāṃsā school of philosophy[44] and Buddhism, and he equated the Nyāya school with Idealism (Cousin 157–8). In fact, Cousin projected indifference and scepticism on all the Indian philosophical systems (213). But he found it particularly prevalent in the Sāṃkhya tradition, which he felt advocated nihilism, fatalism, absurd fanaticism, and pure mysticism (217). As a champion of liberal spiritualism, Cousin viewed the issue of Sāṃkhya's blatant mysticism as most problematic (182). The *Gītā* became important for Cousin because he saw it as the literary monument of Sāṃkhya and, as such, the paradigm for mysticism in Indian philosophy. He, therefore, directed his analysis of the poem to expose what he judged as the moral and metaphysical excesses of Indian philosophy.[45]

The entire thrust of Cousin's reading of the *Gītā* was aimed at proving it to be a text promulgating mysticism according to his understanding of the term as the primacy of intuition over discursive knowledge and the superiority of faith over works. Mysticism particularly peeved Cousin because he believed it led to inaction and indifference. Cousin viewed mystics as individuals who have separated themselves from science, turned from regular study, and embraced contemplation (Cousin 220). He therefore saw in the *Gītā* the same baneful effect of inertia that Hegel had attributed to Indian thought. Reminiscent of Hegel, Cousin also supported a quietistic interpretation of the *Gītā* supported with translations

alone of Asian nations possesses philosophy. Egypt and Persia have only theologies. Cousin ignores China.

[43] Johann Peter Eckermann (1792–1854), German author best known for his *Conversations with Goethe* during the last years of the latter's life.

[44] *Mīmāṃsā* was the first major orthodox philosophical system to develop. The Sanskrit term signifies a 'revered thought'. The word is originated from the root '*MAN*' which refers to 'thinking' or 'investigating'. The word '*mīmāṃsā*' suggests the 'probing and acquiring knowledge' or 'critical review and investigation of the *Vedas*'.

[45] Cousin examines in depth the *Gītā* in the second half of the sixth lesson. He uses A.W. Schlegel's Latin translation of 1823, which Antoine de Chézy reviewed in the *Journal des Savants* (January 1825): 37ff. in addition to Wilkins's rendition.

of excerpts that were contextually unsupportable and fragmentary. In short, Cousin's reception of the *Gītā* replicated Hegel's treatment of the text in both its emphasis on quietism and its manipulation of translated material.

To establish the mysticism of the *Gītā*, Cousin first established what he saw as its demand for *recueillement* and interior contemplation, which for Cousin were the prolegomena of mysticism. Both themes are not supported by the text he cites.[46] Furthermore, Cousin's reading of the *Gītā*'s call for disinterested action as disdain for book knowledge, belittlement of the *Vedas*, and mockery of ceremonies is nowhere justified by the text. In Krishna's criticism of the type of ritual action that aims at the enjoyment and exercise of power (*Gītā* 2.43), Cousin saw a condemnation of action in general. Here too, this message is not at all supported by Schlegel's Latin text from which Cousin worked.[47] In other instances where Cousin is forced to acknowledge Krishna's message of disinterested action, he simply fabricates a subtext. According to Cousin, the author of the *Gītā* has Krishna teach disinterested action in pursuit of duty (*dharma*) only in order not to shock the common sense and virility of a young warrior. But his argument is circuitous. Cousin claims to expose a subterfuge inherent in the *Gītā's* teaching: because one cannot be sure about the disinterestedness of any action, one would tend to abstain from action in general, which in turn engenders inertia and, finally, the ideal of complete inaction.[48] To support this interpretation, he evokes the *Gītā* verse 4.18:

[46] To support such a reading, Cousin (*Cours*, 136–7) cites the *Gītā* 2.46: 'yāvān artha udapāne sarvataḥ saṃplutodake tāvān sarveṣu vedeṣu brāhmaṇasya vijṇānataḥ'. Schlegel translated it more or less correctly. My literal translation is 'As much as there is value in a well, when there is water overflowing on all sides, so much is there (value) in the Vedas for the brahmin who knows'. Schlegel translates it as 'Quot usibus inservit puteus, acquis undique confluentibus, tot usibus praestant universi libri scari theologo prudenti.'

[47] Schlegel, *Bhagavad Gītā*, 136: 'Rituum varietate abundantem . . . sedem apud superum finen bonorum praedicantes.'

[48] Cousin, *Cours*, 223–4: 'Toute commence toujours bien, et le préceptur d'Ardjouna ne lui recommande pas d'abord l'inaction, ce qui choquerait le sens commun et les mâles habitudes du jeune scharita: mais il lui recommande d'agir avec pureté, c'est à dire sans rechercher les avantages de son action, d'agir par la simple considération du devoir, arrive ensuite que pourra. C'est le désintéressement, la pureté intérieure. Rien de mieux assurément: mais la pent est glissante, car la pureté est modeste, ell doit fuir toutes les occasions de chute; et comme on n'est jamais plus sûr de ne pas mal agir qu'en n'agissant point, bientôt on va du désintéressement à l'abstinence et de l'abstinence à l'inertie.'

karmaṇyakarma yaḥ paśyed akarmaṇi ca karma yaḥ sa buddhimān manuṣyeṣu sa yuktaḥ kṛtsna-karmakṛt.

He who see inaction in activity, and activity inactivity, is intelligent among people, active in all activities, he is disciplined.

But when the final pāda of this verse (sa yukta kṛtsnakarmarmakṛt, 'he disciplined, doing all action') contradicts the quietist interpretation, Cousin simply omits it. Moreover, this omission does not stem from any ambiguity in the Schlegel translation—'Qui in opere otium cernit et in otio opus, is sapit inter mortals is devotus cunctis operibus peragendis aptus est' (Schlegel 144). Cousin simply edits Schlegel. The central injunction to perform all actions with discipline disappears and Cousin can erroneously conclude that the *Gītā* teaches the superiority of contemplation over action and works.

For Cousin, the mysticism of the *Gītā* also contributes to its degrading of works, both good and bad. He references the *Gītā* verse 2.50: 'buddhiyukto jahātīha ubhe sukṛtaduṣkṛte tasmād yogāya yujyasva yogaḥ karmasu kuśalam', literally 'he who is bound in intelligence, he casts off both good and evil deed. Therefore, bend yourself to *yoga*, *yoga* is skill in actions.' Schlegel had translated this passage as 'mente devotus in hoc aveo utraque dimittit, bene et male facta' (Schlegel 1823: 137). But here too, Cousin omits its final meaningful quarter stanza, 'yogaḥ karmasu kuśalam' (yoga is skill in actions), found in Schlegel as 'Qare devotioni te devove: devotion dexteritatem in operibus praebit' (136). From his selective and truncated renditions, Cousin concludes that the text exhibits disdain of works that easily leads to madness, even in its most perverse forms (225). This pattern of fragmentary translation continues throughout Cousin's analysis. He asserts that if the Hindu God only counts faith and disdains action, then he must be indifferent to good as well as bad actions (226). Cousin concludes that in such a religious system, the individual can rise to sainthood regardless of sin. Supporting the thesis that the *Gītā* promulgates actions beyond good and evil, Cousin glosses *Gītā* 9.30: 'api cet sudurācāro bhajate mām ananyabhāk sādhur eva sa mantavyaḥ samyag vyavasito hi saḥ' (even if an evil doer, if he worships me and is devoted to no one else then he indeed is thought to be good. Indeed, he is rightly determined). This is translated by Cousin as: 'Le plus criminel, s'il me sert sans partage, est purifié et sanctifié par là' (227).[49] Whereas, the Sanskrit original, as well as in Schlegel's rendition, focuses on the power of *bhakti* (faith or devotion) over moral effects, Cousin's focuses on morality. The *Gītā* does not teach, as Cousin would have us believe, that the individual is destined to advance beyond good and evil, as well as error and truth, and good and bad philosophy.[50] Rather, Krishna enjoins Arjuna to fulfil his *dharma* as a warrior.

Objectively, there are certain instances where Cousin's predisposition to read fatality into the *Gītā* was abetted by Schlegel's translation as in 'cunctus operibus animo dismissis commode sedet temperans mortalis in urbe novem portis instructa, neque ipse agens nes agendi auctor' (Schlegel 147) for verse 5.13: 'sarvakarmāṇi manasā saṃnyasyāste sukhaṃ vaśī navadvāre pure dehī naiva kurvan na kārayan' (Renouncing all actions with his mind he sits happily, a ruler, in the city of nine gates; he is the embodied one, never indeed doing anything or causing anything to be done). The Sanskrit specifically refers to the individual who sits as a ruler and through control has removed all actions 'with his mind'. Although Schlegel clearly expresses that the individual is 'restrained' (*temperans*), he omitted translating 'with his mind' (*manasā*), which ultimately refers to the yogi's ability to perform desireless action. Cousin will render this passage:

> Delivré de tout souci de l'action, le vrai dévot reste tranquillement assis dans la ville à neuf portes (le corps), sans remuer lui-même et sans remuer les autres. (Cousin 229)[51]

In a similar fashion, Schlegel correctly translates verse 2.58 ('yadā saṃharate cāyaṃ kūrmo'ṅgānīva sarvaśaḥ indriyāṇīndriyārthebhyas tasya prajñā pratiṣṭhitā') as: 'sicuti testudo undecunque, sensus abstrahit a

[49] Cousin's text can be translated as: 'The most criminal, if he serves me without division is purified and sanctified by it.'

[50] See, for example, the *Gītā*, 3:27—*prakṛteḥ kriyamāṇāni guṇaiḥ karmāṇi sarvaśaḥ ahaṃkāravimūḍhātmā kartāham iti manyate*. I translate this verse as 'actions everywhere are performed by the *guṇas* of nature. He who is deluded by the concerns of the ego thinks 'I am a doer.' In A.W. Schlegel's *Gītā*, (141): 'naturae qualitatibus peraguntur omni modo opera; sui fiducia qui fallitur, eorum seipsam auctorem esse arbitrator.' In Cousin (227) this verse becomes: 'Le présompteux se croit l'auteur de ses actions; mais toutes ses actions viennent de la force et de l'enchaînment nécessaire des choses' (The presumptuous one thinks that he is the author of his actions, but all his actions come from force and the necessary sequence of things').

[51] Cousin can be translated as: 'Delivered from all cares of action, the true devotee remains tranquilly seated in the city with nine doors (the body) without moving himself or others.'

rebus quae sensibus observantur: tunc apud eum sapiential commoratur' (Schlegel 1823: 138). This verse can be literally translated as: 'And when this one withdraws from the objects of the senses, like the limbs of a tortoise, his wisdom stands firm.'

Schlegel's translation conveys the yogic agenda of distancing the self from involvement and controlling one's thought. The Sanskrit literally refers to the drawing together (*saṃharate*) of the senses. Unfortunately, Schlegel has chosen to render the verb SAM-HṚ as *abstraho*, which leads to Cousin's choice of the term '*se recueillir*', evoking the process of retiring within oneself. Hence the quietist rendition: 'Il se recueille en soi, comme une tortue qui se retire en elle-même' (Cousin 229).[52]

Other examples can be brought forward, such as in *Gītā* 2.69, the Sanskrit reads as: 'yā niśā sarvabhūtānāṃ tasyāṃ jāgarti saṃyamī yasyāṃ jāgrati bhūtāni sā niśā paśyato muneḥ', which literally means: 'What is the night for all beings, in this the restrained one is wakeful, in which beings are wakeful, that is the night for the seeing sage.' Cousin renders this verse as: 'Ce qui est la nuit pour les autres est la veille du sage, et la veille des autres est sa nuit' (Cousin 229), translated as '[t]hat which is night for others, is the night before/vigil for the wise man, the night before/vigil of others is his night'. Cousin translates the Sanskrit *saṃyamī*, 'a man of restraint' as '*le sage*' (the wise man). His translation does not adequately express the status of abstinence present in Schlegel's use of '*abstinens*', rendering correctly the sense of action that is present in the Sanskrit text: 'quae nox est cunctus animantibus, hanc pervigilat abstinens; qua vigilant animantes, haec est nox verum intuentis anachoretae' (Schlegel 138–9).

Although the argument can certainly be made for the mysticism of the *Gītā*, Cousin's thesis that the poem promulgates absolute quietism, indifference, renunciation, and contemplative immobility is simply not justifiable, certainly not when it is clearly stated in 2.47 that action should be one's concern, just not its fruit: 'karmaṇyevādhikāraste mā phaleṣu kadācana mā karmaphalahetur bhūr mā te saṅgo'stv akarmaṇi' (your jurisdiction is in action alone, never at any time in the fruits, never should a motive of the fruits of action arise, never let there be attachments in inaction). Cousin totally distorts this clear message when he writes:

[52] 'He retires within himself, like a turtle who retracts into itself.'

> La dévotion ou logisme consiste, nous l'avons vu, à préférer la contemplation à la science, l'inaction à l'action, la foi aux oeuvres, à se fixer dans la prédestination .... (Cousin 237)[53]

Like Hegel, Cousin ignored the principal theme of the poem, the Hindu mystical identification of the individual soul (*ātman*) with All-Soul (*brahman*). Cousin instead chose to view this recognition as a wholly passive act. Here too, the case can feasibly be made that Cousin was led astray by Schlegel's translation of *yoga* as *devotio* (in the sense of contemplation), but it is a significant distortion to conclude that the fundamental theme of the *Gītā* is quietism. Granted, the message of the *Gītā* is not particularly simple. It teaches a complex game of action, detachment, and devotion. However, the *Gītā* clearly teaches that one is enjoined to behave according to one's own *dharma* (*svadharma*), and that action ought to be completed once one has renounced the fruits of that action. Action is pursued by the unification of the senses and thought, with desire, hope, and fear dispelled. Renunciation separates the actor from the act. The action, in which the subject is not implicated, is then offered up to God. Any serious or neutral reading of the *Gītā* clearly shows that the text does not promote inaction. Neither Hegel nor Cousin was willing to read this obvious message in the *Gītā*.

Conclusion

It is, indeed, curious how Humboldt, Hegel, and Cousin, three thinkers who had such a profound effect on the institutional instruction of philosophy in their respective countries, set out to decipher Indian philosophy (through the *Gītā*) for the West. Humboldt intentionally read the *Gītā* in isolation from other religious and philosophical texts. With his translation of *yoga* as *Vertiefung*, he genuinely sought to convey the nuances implied by the Sanskrit root *YUJ* (to bind): *Frommigkeit* (piety), *Weihung* (devotion), *Widmung* (dedication), and *Anstregung* (effort). Hegel and Cousin, in contrast approached the text through translation

[53] Piety or logism consists, we have seen, in preferring contemplation to science, inaction to action, faith to works, in order to determine one's predestination.

and manipulated it to paint an extraordinary negative and quietist interpretation of the *Gītā*'s message. The personalities involved in the endeavour of translation here (as we shall see elsewhere) are oversized and intrusive; they impose themselves not only on the translations themselves but on the text's reception.

Humboldt, for example, viewed Hegel's response article as directed solely against him and believed that Hegel's point of departure was to show that Humboldt could be called everything but a philosopher (Hegel 1954: 3.406). To a certain extent, Humboldt was correct in his assessment: Hegel, for his part, refused to appreciate Humboldt's attempt, as a philologist, to translate Indian philosophy objectively, without mixing it with Western philosophy, Indian ritual, or contemporary sociological observations. In turn, Humboldt questioned Hegel's philosophical method. Indeed, Hegel had supplemented his knowledge of Indian philosophy with insights from epic, fragments from the *Purāṇas*,[54] and the testimony of British military officials.[55] Although Hegel was virulent against his fellow Germans who sought to discover religious purity in India, in his own research he was not especially critical of the variety or objectivity of the source material he himself used. While he railed at the Schlegels and Humboldt because they did not think conceptually, he never challenged his own historical perspective: Hegel himself mixed philosophy with fable, and modern scholars with missionaries, travellers, and military officials.[56] In fact, his analysis of Indian philosophy was as much a faulty potpourri and a melange of the Indian 'sources' as anything done by the

[54] Ancient Sanskrit texts dealing with mythology, legends, and traditional lore.

[55] For example, Captain Samuel Turner's (1749–1802) travel accounts found in *Asiatick Researches*, 1:197ff., cites ascetical exercises and how they stupefy the adept. Hegel does not question the truth of Turner's assertions. They confirm that 'the Indian withdrawal of the Soul into the emptiness is rather a benumbing, which perhaps does not deserve even the name of mysticism and which cannot lead one to the discovery of truths, because it is without content' (Hegel 1970: 161). H.J. Schoeps ('Die ausserchristlichen Religionen bei Hegel', *Zeitschrift für Religions- und Geistesgeschichte* 7, no. 1 [1955]: 6) believes Hegel's prejudices against the 'amoral' character of the Hindu were due to Abbé Jean Dubois's, *Description of the Character, Manners, Customs of the People of India* (1807). Hegel makes a specific reference to Dubois when he discusses the amoral character of the Hindu (see Hegel 1968: 2: 390–1, cited in Viyagappa 29).

[56] Viyagappa (60) notes that Hegel praised Friedrich Creuzer and Franz Bopp because they had searched for an inner rationality or one idea that governed all aspects of Indian life. Hegel was also influenced by Creuzer's contention that Indian religion exhibited three main features: (1) the naiveté of childhood; (2) religious devotion and reflection; and (3) the element of speculation and philosophy (Viyagappa 55). Hegel found Creuzer's manner of presentation 'of immense interest for himself as well as for the world at large' (Hegel 1954: 2. 218).

Romantics, with the major difference being that Hegel claimed to support his reading with 'science', whereas he chided the Romantics for relying on intuition. Hegel's belief that India was immutable with no possibility of creative originality perhaps justified (in his own mind, at least) his method of inquiry. By cutting away everything that did not suit his argument, Hegel retained from Humboldt's reasoned discussion (Humboldt 1841: 1.31) only the negative, engulfing, emptying aspect of devotion. To a certain degree, Schopenhauer's subsequent assessment of Hegel's attempt to understand world history—that it was naïve and trivial[57]—takes on greater validity when we consider Hegel's reading of the *Gītā*.

In his own analysis, Cousin imitated Hegel's scholarly method of legitimizing a normative reading and his negative assessment of Indian thought. Cousin imposed his own philosophical schematization on the *Gītā*, arrived at through a distorted dissemination of Schlegel's Latin translation into French. Hegel's accusation of *Substanzialität* became Cousin's campaign against mysticism. For Cousin, the *yoga* (*dévotion*) of the *Gītā* consists of union through ecstasy: inaction is preferable to action, and faith to works. Through the indifferent renunciation of all actions, one gives oneself over to the immobility of indifference (Cousin 237). Hegel's theme of quietism also defined Cousin's judgement on Indian philosophy. Although Cousin did not explicitly mention Hegel's article, his lectures reiterate Hegel's critique of the abstract character of pure being. Cousin differs from Hegel only in his belief that this abstraction is a universal trait of mysticism, whereas Hegel views abstraction as historically circumscribed to India.[58]

We might compare these three thinkers' reception of the *Gītā* in terms of their overarching themes and styles. In reference to the seminal theme of inaction, Humboldt offers a sober explication, highlighting the role of action in the *Gītā* while pointing out its problematic relation to the path of contemplation. Although Hegel does not specifically identify

[57] Schopenhauer saw Hegel as a worthless charlatan and a corrupter of minds. He viewed Hegel's philosophy as confused and empty verbiage, as absolute nonsense, claiming that Hegel was unable to see beyond the farce of history (*World as Will and Representation*, vol. 2, chap. 35). Schopenhauer was familiar with Colebrooke's essays, although he himself did not use them. One can only guess whether Hegel's misreading of the *Gītā* contributed significantly to Schopenhauer's negative assessment.

[58] Hegel does not even discuss Indian mysticism, the cornerstone of Cousin's thesis. Cousin, on the other hand, ignores Hegel's extensive discussion of the caste system.

the renunciation of the fruits of action with inaction. his response to Humboldt levels a sharp condemnation of Indian passivity and fatalism. Cousin follows Hegel in his condemnation of Indian inaction, which he identifies with mysticism. By attributing a mystical agenda to all Indian philosophy, Cousin avoids seeing any ambiguity inherent in the text.

However, the greatest mistake in Hegel's and Cousin's interpretations of Indian thought consists of their imposing a Cartesian agenda upon Sāṃkhya, wherein the individual appears as the point of departure and ultimate term of reference. Belief in this Self, that is impassible and inactive, strikes them as nihilistic given their Western metaphysical grounding in subjectivity, of which Hegel's philosophy is the exemplum. Thus, an image of despair runs throughout Hegel's and Cousin's reading of the *Gītā*, an image that appears neither in Schlegel's Latin translation nor in Humboldt's commentary. This misconception (Halbfass 60) can best be summed up by Hegel's infamous metaphor claiming that that Indians could only attain a dreamworld and the happiness of insanity through opium.[59] Viewed in this light, Indians placed themselves beyond good and evil, paying the price of the total destruction of their concrete individuality. Neither Hegel's criticism of the European vanity of the Self nor Cousin's radical humanism deters them from their Western-centred arrogance. For Hegel, Europe represents progress and remains superior to all other nations of the world. Schlegel and, to a lesser degree, the persecuted liberal hero Cousin appear as advocates of this ascendency and the colonialism that such an intellectual posture fostered. By focusing on the literary dimension of this initial reception of the *Gītā*, I have suggested that nineteenth-century translation practices and hermeneutical concerns played a decisive role in the critical dismissal of Indian philosophy in the West and this dismissal had little to do with colonialism; it was, however, motivated by racial animus. The reception of India is far more complicated than postcolonial theory would have us believe.

Humboldt read the *Gītā* in the original Sanskrit. His reading was syncretic. In order to avoid misreadings, he pointed out how Indian speculative thought differed from Western philosophy. Rather than mask the universality of the *Gītā*'s message, he compared in order to highlight this

[59] Hegel 1968: 2. 355, 339; see also Hegel 1928: 9. 205. Hegel also speaks of the dreaming spirit of the Indians (1970: 169–71).

universality. His approach distinguished his interpretation from the hermeneutical impasse articulated in the narratives of Hegel and Cousin. Although Hegel was as well versed in the fledging field of Indology as any non-specialist of his time, he never allowed the message of the *Gītā* to challenge his own philosophy or system. To the end, he insisted on the radical alterity of East–West representations. It was through his manipulation of the text's translation that he cut and pruned the *Gītā* to support the interpretation he sought. Cousin used similar methods to seek a direct assimilation of Indian philosophy. His method erred in the same manner as Hegel's did. He ignored words and phrases in the Latin translation that might pose interpretive problems. In as egregious fashion as Hegel, Cousin also toyed with the translation to support his interpretation. Cousin's metaphysical psychology also suggests the degree to which Schlegel's refractive Latin translation gave access to the letter of the text with diffraction or effraction. However, by presupposing the possibility of total translation, Cousin ended up negating ('foreclosing') the act of translation. Whereas Schlegel and Humboldt spoke of the figurative impossibility of translation, Cousin predicated his reading upon the immateriality of translation (Droit 1988: 187). Languages and their representations are interchangeable. Cousin was content to reposition the Other to fit his view of the Western model.

Hegel's relation to the text, however, was based on his belief in the incommensurability of cultures. He worked from the vantage of the superior position that he ascribed to Western philosophy, with his own philosophy as its acme. As J.L. Mehta noted, Hegel originated the idea that the Orient can be superseded in order for the West to understand it. By contrasting 'Western' truth to that of the Orient, he was the first systematically to set out and prove the Orient deficient in terms of this truth (cited in Halbfass 167). Hegel's project consisted, therefore, of a good deal more than merely distancing India, negating the Other, and avoiding the temptation of viewing the Self in 'an Aryan mirror' (Olender 20). Yet despite his assumption of superiority, there is clearly a defensiveness that appears as a consistent subtext. The Indian exotic (and equally the German Romantic) must be discredited in order to prove that truth is rational and develops historically, even broadening its scope through the only means devised to explicate its meaning—translation.

This initial Western reception of the *Gītā* foregrounded the hermeneutical problems involved in translating the Other. In their remarks concerning the translation of the *Gītā*, each of these thinkers questioned how philosophical thought can be understood outside its own tradition. In a critical detour from Enlightenment universalism which still held sway in the nineteenth-century hermeneutic tradition (and was supported by the work of Humboldt), Hegel foreclosed the very possibility of such understanding when he rejected the notion of a common standard of meaning, and inflicted the standards and methodological apparatus of one culture upon another. The impossibility of understanding the Other without a European mode of understanding is nothing more than a movement to colonize the consciousness of the Other. Any hermeneutical project is thus aborted.

If, as Hegel maintained in his discussion of philosophical terms, understanding is impossible, how are we then to interpret any venture toward the Other? Gadamer posited two essential processes in understanding the Other in its own identity. First, there is the historical reconstruction of the original context as well as the discovery of a message beyond a text's content. The second step necessitates a willingness to accept the message, what Ricoeur would later term 'linguistic hospitality'. In the circular movement of hermeneutical understanding, the text imposes flexible expectations, sharing (in the form of play) in the common meaning of tradition and interpretation. This movement allows for the anticipation of meaning. Within the reader's desire to communicate with the text, there appears strangeness as well as familiarity in the form of prejudices which facilitate or thwart understanding. Thus, the distance between the reader and the text does not appear as an unbreachable obstacle, but rather as what sets the hermeneutical process in motion. It is precisely this process that is short circuited in Hegel's, Cousin's, and subsequent encounters with the *Gītā*. In the following chapter, we will see other instances where the hermeneutical process does not run full cycle or stalls at intervals. The translator/interpreter may refuse to engage in the play or in alternative forms of inquiry. Delectation with some dominant fiction or master narrative (as in the case of Hegel and Cousin) may ultimately be more gratifying than mere understanding. The ensuing privileging of the Self beyond the quotidian may simply prove too seductive. In the case of Hegel, advancing the truth claim of Western philosophy was inseparable from defending his own pre-eminent position. An unfortunate result of this ambition was that the scholarly reception of Indian philosophy was repressed and marginalized. In subsequent Western commentary, the resulting lacuna would be filled by popular notions of the esoteric and the occult East. Scholarship abrogated its responsibility when it capitulated and codified Indian philosophical concepts through such a faulty methodology as one finds in Hegel and Cousin. The field was then opened for a revitalization of Romantic irrationalism with an important legitimization by science (in the form of philosophical and philological discourse), as the subsequent master narratives on India, both in the East and in the West, would show.

PART II

TRANSLATING COMMENSURABILITY, CLASS, AND CASTE

Part II examines the next generation of reception in India and the West. It focuses on the Transcendentalist movement in America, especially the work of Emerson and Thoreau who assume proprietary and Indian nationalists (Vivekananda, Tilak, and Aurobindo), who use the text to foster their political and spiritual agendas.

4

Brahman as the Cosmic Translator and the *Gītā*'s Potentiality in American Transcendentalism

Emerson, Thoreau, and Whitman

Introduction

In the last chapter, we examined how the early European philosophical reception of the *Gītā* imposed a vision of fatalism on Indian philosophy. We saw how this interpretation was facilitated by Hegel's creative use of translation strategies that were then further implemented by Cousin. This 'judgement' regarding Indian metaphysical thought was subsequently popularized in the West and projected onto a fictive India or read into its literature. In this chapter, we will examine the reception of India and the early evocations of the *Gītā* by the American Transcendentalists[1] for whom this Hindu sacred text provided the exotic background for personal, spiritual, and national aggrandizement.

We have seen how Hegel had felt unconstrained in offering imprecise and fragmentary renditions of the *Gītā* with the result that the text supported a judgement on Indian philosophy that was grounded in a defence of Hegel's own philosophical system. In such free and creative use of translation, the foreign text becomes less significant. Sometimes it is even eclipsed by the reader's prejudices, having become a mould into which these prejudices can be poured. The hermeneutic process is derailed and the other is reduced to the same; it is annexed rather than

[1] Let us outline the chronology of the available translations. The Wilkins translation appeared in 1785 with a reprint in 1846–8. There were French translations in 1787 (M. Parraud) and 1788 (Chevalier d'Obsonville). As noted, the A.W. Schlegel translation dates from 1823. In 1855, the year Whitman published the *Leaves of Grass*, J. Cockburn Thomson translated the text anew.

The Afterlives of the Bhagavad Gītā. Dorothy M. Figueira, Oxford University Press. © Dorothy M. Figueira 2023.
DOI: 10.1093/oso/9780198873488.003.0005

encountered. Hegel and his disciple Cousin effected the type of harm that Nietzsche will envision occurs when translation morphs into interpretation. Did a similar process occur in the initial American readings of the *Gītā* in the nineteenth century? While Hegel and Cousin understood that much of the exotic lure India held for Europe had motivations tied to origins, *Urreligion*, linguistic ancestors, and colonial projects (Figueira 1994), for the New England Transcendentalists, those Boston Brahmins and Concord Yankees, India spoke to specific foundational values of the fledging nation. In the US, India could be seen as devaluing material progress and promulgating detachment from the world of cities and their wealth. Moreover, it allowed for a safe (i.e. far removed from Catholicism) contact with the spiritual world and a safe fascination with another form of 'priestly' power. It is important to keep in mind that while German Romanticism had certainly filtered into New England (Van Doren 49–50, cited in Christy 224), other more baroque strains of esotericism also flourished. In Vermont, we find Colonel Olcott, the co-founder of the Theosophical Society, who fostered the spiritualist antics of the Eddy Brothers[2] and received Mme. Blavatsky.[3] In nineteenth-century America, the craving for the otherworldly was in vogue and Indian religious 'wisdom' would present a great source of inspiration.[4] None of the figures examined in this chapter literally 'translate' the *Gītā*, but Emerson and Thoreau made ample and intense use of it in translation, often citing passages directly, to develop their interpretation of it.

[2] William and Horatio Eddy were two nineteenth-century mediums who claimed psychic powers, held seances, and performed ectoplasm materializations. See Emerson 1939: 322.

[3] Mme. Blavatsky (1831–1891) was a Russian occultist who co-founded the Theosophical Society in 1875. Theosophy was a 'science' of the occult with roots in Mesmerism that had been advanced by some rather shady Englishmen and the equally enigmatic Mme. Blavatsky who combined Russian messianism, Egyptian religion, an interpretation of supposedly Tibetan wisdom, Hinduism, and Buddhism. The Theosophical Society was a very significant spiritualist movement. Blavatsky also claimed to be able to contact spirits of the dead.

[4] First before I go any further, let me state that I do not share the general appreciation of many literary scholars for Emerson, Thoreau, and Whitman. Although I literally lived down the road from one of Whitman's houses on Long Island and had the rare privilege of being assigned to Emerson's spacious dorm-room at Harvard Divinity School and duly made a pilgrimage to Walden Pond (and even swam across it), I never really found them to be great seers or profound authors. As a student of religion in the 70s, the Transcendentalists were still required reading, but with respect to their Orientalism, they did not strike me as very different from the Western devotees to Transcendental Meditation and exotic questers who often surrounded me in my history of religion classes. This is the prejudice with which I approach Transcendentalist readings of the *Gītā*.

Emerson

Ralph Waldo Emerson's (1803–82) interest in Indian thought began at a young age. In his journal, 'The Wide World', Emerson noted that one needed to head to the East in order to understand Western civilization as it came to us through Greece. His initial curiosity with India (Emerson 1960: 1:11–12), however, soon gave way to extreme distaste for Hindu spirituality, religious customs, and rituals. Emerson's early disenchantment took form in his graduation talk of 1821, where the 16-year-old senior from Harvard College dismissed Indian thought as perilous nonsense. In preparation for this essay, entitled 'Indian Superstition', Emerson had poured over all the literature available at the time regarding India—especially travel accounts and the works of Sir William Jones. Some of his early knowledge on India also came from his reading of the *Monthly Anthology and Boston Review*, a periodical that his father had edited from 1803–11. Emerson consulted recent articles on India published in the *Edinburgh Review*, *The Christian Review*, the *North American Review*, and the *Christian Disciple and Theological Review*.[5] The young Emerson was particularly influenced by Robert Southey's *The Curse of Kehama* (1810) which had supplied him with further source material (1.340, cited in Hodder 141).[6]

Initially, Emerson was more impressed with Sanskrit literature[7] than with Indian philosophy. 'I want not the metaphysics but only the literatures of them' (Emerson 1909–14: x.248, cited in Christy 6). From his reading, Emerson had concluded that India consisted of ruins, 'where Havoc welters now'.[8] However, by 1830, his initial disinterest in Indian philosophy changed upon discovering in the *Mahābhārata* what he felt

[5] From an examination of the records of the Harvard College Library, as well as those of the Boston Athenaeum, we have a good idea of what Emerson read during these formative years.

[6] It was in an appendix to Southey's poem that Emerson first read excerpts from *The Laws of Manu*. His thoughts on this text were strangely positive, comparing the lawbook's take on truth to the perverted bigotry of the Jesuits (Adiasamito-Smith 137).

[7] In a letter to F. Max Müller, Emerson wrote: 'All my interest is in Marsh's *Manu*, Burnouf's *Bhagavat* [*sic*] *Purāṇa*, and Wilson's *Viṣṇu Purāṇa*, yes, and a few other translations. I remember I owed my first taste for this fruit to Cousin's sketch, in his first lecture, and the dialogue between Krishna and Arjoon and I still prize the first chapters of the *Bhagavat* as wonderful' (Emerson 1939: i.lix).

[8] Emerson 1954: 2. 11–16, 103–12, cited in Cameron 49: 52–3, see also Charles Grant's 'A Poem on the Restoration of Learning in the East', as a source for *Indian Superstitions*, where Vyāsa is joined with Bishop Berkeley, the Idealist philosopher.

was a form of Idealism. He then shifted his focus away from Sanskrit literature to Indian philosophy. This new-found appreciation was also prompted by his reading in 1831 of Cousin's commentary on the *Gītā* (Emerson 1939: 1.lx; 3.292).[9] It was, however, what Emerson saw as the *Gītā*'s theism and its impersonal pantheism that most impressed him. He felt that all philosophies, religions, and their scriptures express fundamental unity, and he believed that Indian religious texts supported this thesis (Emerson 1971–: 4.28, cited in Goodman 641). The *Gītā* was particularly congenial to him, since it expressed loving devotion to God and endorsed a life of labour, both scholarly and manual. In a letter to Elizabeth Hoar (17 June 1845) describing his day-to-day experiences, Emerson wrote of his enthusiasm upon receiving his very own copy of the poem:

> The only other event is the arrival in Concord of the *Bhagavad Gītā*, the much renowned book of Buddhism, extracts from which I have often admired, but never before held the book in my hands. (Cited in Christy 287)

While Emerson might be confused about which religion the *Gītā* promulgated, he was nevertheless glad to finally own a personal copy of what he considered an important book. He appreciated how the *Gītā* challenged Christian piety. After studying his edition extensively, Emerson was even more impressed with Cousin's interpretation of the poem. He was particularly fascinated by the Frenchman's eclecticism, appearing as it did at the end of German Idealism and Enlightenment sensationalism. He felt that Cousin had, in the wake of the Encyclopedists, rejected exclusivity and especially the notion of 'acceptable' ideas. Emerson particularly liked Cousin's attack on knowledge gained from books. This was a theme he had explored in his 'Divinity School Address' (1836) and in 'The American Scholar' (1837) (Goodman 628, citing Emerson 1971–: 1.57). Cousin's mode of rebellion simply entranced Emerson. Perhaps, he even saw in Cousin the beginnings of a practical trend of cosmopolitanism. In any case, Emerson began to envision Transcendentalism as

[9] Emerson 1939 1: lx; 3.292. Emerson was also familiar with Colebrooke's essay outlining Indian philosophy (Richardson 1995: 407).

an American response to such an eclectic synthesis and decided to read Idealism into Hindu practices. It was also for this reason that he and his fellow Transcendentalists undertook the task of grafting onto Indian wisdom the common-sense approach of Yankees facing the demands of a work-a-day world (Christy x–xi).

The poems 'Hamatreya' and 'Brahma' are most often cited as the primary fruits of Emerson's involvement with Indian thought. The title of the poem 'Hamatreya' (1845) evokes Emerson's variant of the spelling of the name of the famous upanishadic female seer Maitreya and her dialogue with the god Vishnu (Hollender 155).[10] 'Hamatreya' presents 'a scornful meditation on the futility of Yankee possessiveness, materialism, and avarice in the face of the evanescence of human life and the inevitability of death' (Hodder 339). However, it was Emerson's poem 'Brahma' that expressed more specifically Emerson's indebtedness to Indian thought as informed by his knowledge of the *Upanishads* and the *Gītā*. In fact, some critics saw this poem as a condensation of the *Gītā* (Burkholder and Myerson 167), especially the second book, or a reworking of the *Kaṭha Upanishad* 2.19 whose verses also appear in the *Gītā* 2.19.

In fact, 'Brahma' was thought to have so closely followed the *Gītā* that contemporary reviewers felt the need to defend Emerson against allegations of plagiarism.[11] It is possible that Emerson had culled his inspiration from the *Kaṭha Upanishad*, which was not as widely disseminated in English as was the *Gītā* at that time.[12] But, it is more likely that 'Brahma' (written in 1857) was inspired by the *Gītā* which Emerson read in 1843 rather than by the *Kaṭha Upanishad* disseminated in the *Bibliotheca Indica* (1853), especially since Emerson so often consulted the *Gītā* and was for

[10] Emerson makes reference in his journal of 1845 to Maitreya (Goren 38).

[11] For a discussion of plagiarism, see 'Defense of "Brahma"' by Charles Godfrey Leland in the *Boston Courier* 23 November 1857: 1, reprinted in Burkholder and Myerson 164–9, where they address the issue of plagiarism: 'the most atrocious of donkey-isms'. In the same volume, see Robert Detweiler, 'The Over-Rated "Over-Soul"' reprinted from *American Literature* 36 (March 1964) 64–8, here 307–9.

[12] The *Kaṭha Upanishad* was available in E. Roer's translation and cited from the *Bibliotheca Indica* (1853), one of the books in a library that a British friend, Thomas Cholmondeley, had gifted to Thoreau, and Emerson had inherited upon the latter's death. Cholmondeley had come to Concord to see Emerson but ended up staying in Thoreau's home for about two months. Cholmondeley corresponded with Thoreau for years afterwards and eventually sent him a 'princely gift' of 44 books of Indian writings for which Thoreau in anticipation, built a box of driftwood (Harding 1965: 346–50, cited in Friedrich 27).

many years, one of the very few Americans to actually own it.[13] Indeed, his copy of the *Gītā* was consulted by Emerson and his friends even more often than students consulted the copy that resided in Harvard's library (Sanborn 481, cited in Christy 23). Emerson widely praised the *Gītā* as a 'transnational book' (Emerson 1971: 9.231–2) that gave him much joy and comfort:

> I owed—my friend and I owed—a magnificent day to the Bhagavat Geeta—it was the first of books; it was as if an empire spoke to us nothing small or unworthy, but large, serene, consistent, the voice of an old intelligence which in another age and climate had pondered and thus disposed of the same questions which exercise us. (Christy 23)

After Emerson resigned from the ministry, he became an even more active reader of Sanskrit texts, writing in 1845 that he had found nothing in the world compared to the wisdom of the *Gītā* (1960: 9.230). Throughout his journals, essays, and lectures up until his death in 1882, Emerson quotes from the *Gītā* (Hodder 341). References to Hindu philosophy can be found throughout Emerson's prose work in such a haphazard and inchoate fashion that Oliver Wendall Holmes was prompted to dismiss Emerson's encounter with India as 'a vacuum of intelligibility . . . the Oriental dreams, born in the land of the poppy and of hashish' (Holmes 397). Even a more generous recent scholar, such as Eric Sharpe (1985) termed Emerson's commentary 'enigmatic and obscure' (25). The poem 'Brahma' stands out in this respect, since Emerson best articulated here what he gleaned from Indian philosophy and he recognized how this poem synthesized all that he culled from his reading of the *Gītā*. When Emerson's publisher, James Fields, wanted him to omit 'Brahma' from the collection of poems, Emerson reportedly told him that everything else could be dropped except that poem (Christy 1932: 164).

[13] He had borrowed from his friend John Cabot a copy and kept it until he received his own. In a letter to John Chapman in May 1845, he wrote: 'There is a book which I very much want of which this is the title, "The Bhagavat Geeta, or Dialogues of Kreeshna & Arjoon" . . . Translated from the original Sanskreet, or ancient language of the brahmins, by Charles Wilkins; London: C. Nourse; 1795.' See Emerson 1939: 3.288.

'Brahma' does, indeed, deliver. It paraphrases the second chapter of the *Gītā* as found in Emerson's copy of J. Cockburn Thomson's translation which reads as follows:

> He who believes that this spirit can kill, and he who thinks that it can be killed, both of these are wrong in judgment. It neither kills, nor is killed. It is not born, nor dies at any time. It has no origin. Unborn, changeless, eternal, both as to future and past time, it is not slain where the body is killed. (Thomson 374)

The Emerson poem in its entirety is as follows:

> If the red slayer think he slays,
> Or if the slain think he is slain,
> They know not well the subtle ways
> I keep, and pass, and turn again.
> Far or forgot to me is near;
> Shadow and sunlight are the same;
> The vanished gods to me appear;
> And one to me are shame and fame.
> They reckon ill who leave me out;
> When me they fly, I am the wings;
> I am the doubter and the doubt,
> And I the hymn the Brahmin sings.
> The strong gods pine for my abode,
> And pine in vain the Sacred Seven;
> But thou, meek lover of the good!
> Find me, and turn thy back on heaven.

The first lines of Emerson's poem simply replicate Thomson's translation of *Gītā 2.19*: 'If the slayer thinks I slay, if the slain thinks I am slain, then both of them do not know well. It (the Soul) does not slay, nor is it slain', and the last lines of Emerson's poem call to mind Thomson's translation of the *Gītā* 8.15–16:

> The high-souled ones, who achieve the highest perfection, attaining to me, do not come again to life.... after attaining to me, there is no birth again.

Beyond the obvious derivative content of this poem, what is interesting is that the 'Brahma' of the title is a misnomer.[14] The poem is not about Brahma, the creator god, at all. But rather it describes the *brahman*, the Absolute, the Universal Soul. The title should have been 'Brahman' (Chandrasekharan 507). The Red Slayer refers to the god Rudra, a name for the god Śiva, the destroyer god, who along with Brahma and Vishnu, the sustainer god, comprise the Hindu trinity. The theme that Emerson is expressing here encapsulates Arjuna's dilemma in the *Gītā*: whether he should kill or be killed. Emerson's poem is recapitulating Krishna's answer to Arjuna that only the body is killed, and the soul (*ātman*) remains, passing over to join itself to other bodies. The Red Slayer, by bringing death to the body *translates* the power of Brahman (Chandrasekharan 507) whose 'subtle ways' regulate how birth, death, and rebirth occur. It is mere delusion (*māyā*) that the Slayer thinks he is slain (*Gītā* 2.19).[15] Nothing ever dies. Energy merely changes form when the body dies. Stanzas 2 and 3 of Emerson's poem address the reality behind *māyā*, where opposites are the same (far and near, shadow and sunlight) as taught in the *Gītā* (Chapter 9) where opposites encompass the whole. Behind this reality is *brahman*, what Emerson later would term the 'Oversoul'. The aim of Hindu thought is to recognize the *ātman*'s oneness with *brahman*: this recognition brings about liberation (*mokṣa*), not the paltry reward of some heaven, after which Emerson's 'Sacred Seven' or the *sapta rishis* (seven sages) of Hindu mythology 'pine in vain'. The sages who longed for heaven did not understand that according to the *Gītā* (6.46) it is not by ritual and austerities that we are liberated, but through love. The *Gītā* teaches that love (*bhakti*) is far superior to rituals and sacrifices. Emerson translates this teaching as the following: He who loves Brahma(n) can turn his back on heaven (note, not Heaven) and be liberated. Even the gods long for salvation in Emerson's poem as they do in

[14] The poem was originally titled 'Song of the Soul'.

[15] While this idea is found in the *Gītā*, it is also found in the excerpt from the *Viṣṇu Purāṇa*: 'What living creature slays, or is slain? What living creature preserves or is preserved? Each is his own destroyer or preserver, as he follows evil or good' (cited in Goren 34).

the *Gītā* (Chapter 11). The strong gods are as dependent on Brahma(n) as we are as humans. The Sacred Seven and humans all 'pine for' *brahma(n)*, realizing that ritual alone is not sufficient. One must surrender to God.

The *Gītā* teaches that nothing can really be destroyed or dissolved because all that exists in the universe has proceeded from *brahman* who 'translates'. His power alternates between two phases of potentialities where one potentiality awaits its next potentiality, 'the subtle ways I keep, and pass, and turn again.' Just as the Absolute regulates the next birth, so too does the translator create a new text with each new rendition. In the poem 'Brahma', Emerson was laying claim to this creative power by taking the *Gītā* and 'bettering' its message. Just as any translator beginning with the Romantics sought to create the potential work, so too Emerson does create in 'Brahma' a new product, a beautiful short poem crystalizing the messages he found most evocative in the *Gītā*, including the wonderful image of *brahman* 'translating' and masterminding the play (*līlā*) of potentialities.

'Brahma' was Emerson's most loved and coherent statement on what he derived from Hinduism[16] and especially from the *Gītā*: a respect for labour (scholarly, contemplative, or physical), which was dear to America's utilitarian pioneer spirit. The *Gītā* was a suitable text for the practical life that the Transcendentalists preached as the American ideal. The unique interpretation that Emerson would bring to the *Gītā* was that of a Yankee India motivated by a Protestant work ethic. Emerson also appreciated how the *Gītā* taught that worship was the height of conduct. He accepted the necessity that Krishna lays on Arjuna—that he must fight. Contrary to the quietism that Hegel had 'discovered' in his reading of the text, Emerson felt that the *Gītā* compelled us to act (Emerson 1975: 11.232). 'Representative Men', in the section on Plato, makes this point sufficiently clear and attributes this theme to the *Gītā*:

> The Same, the Same: friend and foe are of one stuff; the ploughman, the plough, and the furrow are of the same stuff; and the stuff is such, and so much, that the variations of form are unimportant. 'You are fit,' says the

[16] The Emerson scholar, Charles Mallory, in one of those wonderful reversals of valuation that one can find only in a national literature scholar's narrow purview, claims that one discovers by reading the *Gītā* 'the whole of Emerson's philosophy' (Maulsby 127, cited in Goren 46).

> supreme Krishna to a sage, 'to apprehend that you are not distinct from me.' (Emerson 1971–: 4 (1987) 28–9)

The *Gītā* provided Emerson with an ethical and religious counterpart to Christian scriptures. What he claimed to take from the *Gītā*—the belief that there is a common heart and a great universal mind—was more attractive for him than the Calvinist notion of an arbitrary deity.

Emerson's concept of the 'oversoul' was a literal translation of the Sanskrit *adhyātma*, (that which is superior to or presides over the *ātman*). In 'The Oversoul' Emerson taught that we all rest in the great nature which contains everyman's particular nature.[17] Emerson's 'oversoul' evokes a pantheistic vision that was both immanent and transcendent: 'Blessed is the day when youth discover that Within and Above are synonyms.' (Emerson 1960–82: 3.309, cited in Christy 97). It presents God/*brahman* as absolute, unchanging, and unfolding consciousness (Cowley 921). The message of 'The Oversoul' also reflects Arjuna's order to Krishna on the battlefield and the identification of the individual soul with the surrounding world. Similarly, in his 1837 lecture 'The Affection', Emerson defines courage as a belief in the identity of the nature of my enemy with my own nature (Emerson 1975: 2.285, 295, 306), an idea clearly resonating with Arjuna's order to Krishna in the *Gītā*. Even the fatalistic understanding of *karma* that Emerson develops from his reading of the *Gītā*'s is transmogrified into his notion of 'compensation', that he articulates in 'The Oversoul', as well as in other works, such as 'Illusion', 'Compensation', and 'Fate.' Similarly, the theme of *māyā*, initially explored in 'Brahma', reappears in the essay, 'Illusions', where Emerson wrote:

> I find men victims of illusions in all parts of life. Children, youths, adults, and old men, all are led by one bauble or another. Yogavindra, the goddess of illusion, is stronger than Apollo. (Emerson 1946: 228)

And more concretely it appears in the poem 'Maya':

> Illusion works impenetrable,
> Weaving webs innumerable

[17] It has been suggested, given Emerson's interest in Neoplatonism, it is equally possible that the Oversoul derived from the philosophical system of Plotinus (Goren 41).

Her gay pictures never fail,
Crowds each other, veil on veil,
Charmer who will be believed,
By man who thirsts to be deceived.

God's acts are not arbitrary with reference to man's deeds. The life led is the result of past deeds in atonement of past works. Not only in 'Brahma' but throughout Emerson's prose and poetry, he accepts the *Gītā*'s teaching regarding the illusory nature of the world and encourages us to engage in battle as instructed by the *Gītā*. This course of action is advised because everything is an illusion, and it is necessary to act as if one acted not. These two fundamental messages of the *Gītā* will repeatedly resurface in Western readings of the text, particularly in the work of Emerson's friend and disciple Thoreau.

Thoreau

Unlike Emerson, Henry David Thoreau (1817–62) had not read anything about India while a student at Harvard (Christy 186, cited in Sarma 77).[18] What he initially knew about India, he learned from Emerson during a prolonged stay at his home beginning in 1841. Emerson's enthusiasm for Indian literature and philosophy had certainly rubbed off on his friend. Thoreau wrote in his journal:

> One wise sentence [from the Vedas] is worth the State of Massachusetts many times over. (Thoreau 1906: 11,4)

Thoreau subsequently read everything that was available in American private and public libraries: the *Bhāgavata Purāṇa*, the *Upanishads*, the *Bhagavad Gītā*, the *Laws of Manu*, the *Viṣṇu Purāṇa*, the *Harivaṃśa*, *Śākuntalā*, and Burnouf's translations of Buddhist scriptures, portions of which Thoreau edited for *The Dial* (June 1844). He would come to own most of the translations from Sanskrit which were available at the time. He

[18] Christy inspected the borrowing records from the Boston Atheneum and Harvard College Library (Paglia 70).

read the *Gītā* in three separate translations (two English and one French) and would go on to study it during the two years he spent at Walden Pond as well as over the nine years spent editing *Walden* (Friedrich 26). Thoreau directly used the *Gītā* to formulate a cohesive philosophy of life. In *A Week on the Concord and Merrimac Rivers*, Thoreau articulated his understanding of *karma yoga*. He explained the *Gītā*'s teaching that 'action is preferable to inaction. The journey of thy mortal frame may not succeed from inaction' (Thoreau 1985: 109). Thoreau contrasted the 'pure morality' of Christian scripture to the 'pure intellectuality' of the *Gītā* (Thoreau 1985: 110–11).[19] He was convinced that the *Gītā* was unsurpassed. He noted that the 'reader is nowhere raised into and sustained in a higher, purer, or rarer region of thought' than in the *Gītā*. This text had much to teach the West. In Walden, he commented: 'How much more admirable the Bhagavad Geeta, than all the ruins of the East' (Thoreau 1980: 39, cited in Friedrich 26). In *The Dial*, where he was charged with introducing New Englanders to Sanskrit literature, Thoreau judged the *Gītā* as neither sententious nor poetic; it simply presented wisdom that unfolded naturally (i.e. it did not 'perspire'). In the 'Monday' section of *A Week on the Concord and Merrimac Rivers*, Thoreau quoted extensively from the Wilkins translation, filling several pages with citations (Thoreau 1985: 110–13). Besides its vast and cosmogonical philosophy, even Shakespeare seems sometimes 'youthfully green and practical' when compared to the *Gītā* (116). Thoreau was particularly drawn to its 'aspect of discipline' (Sharpe 25–31), and found himself thinking about the *Gītā* at the hour before sunrise (Thoreau 1987–2002: 1.311–2, cited in Friedrich 25). It was such a valid text that Thoreau felt that it should be de-Hinduized for a more generalized audience, particularly since it advocated the universal concerns of discipline and the cultivation of wisdom through contemplation. However, Thoreau most appreciated that the *Gītā* did not discourage action. His extensive quotes from the *Gītā* found in *A Week on the Concord and Merrimac Rivers*, support his reading that the Sanskrit poem enjoined us to 'perform the settled functions' (Thoreau 1985: 109). Its 'wisest conservatism' (109) taught one to perform one's individual duty.

[19] It is quite astonishing that Thoreau scholars, such as Van Doren (1916: 95) and Sattelmeyer (1988: 67–8) deny the influence that the *Gītā* exerted upon Thoreau (Friedrich 29).

'Monday' contains the bulk of Thoreau's commentary on the *Gītā*. Thoreau finds the Sanskrit text's conservatism is sublime (Thoreau 1985: 109–10) since it preserves 'the universe with Asiatic anxiety' (108). The *Gītā* dwells on the 'inevitability and unchangeableness of laws, on the power of temperament and constitution' whose end is the immense consolation and eternal absorption in Brahma [sic] (109). The *Gītā* 'raises the reader to the highest, purest and rarest regions of thought'; it is 'unquestionably one of the noblest and most sacred scriptures' (110–11). The *Gītā* also provided Thoreau with an opportunity to present his own philosophy regarding the continuity of spirituality from antiquity into the modern times, a point central to Transcendental thought. According to Thoreau, the past is not the past but ever present, like the flowing of a river or the mingling of the waters from Walden Pond and the Ganges. The commentary on 'Monday' logically follows the sweeping critique of the Christian church and denunciation of the State that Thoreau articulated in 'Sunday'.

The *Gītā* epitomized for Thoreau the wisdom of India. In a letter to H.G.O. Blake in 1849, he equated his life in nature as equivalent to the practice of *yoga*: 'Even I am a Yogi.' (1906: 6.175, cited in Christy 201 and Sarma 79). Thoreau appreciated what he viewed as the *Gītā's* recommendation to lead an ascetic life and live alone in a secret place without cravings and without possessions. This path was, in fact, what he sought to follow at Walden Pond. Thoreau also recognized that the wisdom of the *Gītā* was hard for the average man to grasp, especially since its message in 6.11–12 (Wilkins 63) enjoins the *yogi* to live as a recluse with subdued mind and spirit. Viewed in this light, the *Gītā* becomes for Thoreau not merely a guide for living. His ability to follow its prompts clearly added credence to Thoreau's belief in his own exceptionality.

Near the conclusion of *Walden*, in the 'Higher View' chapter, we find the parable of the artist of Kouroo (a name that evokes Arjuna's descent; he and his brothers are the sons of Kuru), who was pure, whose art was pure, and whose resulting creation could only be wonderful. In this parable on perfection, the man of discipline is purified of his sins and perfected through many births until he finds a higher way (Friedrich 2008: 78–80). This parable can be read as a translation of Krishna's message of spiritual discipline into artistic terms (Miller 158). The mystical love of nature that brought Thoreau to Walden Pond here is portrayed as a path to self-knowledge and spiritual realization.

> There was an artist in the city of Kouroo who was disposed to strive after perfection. One day it came into his mind to make a staff. Having considered that in an imperfect work time is an ingredient, but into a perfect work time does not enter, he said to himself it shall be perfect in all respects though I should do nothing else in my life. He proceeded instantly to the forest for wood, being resolved that it should not be made of unsuitable material; and as he searched for and rejected stick after stick, his friends gradually deserted him, for they grew old in their works and died, but he grew not older by a moment. His singleness of purpose and resolution, and his elevated piety, endowed him, without his knowledge, with perennial youth. As he made no compromise with Time, Time kept out of his way and only sighed, at a distance because he could not overcome him. Before he had found a stock in all respects suitable the city of Kouroo was a hoary ruin, and he sat on one of its mounds to peel the stick. Before he had given it the proper shape the dynasty of the Chandahars was at an end, and with the point of the stick he wrote the name of the last of that race in the sand, and then resumed his work. By the time he had smoothed and polished the staff, Kalpa was no longer the pole-star; and ere he has put on the ferule and the head ornament with precious stones, Brahma had awoke and slumbered many times. But why do I stay to mention these things? When the finishing stroke was put to his work, it suddenly expanded before the eyes of the astonished artist into the fairest of all creations of Brahma. He had made a new system in making a staff, a world with full and far proportions; in which, though the old cities and dynasties had passed away, fairer and more glorious ones had taken their places. And now he saw by the heap of shavings still fresh at his feet, that, for him and his work, the former lapse of time had been an illusion, and that no more time had eclipsed than is required for a single scintillation from the brain of Brahma to fall on and inflame the tinder of a mortal brain. The material was pure, and his art was pure; how could the result be other than wonderful? (1985: 582–3)

This parable is odd and to the general reader it appears to focus primarily on artistic production and aesthetic perfection. To someone familiar with Thoreau's fascination with the *Gītā*, the parable's conclusion is oddly reminiscent of the cosmic revelation of Krishna to Arjuna. Rather than Krishna showing himself in his expansive and all-devouring form, Thoreau presents us here with the artistic product as manifestation of divine revelation. Thoreau substituted Art for God. We also find in this parable 'Brahma', who at the end of each *kalpa* recreates a more 'glorious' world, Thoreau's artist makes an ever-more-perfect staff. One is hard-pressed not to draw the analogy between Brahma's (correctly the creator god here) ever-more-glorious creation, the artist's more perfect staff, and the translator's perfecting a text through translation. Like Emerson, Thoreau was also signalling in his parable what he felt he was 'doing' with the *Gītā*: crystallizing its message, making it better (to be understood by Americans) and therefore attaining its potential in their 'translations' of it.

Thoreau's admiration for Hindu religious thought permeates his work. But it was Thoreau's indebtedness to the *Gītā* especially that most inspired *A Week on the Concord and Merrimack Rivers*, where he quotes not only extensively from Wilkins's translation but specifically expresses enthusiasm for Krishna's critique of inaction and Hinduism's focus on contemplation and the brahmins' devotion to austerity (Thoreau 1985: 123).[20] At Walden Pond, Thoreau expressly drew the connection between his experiences and the teachings of the *Gītā*. It was particularly on a visit to the well at Walden Pond, where he evokes the latter in two rather mystical episodes. In 'Pond in Winter', Thoreau goes to the well for water and imagines himself communing with the servant of a brahmin priest and envisions Walden Pond mingling with the Ganges. Both the Hindu priest and the Concord seeker are involved in identical quests for religious truth. Thoreau universalized his experience at Walden Pond with that of the devout Hindu on the Ganges. Both are immersed in the wisdom of the *Gītā*. The pure water of Walden Pond quenches the spiritual thirst of the world. The inhabitants

[20] Sharpe points out that *The Portable Thoreau* (1977) offers an abridged version of *A Week on the Concord* with all the references to the *Gītā* omitted.

> of Charleston and New Orleans, of Madras and Bombay and Calcutta, drink at my well. In the morning, I bathe my intellect in the stupendous and cosmogonical philosophy of the Bhagavad Geeta, since whose composition years of the gods have elapsed, and in comparison with which our modern world and its literature seem puny and trivial; and I doubt if that philosophy is not to be referred to a previous state of existence, so remote is its sublimity from our conceptions. I lay down the book and go to my well for water, and lo! There I meet the servant of the Brahmin, priest of Brahma and Vishnu and Indra, who still sits in his temple on the Ganges reading the Vedas, or dwells at the foot of a tree with his crust and water jug. I meet his servant come to draw water for his master, and our buckets as it were grate together in the same well. The pure Walden water is mingled with the sacred water of the Ganges. (112–3)

It is noteworthy that Thoreau, like any reader working from his prejudices, sought in the *Gītā* points of comparison for the very things he sought in Christianity. The *Gītā* is a 'good book' that 'deserves to be read with reverence even by Yankees, as part of the sacred writings of a devout people'. Even the 'intelligent Hebrew will rejoice to find in it a moral grandeur and sublimity akin to those of his own scriptures' (Thoreau 1985: 115). Not only did Thoreau elevate the *Gītā* to the ranks of a masterpiece of literature, comparable to Shakespeare, but he places it on a par with Jewish scripture and the New Testament. The God of the *Gītā* can be said to have been 'brought down to earth and to mankind' by Christianity in the form of Christ (110). Hindu scripture, as exemplified in the *Gītā*, offered Thoreau a vision of the Divine he found attractive and relatable. The *Gītā*'s intellectuality could be compared to what Thoreau saw as mere practical guidance and sensible morals in the New Testament (115).

> The New Testament is remarkable for its pure morality, the best of the Vedic scripture, for its pure intellectuality. The reader is nowhere raised into and sustained in a bigger, purer, or rarer region of thought than in the Bhagavat Geeta. The Geeta's sanity and sublimity have impressed the minds even of soldiers and merchants. (110–11)

Most importantly, Thoreau saw in the *Gītā* a common connection between India and the world. 'In every man's brain is the Sanskrit' (121, 123–4). While he suspected that the British and the Germans would fail to appreciate fully the genius of the Indians (115–16), the open-minded Americans would be more receptive to the *Gītā* (115). Here too, Thoreau was a proponent of American exceptionalism.

Thoreau, however, did not read the poem uncritically. He took issue with certain teachings he found expressed in the poem. He felt, for example, that the *Gītā* showed that Indians lacked freedom and flexibility and that Christians were more humane and practical than Hindus (Thoreau 1985: 110). The *Gītā* exemplified how Indians fixated on unchanging laws, the qualities of nature, the role of birth, final union with *brahman*, meditation, the mystical *OM*, and identification with the Absolute who was wise but inert (110). Thoreau, however, reserved his most comparative and critical assessment of the *Gītā* to its discussion of caste. He stands out among modern readers, both Indian nationalists[21] and Westerners alike, in recognizing the issue of caste as central to the *Gītā* and voicing a muted critique of it (Hijiya 2000: 134). While he praised the *Gītā's* conservatism in its refusal to assign the same *dharma* to every human, and to order hierarchically according to the role determined by family, age, and training, Thoreau recognized in the *Gītā* a form of 'brahmin passivity' in confrontation with the reality of caste, fate, and time. He recognized the social ramifications of such a system (109–10). The brahmin 'never proposes courageously to assault evil but to starve it out because his active faculties are paralyzed by caste.' Here again we have the acknowledgement of a perceived Hindu notion of fatalism and inertia. In noting that Krishna gives no 'sufficient reason not to fight' (113–14), Thoreau deems Krishna's argument defective. Moreover, he finds the *Gītā*'s concept of duty to be vague. Virtue, for the brahmin, consists in doing not right, but arbitrary things. Thoreau feels that the text leaves many questions unresolved. He asks: 'What is 'action', what are the 'settled functions'? What is 'a man's own religion'? 'Why is it better than another's? What is a man's particular calling? What are the duties appointed by one's birth?' Thoreau clearly has issues with the *Gītā*'s defence for the institution of caste (114). While he admits that caste is also

[21] With the exception of Ambedkar; see Chapter 7 in this volume.

found in the West, it is 'faint' and construed as 'conservatism here'. In the West, caste is rendered as not forsaking a calling, not outraging an institution, not using violence or rendering bonds. The State here is the parent, and caste offers a sense of virtue and manhood that are 'wholly filial' (114). Thoreau understood well how the *Gītā* defended caste. For all the *Gītā*'s mystical value, that he fully acknowledged, this one specific point troubles our New England radical.

> Thank God, no Hindoo tyranny prevailed at the framing of the world, but we are freemen in the universe, and not sentenced to any cast [sic]. (1980: 148)

His distaste for caste led Thoreau perhaps to focus more on the wisdom and nature of duty expounded in the text, rather than on its social implications. The *Gītā* offered not absolute law, but rules particular to each person, according to the *dharma* of the *varṇas* (18.41–4). One should do one's duty and no one else's (3.15, 18.47). Like Emerson, Thoreau took Sāṃkhya philosophy as a way of remaining in the world and doing one's duty. He recognized that it was not the path for all. But he understood it as the higher path taught by the *Gītā* and, perhaps, the 'private business' he needed to undertake at Walden Pond.

> My purpose in going to Walden Pond was not to live cheaply nor to live dearly there, but to transact some private business with the fewest obstacles. (Cited in Sarma 79)

What exactly that private business was, we can only glean from what Thoreau says. But it is very reminiscent of the *karma yoga* expressed in the *Gītā* (12.11):

> By the conscious effort of mind, we can stand aloof from actions and their consequences; and all things good and bad go by us like a torrent. We are not wholly involved in Nature. I may be either the driftwood in the stream or Indra in the sky looking down on it. I may be affected by an actual event which appears to concern me much more. (Cited in Sarma 82)

Or

> The true husbandman will cease from anxiety as the squirrels manifest no concern whether the woods will bear chestnuts this year or not, and finish his labour with every day, relinquishing all claims to the produce of his fields, and so sacrificing in his mind not only his first but his last fruits also. (Cited in Sarma 82)

For Thoreau, the *Gītā* charted a path for an enlightened elite (to which he belonged by virtue of his education). In this respect, Thoreau fully represented the implied reader (exceptional, artistic, entitled) of the *Gītā* for generations of Westerners to come. Already its exotic and elitist allure was firmly established. It would be the text for those who felt that while truth and wisdom might exist theoretically for all humanity, only a chosen few could access it. Nowhere is this potential in all its pretentiousness and superficiality more apparent than in the work of Walt Whitman, the Transcendentalist poet also associated with having been inspired directly by the *Gītā*.

Whitman

Perhaps the first literary reference to the *Gītā* in American literary criticism was Emerson's comment that the *Leaves of Grass* was a 'mixture of the *Bhagavad Gītā* and the New York Herald'.[22] Thus, from the very beginning of its reception in America, parallels were sought between the Sanskrit mystical poem and Walt Whitman's poetry (Allen 457). The Indian holy man, Swami Vivekananda, who had never even met Whitman (1819–92),[23] nevertheless referred to him as an 'American Sannyasin'[24] (Sarma 76). In a letter to Harrison Blake in December 1856, Thoreau remarked that Whitman's poems were 'wonderfully like the Orientals', and he asked Whitman whether he had ever read them. Whitman replied, 'No, tell me about them' (Thoreau 1894: 347, cited in Preston 1998: 186). While T.R.

[22] Frank B. Sanborn, 'Reminiscent of Whitman'. *The Conservator* 8.3 (May 1897): 37–40, here 38, cited in Preston 256, see also Zweig 1984: 8.

[23] Vivekananda arrived in the US in 1893, one year after Whitman had died.

[24] The *saṃnyāsin* is a holy man who has renounced the world.

Rajasekharaiah views this denial as a ruse on Whitman's part to hide his true indebtedness to Hindu scriptures (Allen 458), his response may well have been true, given Whitman's method of perusing dozens of books at a time, reading a few pages here and there, and seldom getting sufficiently interested in any volume in order to read it in its entirety (Lốpez 2011: 5). But we do know that Whitman owned a copy of the *Gītā*, since he had told one of his literary executors, Horace Traubel, that he was very familiar with the poem and saw it as a formal classic (Allen 458). The existence of this copy was confirmed by Traubel's widow (Mercer 32). Whitman had received his copy of the Cockburn Thomas translation of the *Gītā* in 1875, from an English cork-cutter named Thomson Dixon as a Christmas present (it is now to be found in the Feinberg Collection).[25]To what degree were Emerson's comments on Whitman's indebtedness to the *Gītā* valid?

There is no verifiable proof that Whitman ever read the *Gītā* before the publication of the *Leaves of Grass* in 1855 and his denial of any knowledge of the text has troubled those critics who wanted to see some resemblance to its teaching in his poetry. In her dissertation on the Indian influences on Whitman's poetry, Helen Mercer claims that Whitman's knowledge and use of the Sanskrit text in his own poetry is indefinable. She speaks rather of the 'literary atmosphere' of Transcendentalism that was charged with Vedāntic philosophy (cited in Rayapati 1973: 14). Whitman did not have the access to the numerous books on Indian philosophy and Sanskrit literature that Emerson and Thoreau enjoyed, but he would have been able to gather a significant amount of information regarding Indian thought and poetry from the translations that appeared in *The Dial* between July 1842 and January 1843. While Whitman might claim originality, he is known to have appropriated or surreptitiously borrowed ideas from other sources in other instances without properly acknowledging his debt, thus begging the question of whether the *Gītā* in any way really influenced his work.

In 'A Backward Glance O'er Travel'd Roads' (1884), Whitman claims to have knowledge of 'ancient Hindoo' poems (1965: 569). If he is to be believed, he must have meant the *Gītā*, since it was the only significant

[25] Whitman's marginal notes do not reveal any previous reading of it. See Hendricks 12–14, cited in Rayapati 13.

'poem' translated during the preparation of the 1855 edition of the *Leaves of Grass*. He may well have read it before the first edition of the *Leaves of Grass*. There is some speculation that it was even a far more important text for him than he let on. In fact, it is reported that when Whitman was found dead in his bed, a translation of the *Gītā* was discovered under his pillow (Hendricks 1959: 12–14). But the issue is actually moot, since any study of Whitman's work reveals only echoes of Indian philosophy and some superficial references to Sanskrit words (Mercer 26). In the 1855 edition of the first version of the 'Song of Myself', Brahma appears in a list of gods Whitman calls 'the old cautious hucksters'. There are occasional evocations of Sanskrit terms, such as Whitman's mention of the 'Shastas (sic) and the Vedas' (line 1105), 'gymnosophists' (line 1103), and 'Hindu avatars'. In 'Salut au Monde', Whitman speaks of Indian holy cities (line 142), and their plagues (line 207). Such references appear among references to and evocations of other traditions and gods. Some of these references to India could have easily been gleaned from 'Excerpts from the Heetopades of Veeshnoo Sarma' found in *The Dial* in July 1842, which Emerson, as editor, chose to publish.

Pinpointing the influence of Indian thought on Whitman's work has occupied several generations of Whitman scholars. T.R. Rajasekharaiah who has examined all the Sanskrit literature in circulation at the time of composition of *The Leaves of Grass* (1840s–1855), including periodical material from which Whitman took clippings, concludes that Whitman's knowledge before 1855 came from second-hand sources. Reviews in *The Dial*, along with other magazines and the writings of Emerson and Thoreau could amply supply Whitman with his references. In accordance with Dorothy Mercer's assessment, Rajasekharaiah felt that Whitman's idea of the soul, immortality, God, and divine immanence can equally be found in Christianity as well as in Romantic poetry, but he noted that for a Hindu or someone with knowledge of Hinduism, it is easy to see in the 'Song of Myself' a god-like Self, resembling the cosmic person found in the *Gītā* and the *Upanishads*. That association, combined with Whitman's superficial evocations of Sanskrit terms, gives the impression of a more direct inspiration to Indian thought than perhaps existed.

We can ascertain that Whitman read a collection of periodical articles preserved in his papers, excerpts from the *Laws of Manu* published in the *Whig Review* in May 1845, and an anonymous review of a translation from the *Mahābhārata* and the *Rāmāyaṇa* entitled 'Indian Epic Poetry' that appeared in the October 1848 issue of *The Westminster Review*. These texts alone can be seen to account for all the Indian terminology found in *The Leaves of Grass* (Rajasekharaiah 75). It is also possible, as Rajasekharaiah concludes, that Whitman owed far more to these sources than he was willing to admit. Whitman's affinities with Indian philosophy seem more than accidental; they appear to reflect a second-hand knowledge. Significantly, Whitman never mentions the *Gītā* by name, even though it was a text which he owned.

After the 1855 publication of *Leaves of Grass*, however, Whitman purchased a number of books dealing with Indian culture, such as Whitney's *Oriental and Linguistic Studies: The Veda, The Avesta*, and J. Muir's *Religious and Moral Sentiments metrically rendered from Sanskrit*. From this point onward, his references to India multiply considerably. 'Nirwana' is evoked in 'Twilight', and 'avatara' in 'So Long'. In 'Chanting the Square Deific', he identifies with the *śūdra* and claims to be Brahma. *Democratic Vistas* (1871) refers to the *Mahābhārata* and the *Rāmāyaṇa*, but these references could have easily come from *The Westminster Review*. *Specimen Days* (1882) talks of a brahmin leading his son, but this description probably came from Monier Williams's *Indian Epic Poetry* (1863) (Preston 248). Whitman also wrote about India's mystic tradition, particularly in his review of Emerson's poem 'Brahma' in the *Brooklyn Daily Times* 1857, where he offered an explanatory note showing some familiarity with the idea of the universal soul. Although he denied to Thoreau that he had read the 'orientals', *November Boughs* is the one text showing that Whitman had in fact read the epics first hand (Preston 248).

The problem in assessing the *Gītā*'s influence on Whitman is the following: What sounds derivative of the Sanskrit text may in fact just be universal religious thoughts that are not exclusively Indian but can, as in the case of his image of the permanent passive Self as a spectator, be attributed to Indian philosophy (Mercer 40). Both the *Gītā* and Whitman ('Elemental Drifts') teach that the subject and object share the same identity. We also find in Whitman an image of the eternal Self, similar to that found in the *Gītā* (Mercer 41) as well as the notion of the Self as potentially God (41). The soul appears as immortal in 'Walt Whitman' (42), and in 'So Long', we have the image of rebirth (45). The concept of *māyā* can be read into 'Of the Terrible Doubt of Appearances' and 'Are You the New Person Drawn toward Me' (46–7) where he concludes, 'Have you thought, O dreamer, that it may be all maya, illusion?' (Whitman 1965: 123). In 'Chanting the Square Deific', there is reference to the *śūdra*:

> Aloof, dissatisfied, plotting revolt,
> Comrade of criminals, brother of slaves,
> Crafty, despised, a drudge, ignorant
> With sudra face and worn brow,
> Black but in the depths of my heart
> Proud as any.

However, certain issues mitigate against any more direct and substantial connection between Whitman and the *Gītā*. Whitman's early poetry was ego-centred, rather than God-centred. His equation of the Self with God fits the Vedānta better than the Judaeo-Christian traditions, and Whitman's later poetry is pantheistic ('Passage to India', 'Prayer of Columbus'), like the *brahman* of the *Upanishads* or the Lord of the *Gītā*. But this pantheism is equally traceable to Western sources. It is important to note that the 'Passage to India' presents this geographical site as a general symbol of man's spiritual quest. That it does so with a style exhibiting declamatory flow and paradoxical structure that someone familiar with Sanskrit might see as similar to the effusions found in the *Gītā* and *Upanishads* is less convincing. The poem 'Eidolons' can be seen to approximate the Vedāntic idea that the spirit of the Self is as real and objective as the universe is an illusion. But, here too, there is no lexical proof or legitimate grounds for these comparisons.[26] We cannot even categorically claim that Hinduism had a significant impact on Whitman's philosophy (Preston 251); it appears as an awareness, never a focus (Preston 249). Whitman merely evokes India, borrows Sanskrit terms, and cribs its seemingly profound and exotic allure. India is certainly not central to his poetry.

Yet, Whitman's idea of the soul is like the Vedāntic (i.e. *Upanishads* and *Gītā*) concept of the Self: a unifying energy that is permanent, indestructible, eternal, and all-pervading (Mercer 110). But such a vision of a

[26] Chari 1964 agrees with Mercer on the question of influence.

cosmic Self merging with all creation is also not unique to Indian thought. It is simply common to all mystical literature. While Whitman's idea of the unity of the Self and the universal spirit can be considered Hindu, it is not exclusively Hindu, nor is Whitman's belief in metempsychosis and his pantheistic worldview exclusively Indian. More importantly, Whitman did not believe in certain central tenets that are absolutely central to Hinduism, and particularly to the *Gītā*. He did not discount the physical body or in any way advocate the subjugation of the senses, as one finds in all Vedāntic texts. In fact, Whitman called for a surrender to the senses. Here too, his indebtedness to the *Gītā* and India was more a part of his evocation of exotic images in order to valorize his pantheistic worldview. He was a nineteenth-century exoticist, like so many others. The influence of the *Gītā* was not only indirect, but filtered through German, French, and English Idealists, who were widely read in the US in the latter half of the nineteenth century (1,7). It is even less reasonable to see Whitman as a mystic[27] who reproduced Hindu mysticism from his own illumined state,[28] particularly since he never made claims to have had a mystical experience.

While the notions of immortality, divine immanence, the essential oneness of all and the identity of the individual soul with the cosmic spirit are common to both the *Gītā* and Whitman, ideas of self-absorption, individualism, equality, sex, comradeship, revolt, and convention, so central to Whitman's poetry find no equivalent in the *Gītā* or Indian thought for that matter (Mercer 154). Moreover, a number of very important ideas in the *Gītā* that were picked up by other early Western readers of the text (the system of Sāṃkhya and Yoga, the *guṇas*, *yoga*, mental discipline, and *dharma*) find no resonance in Whitman's poetry. Unlike Arjuna at Kurukshetra, Whitman did not doubt his duty in the Civil War. But, in *Democratic Vistas,* he did assert that everything of old needs to be rewritten or restated in terms consistent with the institutions of the United States. In short, India does not appear to hold timeless truths for Whitman. He situates it rather within a historical progression that will come to fulfilment eventually only in the American continent. India, like

[27] Chari and Sarracino try to find a unified Vedāntic view; Rajasekharaiah sees Hindu sources for everything Whitman wrote.

[28] For an overview of such hagiography or attribution of deep yogic initiation, see Bucke, Nambiar, and Cowley, all cited in Preston 256.

so much else in Whitman, appears as the progenitor to be reworked and find fruition in the United States. The *Gītā* in translation, like all translations, must always be a potential text, the third text, a fulfilment to be found in some subsequent iteration, reworked to suit its reader's needs and desires. This is an important point regarding translation in general and specifically the translations of the *Gītā* we examine in these pages. What is important to take away from Whitman is that he says nothing profound about India or the *Gītā*. But the *Gītā* was by this time perhaps sufficiently well known to Americans and admired as an exotic text of great wisdom that any banal or superficial reference to India must have come from it, as the primary source of all things Indian. Certainly, from the Transcendentalists onward, any exotic terminology evoked by American authors was assumed to signal some profound Indian wisdom that had its source in the *Gītā*. Similarly, any spiritual reference, even when not exclusively Indian, also presumably came from the *Gītā*. By 1855, the *Gītā* had such stature in America that Whitman's 'philosophical' religiosity was attributed to the *Gītā*, even when his references were clearly facile and uninformed. Evocations of exotic terms sufficed. Moreover, Whitman's egotism and grandiosity are particularly instructive here. They bring into glaring focus first how some self-serving and superficial authors would appropriate this 'exotic' text, as opposed to others who were more serious in their approach to it. A willingness to engage the otherness of the *Gītā* had already been challenged by Hegel in his treatment of the text, where the hermeneutic process was derailed and there was no effective engagement with the Indian Other. Whitman is the exception to the rule: he never mentioned the *Gītā*. But, even so, he is worthy of our attention because of how the sustained and superficial references to India we find in his work are really no different from several of the discussions of the *Gītā* we examine here. The *Gītā* is referenced because it lends its authority to vouchsafe for the beliefs and postures of the Self. Referencing the *Gītā* or, in Whitman's case, India, serves the function of maximizing the potential of the exotic, specifically, what it says about those referencing it (their cleverness or spirituality). Those who are just questing after the exotic have no intention of actually engaging it.

Conclusion

Emerson and Thoreau approached the *Gītā* in translation with what we might term a German Romantic focus. They saw its appearance in translation as a potentiality, not an end in itself. Emerson's main statement on Indian thought appeared in 'Brahma,' where he presents the entire universe as an ongoing translation (not of words, but of souls), with the Absolute as the Translator-in-Chief. Thoreau, in his elusive parable of the artist of Kouroo repurposes this trope. We are still discussing translation. Once again it is not an issue of words, but each successive artwork (the staff) as a potentiality, with each rendition (up until then) appearing as a *Verbesserung*, to use the terminology of German translation theorists. In the Transcendentalist readings of the *Gītā's* translations, there was on the part of Emerson and Thoreau an attempt to grasp its essence. But they approached the *Gītā* not to learn from it as much as to have confirmation of what they already believed (Sarma 29). The *Gītā*, as a book of old intelligence, 'poses the same questions which exercise us' (Emerson 1975: 10.360). Its voice was the same as Emerson perceived his own to be. In the opening of 'Self-Reliance,' Emerson wrote: 'In every work of genius we recognize our own rejected thoughts: they come back to us with a certain alienated majesty' (Emerson 1971–: 2.27, cited in Goodman 645). The important point is that 'we' had also experienced this insight but chose to reject it. How superior does that make us?

Emerson and Thoreau absorbed the *Gītā* and, in the process, set in place a view of India that exists even today. They cut the *Gītā*'s roots and transplanted it in a different soil, making it a different text (Sharpe 26), a translation that presumed to improve on the original and reach a transnational audience. There was no concern for potential loss, only gain. The *Gītā* in translation could thus be expropriated and colonized. One stood outside the work, had feelings for it, but saw it primarily as a useful source for potential reworking. For Emerson and Thoreau, the text was as much the source material for an ultra-text, as F. Schlegel asserted all translations in effect were. One invades it, extracts from it (and in the case of Emerson, plagiarizes it) and, to paraphrase Steiner, then brings it home. This aggressive use of appropriation brings to the fore the manner in which the exoticism involved in this reception of the *Gītā* functions: exotic quests are not by nature egalitarian—they presuppose and foster elitism. Take for example Emerson's treatment of caste, which he had initially criticized in *Indian Superstition.* Like Thoreau, Emerson would oppose caste, comparing it to culture in *The Conduct of Life* (1860). While culture risks self-involvement, it nevertheless frees the individual from castes, here seen by Emerson as rigid determinations imposed from without. But he ended up explaining caste away as a product of fate and India's immovable institutions (Emerson 1971–: 4 (1987).30, cited in Goodman 6423). Culture allows for the redistribution of power. It redresses the balance and puts one among one's equals *and* superiors (6 (1968): 137). But as Russell B. Goodman points out, it imposes a new caste among one's superiors (Goodman 643). This is a crucial point in the non-Indian encounters with the *Gītā.*

It is the exotic, in the form of the *Gītā,* that suits the Emersons, Thoreaus, and Whitmans who, as American everymen, still recognize their due as exceptional beings for whom the quotidian experience does not suffice. Although beneficiaries and admirers of American democracy, they nevertheless seek the super-ordinate in order to invest their individual existences with greater value and intensity. These are the armchair yogis or homespun philosophers who truly believed (rather arrogantly) that while the divine spark is present is all humanity, not all humanity is capable of reuniting his/her spark with the divine. Emerson exemplifies this elitist tendency (but it is also found in self-identified champions of the common man, such as Whitman). In a letter of 19 October 1856, Emerson wrote to William Rounseville Alger:

> When it was proposed to me once to reprint the *Bhagavad Gītā* in Boston, I shrank back and asked for time, thinking it not only some desecration to publish our prayers in the 'Daily Herald', but also those students who were ripe for it would rather take little pain and search for it, then throw it on the pavement. It would however be as neglected a book, if Harper's published it, as it is now in libraries. (Williams 1923: 483)

In reading this letter today, one is taken aback by Emerson's exalted vision of his intellect and his spiritual as well as his proprietary stance. When did he come to 'own' the *Gītā* or become its custodian and decide if and how it should be disseminated to *hoi polloi*? Even though he was the 'best of the brahmins' according to Protap Chunder Mazoomdar in 1884 (Sanborn 1971: 371), the book's fate was not in his hands. Or was it?

Emerson saw his task as listening for the 'authentic utterances of the oracle' and matching the author's 'creative writing' to the act of 'creative reading' (Emerson 1971–: 1. 57, 58, cited in Goodman 645). But such an understanding raises important questions that we will investigate in the coming chapters concerning the status of the exotic text and its content. What does it really mean to read, translate, or interpret such a text?[29] And what do these acts say about the people performing them?

[29] For analysis of such concerns, see Cavell 14ff.

5

Nationalism, Sedition, and Mysticism

Vivekananda, Tilak, and Aurobindo

Up to this point in our investigations, we can identify several operant features in the reception of the *Gītā* in the West. The text is complex, rich, and flexible enough to lend itself to a variety of interpretations. As the first complete text translated from the Sanskrit into English, it inspired among Westerners elaborate discussions on the role, feasibility, and mechanics of translation. Such theoretical issues were then worked out in the various acts of translation. It quickly became apparent that translations of the *Gītā* could be unmoored or untied from the letter of the Sanskrit original. The *Gītā* could then become interpreted to say anything anyone wanted to impose on it. It could foreshadow Hegel's philosophy of history or express in more mystical terms Emerson's concept of self-reliance. Even in those instances when interpretation hewed to the text or its translations, the translation could be doctored to justify the desired reading. Authority became less invested in the meaning of the Sanskrit terms translated and more in the text's true, authentic, and hidden meaning that allowed for disparate readings. It was the theories of translation that developed (its aims and capabilities) and the methods of translation subsequently adopted that enabled free-floating translations and interpretations to circulate.

In India, translation remained a key issue in the modern reception of the *Gītā*. The Sanskrit text was not readily available to all. Many educated Indians were disconnected from their tradition and ignorant of the *Gītā*, since it did not impact on their customary rituals, even if they were observant. It was only during the late colonial period that the *Gītā* became a pre-eminent text in India that allowed for the conceptualization of the ethical. It also became a source par excellence to reformulate political action. In general, Indians in the nineteenth century did not focus (to the

The Afterlives of the Bhagavad Gītā. Dorothy M. Figueira, Oxford University Press. © Dorothy M. Figueira 2023.
DOI: 10.1093/oso/9780198873488.003.0006

degree that Westerners did) on issues of human agency and subjectivity. In addition to being imprisoned in structures of industrial society, they were alienated through caste. Notions of agency had further dissolved into passivity under colonialism (Kapila 443). But under foreign rule, Indians increasingly felt the need for freedom, either through the Self, preferably with the Vedānta and with the *Gītā* in particular as their source of inspiration, or through a renunciation of the present material world. The *Gītā*'s legitimization of caste, a theme that was even recognized by a foreign reader such as Thoreau, would either have to be ignored or be managed in order to ensure the continuation of the Indian social order.[1]

Vivekananda

Narendranath Datta, known as Swami Vivekananda (1834–86), directed his reading of the *Gītā*, not initially or primarily at an Indian audience, but packaged it instead for upper-class American matrons and the often-naïve American academics and men of the cloth he encountered in Chicago, Illinois, and Cambridge, Massachusetts. His reception of the *Gītā* can be seen in his talks and speeches on Hinduism and Indian national identity that were delivered across the United States. Vivekananda had first wowed the participants of the World Parliament of Religions in Chicago in 1893, where he astounded all gathered with his charm, good looks, particularly stylish attire, and impassioned presentation of the sophistication and enlightened vision of Hinduism that he introduced. He was so impressive that funding soon came his way to tour the north-east United States, visiting Maine, Harvard University, and other venues. This six-month tour soon turned into three years. He 'performed' Hinduism prodigiously. In 1896, Harvard University offered him a chair of Eastern Philosophy, which he declined. One of its Greek professors, W.H. Wright, noted that he felt Vivekananda was more learned than all the learned

[1] This system, the *varṇāśrama*, identifies the four basic material occupations of duties (*varṇas*)—the brahmins comprised of priests and intellectuals; the *kṣatriyas* who are the warriors and administrators; the *vaiśyas* who comprise the farmers and merchants; and the *śūdras*, the manual laborers and general assistants. There are also four spiritual stages of life: the *brahmacarya* (celibate student), *gṛhastha* (married life), *vānaprastha* (retired life), and *saṃnyāsa* (renunciation). Outside this order are the Untouchables who are denied all rights and privileges.

professors at Harvard put together (Gupta 119, cited in Hodder 338). But Vivekananda had a different trajectory in mind for his career in the States. In his self-promotion as a godman and his successful marketing of Indian spirituality, he would unseat Emerson as the 'Best of the Brahmins'. That role could now be assumed by a real brahmin!

Vivekananda had no intention of burdening himself with the responsibilities of teaching Harvard's students, when he could tour California and return to Chicago, lecture on Indian thought and be feted in both venues by his fan base as well as spend time in New York City where he founded the Vedanta Society of New York in 1894. In these locales, Vivekananda taught that the *Gītā* was the loftiest of all scriptures. It had already been introduced to educated segments of American society as an inspirational text by Emerson and Thoreau. So, Vivekananda could easily present it as the primary source material for the Transcendental Movement (Vivekananda 1985: 95, cited in Robinson 89). Since many broad intellectual and spiritual movements in America were tied to Transcendentalism, it was very gratifying for America's elite to hear from an actual Indian holy man how their homegrown philosophy had so cleverly delved into the wisdom of the esoteric East. Vivekananda slyly suggested that America should take heed of and recognize how much of its contemporary spirituality it owed to India (Hoddard 338–9).

Vivekananda also tailored his US appearances to suit the Christian yearnings of his American audiences (Figueira 2002: 133–8).[2] Hinduism taught the world tolerance; it did so brilliantly on a sliding scale of higher and lower truths (Vivekananda 1994a: 17). The *Gītā* advocated action. But it also showed how one should lead one's existence according to one's own path, since there were different paths and one should only perform the action that best befits one's specific condition (457), as determined by one's individual nature (440, 472–3). The *Gītā* taught that it is better to do one's own duty and not another's (*Gītā* 3.33). The *Gītā* also instructed (3.35) that spiritual fulfilment could be achieved through non-attachment with the aid of a political or military leader (Vivekananda 1994b: 439) who likewise would be following his own assigned path. It all sounded so logical and lofty. The unsuspecting American public might not recognize

[2] Robinson cites four pertinent speeches on the *Gītā* dating from 1895–7. '*The Gītā I, II, II*' given in San Francisco in 1895 and 'Thoughts on the *Gītā*' given in Calcutta in 1897.

in Vivekananda's pronouncements how he deftly sidestepped the issue of caste and the *Gītā's* justification of it. Besides, no American would understand the degradations imposed on Untouchables by this system, especially those who without qualms sanctioned the horrific treatment of Blacks in America at the time and nativist rhetoric directed against immigrants. In fact, Vivekananda carefully avoided the issue of caste during his lectures in America. When he spoke to California and Chicago matrons, he chose to stress Hinduism's tolerance and universal acceptance, just as he had done at the Chicago Parliament (Vivekananda 1995b: 242). Vivekananda presented the *Gītā* to Americans as the all-purpose book of knowledge for Hinduism; he claimed that it offered not only a commentary on the *Vedas* (Vivekananda 1994a: 8; 1995b: 244–5, 261), but also gathered together all the wisdom of the *Upanishads* (Vivekananda 1995a: 189).

When he subsequently 'preached' in India, however, Vivekananda focused on the need for practical activity[3] and generally downplayed the issue of social tolerance he so strenuously touted in the US. He specifically emphasized the *Gītā*'s injunction to perform worldly duties while simultaneously pursuing spirituality. The *Gītā's* advocacy of action, was thus seen to necessitate a strong moral imperative and sanction violence on ethical grounds. This reading would prove particularly popular with Indian nationalists, such as Bankim Chandra Chattopadhyay (1838–1894)[4] who shared Vivekananda's advocacy of justifiable violence for self-protection (Gowda 39), adherence to caste distinctions, and segregation (Gowda 30). Performing duties with desireless action would be propagated by those political activists who wished to foster nation-building. Radicals such as Bankim could view nationalist violence not only as justified, but also as an appropriate path to the Divine.

But Vivekananda was not suggesting anything so revolutionary. He marketed himself as a god-man seeking to liberate the masses from Vedic ritual and make salvation available to all, with the desired consequences

[3] He noted, for example, that one was closer to Heaven by playing football than by studying the *Gītā* (Vivekananda 1995b: 242).

[4] Bankim, as an Indian poet, novelist, and activist in the Independence struggle, felt that it was important to focus on Krishna as a historical figure. In Bankim's historical fiction, *Dharmatattva* and *Krishnacharita*, the *Mahābhārata* War is presented as a concrete historical event and Krishna is a real historical figure.

of an eventual return to some form of Vedic religion (Gowda 91). There was nothing anti-brahmin about his project. Vivekananda was not suggesting radical reform. He was merely proposing, as did other reformers in nineteenth-century India, that the true and original genius of Hinduism had been overlaid with accretions over the years and one needed to return to the pristine past and reinstate the original truth by paring away the ceremonies and rituals that had obscured it (Figueira 2002: 105–19). His reading of the *Gītā* sought to provide an ethical template (for the world) that could be used for just such a rejuvenation.

In his interpretation, Vivekananda focused on *Gītā* 2.2–2.3, where Krishna tells Arjuna that his dejection is un-Aryan and will not lead him to heaven. In modern parlance, Krishna exhorts Arjuna to 'man-up'. His behaviour is unbefitting and he must cast it off. To support his argument, Vivekananda also cites *Gītā* 13.27–8, where Arjuna is told that he who sees the Lord in all perishable beings is imperishable. By seeing the Lord everywhere, one is not subject to harm and attains the highest goal. Vivekananda uses these verses to equivocate on the issue of caste by making Arjuna appear as everyman: all are seen to partake of the same truth regarding the *ātman*. The downtrodden are uplifted, since the poor are not deemed inferior; everyone is equal; brahmins are not superior to lower castes and Untouchables. Salvation is available to everyone. As noted, this slight-of-hand reading of caste made for convincing rhetoric, when directed at Western audiences who around the turn of the twentieth century were fairly ignorant of caste restrictions. It is also important to note how Vivekananda's comments were purely theoretical. He proposed no programme for the abolition of caste inequalities in the real world. It was enough to say that, ideally, the *Gītā* promotes equality among all peoples. The problem was not with Hinduism or its holy books, but with the brahmins who misinterpreted them. Over the centuries, priests have abused their privileges and exploited the poor in violation of the *Vedas* which had already been distorted by superstition. In an initial lecture on the *Gītā* in San Francisco (26 May 1900), Vivekananda claimed that the *Upanishads* had originally tried to alleviate suffering by challenging priestly machinations and ritual minutiae, to little avail. The *Gītā* then sought to reconcile the teachings of the *Vedas* and the *Upanishads* by harmonizing ritual and philosophy as well as mediating between the priests and the people (Vivekananda 1994a: 455–6). The *Gītā* thus presents an allegory representing the struggle between philosophical and religious systems. Its theme of non-attachment was directed primarily against priestly abuse. According to Vivekananda, the *Gītā*'s teaching on non-attachment challenged the role that priests and religious practices play in the repressive exploitation of the poor. As in most Hindu reform movements, here too the Vedic and the Upanishadic religions are 'revealed' as originally pure (Figueira 2002: 96–9, 105–20); they only became elitist because of the machinations of priests (Vivekananda 1994b: 172–3). Religion declined as priestcraft gained ascendency (Vivekananda 1994a: 428). Vivekananda claimed that he was merely seeking to reverse this deterioration.

The message that Vivekananda raised throughout his tours of America was tailor-made for his gullible audience. The *Gītā* is shown to democratize Hinduism. Its message was all-inclusive; everyone is addressed by the teaching of the *Gītā*. Vivekananda pretends that all are equal according to the *Gītā*. Concern for the poor was once also found in the *Vedas* and the *Upanishads*, but their focus was primarily on ethics and morality and not on economics (Vivekananda 1994a: 454–5). While these texts prioritized the role of the *saṃnyāsi* (religious mendicant), the worshipping of idols, and the priestly version of Vedic religion, the *Gītā*, in contrast, focused on *niṣkāma karma* (desireless action) and service to the poor (441–2). Vivekananda actually cast Prince Arjuna as the symbol of the poor and downtrodden who are likewise exhorted and given moral support by Krishna. In Vivekananda's reading, the *Gītā* functions as an inspiration to all, even the *tamasvik* (those whose minds are coloured by confusion and dullness): the poor, women, the weak, Untouchables, and cowards. It specifically enjoins these groups to not accept humiliation and to choose the right path (Vivekananda 1985: 108–9). Vivekananda even attributes an infinite soul to women and children, regardless of their caste, vouchsafing them infinite possibilities and infinite capacities (Vivekananda 1995b: 193–4). But it is important to note, once again, the audience to which he directed these comments were not the upper-caste Hindus in India, nor the Untouchables murdered for seeking water from a village well, but the God-fearing Christians in America. Hence, we have a *Gītā* permeated with Christian compassion and a Protestant ethic. For Vivekananda, even more than for the Transcendentalists, the *Gītā* becomes a book of self-reliance. The weak should not view the learned as givers of service (Vivekananda 1994a: 442); they need to help themselves (478), pull themselves up by their bootstraps just like the many wealthy Americans Vivekananda is addressing pretend to have done. Vivekananda spoke to those Americans who really believed (and many continue to believe), thanks to the Protestant work ethic and general materialism, that the rich are better human beings and the poor somehow deficient. Hinduism, not known for overemphasizing compassion, becomes in Vivekananda's hands a religion of self-reliance and caring. Just as Christ and Buddha open the door to all (Vivekananda 1994a: 438), so does Krishna elevate women and *śūdras* to share in the equality of upper-caste men (Vivekananda 1995b: 427). If the wisdom of the *Vedas* is difficult for people of low intelligence to grasp, then the *Gītā* provides an alternative solution in the diversity of practices it deems accessible to those with a variety of skills. One should find one's own link in the chain of approaches presented in the text and hold on to it (Vivekananda 1994a: 439). Krishna knows that different people have different needs, so he seeks to satisfy them all. You can choose the method that best suits you and your capacities or, if you cannot, just take refuge in Krishna, reject Vedic ritual as work with motives and adopt the *Gītā*'s path of work without motives (Vivekananda 1994b: 178–9).

So, ultimately, Vivekananda's interpretation of the *Gītā* as a democratizing text, tailored for a consumerist and capitalist America, relied on old-fashioned orthodoxy. Since there are too many confusing religious teachings in modern Hinduism, people should simply just return to Vedic religion as the *Gītā* instructs with its philosophy of non-attachment. Vivekananda viewed the *Gītā* as harmonizing the ideas and institutions of the Vedic religion, even if they had degenerated. He presented it as reconciling discordant religious elements and as unique among Hindu scriptures in achieving this balance (Vivekananda 1985: 106). The *Gītā* teaches a life of enjoyment with renunciation (Vivekananda 1994a: 446–58); it upholds *karma* (action) with a lower motive-based sliding-scale and sustains *jñāna* (knowledge), but not its rejection of the material world. Following the *Gītā*, you can gain your highest goal, work for the nation, be a leader, or command the army (439). In short, with this reading of the *Gītā*, Vivekananda claims that the great struggle of Indian religion is resolved (455; 1985: 106–7). It distinguishes *yoga* from *jñāna bhakti* (devotional/mystical knowledge) and reconciles them harmoniously. It takes the best of all Hindu practices and seamlessly threads them together (Vivekananda 1985: 106–7), including wisdom that can also be found in the New Testament and in the teachings of the Buddha (Vivekananda 1994a: 444–5). The *Gītā* is universal. Its philosophy of *niṣkāma karma* should be the guiding principle for the Indian nation, since it undermines inequality and upholds equality. Once again, caste is erased from this picture.

Vivekananda's interpretation of the *Gītā* flirts with the possibility of interreligious dialogue, especially if one accepts that the *Gītā* enables India to become the spiritual teacher of the world. Vivekananda's project here is straightforward: he marketed India in the form of the *Gītā* to the West and sought to render Hinduism attractive to Americans by praising its democratic and consumer-friendly principles. In the process, he designated himself as the spokesperson abroad for an India that existed primarily in the exotic fantasies of his American interlocutors. In India, he claimed a reform project that ultimately reformed nothing (in keeping with the desires of a large segment of India's orthodox elite). It was a win-win strategy. Vivekananda pretended that all Indians were equal. In this respect, he differed from Bal Gangadhar Tilak (1856–1920) who in his translation and commentary of the *Gītā* clearly delineated two kinds of individuals, the weak and the strong in mental strength. Tilak would claim that India needed the strong-minded *sthitaprajña* (he who controls his senses) and is well versed in religion to lead the masses. This image too would also become a compelling fantasy of Indian masculinity. For Vivekananda, the *Gītā* and its call for action was not limited to the *kṣatriya* but could be accessed by all for the workers of the nation, whether leaders or followers. For Tilak, however, (and for Gandhi), instead of the *kṣatriya* of the *Gītā*, the *sthitaprajña* would become the star attraction.

Tilak

Just as Vivekananda spoke for a Hinduism made palpable for export abroad, 'Lokmanya' ('accepted by the people as a leader') Tilak represented the orthodox community at home. Western-educated, Tilak could communicate with and understood British civil authorities. He was also deeply connected to his community. As a religious firebrand in Maharashtra, and the editor of the arch-conservative journal *Kesari*, Tilak was the voice for Mahratta traditionalism and supported all the significant Hindu orthodox battles of his day (*sati*, prohibition of widow remarriage, child marriage, etc.).[5] Maintaining the supremacy of brahmins was at the heart of Tilak's activism. He wrote the *Śrīmad Bhagavadgītā Rahasya* (1910–11) (*The Secret Teaching of the Gītā or Karma Yoga Śāstra*), two volumes of 1,300 pages, in five months (2 November 1910–30 March 1911) while serving a prison sentence for sedition in Mandalay, Burma. Unlike his earlier books, *The Orion, or Research into the Antiquities of the Vedas* (1893) and *The Arctic Home of the Vedas* (1903), which were written in English, the *Śrīmad Bhagavadgītā Rahasya* was written in Marathi and then translated into other Indian languages and English.[6] It was a book for the people and meant to present the *Gītā* as a living tradition (Seth 140).

The *Śrīmad Bhagavad Gītā Rahasya* is a bloated work, consisting of Tilak's translation of the *Gītā* along with of two distinct and traditional forms of commentary (*bhāṣya*) and criticism (*tīkā*). Before presenting his commentary and critical assessment, Tilak first addressed the previous authorities on the *Gītā* scholarship. He needed to 'kill the fathers'[7]—the authors of the traditional commentaries: Śaṅkara, Rāmānuja, Jñānadeva, and Madhva. Each commentator had dealt with the three paths to salvation examined in the *Gītā* (*karma*, *jñāna*, and *bhakti*) in their own way, prioritizing one over the others. Tilak not only needed to dismiss these orthodox commentaries, which posed major obstacles to his own reading, translation, and reform programme, but he had to lay claim to his preferred choice among the three paths to liberation. He had to neutralize Rāmānuja and Śaṅkara in particular, since they had read the *Gītā* in what might be termed an anti-activistic manner. To compromise

[5] He differed from his rival in the Nationalist movement, Gopal Krishna Gokhale (1866–1914), who was wedded to the tradition of British parliamentary procedure (Brown: 197). For a discussion of Tilak's political action in support of brahmin orthodoxy, see Figueira 2002: 121–32.

[6] Tilak's translation and commentary were first published in 1915, with translations in Hindi, Gujarati, Bengali, Telegu, and Tamil soon following. The Hindi and Marathi versions sold tens of thousands of copies (Kapila: 439#5).

[7] Do I dare hazard to propose that this is a particularly gendered discursive strategy? None of the female readers examined here were moved to clear away their precursors before engaging in their own flights of fancy with the *Gītā*.

their interpretation, Tilak essentially did what he accused them of having done: he translated the text nonobjectively to promote a sectarian bias. This was a clever ploy. Tilak chose not to disagree with these commentators, but rather with their interpretations and translations of certain key passages. He attributed to them errors that he now sought to correct. Their errors had caused wrong readings (contributing to the rise of Buddhism and Jainism) that, in turn, had further encouraged renunciation.

According to Tilak, the true message of the *Gītā* was activism, since Arjuna's task is really the task of everyone. Krishna's advice to perform action is universally applicable. This is the 'secret teaching' (*rahasya*) that Tilak will reveal in his translation and commentary. Tilak noted that this message had not been properly understood in the traditional commentaries. Śaṅkara had interpreted the *Gītā* as promoting the renunciation of action (*Bhagavadgītābhāṣya* 6.3). Rāmānuja had read it as stressing devotion (*bhakti*). Madhva, similarly, did not promote an activist reading. Tilak identified the problem with their interpretations as stemming from their readings of *Gītā* 18.43—where Krishna enjoins Arjuna to fight/act (Tilak 1195). To make the case for general activism, Tilak needed to interpret the action demanded of Arjuna as applicable to not just the warrior caste (Brown: 197–8). He needed to translate the text so as to apply the *karma yoga* to all Hindus (Brown: 201). But, to make this reading universal, he first had to debunk Śaṅkara's quietist interpretation. He did so by enlisting Jñānadeva and Rāmānuja to support the activist reading. He further legitimized his interpretation with his translation and commentary.

Śaṅkara (AD 800),[8] read the *Gītā's* teaching to be that of knowledge and renunciation of all action (Tilak: 18, 20, 510–11). This interpretation was shared by Sanskritized literati (Harvey 322). Śaṅkara saw action as the path of the ignorant and held that the *Gītā* advocated a release through our knowledge and devotion (Tilak: 15–21). Tilak repudiated this thesis, claiming that Śaṅkara had thus accommodated heresies and even helped integrate them into orthodox Hinduism. For Śaṅkara, release (*mokṣa*) occurs by turning one's back on the world of action which binds us to an illusory world. One must simply renounce the world of illusions and

[8] The proponent of the Advaita school of the Vedānta that posits non-dualism. The *brahman* (All-Soul, Divine) and the *ātman* (soul) are identical; all reality is interconnected oneness.

binding action. This Vedāntic vision was popular, perhaps even the prevailing teaching of Indian philosophy in Tilak's time. So, to counteract it, Tilak had to delegitimate Śaṅkara's renunciate philosophy in order to establish his activist philosophy of *karma yoga*. To achieve this end, Tilak enlisted Jaimini, the traditional founder of the Mīmāṃsā school, to show how action is essential (Tilak: 479). The *Upanishads* had focused on *jñāna* (translated by Tilak as renunciation, rather than its customary translation as 'knowledge'). Tilak saw the genius of the *Gītā* to be its reconciliation of *jñāna* with 'activism', his translation of the term *karma* (Tilak 480).

To refute Śaṅkara further, Tilak next turned to his fellow Maharastrian Jñānadeva (1275–96) who was considered particularly pious. He addressed Jñānadeva's commentary on the *Gītā*, the *Jñānesvarī*, along with portions of Jñānadeva's anti-Śaṅkara philosophical treatise, the *Amṛtānubhava* (Tilak 345–6). In the *Jñānesvarī* (18.867), Jñānadeva had rejected Śaṅkara's renunciation as illusory and asserted that the world of action, phenomena, and materiality were true and authentic reality (Brown 203). Since Jñānadeva devised this philosophy from his own mystical experiences, *bhakti* (devotion) was especially important. Tilak could accept Jñānadeva's valorization of *bhakti*, as long as it could be bundled together with his rejection of Śaṅkara's vision of the world as *māyā*. Tilak then claimed that Jñānadeva had actually advocated a form of social action for universal benefit (*lokasaṃgraha*) (Brown 204).

Tilak also availed himself of Rāmānuja's commentary on the *Gītā*, the *Gītābhāṣya*. A proponent of the *viśiṣṭādvaita*[9] school, Rāmānuja (AD 1000) had also held to a devotionalist view, claiming that the *Gītā* primarily developed a religion of devotion (*bhakti*) to Krishna. In his commentary to the *Gītā* (specifically 18.47–8), Rāmānuja argued that pursuing *karma* was the only possible path and *jñāna* was not possible because of the nature of things. Action, while doing one's duty, was not binding. *Jñāna* is inferior to *karma* and the renunciate's non-action is just an illusion. Tilak thus interprets Rāmānuja as advocating that action is indeed the proper path set forth in the *Gītā*. He ignored, however, what Rāmānuja meant by the term *karma*. Rāmānuja saw it primarily as ritual acts devoted to Krishna. Tilak, however, translated the term *karma*

[9] Non-dualist school of Vedānta philosophy in which *brahman* alone exists but is characterized by multiplicity.

differently (i.e. as activism). Tilak basically intended to adapt Rāmānuja's devotionalism, since compared to Śaṅkara, he felt that it was the lesser of the two evils. His main concern was to counteract the hold of renunciation. Rāmānuja's commentary in the *Gītābhāṣya* on the *Gītā* verses 18.47–8 would prove to be a manageable fit for Tilak to achieve this goal, even though it minimized action (Tilak 22–37).[10] He could accept Rāmānuja's understanding of nature and the necessity of both action and duty as unavoidable.

By thus accommodating Rāmānuja's reading of the *Gītā*, Tilak was able to remain somewhat within the traditional and orthodox camp of interpretations and still reject Śaṅkara's more problematic approach that advanced the renunciation of action, condemning it as an illusory path to *mokṣa*. Tilak also adopted Rāmānuja's advice to follow the path of *karma yoga* because it was a practical and possible path for *mokṣa*. He ascribed to Rāmānuja's claim that the *Gītā* admonished one to perform action as the only possible path due to the nature of living beings and all matter. This action, performed while doing one's duty, was moreover seen as non-binding. Tilak could also accept Rāmānuja's understanding that the *Gītā* taught how *jñāna yoga* was not possible because of the nature of living matter. Even if one could follow the path of renunciation, it was still inferior to *karma yoga* because all action was surrounded by a binding potential. Renunciation's non-action was essentially illusory (Harvey 324). Tilak thus read Rāmānuja as advocating that it was only by performing non-binding actions that one can escape bondage. As far as Tilak was concerned, Rāmānuja supported the thesis that *karma yoga* was the correct path.[11] Throughout the *Gītārahasya*, Tilak will strategically coopt Rāmānuja's pronouncements and terminology for his presentation of *karma yoga*. He will then posit his own translation of key terms as the most reliable and preferable authority on the *Gītā* and the basis for his judgement that the *Gītā* is 'essentially a treatise on Right or Proper Action (*karmayoga*)' (Tilak xxvi). He would also interpret the *karma yoga* propounded in the *Gītā* as supporting nationalism (Robinson 58).

[10] Tilak made the same claim for Madhva (Tilak 23).

[11] Rāmānuja could also be seen as close to Jñānadeva in his devotional interpretation of the *Gītā*. He saw *karma yoga* as generally entailing personal and liturgical acts of devotion.

In such an activist interpretation, the *Gītā* can be seen to promote violence as a method of achieving freedom.

Tilak claimed that the *Gītā* was the scripture par excellence of what he called the Bhagavata religion (Tilak 12–13) which he understood in terms of Energism (13–14) or Action-Energism (39). Tilak admitted that he had initially thought the *Gītā* was a text about salvation through devotion (xv–xviii). But he discovered, when he actually studied it, that it was really about action (xliii) and how it was better to perform action than to abandon it. Activism is simply better than renunciation (431–3, 440). In fact, Tilak claimed that this Bhagavata religion promoted action as a duty to the exclusion of renunciation. It combined the householder ideal with the valorization of knowledge *(jñāna)* and devotion (*bhakti*) (480). Tilak cautioned that even *jñāna* and *bhakti* were subordinated to action. He explained that Vedic religion had initially been based on action, but this focus was overlaid and supplanted by a philosophy promoting renunciation (486–9). Tilak sought to reclaim what he termed the original Vedic nature of the *Gītā*. Its promotion of action with liberation attained through knowledge and devotion (Tilak 713).

He then made another important distinction. While public duty is traditionally specifically applicable to the *kṣatriya*, Tilak contended that the *Gītā* teaches that it is applicable to all four castes (Tilak 697), particularly in times of national crisis, when India is threatened by internal decay and external oppression. Indian Energism is pure (*sattvika*) as opposed to the rage-based (*rajasvik*) violence one finds in the West (700). However, since we live in the *Kali Yuga*,[12] the renunciation of action should, according to Tilak, really be prohibited (701). The nation's leaders must support action (700) and this action must be selfless in order to avoid bondage and be effective. Moreover, this action necessitates violence, especially in times of national crises. But such violence must be consistent with the guidance of the wise (510–65). Leaders are, therefore, needed and must function as activists (700).

Throughout his translation and commentary, Tilak emphasizes that the *Gītā* is not about non-violence. In fact, Tilak claims violence as the natural by-product of the *Gītā*'s advocacy of duty to the hereditary tasks that bring about societal welfare (Tilak 556). The *karma yoga* expressed

[12] Literally, the 'Age of Kali' or the 'Age of Vice and Misery' or 'Age of Darkness.'

in the *Gītā* is, of necessity, nationalistic and Tilak laments how the *Gītā*'s call for action (and violence) had for so long been misconstrued and ignored, especially in his era (713), forcing him to compose the *Gītārahasya* in order to teach that real Hinduism is not quietist and does not teach the renunciation of the world. Rather, the *Gītā* endorses action in the world, especially political activity, and views such action as patriotic. Tilak distinguished this obligatory daily action in the world from what he saw as the much rarer form of detached action marshalled occasionally as sacrifice (510–65). Also, Tilak emphasized that the violence endorsed by the *Gītā* is not directed at an outsider, but rather at an intimate.

Tilak had no problem with the fraternal being converted into enmity, since the fraternal was indeterminate and not permanent. He saw the fraternal killing advocated in the *Gītā* as consonant with the restoration of *dharma*. The West, according to Tilak, erroneously focuses on happiness, whereas India rightly emphasizes duty. To protect the family, the individual may be abandoned; to protect a town, a family may be abandoned, to protect the *ātman*, even the earth may be abandoned (Tilak 558). Discriminating what action to take was considered paramount. It was also necessary to be able to distinguish the normal time of ethics from moments of exception when rules must be suspended. One needs discriminatory knowledge in order to recognize and declare such a state of exception. The *Gītā* provides this knowledge. Tilak exhorts his readers to recognize and declare just such a state of exception (41–9). His valorization of fraternal enmity would be embraced by radical nationalists and become an important factor in modern Indian politics.

Tilak opposed all those readings of the *Gītā* that presented *jñāna* and *bhakti* as the paths to self-realization and freedom, because they privileged renunciation. He claimed that such readings were the product of different sects (Tilak 18). These various interpretations, ranging from Śaṅkara's interpretation of the *Gītā* as supporting knowledge to Rāmānuja's advocacy of devotional practices or his message of desireless action as a technique towards *mokṣa* rather than an end in itself, seemed to Tilak as false readings based on faulty translations. Tilak noted that one cannot just take from the *Gītā* what one wants (28), although he himself did that very thing. All the earlier commentators, according to Tilak, had ignored the beginning (*upakrama*) and conclusion (*phala*) of the *Gītā*. He accused Śaṅkara particularly of exhibiting sectarian bias and self-interest

(33). Tilak claimed that he himself had avoided this trap by intentionally not focusing on love for union with God as a form of detachment from conjugal attachment. He did not pursue *jñāna*. He eschewed the rigours of discipline as forms of self-emancipation. Rather, he focused exclusively on Arjuna's dilemma to kill or not kill, making it the central event of his analysis (Kapila 447). Tilak posited truth (his truth) and violence as the pillars of the text. Violence performed and predicated on vows are alone true (Tilak 52).

Tilak claimed that in a period of crisis such as India then found itself, the *sthitaprajña*, like Arjuna, is exhorted to kill in order to restore the moral order and protect the perpetuation of the good life from the irruption of evil (Tilak 70–94). *Ahiṃsā* (non-violence), therefore, must be suspended. Kinsmen must be transformed into enemies. This transformation becomes a matter of judgement that exists in and during the event. At the end of the event, there is the resumption of the normal course of *dharma* and enemies can be reconverted back into kinsmen, as in the *Śāntiparvan* of the *Mahābhārata*, when those who have killed their kin subsequently perform the death duties for them. This is the state of exception described in the epic and operant for India under colonial rule where it finds itself in a permanent state of exception. For Tilak, the *Gītā* actually describes the contemporary course of action needed. Indians must reject the quotidian (as represented by the British) and boycott their mundane world of employment, education, food, and clothing. In this state of exception, there could be justification for the murder of the British colonial administrators, as in case of Mr. Rand and Lt. Ayerst on Queen Victoria's Diamond Jubilee (27 June 1897) by Damodar Chapekar whom, it was claimed, Tilak had worked up into a state of 'murderous frenzy' with his denunciations of British oppression (Chirol 100ff, cited in Sharpe 72). With that assassination, the *Gītā* became directly associated with revolutionary violence and future acts of anti-colonial violence.

As part of his general activism, Tilak had become deeply involved in creating popular festivals for figures from the mythical and historical past. The most important of these initiatives was the festival for the seventeenth-century Maratha general Śivāji who had fought against the Muslims. Tilak claimed that Śivāji had been inspired by the *Gītā*. But the problem in glorifying Śivāji was that his famous engagement with Afzal

Khan[13] in 1659 was, from a moral perspective, problematic, and some might say, even dirty and treacherous. Śivāji had besieged his enemy's fortress and after considerable fighting, called a truce. Śivāji agreed to meet Afzal Khan face to face in order to discuss the terms of surrender. However, at this encounter, Śivāji took the opportunity to kill his adversary.[14] Tilak justified Śivāji's rather unheroic actions by claiming that in acting as he did, he was adhering to the precepts of the *Gītā*. The implication was clear. What was good for Śivāji was good for all Hindus. They could justifiably break the rules of combat, just as Śivāji had done.

Tilak's *Kesari* of the 15 June 1897 had delineated the moral and ethical aspects of Afzal Khan's murder and fuelled a debate surrounding Tilak's establishment of the Shri Śivāji Coronation Festival. If the *Gītā* is seen to teach that good men are above the common principles of morality and even teachers and kinsmen can be blamelessly killed as long as they are destroyed not out of any desire to reap the fruits of the deed, then Śivāji had done well when he killed Afzal Khan for the good of others. While such an act might be seen as 'legally wrong', it was nonetheless morally defensible in Tilak's estimation. Tilak even urged Hindus to jettison the *Penal Code* and enter into the extremely high atmosphere of the *Gītā*, where such lessons were taught (Sharpe 71). Śivāji's action was simply not a sin according to Krishna's teaching to Arjuna. The *Gītārahasya* and Tilak's promotion of Śivāji are of a piece: they both advocate violence. Even if the conventional account of Śivāji's encounter with Afzal Khan raised moral questions, Tilak found it acceptable and claimed that it corresponded to the same justifiable violence advocated in the *Gītā*. Moreover, Tilak proposed that what he envisioned as the 'Śivāji spirit' needed to be revitalized and emulated (Sharpe 71) by the nationalist action that Tilak read encoded into the *Gītā*. India could become great again if only it followed this original principle of the Hindu tradition set forth in the *Gītā*. Tilak advocated that Krishna's exhortation to Arjuna should become the rallying cry for Hindus to fight the British by any

[13] A general of the Adil Shahi dynasty of Bijapur Sultanate, he had subjugated the Nayaka chiefs who had taken control of the former Vijayanagara. He was then sent to subjugate Śivāji in 1659.

[14] Some Marathi accounts claim Afzal Khan attacked first with a concealed weapon. But the more popular story is that Śivāji had concealed *bagh nakh* (tiger's claws) and treacherously killed his opponent during their negotiated encounter.

violence necessary in order to regain political supremacy. In fact, the *Gītā* alone unambiguously presents the Hindu values necessary for this fight, while the *Vedas* and the *Upanishads* had merely focused on *jñāna*. The *Laws of Manu* further fostered this upanishadic vision. Finally, Buddhism and Jainism promoted atheism and rejected the *Vedas*. For these reasons, Tilak stood by the *Gītā* as the most reliable Hindu text. Hindus need not read any other *śāstras*. The *Gītā* alone sufficed to revitalize Hinduism and legitimize political activism. It was important that the modern Indian nation not be founded on any source other than the *Gītā*. It did not need any other masterpieces of the Hindu tradition and it certainly did not need the wisdom of the West if it had a text like the *Gītā*. Although not a part of the earlier canon, the *Gītā*'s core nevertheless derived from it and encapsulated the original teachings of the Hindu tradition.[15] Moreover, the *Gītā* supplied the wisdom that could be found in other cultures as well. The Bible, for example, was derivative of Buddhism (831), which in turn borrowed from the *Gītā* (822).

Tilak's method of translation played a key role in his analysis of the *Gītā*. As Mark J. Harvey has shown, Tilak's argument rests on his translation of three key terms: *karma*, *yoga*, and *dharma* (Harvey 325). To develop his thesis, Tilak gave each of these terms a new meaning. *Karma* derives from the root *KṚ*, 'to do' or 'to act', of which there are two broad divisions distinguished by the Sanskrit grammarians that Tilak used. The first involves *yajñakarma* or action for sacrifice which is not binding. The second is *puruṣārthakarma* or action for the purpose of the subject which is binding. In Hinduism, sacrificial actions are viewed as meritorious. They do not contribute to the accumulation of *karma* which is seen to bind one to the world (Tilak 72–5). However, actions performed for the self are deemed selfishly motivated by greed and lust; they entail a heavy accumulation of *karma*. Arjuna did not want binding actions (Harvey 326): he sought to avoid them in order to gain liberation. In addition to not being seen to advocate inaction or renunciation (as in the reading by Śaṅkara), the *Gītā* must also be read as advocating a special kind of action, a personal form of action performed with an unattached frame of mind, what Tilak terms 'equable reason'. Tilak proclaims that

[15] See the conclusion of Tilak's opus for the texts Tilak believed were synthesized by the *Gītā*.

anyone who performs action in this way attains liberation, perfection, or release (Tilak 897–8).[16]

The term '*yoga*' means 'to yoke' or 'to join.' Tilak used this term in the sense of skilful means or the skilful use of action (Tilak 76–81). He based this interpretation on his translation and commentary to the *Gītā* 2.48–50 (Harvey 326). The Sanskrit of the *Gītā* 2.50 as follows:

> buddhiyukto jahātīha ubhe sukṛtaduṣhkṛte tasmād yogāya yujyasva yogaḥ karmasu kauśalam

Tilak translated this passage as:

> He who is steeped in the (equable) reason remains untouched both by sin or merit in this (world); therefore, take shelter in yoga, the cleverness (skillfulness or trick) of performing Action (without acquiring merit or sin) is known as (*karma*) *yoga*. (Tilak 897–8)

Let us compare this rendition to Harvey's literal translation:

> Here (one possessed of mind) gives up both bad and good, therefore prepare yourself in *yoga*; *yoga* is skill in action. (Harvey 327)

Harvey views Tilak's translation neither essentially wrong nor a contradiction. Tilak just 'over-translates' the text to support his *karma yoga* thesis. One can cite other idiosyncracies with Tilak's translation, such as 2.49, where Tilak reads that *karma* as far inferior to the '*yoga* of reason'. Here, Tilak's translation actually contradicts his premise that *karma yoga* was more important than *jñāna yoga* (Harvey 327). Tilak needed to remedy this contradiction. He needed to establish *karma yoga* as the supreme path of the *Gītā*, so he simply claims that the interpretation proposing that *karma* is less important than *jñāna* is not correct. Those who say reason is superior to action are simply wrong.

[16] Just as he translated *karma* and *yoga* in a rather unique way, so too did Tilak reinterpret the concept of *saṃnyāsa* (renunciation), changing it from its historical meaning of the renunciation of all actions to mean, rather, the renunciation of the ends/fruits of action.

There is also a problem with the translation of *buddhi* (reason) as meaning *jñāna* (knowledge). Tilak's reasoning is as follows: because the description of equability given in the 48th stanza is continued in the 49th stanza and subsequent stanzas, the word *buddhi* must be translated as meaning an 'equabilising *buddhi*'. The goodness or badness of an act does not depend on the act itself, although the act may be one and the same; it becomes good or bad according to the good or bad intention of the doer; reason is therefore superior to action. Krishna says that when a man performs action in this way with an equable reason, there is no neglect of worldly activities, and complete perfection or release is achievable (Tilak 898). Usually, *buddhi* simply means 'wisdom' or 'knowledge'. But, in Tilak's commentary, *buddhi* is a special kind of reason or knowledge that is unattached and balanced (Harvey 327).

The final problematic term that Tilak translates is *dharma*, deriving from the verb *DHṚ*, 'to uphold or bear'. *Dharma* signifies the duties of the four *varṇas* (brahmin, *vaiśyā*, *kṣatriya*, and *śūdra*) to uphold society. Tilak curiously identifies two operant *dharmas*: one *dharma* of this world and one of the afterlife (*mokṣadharma*). He claims to have derived this distinction from the *Mīmāṃsā* school of philosophy.[17] For Tilak, it was everyday *dharma* that was the most important (Tilak 88–101). One must work out in this world one's own salvation from life to life (885). According to Tilak's translation of *Gītā* 18.17 and 18.59–60, it is the frame of mind one uses in doing action that matters, enjoining one to act so as not to be bound (Harvey 329). While *karma* is the inevitable concomitant of human nature, it was the *buddhi* or mental state of desiring or not desiring the fruits/goals that determine whether an act is binding or not. In his translations of the key terms, *karma*, *dharma*, and *yoga*, Tilak attributed to them explicit social content and placed them in a political context. His creative reinterpretation linked them together as *karma yoga dharma* (skilful use of action in this world). If Indians do their duty in society with single-minded purposefulness and a desireless frame of mind (Harvey 329), then society will be liberated and prosperous (Tilak

[17] Mīmāṃsā presents a critical investigation on the meaning of the Vedic texts. *Dharma* is not accessible to reason but must be inferred by the *Vedas*, so Mīmāṃsā offers rules for the interpretation of the *Vedas*.

700–13). As Tilak read it, the *Gītā* called for the betterment of society through unselfish service in this world of fellow beings (*lokasaṃgraha*).

Just as in the case of Tilak overtranslating to support his *karma yoga* thesis, so to an even greater degree did he supplement his entire translation and commentary with references to *lokasaṃgraha*. This concept which only appears in a few fleeting instances in the Sanskrit original becomes in Tilak's translation a recurring theme. The reference to sacrifice (*yajña*) in 3.9 is glossed 'also all worldy actions' (Tilak 918), and the '*yajña cakra*' or 'cycle of sacrifices' (*Gītā* 9.12) is translated as 'a land of universal service (*lokasaṃgraha*), that is, action productive of universal welfare' (919). In *Gītā* 4.23, the '*yajñayacarataḥ karma*', or the 'action undertaken for sacrifice' is destroyed because it is not done for the sake of the *lokasaṃgraha*. Only through action for the *lokasaṃgraha* can one be liberated from the consequences of action and attain release (955) with reason, what Tilak qualifies as 'equitable reason' (963). *Lokasaṃgraha* is brought into discussions in these instances and others even when it does not appear in the text (as in Tilak's commentary to *Gītā* 4.33). Tilak claims in his commentary to *Gītā* 14.74 that since *lokasaṃgraha* 'is the chief question' of the *Gītā*,' he feels justified in adding it at will to the text, translation, and commentary. He does so freely. Similarly, while also not specifically in *Gītā* 4.10, Tilak supplements this text by explaining that *lokasaṃgraha* is the reason why the Blessed Lord even became incarnated (in the form of Krishna) (944). *Lokasaṃgraha* appears unannounced in most instances where *yajña* or *karma* are discussed.[18]

As Tilak notes in his commentary to 3.22, *lokasaṃgraha* is 'not some humbug' (Tilak 928). It refers to the *dharma* of all, even the *jñānin* (renunciant or possessor of wisdom) and ordinary people (930). It is, however, the task especially of the *jñānin*. In fact, we are told that the message of the *Gītā* is that the *jñānin* should perform action to teach others and improve them (931). Clearly, Tilak sees the *Gītā* as the text par excellence to motivate the entire Indian population to fight, not just the *kṣatriyas*. But, citing 3.12, he prioritizes the salutary role to be played by the intelligentsia and the brahmins. The reference here to Janaka is significant

[18] In 2.71, the verb '*carati*' which can mean 'move', 'live', 'beg', becomes 'takes part in worldly affairs' (906–7) or when the term '*karma*' necessarily implies *lokasaṃgraha* as in his commentary to 4.41 (968).

since he was a *kṣatriya* who claimed he could perform sacrifices without brahmin help. In his commentary, Tilak uses this verse to make the point that the *jñānin* (i.e. not the warrior, but the renunciant or brahmin) must defend the entire world, since it 'falls his lot' (927) as Tilak forcefully noted in his commentary (456).

Tilak claims that the *Gītā*'s vision is not narrow. It does not merely speak to the warrior. While the Sanskrit might address one's 'in-born action', Tilak shifts the focus away from one's profession to invite all professions as long as one had (or is enjoined to activate) the proper frame of mind for performing action (Tilak 1198). In Tilak's translation and commentary of *Gītā* 18.48–9, he also specifies the mobilization of the man 'endowed with spiritual and empirical knowledge as much as the brave warrior, merchant, labourer, carpenter, ironsmith, potter, butcher'. The message is clear. While Tilak asserts the importance of his own caste by prioritizing the role of the brahmins in the action that must be done, he calls upon all Indians also to fight for the welfare of the nation, as stated in the *Gītā* 3.20: 'Lokasaṃgraham evāpi saṃpaśyan kartum arhasi' ('Beholding the mere holding together of the world, you should act'). It is also worth noting in passing that Tilak's general mobilization of the entire population is mandated without any limitations or qualifications placed upon the traditional functioning of the caste system. Caste is left intact in Tilak's revolutionary call to arms.

Tilak, therefore, expands the traditional understanding of *dharma* from a specific caste's duties and makes it a pan-Indian duty (with brahmin ascendency reinstated) through which Indians should strive for Home Rule as the implementation of his specific understanding of *karma, yoga*, and *dharma*. Tilak cleverly acknowledges the significance of Jñānadeva's and Rāmānuja's interpretation of the *Gītā*'s presentation of *bhakti* and Śaṅkara's understanding of its call for *jñānasaṃnyāsa*. He judges them as valid messages for their times. But he maintains that the historical circumstances had radically changed, and that the world was now active and lively; the India of his day needed a path for liberation that was in accord with the changing times. Tilak's world needed *karma yoga*, the activism advocated in the *Gītā*. For Tilak, the *Gītā* called for activism, and not renunciation.

In addition to legitimizing his activism, making it *the dharma* for all Hindus, Tilak also sought to revitalize tradition. Tilak established new norms that were both political as well as religious (Harvey 331) His translation of the *Gītā* in the *Gītārahasya* claims to interpret the philosophy of *brahman, ātman, karma, jñāna, bhakti,* and the escape from *saṃsāra*, not only according to the *Gītā* itself, but in conjunction with all the other pertinent literature, from the *Vedas* through to Buddhist scripture. But Tilak's main aims in writing his opus were clear: he sought to bridge the gulf he felt existed between external knowledge and Sāṃkhya philosophy. Since he had been young, Tilak held the opinion that the *Gītā* was universally acknowledged as containing all the principles of the Hindu religion and that the interpretations of the *āchāryas* (renowned commentators) were doctrine oriented (Tilak 24f.). But he now realized the extent to which all previous translators (the same *āchāryas*) had got it wrong. Tilak felt they were all biased in favour of their individual ideologies. He sought, therefore, to reveal what he considered the *Gītā*'s hidden truth: the morality necessary for nationalism. Tilak was not overly concerned with any inconsistencies in the text that might detract from his thesis. He drew his conclusions from his translation, where his qualified renditions of key terms and supporting citations from other canonical works were enlisted to support his interpretation.

For Tilak, *karma yoga* was the *Gītā*'s central teaching. It combined knowledge for the absolute (*jñāna)* with the performance of duties (*karma*) and dedication to the divine (*bhakti*). The *sthitaprajña* (the one who gains control of his inner self) is the integrated person practising *karma yoga*. Tilak proposed the *sthitaprajña* as the model for the new Indian who would create a new Brahmanism. Tilak's *sthitaprajña* has a heroic personality and is a member of the elite. Only the *sthitaprajña* can justify acts because they come from his desire for universal welfare and because he acts with a desire for *lokasaṃgraha* (Tilak 550).[19] His action, therefore, can be considered non-violent, even if it is violent.[20] Tilak accepts *hiṃsā* as an integral part of life. He criticizes Buddhism and Christian ethical commandments. He maintains that non-violence is not violent if it is done for the protection of society and social order (548–9). Besides, high moral values, such as *ahiṃsā,* should not be seen as universals (42).

[19] The *sthitaprajña* is clearly gendered as male here.

[20] The notion of the elite as the implied reader, whose violence carries no guilt, can also be found in the later German National Socialist readings of the *Gītā*.

Ahiṃsā is not justifiable, since India under colonialism cannot be viewed as a perfect and harmonious place (546). The *sthitaprajña*, consequently, has the moral duty to punish evil (550).

As far as Tilak is concerned, India simply cannot continue to support other readings of the *Gītā*, such as Śaṅkara's, because they primarily promote the apathetic Vedic *saṃnyāsa*. India needs both active and responsible men (Tilak 555–6) who meet violence with their own ethically justified violence and not with non-violence. For Tilak, the demand for general welfare replaces any concern for the individual. Violent acts become morally just (554). While Tilak judges all earlier interpretations of the *Gītā* as doctrinal, he maintains that his own is not; it is, as he claims, an unbiased discourse of nationalism. He views his reading of the *Gītā* as a necessary corrective to the quietism and renunciation that had taken root in India in the fifth century BC with the rise of Jainism and Buddhism. Tilak viewed these belief systems as heretical sects that advocated an open 'door of Renunciation to all castes' (703). Their levelling out of caste and advocacy of quietism had to be stopped. It is important to note how in the various nationalist discussions of the *Gītā*, the issue of caste, its centrality, and the need to reform it are largely ignored or disregarded. Tilak's commentary on the *Gītā* is no exception. The nationalist readings of the *Gītā* always seem to observe the subtext of caste, and sanction the maintenance of its sway over India by folding it into discussions of worth or exceptionality, as in the case of Tilak's rhetoric on the *sthitaprajña*.

According to Tilak, the *Gītā* teaches that action is violent and must be performed for the sake of the greater good of the community and it should be done selflessly. When this message had been lost to generations, India had suffered. So Tilak set out to resuscitate it by advocating a vision of a national community constructed upon a truth that was found in the *Gītā*, and particularly in his reading of it. This necessity for violent action would subsequently be taken up by other nationalists such as Bankim, Savarkar, and Aurobindo. However, this was a notion of community with which Muslims and non-Hindus would have difficulty identifying. It consisted of an exclusively Hindu vision of nationalism, where caste distinctions are elided within the nation. The issue of caste is never far from any of these readings even, as an absent theme of the narrative. Krishna's advice to Arjuna, his admonishment to fight (act), was based on Arjuna's specific caste obligation as a *kṣatriya* (warrior). Since this interpretation was set out very clearly in the *Gītā* 18.43, Tilak needed only to find a justification that would make the act of fighting the duty of all individuals, regardless of caste. He therefore sought to make *karma yoga* applicable to India as a whole (Brown 197–8). Caste was always present. But for Tilak, it was not really an issue given his orthodox brahmin perspective, he need not even directly address it. Caste merely had to be adapted in this instance and folded into Tilak's nationalism.

The new Indian of Tilak's nationalism practises *karma yoga*. Unattached, he takes part in activities based on reason and concern for social welfare (Tilak 548). Tilak's *sthitaprajña* appears as an exemplar to be envied and emulated. Just as Śivāji was justified in his killing of Afzal Khan, so too is Tilak's *sthitaprajña* justified in the use of violence against the British colonizers, especially since nationalism is not an end in itself. Its final goal is universal welfare (556). An imperialist country has no ethical right to expect non-violence as the response from those they subjugate (557). Tilak reasoned that such violence serves a larger public good. If people behave unjustly, others have an ethical right to protect themselves (557, 560–1). It is *karma yoga*, rooted in family relations, village, and country, that will lead Indians to a higher state. Tilak viewed such a nationalism as being able to raise an imperfect country, such as India, to perfection and enable it to fight injustice (556). While he notes that the path of knowledge can work for some (567), clearly it cannot work for all. It is primarily the path for an elite. But, in order to mitigate elitism, the *Gītā* has given us another path to the Divine (*brahman*) through *bhakti* (556–7), the *Gītā*'s special leveller (582), the path for the ordinary and unendowed. Thus, Tilak's *sthitaprajña* nominally combines all the virtues Tilak reads into the *Gītā*: *bhakti, jñāna,* and *karma* (578). Tilak's *Gītā* is particularly convenient. It combines self-interest and sectarianism and leaves caste untouched.

In Tilak's commentary of the *Gītā,* he replaced the brahmins, whom he tirelessly championed, with the *sthitaprajña*, who will serve as the model for the nation. It is, of course, a given that Tilak's vision of the *sthitaprajña* hailed from the traditional elite. Tilak was thus able to elide caste elites now with moral elites. He discredited the renunciant (*saṃnyāsi*) and assigned devotion (*bhakti*), rather than pursuit of knowledge (*jñāna*), to the masses, thus making it a precondition for the *sthitaprajña*. Tilak's new elite can be seen to show, at least superficially, a connection with the masses who still remain virtually absent from any real power. Tilak fostered a nationalist discourse on compassion for the inferior and disenfranchised which would, of course, reach its acme in Gandhi's reading of the *Gītā*. But, first, Tilak's vision of the *Gītā's* justified violence needed to be adopted and implemented by even more radical thinkers. His translation and commentaries were deemed so authoritative that their promotion of *lokasaṃgraha* could readily be employed to justify both mystical and violent variations.

Sri Aurobindo

Sumit Sarkar once wrote that 'the conventional image of the Bengal revolutionary as advancing with a bomb in one hand and the *Gītā* in the other seems more than a little overdrawn' (Sarkar 1973: 484, cited in Sharpe 81). But the reality is, as Sarkar also acknowledged, that the *Gītā* was really used to this effect. Although Aurobindo Ghose (1872–1950), subsequently known as Sri Aurobindo, denied that the *Gītā* had become the gospel of terrorism, his brother (Barindrakumar) ran a religious school/bomb factory in Maniktala, a suburb of Calcutta, that focused on spiritual exercises based on the *Gītā* and bomb-making (Sarkar 486). The *Gītā* was chanted as vows for initiation into revolutionary secret societies (Sarkar 485) and, as we have seen, from around 1879 onward Indian nationalists began using the *Gītā* to justify the killing of their imperial masters (Sharpe 70). In his own life, Sri Aurobindo would play a slippery game, juggling the dual roles of the worldly activist and the holy man removed from the world. Aurobindo acknowledged violence as part of nature and directed his reading of the *Gītā* to justify its use. At a time when teaching and possessing the *Gītā* was deemed suspicious by the British government, Aurobindo advocated using it as India's 'hope for the future, our great force for the purification of the moral weaknesses that stain and hamper our people' (Aurobindo 1972b: 400ff, cited in Sharpe 82). Granted it was the *kṣatriya's* duty to fight, but he felt that the *Gītā* provided the moral basis for the hero, soldier, or the king to join in. The *Gītā* was a necessary text, since its teaching absolved these combatants from being considered criminals. Aurobindo did, however, admit that the message of the poem could be perverted by terrorists.

Aurobindo Ghose was born in Calcutta. His father, a well-to-do surgeon, sent him to England at the age of seven to receive a Western education, culminating in his graduation from King's College in 1893. When he returned to India, he began publishing in revolutionary journals and became involved in the freedom struggle. One can identify three phases in Aurobindo's life. First, there was his militancy within the Indian National Congress, where he had become the leader of the radical wing and turned to instigating armed revolution. Then, there was his contact with Tilak from 1902–06. During this time, he became interested in *yoga* (primarily the breathing exercises and not the philosophical school) and the Shakti cult, where the Divine Mother is seen as the Supreme Goddess. Aurobindo believed that it was the lack of devotion to the Mother Goddess that had made India effeminate and had resulted in its subjugation by the British. For this reason, Aurobindo exhorted Bengalis to revere the Mother Goddess rather than the more traditional worship, especially since she was seen to sanction the use of force in order to reach one's desired goals. Aurobindo's militancy was not just rhetorical. Between 1906 and 1908, he served a prison term for complicity in a bomb incident. During this stint in prison, he began to read the *Gītā*[21] and, as he wrote in the journal, *Bande Mataram* (26 December 1906), Aurobindo now saw this text as providing the best answer for those who shrink from battle as a sin. Aurobindo had also been inspired by Tilak's nationalism. He viewed the Śivāji festivals as useful, not just as excuses for revolt, but as exercises in the cultivation of courage (Ghose 1972a: 476).

After the defeat of the Swadeshi mobilization (1905–1908), however, Aurobindo underwent a radical change in his political stance (Santori 314). Previously, there had been no sustained discussion of the *Gītā* in his written work, since he hardly knew the text.[22] After May 1909, however, the *Gītā* gained prominence in Aurobindo's thought. He now saw it as representing the core of Hinduism (Ghose 1972b: 3, cited in Sharpe 79).

[21] Aurobindo did not access the text in Sanskrit or even in the Bengali (he could not then even speak it) translation. He probably read it in the English translation of the Theosophist Annie Besant (Sharpe 80).

[22] During his most active years of political involvement (1900–10) in the almost 1,000 pages of the Sri Aurobindo Birth Centenary edition of his works (vol. 1 dealing with his output up to 1 May 1908), there is no mention of the *Gītā*. An exception can be found in Aurobindo's journal *Karmayogin*, where Krishna instructing Arjuna on the battlefield, appears as the picture on the cover. The revolutionary paper *Juguntur* quoted the *Gītā* 4.7 as its motto.

Always an ardent nationalist through his contact with the militant wing of the Indian Nationalist Congress, Aurobindo was beginning to move away from advocating armed revolt. It was during this time that he developed the concept of the Motherland in order to connect the divine with the earthly life. Aurobindo wanted to transform Indians from peaceful nationalists into revolutionaries.[23] But, he realized, particularly through his involvement with *Bande Mataram* (1909–10), that his nationalist activities could only bring him so much and he increasingly turned to the spiritual. His concept of the Motherland now took on a different focus.

From 1910–14, Aurobindo withdrew from politics. On the run because of his activism, he fled to the French territories and ended up in Pondicherry, where he would subsequently build an ashram and create the experimental township dedicated to human unity and evolution, Auroville. Between 1914 and 1921, he wrote the *Essays on the Gītā*, a collection dealing with spirituality and nationalism. The *Essays* were a continuation of his nationalist project and increasingly begin to show (particularly in 1916–20) Aurobindo's process of recreating himself, moving from the ideal nationalist to the persona of a cosmopolitan guru. As noted, the *Gītā* had previously played no role for him when he began his nationalist endeavours. However, it now became the primary text for him once he retired from politics. He urged his followers to revisit the *Gītā* (Ghose 1966: 1–3). *The Essays on the Gītā,* originally published in the monthly journal, *Arya*, promoted Aurobindo's belief that India had to desist from imitating the West before it could restore the 'Aryan' way of life that it had lost. Aurobindo blamed the British for having destroyed Aryan spirituality. He felt that it could only be re-established by ejecting the British. However, his strategy for achieving this aim was oddly deracinated.

Aurobindo had co-founded *Arya* in 1914 with a minor French occultist socialist Paul Richard, whom he had met on a trip to Pondicherry in 1910. Aurobindo was very impressed with Richard's wife, Mirra Alfassa, a Parisian bohemian daughter of Sephardic Jews, and he renewed contact with the couple when they returned to India in 1914, when Paul was seeking election to the French Chamber of Deputies from Pondicherry and then again in 1920. Richard's wife, who claimed to be a mystic, would

[23] Until he left Bengal in 1910, he stayed in contact with revolutionary groups.

become the central figure in Aurobindo's project of reconnecting with Aryan spirituality. He personally designated her as the Mother and put her in charge of the ashram he had established. So, in effect, Aurobindo's idea of returning to a pure Aryan past consisted of his collaboration with a French bourgeois esotericist and his Parisian occultist wife and his handing over of his ashram to her direction. He would leave the entire material and spiritual operation of the ashram to the Mother after he retired from managing it and went into seclusion around 1926. This was his plan for restoring the 'Aryan' way of life: he replaced the British cooptation of India with a French variant of the occult, replete even with French and Middle Eastern[24] anti-Semitism.[25]

The Essays on the Gītā (1921) consist of 48 chapters written in 48 months (Ghose 1916–1920).[26] Twenty-four essays deal with the first six chapters of the *Gītā*, especially the notions of *karma* and *jñāna*. The next 12 essays deal with *bhakti* and its relation to *karma* and *jñāna*, interspersed with Aurobindo's thoughts on the cosmos. The final 12 essays deal with the last six chapters of the *Gītā*. The main thrust of this commentary is that it was wrong to read the *Gītā* as preparation for the life of a renunciant (Ghose 1966: 26–34). While the Gītā presents a synthesis of *bhakti*, *jñāna*, and *karma*, the action of *karmayoga* takes precedence over both *bhaktiyoga* and *jñānayoga* (Brown 203). In fact, the *Gītā* sanctions violence in a righteous cause.

The *Essays* also articulate Aurobindo's discontent with the contemporary world, where spirituality and religious teaching are viewed as superstitions and contemporary science is elevated to a creed and seen as the only way to truth. But first, he advised readers to set aside their ego. Unlike Vivekananda, he did not advocate spiritual pride, nor did he feel a need to feign inclusion. He forthrightly admitted that *śūdras* and women have significant spiritual disabilities. He made no attempt to promote the argument that there existed pure, pristine *varṇas* in some ideal past. Caste becomes a principle of universal validity.[27] Like other reformist thinkers

[24] The Mother was of Turkish and Egyptian descent.

[25] Personal reminiscences of French friends who visited the ashram in the 1960s.

[26] The First Series was published in *Arya* in August 1916–July 1918 and August 1918–July 1920. This First Series was revised and subsequently published by Calcutta's Arya Publishing House in 1922 as a separate volume. The Second Series came out of the same publishing house in 1928.

[27] He went so far as associating the Untouchable with the proletariat in Europe. See Ghose 1943: 1.42.

who sought to minimize the determinism of caste, Aurobindo also pretended that the Untouchable could climb straight to spiritual liberty and perfection (Bolle 1989: 146). Aurobindo supported the caste system even though at no point in the *Essays* did he use the term caste, *varṇa*, or *jati* (tribe, community, clan, sub-clan). He justified caste as serving social, cultural, and spiritual purposes in creating a functional society (Ghose 1966: 46). He repurposed racial superiority in the garb of spirituality with difference depending on the working of the *guṇas*, a common explanation among caste apologists. Besides, India needed a caste such as the *kṣatriyas*, just as the Japanese needed samurais (46).[28] They fulfilled a political role. In 'The Morality of Boycott' Aurobindo had shrunk away from battle aggression, seeing it as lowering morality (1972a: 124). But subsequently, he would interpret the *Gītā* to formulate a doctrine of resistance. The action promulgated by the *Gītā* is not what it is understood to be by the modern mind, controlled as it is by personal, social, and humanitarian motives and ideals (1966: 30–31). There are those (and here he perhaps means someone like Tilak) who make the *Gītā* transform the ideal of disinterested performance of social duties into a modern ideal of social service. Aurobindo saw this approach as misguided. He believed that the *Gītā* does not teach human action but divine action; it does not demand the performance of social duties, but rather the abandonment of the standards of quotidian activity.

Essays such as 'Man and the Battle of Life' (Ghose 1966: 42–50) or 'The Creed of Aryan Fighter' (51–60) valorize violence as God-given work. In these essays, Aurobindo connects the ideal of the *kṣatriya* to its corresponding reality. Good and evil clash, yet the ideal *kṣatriya* fulfils his function of protecting the sage. Unfortunately, this ideal can degenerate. Aurobindo also emphasized that one must abandon limited notions of duty, the illusion that we possess agency, and take refuge in the Supreme. 'Seek refuge in Me alone. I will release you from all sin; do not grieve' (Ghose 1997: 37, cited in Palshikar 62). According to Aurobindo, the *Gītā* contributed to the process of such self-overcoming and led to the advancement of the will of God. It encouraged one to perform violence as bidden. Just as with his presentation of caste, Aurobindo also clothed his

[28] It is significant that the Mother spent the four years of the First World War in Japan. She may be responsible for Aurobindo's understanding of the samurai tradition.

understanding of violence in spirituality. Violence was a necessary part of divine work (1970: 72:13.42). In the chapter 'The Gist of the Karmayoga' (1966: 224–38), Aurobindo claimed that action done without ego constraints, both intellectually and spiritually detached from its fruits, is the equivalent of the supra-cosmic reality. This interpretation of *karma yoga* allowed Aurobindo to address the condition of modern man. In 'The Core of the Teaching' (30), for example, Aurobindo maintained that the *Gītā* held great potential that could be harnessed to create soldiers, lawyers, and politicians for India. It was not merely a religious text but should become part of the modern educational institution, instructing future citizens in the existence of both *ahiṃsā* and *hiṃsā*. While Aurobindo admitted that non-violence was sometimes better than violence, he continued to affirm that violence is truly the right course of action (72:22.491) and maintained that the *Gītā* offers the best theory to instruct those who wrongly view battle as a sin and shrink from violence (72:1.124).

Aurobindo felt that India needed a spiritual awakening of the Self in order to bring about a national reconstruction. He rejected contemporary *karmayogic* readings of the *Gītā* that he deemed materialistic and prejudicial. He claimed that the *Gītā* was not about the disinterested performance of duty in any social sense; rather, it advocated the performance of duty in a spiritual sense so that one might access what Aurobindo's termed 'Brahmanic consciousness' (Ghose 1966: 28–32). Aurobindo maintained that other readings of the *Gītā* ignored this spiritual message. Certainly, the *Gītā* prefers action to non-action, but it does not rule out the necessity of inaction as the path to spiritual life (29–31). In Europe, the social took precedence over the spiritual to its detriment (28), and Indians, who have been seduced by this Western attitude, needed to reject it. Reminiscent of Vivekananda, Aurobindo compared the enlightened East to the decadent West. Europe was enslaved to materialism, power, and progress; it had exiled the eternal and the spiritual. India needed to renounce such foreign notions.

While Tilak and Vivekananda viewed *dharma* in terms of social welfare, Aurobindo generally refuted such altruistic and utilitarian readings of the *Gītā* (Ghose 1966: 31–2). He preferred mystical and spiritual interpretations of the text. The *Gītā* for him was not an allegory of the fragmented and colonized Self. Rather Krishna is the divine exemplar sent to resuscitate man and lift him towards his real divine nature (150–1).

Krishna was the *avatar* sent to renew *dharma*, through a revival of the Aryan way of life. In this respect, Aurobindo's idea of *dharma* differed from that seen in other nationalist commentaries of the *Gītā*. The avatar appears during a crisis of consciousness (159), not just for the sake of *dharma*. While Tilak used the *Gītā* to justify violence on ethical grounds, and Gandhi would proclaim it as a text on non-violence, Aurobindo claimed that the *Gītā* is a text on violence, not nonviolence. He viewed violence as natural and an innate aspect of the universal project of emancipation. Arjuna was asked to do violence; he was not instructed to engage in non-violent activities.

For Aurobindo, the *Gītā* presented life as a clash between good and evil, symbolized by the protagonists of the epic battle, the Kauravas and the Pāṇḍavas. He viewed such clashes as essential for the functioning of cosmic cycles. Things have meaning only in relation to their opposite forces. Without good, there is no evil. There is no high spiritualism, without egocentric action. In order to advance spiritually, one must accept these truths. Although the issue of caste is avoided or, rather, occluded by spiritualized discussions of the *guṇas*, there is no doubt that Aurobindo read the *Gītā* as supporting the social order. He viewed man as a spiritual being for whom the social hierarchy provides a device for spiritual development (Ghose 1966: 51–60). The *Gītā* implements the 'Aryan' social order, established by the workings of the *guṇas*, to reduce the individual's burden of activity.

Aurobindo differed from his contemporaries and their ethical readings of the *Gītā* in other respects too. He did not read into it any argument promoting *niṣkāma karma* or *lokasaṃgraha*. He did not feel that the *Gītā* should be read in any sociological or ethical–moral manner, since any involvement in social action precludes desirelessness (Ghose 1966: 89–90). Aurobindo saw the *Gītā* as teaching the desirelessness needed for the acquisition of 'Brahmanic consciousness'. Whereas social consciousness brings man down, Brahmanic consciousness leads to liberation (93–4). Even if the Sāṃkhya philosopher interprets *niṣkāma karma* as Vedic sacrifice and the modern ethicist might see it as the disinterested performance of social duty, neither understands the true intent of the *Gītā* and, according to Aurobindo, they violate the text's assertions of spiritual elitism. For Aurobindo, the *Gītā* is a text for mastermen and supermen (not in the Nietzschean or Olympian sense). He views it as a text directed toward the individual whose whole personality is dedicated to finding its greater Self (130).

In no way does Aurobindo seek with his interpretation of the *Gītā* to address the masses who constitute the nation. In fact, he marginalized human freedom in his drive to exalt divine will. Aurobindo had no difficulty upholding caste as functional. His position on caste can be seen as a form of spiritual racism, in the manner in which he delineated a gradation of souls (Gowda 162). Aurobindo's reading of the *Gītā* projects an ethos that is unconcerned with any socio-political and ethical challenges facing India. He rejected those readings of the *Gītā* that focused on activism as social duty, rather than as a spiritual desideratum (Ghose 1966: 31). Aurobindo admitted that the idea of the warrior's duty to kill could be subject to corruption, but he dismissed this concern since the *Gītā* taught that no sin is incurred if an act is selfless and dedicated to the divine.

Aurobindo did not want a narrow literal interpretation of the *Gītā* which would deny its universality and spiritual depth (Ghose 1966: 3). Rather he promoted reading the *Gītā* as a call for inclusive and synthesized action, with knowledge and devotion as paths to the Divine (Ghose 1966: 5). By advocating action that sought spiritual understanding, Aurobindo tried 'to resolve the contradiction between devotion to one's individual *dharma* and the life of the nation, or between the Indian national destiny and the destiny of the whole' (Bayly 7). He was particularly critical of readings that focused on the *Gītā's* stress on action over knowledge and devotion. For Aurobindo, the *Gītā* was not a book of practical ethics (28). In 'The Message of the *Gītā*,' action is presented as a sacrifice culminating in self-surrender to the Supreme Spirit (540). One acts in service of the Divine and is directed by divine guidance. This truth, that is known within, relativizes the authority of scripture.[29] Eventually, even the *Gītā* is superseded in Aurobindo's estimation by the mystical. Later, in works such as *The Life Divine*, Aurobindo makes only passing reference to the *Gītā* with short quotations. Around 1926, as noted, Aurobindo completely withdrew from worldly activities. He had handed over the leadership of what would become the International Aurobindo Ashram

[29] Throughout the *Essays on the Gītā*, Aurobindo privileged experience over scriptural authority.

to the Mother and went into seclusion for the rest of his life. The exercise of violence ultimately became less important than spiritual growth.

We can briefly compare a figure like Aurobindo to his activist contemporary, Vinayak Damodhar Savarkar (1883–1966), who never doubted for a moment what was commonly understood among their nationalist contingent when they read the *Gītā*'s message of justified violence. Savarkar was the creator of the theory of *Hindutva* (Hinduness) as the basis for the then and current Indian state. He praised the 'Geeta' as the text of Hindu unity (Savarkar 1949: ii) but did not offer any systematic critique of it (Chaturvedi 418). However, he did claim that the *Gītā* provided a justification for understanding the past and plotting a politics for the future (432). He envisioned this future as one of a permanent state of war, as it had historically always been in his estimation. Savarkar maintained that Hindus were always turned to warfare against foreigners. Citing instances from India's history, Savarkar showed how Hindus regularly used violence as an ethical response to aggressors. The assimilation of foreigners to the Hindu polity taught that conflicts in early India had always been political and not religious, thus rendering Hindu polity fragile and vulnerable. Savarkar felt that Hindus themselves were to blame, since they had lacked a reasonable war strategy. In fact, he held that those Hindus who promoted extreme non-violence had a perverted conception of virtue. They had twisted the message of the *Gītā* and abandoned its principles (Savarkar 1971: 168, cited in Chaturvedi 432). Savarkar was alluding, no doubt, to Gandhi, who (as we shall see in the next chapter) claimed Savarkar promoted violence as an erroneous reading of the *Gītā*. A common theme among interpreters of the *Gītā* was that the text is always misread by other interpreters and actually means something totally different. It comes down, once again, to a problem of translation and interpretation. This assessment is particularly ironic in the case of Gandhi, a Western-educated Indian, who was introduced to the *Gītā* by Westerners (and rather unique exoticist Westerners at that) and, who like Aurobindo had, accessed the text initially in English. In Gandhi, we have an Indian who not only fell in love with the text in Arnold's flowery baroque English translation but read it in the manner of foreign Theosophists![30] These

[30] As an esoteric cult, Theosophy sought to co-opt Eastern wisdom for very pragmatic exoticist aims. It had a wide geographical spread, and it says volumes for Gandhi's disconnect with his own culture that Theosophy informed his reading of one of its paradigmatic texts.

nationalists, Vivekananda, Tilak, and Aurobindo, were all English educated. They all represented the new Indian elite which had emerged from the British educational reforms of 1835 with the victory of Macauleyism. These nationalists were indebted to the Orientalists who had revived the study of Sanskrit, introduced printing and the production of newspapers, encouraged the development of vernaculars, and brought the classicist and Enlightenment ideology to this elite, fostering a new respect for Indian culture. But their respect would be for a re-enculturated scripture of Indian culture, radically disconnected from what the *Gītā* might literally say. Savarkar's disciple, Naturam Godse, put the lie to Gandhi's allegorical reading of the *Gītā* as a text of *ahiṃsā* when he carried a copy of the text with him to the gallows after having murdered the Mahātma.

PART III

THE DEFEAT OF TRANSLATION AND THE END OF CRITICISM

6

Gandhi's Convenient Text

Se vogliamo che tutto rimanga come è, bisogna che tutto cambia.[1]

Tomasi Giuuseppe di Lampedusa, *Il Gattopardo*

Introduction

Mohandas Karamchand Gandhi's (1869–1948) initial knowledge of the *Gītā* is significant, given the role it would subsequently play in his life. We have noted that he first read this text in 1889 in the form of Edwin Arnold's baroque and flowery English translation and at the urging of two Theosophical friends,[2] while he was studying law in London (Gandhi 1984: 36:60, 481). It is noteworthy that he read the Arnold translation, since it was not actually a translation at all but a free-verse paraphrase of the English translation of 1882 by John Davies (Sharpe 81). Gandhi based his reading on a paraphrase of a translation, considerably removed from the original. As in the case of Aurobindo, it was through Westerners and notably Theosophists that Gandhi had to learn initially about this fundamental Hindu text. Also, like Aurobindo, but unlike most other nineteenth-century educated Indians, Gandhi initially read it neither in the original nor in any Indian language.[3]

1 'If we want that things stay as they are, everything must change.'

2 These same Theosophists, two brothers, also convinced him to read Mme. Blavatsky and he became an associate member of the Theosophical Society (Sharpe 116). This is not the place to discuss the fraudulence of Theosophy. Suffice it to say that Mme. Blavatsky and her cohort believed in all the mesmerist fantasies of their time and the esoteric wisdom of Tibetan *Arhats* and Egyptian seers that they channelled in their spectral form. Annie Besant, Mme. Blavatsky's successor in India and Britain, after her flirtations with Fabian Socialism and eugenics, was known for her involvement with the Indian nationalist movement. She used the *Gītā* politically, repeatedly drawing parallels between it and the Indian freedom struggle.

3 Gandhi admitted to these friends that he was not familiar with the *Gītā* in either Sanskrit or in his native Gujarati (Gandhi 1957: 67, cited in Bolle 1989: 139).

The Afterlives of the Bhagavad Gītā. Dorothy M. Figueira, Oxford University Press. © Dorothy M. Figueira 2023.
DOI: 10.1093/oso/9780198873488.003.0007

Gandhi admitted that his first thoughts on the *Gītā* were shallow. He nevertheless judged the poem to be 'the book par excellence for the knowledge of Truth' (cited in Majeed 2006: 306). But, as we shall see, this truth was quite personal and unique to his interpretation. In 'The Meaning of the *Gītā*', Gandhi wrote: 'Mine is but to fight for my meaning, no matter whether I win or lose.'[4] From the beginning, Gandhi chose to impose his personal interpretation on the text. After this initial encounter, he would not reread the *Gītā* until 1903, 10 years after his arrival in South Africa and, although he wrote nothing on it during his two-decade long stay there, he still claimed that the *Gītā* had already become his 'infallible guide of conduct' (Gandhi 1957: 265). He maintained that it was his dictionary of daily reference. However, Gandhi only really began to use the *Gītā* as a source of inspiration after his return from South Africa (Jordens: 88, 90). Until then, the *Gītā* had been for Gandhi a text evoked more for its authority than for its content.

In 1890, a Theosophy-inspired English translation of the *Gītā* was produced by William Q. Judge,[5] replacing a Theosophical reprint of Wilkins which had for almost a century been the only English version readily available in India. Judge's translation presents the religion of the *Gītā* as the counterpoint to the 'materializing influence of Western culture' (Judge 1918: 3, cited in Sharpe 104). But this focus was of little import since Judge maintained that the true spiritual meaning of the text was to be found 'between the lines'. Judge held that customary linguistic methods were of no use, since one must seek the 'inner sense' of the text, related to the outer as the soul is to the body (Sharpe 104). Judge proposed that reading in this manner provided the only path for sincere students to read Hindu scripture (1918: 6, cited in Sharpe 104). He encouraged his readers to unveil the undisclosed science (*veda*) hidden in the *Gītā* (1918: 7, cited in Sharpe 105). This was the standard method by which Theosophists read their fantastic interpretations into texts. In their quests for esoteric content and hidden meanings, Theosophists read allegorically.[6] So, any meaning the *Gītā* would provide to a Theosophist would be

[4] See 'The Meaning of the *Gītā*', *Young India: A Weekly Journal* vii/46 (12 November 1925): 385–6, cited in Sinha 2003: 39.

[5] Judge was the chief American proponent of Theosophy after Mme. Blavatsky. His translation predated the most popular Theosophical translation, that of Annie Besant, by 14 years.

[6] Judge noted that even brahmins could not know the true meaning of the *Gītā* because they were pernicious untrustworthy priests.

hidden in the form of an allegory. In short, Judge advised that the *Gītā*'s message was occluded and needed to be discovered. In his interpretation of the *Gītā*, Gandhi would follow this theosophical mode of reading and seek to reveal the text's hidden and allegorical core that should magically and mystically be revealed to him.

This call to read religious texts allegorically was a challenge shared by other religious groups at the time. In South Africa, Gandhi had been in contact with evangelical Christians, and he was in the habit of discussing religion with them, using arguments previously put forth by Edward Maitland, the founder of the Esoteric Christian Union, who regularly presented allegorical readings of the Gospels and believed in the fundamental identity of all religions (*Navajivan* 1927: 99, cited in Jordens 90). So, even before Gandhi had any contact with the Theosophists or Judge's translation, he had already been exposed to allegorical readings of scripture by other esotericists. It should come as no surprise then that when he came to read the *Gītā,* he would follow this methodology. Specifically, he interpreted the *Gītā* as presenting an allegory of the struggle in human nature (Judge 1918: 15), where we are brought face to face with ourselves (28, cited in Sharpe 105).

There was, of course, another reason allegorical interpretations were popular with Theosophists (such as Judge, Subha Row, Annie Besant, and others): they made no demands on the reader with respect to any knowledge of the text, its reception, or context. The text could be easily accessed without addressing or needing to challenge earlier interpretations and more readily made to fit the reader's individual vision or intended message. This use of allegory presents a facile interpretive strategy; it is not surprising that Gandhi would have chosen it if he wanted to fit the *Gītā* to an idiosyncratic reading. There was, of course, also a tradition in Hindu scripture (and amply documented) of reading texts allegorically and on different levels (Sharpe 117). But it is fairly certain that Gandhi was not familiar with existing Sanskrit hermeneutical practices. We can safely conclude that his decision to read the *Gītā* allegorically, to 'imagine' its message, or let it be 'revealed' imaginatively rather than tied to the letter of the text was a tactical choice on his part. It was certainly odd for someone who claimed to seek Truth, to have borrowed his method from Western occult practitioners, such as the Theosophists who, even in his time, were seen as exoticist foreigners 'colonizing' Eastern thought. One thing is certain: Gandhi was so deracinated from his own religious tradition that it took these rather disreputable Westerners to introduce him to this Hindu classic. It is also noteworthy that, while Western Orientalists and Indian proto-nationalists were avidly reading the *Gītā* in the latter years of the nineteenth century and early twentieth century, Gandhi really did not know the text at all. It was only through his reading of the text in Arnold's paraphrase of a translation at the instigation of foreign esotericist friends that Gandhi discovered the *Gītā*.

Gandhi presents us here with a perfect case study in re-enculturation, what Agehananda Bharati has called the 'pizza effect': The original and authentic Neapolitan pizza was essentially just bread, a focaccia of sorts, with no toppings. The pizza came to America where it received a new configuration with sauce, cheese, and toppings. After World War II, it went back to Italy in this new form. So too for Gandhi's *Gītā*. It came back to India in the form of Arnold's Theosophical paraphrase of an English translation (Bharati, cited in Larson 663–4). Thus, mediated through the Arnold 'translation', the *Gītā* becomes the primary religious text (and symbol) of the Indian freedom struggle, even though in this mediated form it embodies the very tradition against which the text is directed in its re-enculturated form (Larson 665). For Gandhi, the *Gītā* becomes a symbol of a new cultural identity for modern India, only having passed through a radical cross-cultural mediation and transformation. So, it should come as no surprise that Gandhi should devise a reading of his re-enculturated *Gītā* that was considerably disconnected from all other nationalist interpretations.

Over the course of his life, Gandhi would compose several works on the *Gītā*. His first statement regarding the text's meaning can be found in the '*Satyagraha* Leaflet' (#18) of 8 May 1919 in which Gandhi called for the *hartal*[7] of Sunday May 11. When he told the people to fast and read the *Gītā*, some questioned how this advice was appropriate for such an occasion, since they understood that the *Gītā* promoted violence. Just like the nationalists examined in the previous chapter, these satyagrahis also saw the text as a call to armed conflict. When challenged with this seeming contradiction, Gandhi devised a rationalization that would guide his future use of the text: a literal reading of the *Gītā* shows

[7] Mass protests involving the shutdown of workplaces.

confusion in the present, when people are distanced from its spiritual truths. Gandhi simply instructed the satyagrahis to adopt *his* interpretation which he claimed presented the real truth and evinced no such confusion. His reading of the text would specifically show that the war depicted in the epic was only meant as a metaphor for the war inherent in our bodies (Gandhi 1994: 15.288). He claimed that the *Gītā* described inner strife and not actual conflict. Like Tilak, Gandhi focused on the role of the *sthitaprajña*, the one who achieves control over his inner self (28.16). Gandhi also encouraged the satyagrahis to follow the wisdom of Krishna who combined the qualities of a hero statesman, warrior, and philosopher. The degree to which Gandhi himself would identify with this persona became clear over time.

Gandhi next encountered the *Gītā* when he was in prison in 1922–4. During his confinement, he read a lot and began to learn Sanskrit. Then, in 1926, he spent a year in retreat. During this time, specifically between 24 February and 27 November 1926, he concentrated on reading the *Gītā* and engaged in public meditations on the text during the morning prayer sessions he held at the Sabarmati Ashram near Ahmedabad. His communal recitation of the *Gītā*, in fact, became the principal religious ritual in the ashram (Jordens 88). Daily, after his morning prayers, he addressed his followers about 'its content and meaning as it unfolded before him' (Gandhi 2000a: 10). These readings of the *Gītā* had so impressed Mahadev Desai (1892–42), Gandhi's secretary and devoted friend,[8] that he felt there needed to be a published record of them.

Gandhi's next treatment of the poem occurred while he was serving a subsequent sentence in Yeravada Prison in 1929. At this time, Gandhi translated the *Gītā* into Gujarati with an introduction and commentary of selected verses. He entitled this translation and commentary *Anāsaktiyoga* (1930) (Yoga of Detachment) (Gandhi 1984: 42.90–101). This version was later translated from Gujarati into English by Desai and became *The Gītā According to Gandhi* (1946). Desai added to this translation of a translation a commentary composed from notes that he personally had taken from Gandhi's earlier daily readings from the *Gītā* at the Sabarmati Ashram. By its very compositional nature, this rendition gives

[8] Desai was the closest person to Gandhi and had unrestricted access to him. He maintained a daily diary of his interactions with Gandhi for two decades.

us Gandhi's reading of the *Gītā* twice removed. Desai's English translation of Gandhi's Gujarati translation was a book intended for India's English-speaking population, specifically for the English-medium-trained high-caste youth of future India whom Gandhi envisioned as those who would govern the country once it was freed from colonial rule. This volume was not meant for the common folk,[9] but rather for an elite audience who would rule India once the British left. It is also significant to note that Gandhi's principal work on the *Gītā* was as far (if not more) removed from the original text as the European commentary of Schlegel's Latin translation from the Sanskrit. Although Gandhi believed himself to be (and claimed it on numerous occasions) a devout Hindu and man of the people, his reading of the *Gītā* was no closer to the actual text than Hegel's commentary.

Gandhi returned again to the *Gītā* in 1930–2, when sentenced to another prison stay in the same jail where he had earlier composed the *Anāsaktiyoga*. During this incarceration, Gandhi sent weekly letters on the *Gītā* to be read at his ashram. These communiqués were published as the *Letters on the Gītā* (*Gītābodh*) (Gandhi 1984: 49). Here, Gandhi once again 'revealed' the message hidden in the text. Another chapter-by-chapter commentary explaining the *Gītā's* exposition of *anāsaktiyoga* was also published by Desai as the *Discourses on the Gītā*. Gandhi envisioned all these various publications as works which were not written to be studied academically, but rather as helpful guides derived from his life experiences (Robinson 153–4). They were not literary interpretations, since Gandhi felt such readings were illegitimate precisely because they engaged the letter of the text and Gandhi found such a practice of literal interpretation unacceptable (Gandhi 1984: 21.337). Written 36 years after he had first read the *Gītā*, these subsequent publications present the extent of Gandhi's creativity with the text. They comprise, all told, approximately 360 pages of a compendium of his thought on the *Gītā* up to 1932 (Clough 61) and offer more commentary than he had written on any other topic or text (Jordens 1986: 88).

Around the same time that Gandhi was writing his daily meditations on the *Gītā*, some three months before the nine-month public offerings

[9] Gandhi claimed that women and *śūdras* have no equipment or desire to read the *Gītā* (Desai 1948: xvi, cited in Adluri and Bagchree 440).

of his meditations, he had also been writing weekly instalments of his *Autobiography*[10] The two narratives were interrelated. In fact, his life story was inextricably bound to his reading of the *Gītā*. Gandhi legitimized his life through his interpretation of the *Gītā* (Koppendrayer 48) and legitimized his reading of the *Gītā* through his life. In the *Autobiography*, he describes his personal spiritual journey to become a *sthitaprajña*. It is this same figure that he envisions extolled in the *Gītā*. He needed to promote the persona of the *sthitaprajña* because he felt that human passions had led him (just as it had others) away from spiritual growth.

Allegory and Experience

For Gandhi, the *Gītā* was the text by which one should examine oneself. In 'A Revolutionary's Defense', he claimed to have found profound inspiration in the *Gītā* (Gandhi 1984: 26.140), not as a historical work (15.288–9) but rather as the book through which one gained the knowledge of truth. As noted, Gandhi had not initially studied the *Gītā* seriously. It was only after some years and a period of confinement that he began reading it daily (Gandhi 1969: 50, cited in Sharpe 116). He interpreted it as primarily teaching action; the *Gītā* enjoined one to be selfless and non-violent through detachment (Gandhi 1960: 21, cited in Robinson 61). In response to the logical question of why a text preaching non-violent action was set on a battlefield, Gandhi answered that the martial setting of the *Gītā* was purely allegorical, representing inner conflict (Desai 1946: 127–8). The forces of evil depicted in the *Gītā* are just personifications of virtues and vices that we all possess in ourselves (Gandhi 1984: 37). The epic's heroes are not historical figures nor does the poem they inhabit relate historical events (Gandhi 1950, cited in Sawhney 111). Everything is allegorical. Duryodhana represents the baser instincts in man. Arjuna represents our higher impulses. The battlefield represents our body. Gandhi reads the *Gītā* as an allegory of the ceaseless spiritual war going on in the human Kurukshetra of the Self (Gandhi 1984: 20.129). The war depicted in the epic was meant as a metaphor for the war in our bodies (15.288). It described our inner strife.

[10] He was 56 years old when he started his *Autobiography*.

Gandhi repeatedly attested that the *Gītā* was not about war. He even advised us not to read the *Gītā* for its plot, since plots are sensually alluring. One needs to read a text for its spirit, and the *Gītā*'s spirit spoke of *ahiṃsā* (non-violence) *satya* (truth), *brahmachārya* (chastity), *aparigrahi* (non-passion), and *asteya* (non-stealing). Only with a grasp of the *Gītā*'s spirit can one interpret it correctly (Gandhi 2006: I.90). Gandhi claimed that the text demanded a slow conversion from literal to bodily work on both the individual and the collective level (Iyer 1985: 92–100). In the fullness of time, the corporal referent in the text expands to become its spiritual referent. Gandhi, in fact, advocated the actual rejection of the text itself as well as its contents. While intentional misreading or not reading a text at all may seem as a perverse hermeneutical gesture to readers today, it did not appear so to Gandhi who portrayed this course of action as the dutiful growth of spiritual inheritance. As one becomes more enlightened, the meanings that one attaches to words become more enlightened (Gandhi 1984: 37.133–4). So, the *Gītā* is not to be read for its martial plot, enjoining violence. In fact, if we read it for what it describes, we indulge our base instincts. Rather, we should perfect ourselves through restraint, which in turn will reinforce a correct interpretation which will be revealed progressively, rather than through what Gandhi termed the self-indulgence resulting from reading the text and its advocacy of permissible retaliation.[11] Gandhi's convoluted reasoning and self-justification are simply astonishing. They bear witness to his political and spiritual clout at the time. It is also quite astounding that Gandhi's strategy of interpretation has not solicited more commentary in the intervening years.

Gandhi did acknowledge, however, the more customary reading of the *Gītā* as a text promoting non-attachment (*anāsakti*) and attributed the other important themes he read in the *Gītā*—non-violence, non-cooperation, and satyagraha—as deriving from it. He saw these themes most forcefully expressed in *Gītā* 2.3–4. In fact, he had elevated the last two stanzas of Chapter 2 to a position of centrality, revealing the core

[11] By this logic, all epics must then teach non-violence, since they all at some point criticize the nature and value of war, as in the case of the *Iliad* or the *Lusiads*. The logic simply does not hold true, especially for the *Mahābhārata* with its massive verse depiction of war, with the *Gītā* being a later addition to the base epic. For a history of the place of the *Gītā* in the epic, see van Buitenen (1962).

meaning of the entire work. He prioritized these stanzas also because they defined most clearly what he saw as the key figure described in the *Gītā*, the *sthitaprajña*, (Gandhi 1984: 28.16). Gandhi downplayed the *Gītā*'s justification of caste; he did not even comment on how readers understood caste as it was codified in the *Gītā*. In discourses 3 and 4 on *karmayoga*, for example, Gandhi merely noted that God did indeed establish the fourfold order according to the *guṇas* (innate qualities) and *karma* (action) (Desai 1946: 65–6). But Desai clarified his intent: we must look beyond caste to find its deep spirituality (41). It is only *māyā* that confuses us regarding caste (Desai 1946: 41). This explanation is insidious, given the sanctioned violence that Untouchables (or as Gandhi rather sanctimoniously called them, '*Harijans*' i.e. 'children of God') suffered at this time. Ignoring the evils of caste and focusing on its philosophical source were the strategies Gandhi and his amanuensis employed. Gandhi further bypassed the issue of caste with a curious postulate of his own invention, the notion of trusteeship, another political strategy for managing caste without acknowledging its horror.

From the outset, Gandhi approached the *Gītā* from a unique perspective that raised serious hermeneutical issues. He did not assume any faith-based approach to scripture (Gandhi 1984: 41:90–92). Significantly, he undervalued the text's divine inspiration and overvalued his own (unique) interpretative skills. In a letter to Sakarlal Dave, written after the *hartal* on 19 May 1919, Gandhi emphasized his personal qualifications for reading the *Gītā*: 'I have something far more powerful than argument, namely, experience' (15.288). Even as early as 1919, Gandhi had already defined how he would read the text allegorically with this 'experience' serving as his primary qualification to be its true interpreter. Since Gandhi claimed that the *Gītā*'s meaning transcended the letter of the text, he urged his interlocuters to move beyond what was literally and objectively enunciated in the *Gītā*. Besides, the *Gītā* need not even express what its author(s) had intended: it can say something completely different (45.96). Gandhi saw his right to interpret this text authoritatively as stemming from his moral sensibility. He posited his philosophy as the equivalent to the true meaning of the *Gītā* (26.140). This (his) truth transcends whatever the text says. Gandhi assumes brahminical authority over the text because he claimed to determine its truth. I term this process of interpretation that Gandhi adopted as 'brahminical' because it asserted an authority that was defined primarily by the brahmin's role as the implied and legitimate reader. As such, one might think that it would be susceptible to the same type of criticism that brahmin priests encountered from reformers, that is, that they were unreliable custodians of scripture who abuse their interpretive power. But I have found no such criticism of Gandhi's readerly strategies. In modern theoretical terms and outside the Indian context, one might even say that Gandhi was Derridean *avant la lettre*, because he asserted that meaning is not initially revealed by the text but needed to be deconstructed.

As noted, Gandhi's privileging of the allegorical reading was aided and abetted by Arnold's poetry as well as the quite odd mystical allegories of his Theosophist friends who introduced him to the *Gītā* in the first place. Gandhi's allegorical reading calls for the reader to follow what he feels experientially and judges to be its spirit, not what the text might overtly seek to communicate (Gandhi 1978: 39–40, cited in Robinson 61). Gandhi's intuition or spiritual acumen overrides what the text literally might say; his account of what he experiences trumps any other claim to the text's meaning (43). What Gandhi is here positing is that meaning depends rather on the spiritual qualities or capacities of the reader (Gandhi) or the exegete's (Gandhi's) realization of the text's truth (Gandhi 1984: 10. 127). He noted that he applied 'the test of Truth and *ahiṃsā* and rejected what was inconsistent with that test' (Gandhi 1950: 9). In a final flourish, Gandhi hedges all his bets: even a literal reading can be seen to support his interpretation and reconcile violence with selflessness, where non-violence becomes a corollary of selfless action (Desai 1946: 133–4).

Gandhi as an Interpreter and his Theory of Translation

In *The Task of the Translator* (1923), Walter Benjamin wants translation to give voice to the intentions of the original, not as a reproduction but as a harmony, as a supplement to the language in which the text expresses itself. Benjamin notes that a literal translation cannot reproduce the meaning of the original. The translator must refrain from wanting to communicate something, 'from rendering the sense because the original has already relieved the translator and his translation of the effect of assembling and expressing what is to be conveyed (Benjamin 78–9). Benjamin here develops upon the German Romantic understanding of translation. What for Benjamin was the notion of translation as a supplement, for Germans from the Romantic period onward was an action wherein the text became complete and perfected. The translation grasps the essence of the text; it brings out its potential, as F. Schlegel noted. The translation is an 'ultra' text. Gandhi saw his translational work in similar terms.

As we have seen, Gandhi did not believe a translation was meant to render the text of the *Gītā* literally. The literal interpretation, he felt, 'puts on a sea of contradictions'. Gandhi called upon the reader rather to just try and understand the spirit of the text, what he deemed its total context (Gandhi 1984: 38.318). He accepted that all interpretations are new interpretations and expansions of the text's literal meaning. You do not discover any literal meaning but expect meaning for new life circumstances (Jordens 95).

> You might ... say that the Poet himself was not against war or violence.... But ... the poet ... is not conscious of all the interpretations his composition is capable of. The beauty of poetry is that the creation transcends the poet. (Gandhi 1925: 386, cited in Sinha 2010: 311)

A devaluation of literal meaning or the belief that interpretation is informed by one's prejudices as they derive from one's historical consciousness (*wirkungsgeschichtliches Bewusstsein*) is a common hermeneutical stance (see Gadamer, Ricoeur, Steiner). Gandhi says something similar when he claims that the *śāstras,* although deemed authoritative (Gandhi 1984: 52.9), suffered from historical limitations (35.98, cited in Jordens 91). Nor is Gandhi alone in viewing a text's historical character altering it as a product of a particular time. He agreed with Hindu reformers of the nineteenth and twentieth centuries who viewed their religious texts as compromised by time and ensuing accretions (Figueira 1993). In *Young India,* Gandhi even noted how the *Mahābhārata* account underwent many emendations over time (1950: 18, cited in Sawhney 111). Scripture conveyed, not eternal truth, but rather the practices of their era (Gandhi 1984: 29.444, cited in Minor 91), first through a human prophet and then through commentaries of interpreters, not from God directly (Gandhi

1984: 64.75). Where Gandhi diverges from interpretive practice is when he claims that hermeneutical criteria should ultimately reside in a text's ethical teaching. Since religion is about action in day-to-day practice (41.98), one must use its ethical standards to peel away the unacceptable, historical layers, and distortions in a text (Jordens 92).

Gandhi envisioned his reading as totally authoritative, since he claimed that he alone among translators truly lived the meaning of the *Gītā* in his own life (Gandhi 1984: 41.92). 'Living the text' made his interpretation qualified and just (43.85). Objectively, his qualifications were scant. He admitted that he had no scholarly skills. But he did not need them, since the *Gītā* was not composed as a learned treatise (34.88, cited in Jordens 96). In fact, profound scholarship is irrelevant to a text's interpretation (Gandhi 1984: 43.85). Learned commentaries are always of less value than experience. One only needed a 'well-cultivated moral sensibility and experience in the practice of truth' (38.316–7) to read and interpret. Living according to a text's teaching (34.89) provides the required experience and that too must be determined by the authoritative reader (Gandhi himself).

Gandhi did not find it problematic that his Sanskrit was perhaps insufficient to read the *Gītā* or that he worked exclusively from English translations and only had a slight knowledge of them (Majeed 2006: 306). He felt that translating a translation was a completely legitimate practice. In 1908, he had rendered Plato's *Apology* into Gujarati from an English translation and not from the Greek. In his Preface to this translation, he claimed that a second-hand translation did not in any way compromise the 'truth' of the text or his task as a translator. Rather, Gandhi saw it as renewing the life of the text in a new context. He felt that his translation of the *Apology* was not in any way limited, but that he had enhanced and deepened the Greek original by the act of secondary translation. What he claimed was 'an elixir' (Gandhi 1984: 10:174, cited in Majeed 327), was, in fact, just a summary of the text that called attention to the secondary nature of his already secondary translation. To a certain degree, Gandhi envisioned translation as some of the theorists discussed in Chapter 1 had understood it, as a culmination of the text and improvement or perfection of it over time. However, he did not even model his translation on a willingness to view the text in its entirety. He could focus on a part of one single chapter, if he felt it adequately expressed his experience. Gandhi was actually quite removed from the actual text of the *Gītā* and, as we noted, his reading was as distant (translations of translations) and as incomplete as Hegel's.

The role of translatability (also a key topic for Hegel) is crucial in any examination of Gandhi's reading of the *Gītā*. Gandhi's tied his translation and interpretation to his quest for 'Truth' and the persona he created for himself as a translator.[12] Because Gandhi claimed that he translated the *Gītā* into his life, his commentary of it as a book of daily reference was equally a commentary on the text of his life (Majeed 2006: 331). Gandhi maintained that he lived life according to his understanding of the *Gītā*. His experiments with 'truth' and his experiences of life alone animated the text's meaning. The fact that this understanding of the *Gītā* diverged from all other readings was not an issue for him, since the *Gītā* was not a stable text (Majeed 2006: 303). Its status as a repository for truth was tied to Gandhi's evolving vision of himself and his understanding of translation as a process.

This role as a translator was important to Gandhi. He had initially presented the Phoenix Settlement and Tolstoy Farm partly as sites for multilingual experiments where various Indian languages were taught.[13] He ended up, however, judging these ashram language-teaching ventures as failures (Gandhi 1984: 39:117). They were as dismal as his personal attempts to learn languages. At Tolstoy Farm, for example, Gandhi presumed to teach Tamil and Urdu with only a rudimentary knowledge of these languages. Even his Gujarati, as he noted in the *Autobiography*, was

[12] Gandhi calls himself a translator in his various autobiographical texts (see specifically *An Autobiography of the Story of My Experiments with Truth* (1927–9) (2018: 524–6).

[13] Phoenix Settlement consisted of 100 acres. Subsequently, one of Gandhi's benefactors, Hermann Kallenbach gave him 1,000 acres with 1,000 fruit trees on it for a second commune dedicated to self-reliance. The vaunted simplicity of these ashrams relied on the largesse of Kallenbach, an architect, avid sportsman, and bodybuilder. A German–Lithuanian Jew, Kallenbach was very close to Gandhi. It is speculated that they were romantically involved. Kallenbach's relationship with Gandhi recently entered the news with the story of how in 2012 the Indian government spent 1.3 million pounds to stop the auction of Gandhi's letters to Kallenbach. The purchase of these letters, some one thousand in number, at such a price was to avoid their being auctioned off by Sotheby's. The Indian government claims that the purchase was for scholarly use. There has been speculation that the government did not want to 'out' what was a physical relationship between the two men. Although Gandhi felt Kallenbach was his soulmate, they grew apart politically. Kallenbach did not share Gandhi's pronouncements on how Jews should deal with Hitler. He became a Zionist and emigrated to Israel. See *The Huffington Post's* review (13 July 2012) of Joseph Lelyveld's book *Great Soul: Mahatma Gandhi and His Struggle With India*.

only on a high-school level (Majeed 2006: 304). He set very low standards for language proficiency. Even the slightest linguistic skill was acceptable to him since interpretation was all just an experiment with Truth. In his translation endeavours, it is questionable whether Gandhi was actually experimenting with truth or rather just experimenting with control, as in an early episode when Gandhi served as the self-appointed translator of Gopal Krishna Gokhale (1866–1915)[14] during his tour of South Africa. During this visit, Gandhi insisted that Gokhale speak in Marathi, even though he admitted to Gokhale that he would be translating him and did not know the language from which he was translating.[15] He felt he could translate Gokhale's words, give them life and meaning, solely in terms of his own vision of the truth they must convey. It is quite astonishing the extent to which Gandhi, lacking the simplest linguistic expertise, manufactured an image of himself as a translator. His persona as a reader, translator, and language teacher was self-consciously rooted in his lack of knowledge of the languages with which he insisted on working (Majeed 2006: 304). In fact, these personae rather celebrated his lack of interpretive skills and grounded themselves in his claims to truth and sincerity. His self-appointment as ultimate and authoritative arbiter of all veracity was based on his understanding of his self-worth and the value he placed on his personal experience.

There were clearly issues of control and manipulation involved in Gandhi's translating exercises. His insistence on dealing with languages over which he had no mastery also reflects another central posture Gandhi assumed: his vulnerability (Majeed 2006: 304, 306), a topic highlighted in the various psychoanalytic readings of Gandhi formulated by Ashis Nandy, Sudhir Kakar, Aijaz Ahmad, and others. Gandhi certainly was consciously creating a self-image that consisted in his presenting himself as honest, even to the point of shining unfavourable light on his behaviour and weaknesses. But an alternative interpretation is that he simply needed to be in control and that entailed the necessity of valorizing his vision of translation as grounded in what he claimed to experience as truth. The fact that this truth was unmoored from linguistic

[14] Gokhale was the founder of the Indian Independence Movement and leader of the Congress Party.

[15] Just as he could not speak a word of Marathi, so too could Gandhi not speak Hindustani.

knowledge and commentary was secondary. The goal was the promotion of his political agenda. Gandhi's willingness to highlight his linguistic ineptitude in reading the *Gītā* and expounding upon it becomes part of his political self-positioning. That he was so thoroughly ill-prepared to presume to teach the world what the *Gītā* meant made his 'life experiments' with the text even more 'real', authentic, and subsequently significant.

His interpretation of the *Gītā*, in essence questioned the 'real' source of knowledge—did it come from reading a text or from another form of knowledge all together? Gandhi was primarily challenging scriptural and textual authority (Gandhi 1984: 41.90–2). By claiming that his life was a commentary to the *Gītā*, he could reduce the teaching of the *Gītā* to whatever he chose to understand it to be (41:91). In this reorienting of the *Gītā*, he could preserve its authority (Sawhney 88) or rather, fabricate his reading as a justification/apologia for his life choices. More significantly, his interpretation of the *Gītā* became the convenient and authoritative structure for him to promote and sanctify his politics.

> I am not aware of [any] claim made by the translators of enforcing their meaning of the *Gītā* in their own lives. At the back of my reading, there is the claim of an endeavor to enforce the meaning in my own conduct for an unbroken period of forty years (41.92, cited in Koppendrayer 67).

What I find interesting here is how Gandhi claimed that his rather distorted reading was legitimate because he supposedly lived his life in accordance with it. The reading is valid, even if its message is not found in the text. It is valid because it is how Gandhi claimed to live. It is also significant that his interpretive strategy was largely accepted. Let us also not forget that he assumed brahminical authority as the custodian of the text and he was inspired in his reading methodology by rather discredited authorities, those rather disreputable Theosophists, who claimed to receive messages on paper dropped from the heavens by Tibetan Arhats but were actually dropped from holes drilled in the ceiling.

Gandhi's public ruminations on the *Gītā* were also intimately tied to his political endeavours. He had been drawn back into active politics in 1928 for various reasons, one being Katherine Mayo's book, *Mother India*, which catalogued India's social horrors. Gandhi took Mayo's book as a personal slanderous indictment of him (Weber 53). In response, he convened the best and the brightest of the satyagrahis from the Sabarmati Ashram who were daily listening to his recitation of the *Gītā* to examine how the *sthitaprajña* was the state-of-being incumbent on each of them. When he initiated the Salt March (12 May 1930) along with 78 of his closest followers, they set out carrying with them his translation. The beginning of the Salt March was marked, in fact, by the release of Gandhi's book (Gandhi 1984: 41.90).[16] He thus made his very idiosyncratic reading of the *Gītā*, derived from his very idiosyncratic theory of translation, central to the process of *swarāj* (self-rule).

It was possible for Gandhi to disregard the interpretations of others because he had defined translation as not tied to the text. Like Tilak and Aurobindo before him, Gandhi saw himself as a public commentator on the *Gītā*. Unlike them, however, he did not feel constrained by its actual text. Seeking the authority of scripture in the form of the *Gītā* was a tactical choice for him at a time when he had lost considerable political clout. In 1920, he had received Congress's endorsement to launch his campaign of non-cooperation, massive civil disobedience, and boycott of the government of India and its institutions. He had tried to shut down the British administration, but this venture did not work. The British carried on, and there was such violence that Gandhi was forced to call off his boycott in February 1922 (Gandhi 1984: 22.377). Congress then decided there would be no more of this particular form of Gandhi-style politics. So, Gandhi needed another means of asserting himself, promoting his message, and developing his political agenda. His translations and commentaries of the *Gītā* provided the path for him to express his vision of what he felt India should be and present it to the public in *Hind Swaraj*.[17]

Along with his various commentaries, Gandhi constructed a theory of translation that would allow him to answer any criticism relating to his interpretation. When challenged by Swami Anand about his conclusion that *ahiṃsā* was the central message of the *Gītā* on the basis of 'just a few verses', Gandhi justified his interpretive process and the manner in

[16] This launch of his Gujarati translation of the *Gītā* on the day of the beginning of the Salt March was quickly followed by translations into Hindi, Bengali, Marathi, and English.

[17] Gandhi's notion in *Hind Swaraj* was that one could return to the traditional India, built on morality coming out of mastery over the human mind and passions (Gandhi 1984: 10:37). It is significant to note that Gandhi is totally silent on the Untouchables in *Hind Swaraj* (Kumar 2015: 100), as if they did not exist.

which he privileged his reading: those sections that did not conform to his vision of the central message of the *Gītā* (i.e. the control of the senses) can and should simply be rejected. Moreover, such an interpretation was not only correct, but it was absolute, since it derived from Gandhi's lived experience which made it real. But his practice of translation as interpretation, unmoored, and emancipated as it was from the text, did not reflect the *Gītā*'s status as a *dharma grantha* (a religious treatise). Gandhi could treat it as if it were not 'holy', yet he authoritatively wielded its sanctity to make it serve as the ethical foundation for the future nation that he envisioned. *Anāsakti* (non-attachment) was the *Gītā*'s primary theme. From *anāsakti*, Gandhi could develop the notion of satyagraha (dispassionate action adhering to *ahiṃsā* and attaining self-realization), non-cooperation (non-engagement in others' duties) (15.312–3), and even the spinning of fabric and the wearing of *khadi* (16.112).

In addition to teaching the value of *anāsakti*, *ahiṃsā*, satyagraha, and renunciation,[18] Gandhi's reading of the *Gītā* also supported the *varṇa* system. He championed *varṇa* as an acceptable means of attaining selflessness. The *Gītā* promoted the idea that it is better to do one's *svadharma* (or even better, to die), than perform a duty that is foreign to one's nature (Desai 1946: 102–5). Gandhi supported the *Gītā*'s teaching on *varṇa*, but he claimed not to support caste, which he maintained was not the same thing as *varṇa*. In fact, he held that *varṇa* had degenerated into caste and caste was a perverted form of *varṇa* (Desai 1946: 102). This situation was, according to Gandhi, unfortunate. Gandhi then took this reasoning further. In the world of the *Gītā*, as Gandhi interpreted it, individual *svadharma* was based on the notion of the *guṇas* (innate character traits) as temperamental qualities predisposing each social group. Since one cannot choose one's *guṇas*, one can also not choose one's caste. The *guṇas* determine who we are and what we are born to be. Thus, Gandhi adeptly sought to dissociate *varṇa* from the reality of caste as it functioned in the real world, by presenting it as he imagined it to function in some ideal

[18] His message is meant to 'correct' Tilak's vision of the *Gītā* as espousing *karmayoga*. Gandhi felt that Tilak's *Gītārahasya* fell into the group of literary interpretations (Gandhi 1984: 26.289) and he accused Tilak of being too influenced by European philosophy (Gandhi 1984: 14.126). There is no trick that Gandhi does not try. He accused Tilak of using the *Gītā* for a political programme, such as terrorism. Gandhi sanctimoniously noted that time will tell who was right (63.319–20).

world present in the *Gītā* that he hoped to recreate. Gandhi adroitly circumscribed the problem and the reality of caste by pretending that there are determinants of social division that are not 'exclusive' (102, 104) to the group to which they are ascribed (Desai 1946: 376), but this, in turn, depends on the *guṇas*. In other words, caste is justifiable, because it is determined by the individual's *dharma* and appropriate to one's inner qualities and skills as aligned with different types of work in the external world. For Gandhi, the *Gītā* promotes an occupational *varṇa* that had unfortunately degenerated into caste but was once a really good thing. In the face of a brutal caste system, where there existed many levels of degradation to which Untouchables were subjected, Gandhi's interpretation here is worthy of note. It shows the measure of the man, his political rather than his 'great-souled' character, that Gandhi promoted this fairy-tale vision of caste Hinduism as something that was actually good, logical, and just, merely a little off kilter. Here, perhaps, some contextualization on Gandhi's racial attitudes is warranted.

As Arundhati Roy has catalogued, Gandhi did not have enlightened views on other races. He was not colour-blind. She cites the negative comments he made throughout his life about Blacks, Untouchables, the Chinese, and assorted labouring classes (Roy 2016: 134). The first thing to understand is that Gandhi's activism in South Africa had nothing to do with the treatment afforded to Black Africans. At the Phoenix Settlement in Natal, there were no Black Africans present in the commune. His activism in South Africa was exclusive: it was geared toward fighting for Indian merchants' rights, so that they could compete equitably with British merchants (79). He even distinguished these merchants from Indian bonded labourers (Gandhi 1984: 1.192–3, cited in Roy 2016: 66–71). The burning of identity passes in a public bonfire followed the passing of the Transvaal Asiatic Amendment Act, which only violated the rights of Indian merchants and professionals.[19] It was not a universal liberation agitation. In fact, a significant act of Gandhi's satyagraha involved his fighting against Indians not having to share the same door at the post office with Blacks. That Indians should be treated like Blacks was totally unacceptable to him. Gandhi held that Indians should not have

[19] This particular narrative of Gandhi's agitation for the poor and disenfranchised Blacks of South Africa finds expression in Glass's *Satyagraha*.

to share a door with 'Kaffirs',[20] since as Gandhi explained in a letter to the Natal Legislative Assembly (19 December 1894), Indians and English come from the same racial stock. In other words, Gandhi's focus was not on the treatment of Blacks in South Africa, but rather about the treatment of Indian merchants. He militated that they not be treated like black Africans. He even protested when he personally had to share a prison cell with them:

> ... but to be placed on the same level with the Natives seemed to be too much to put up with.... They are troublesome, very dirty and live almost like animals. (Gandhi 1984: 8. 198–9, cited in Roy 2016: 73)

Indians should not be imprisoned with Blacks, since there was racially no common ground between the two groups (Gandhi 1984: 9.256–7). While detained, Gandhi personally refused to use the same blankets that Blacks had used and 'defiled' (9.274). He also felt that imprisoned Indians deserved to eat rice with ghee, rather than the 'mealie pap' doled out to the Blacks. He and other imprisoned Indians certainly deserved separate toilets from the Blacks (9.270, cited in Roy 2016: 74).

Gandhi's non-violent satyagraha in South Africa was actually a failure. There had been considerable rioting, arson, and bloodshed. But, in the end, all Gandhi achieved was a settlement he signed with Jan Smuts promising to provide free passage to Indians who might want to repatriate back home (Roy 2016: 86). No concession was ever made to the Blacks or other exploited labourers, such as the Chinese. So, his fame (which garnered him a hero's welcome back home)[21] is a testament to his self-promotion and rests on very little tangible reform. He did nothing for black Africans and worked rather ineffectually for Indian merchants. His work for poor Indian labourers in South Africa was non-existent (86–7). His clientele were mostly rich Muslim merchants. So, Gandhi's discourse on caste, therefore, takes on a different hue in light of this activity and his racial attitudes. Similarly, we should read his encouragements to other precarious

[20] An insulting term used for a black African.

[21] One need only compare this homecoming to that of the Untouchable B.R. Ambedkar's ignominious treatment upon returning home from abroad to work as a newly minted lawyer and Ph.D.: he was spat upon by caste Hindu law clerks and could not even find housing!

groups (the Jews under Hitler) to adopt satyagraha as their preferable course of action in light of his general racist attitudes.

Let us note his respect for Mussolini and admiration for Hitler.

> But I do not consider Hitler to be as bad as he is depicted. He is showing an ability that is amazing and he seems to be gaining his victories without much bloodshed. (Gandhi 1984: 78.219)

As late as 1940, he would write:

> We have to live and move and have our being in *ahiṃsā* as Hitler does in *hiṃsā*.[22] It is the faith and perseverance and single-mindedness with which he has perfected his weapons as a monster is immaterial for our purpose. We have to bear the same single-mindedness and perseverance in evolving our *ahiṃsā*. Hitler is awake all the 24 hours of the day in perfecting his *sādhana*.[23] He wins because he pays the price. His devotion to his purpose should be the object of our admiration and emulation. Although he works all his waking hours, his intellect is unclouded and unerring. (Gandhi 1984: 78.349, cited in Roy 2016: 209)

Indians should emulate Hitler. Persecuted Jews should become satyagrahis as Gandhi notoriously advised them during the war, when they were being deported and butchered. Jews should 'summon to their aid and the soul-power that comes only from non-violence' (Gandhi 1984: 74.298) and Gandhi assured them that Herr Hitler would '[b]ow before their courage' (74.298). He also urged the British to 'fight Nazism without arms' (78.387). The oddness of this stance is more glaring when we compare it to Aurobindo's comments regarding Hitler and his opposition to Gandhi's advice. Aurobindo felt that by refusing to impede evil-doing, Gandhi encouraged someone to cause greater harm (Ghose 1970: 13.39). He also felt that Gandhi's presumptions emboldened and increased the harm of evil-doing through further retaliation. Aurobindo felt it was more merciful to use force against an evil doer. By ignoring

[22] The Sanskrit term for 'violence.'

[23] Literally, a means to accomplish something. It can also mean religious discipline or exercises for attaining detachment from worldly things.

violence, one refuses to participate in creation which is always mixed with destruction (13.40). Aurobindo wrote: 'Evil cannot perish without the destruction of much that lives by evil' (Ghose 1997: 42, cited in Palshikar 61). He added: 'I have supported justifiable violence on justifiable occasions, e.g., Kurukshetra and the war against Hitler and all that he means' (41–2, cited in Palshikar 71). He also chided Gandhi as egoistical, setting up impediments and overthinking *ahiṃsā*. In *Harijan* (November 1938), Gandhi responded to letters criticizing what he thought about the happenings in Germany:

> If there ever could be a justifiable war in the name of humanity, a war against Germany, to prevent the wanton persecution of a whole race, would be completely justified. But I do not believe in any war.... Can the Jews resist this organized and shameless persecution? Is there a way to preserve their self-respect and not to feel helpless, neglected and forlorn? I submit there is. If I were a Jew and were born in Germany and earned my livelihood there, I would claim Germany as my home even as the tallest Gentile German might, and challenge him to shoot me or cast me in the dungeon; I would refuse to be expelled or to submit to discriminatory treatment. And for doing this I should not wait for the fellow Jews to join me in civil resistance but would have confidence that in the end the rest were bound to follow my example. If one Jew or all the Jews were to accept what the prescriptions have offered, he or they cannot be worse off than now. And suffering voluntarily undergone will bring them an inner strength and joy which no number of resolutions or sympathy passed in the world outside Germany can. Indeed, even if Britain, France and America were to declare hostilities against Germany, they can bring no inner joy, no inner strength. The calculated violence of Hitler may even result in a general massacre of the Jews by way of his first answer to the declaration of such hostilities. But, if the Jewish mind could be prepared for voluntary suffering, even the massacre I have imagined could be turned into a day of thanksgiving and joy that Jehovah had wrought deliverance of the race even at the hands of the tyrant. (Gandhi 1942: 170–2)

In an open letter on 24 February 1939, Martin Buber took Gandhi to task for his frivolous equation of Indians in South Africa with Jews under

Hitler (www.jewishlibrary.org). As Hannah Arendt would note, Gandhi's vision of non-violence worked because his enemy was not Hitler, Stalin, or the Japanese, but the British. Had it not been the British, the outcome would have been not decolonization but massacre and submission (Arendt 1972: 159). Gandhi's lack of sympathy for the Jews persecuted by the Nazis (whom he literally advises to sacrifice themselves) is of a piece with his contempt and disregard for the Blacks in South Africa. Similarly, his discourse on *varṇa*/caste as found in his commentary on the *Gītā* should be seen in the context of this documented insensitivity to the suffering of others.

In this commentary on the *Gītā*, Gandhi translated *varṇa* into the vocabulary of modern social science as a vocational sort of trade union. He made no attempt to compare this assessment to the actual existences lived by the sub-castes. He also translated *varṇa* into a modern Western phenomenon to better ignore its Indian reality. He even pretended that in pre-Independence times, you could freely follow your aptitude and character and thereby serve society as a whole. Gandhi's perverse rendition maintains that an Untouchable has as much right to knowledge as a brahmin but he falls from his estate if he tries to gain his livelihood from teaching (cited in Nandy 1987: 326).[24] In addition to the historical inaccuracy and distortion of this view (Bolle 98–9, 143), with respect to the reality of Untouchable suffering, it was absurd to make such a projection of arcadian simplicity and utopian socialism (Bolle 1989: 144). Equally irresponsible was the vision of society that Gandhi evoked—that three or four vocations were all that were needed ('that was all then') and the assertion that it could be relevant in the twentieth century (143). But Gandhi was not naively engaging in nostalgia. He was showing his hand. Under the guise of returning to the ideal past's values, he intended to maintain the status quo. If everyone keeps to his place, then society will be perfect.

According to this logic, caste used to work well, but it had presently fallen on hard times. It could work well again if we just simplified things. The division of the *varṇas* met the requirements of the then-existing society. They were broadly divided into the intellectual and spiritual,

[24] In a talk in Tokyo in 1944, the Indian nationalist Subhas Chandra Bose (1897–1945), who was allied with Nazi Germany and Japan, maintained this distortion when he claimed that any caste member can take up any profession, since caste will not be a problem in free India (Bose and Bose 1998: 320, cited in Sawhney 118).

defence, and the production of wealth as determined by an intelligent economy and by labour (Desai 98–9). One just had to follow the original idea of a vocational caste, something curiously, Gandhi himself did not do as a *kṣatriya*. He was, in fact, living proof that sticking to one's duty, was not feasible in the modern world. The reality was that Gandhi did not offer any proposal to improve the existing caste system besides bemoaning how it had degenerated from the ideal he envisioned. Untouchables still could not drink at wells or enter temples. There is no amount of lamenting the degeneration of the pure past in the present that would change that reality. What had been perfect, Gandhi presented as something that had now unfortunately decayed, hinting that this situation was impermanent and reversible. It can always be changed, but Gandhi offered no plans for changing it just then.[25] It sufficed to evoke the perfect past. Even if it did not correspond to the present, it still had relevance (Bolle 1989: 143). The problems were actually not insurmountable: access to water, physical safety and well-being, human dignity, and freedom to worship. But Gandhi was not demanding that they be rectified. Rather he was obfuscating and avoiding the serious disabilities of the low castes. He clothed the evil of caste in a veneration of a pure past that had degenerated a bit and needed some tweaking.[26] He sidestepped the whole issue of caste discrimination with his nostalgia of an early India, where people were treated with dignity in an ordered hierarchized and well-tuned society.

The time frame here is important. We should place Gandhi in the context of his era and its prevailing attitudes. V.D. Savarkar, the author of *Hindutva*, told Gandhi that the *Gītā* meant exactly the opposite of what he ascribed to it (Gandhi 1984: 11.82). As noted, Aurobindo also told

[25] One is reminded of St. Augustine's 'Da mihi castitatem et continentiam, sed noli modo.' (Give me chastity and continency, but not yet.)

[26] In Desai's *Gospel of Selfless Action*, he claims that in talking about the *Gītā*, it was 'no place' to make a 'case for or against the so-called "caste system" ... '. He chose not to comment on a thing which is just a shadow of what existed ages ago. There was a system which existed in the ages gone by, which served the then existing social organism magnificently, which was elastic and hence made it possible for a number of different groups of the same race and several races to live together in amity and peace. What we see today is its travesty, a fossil formed out of the incrustations of customs and practices of several centuries.... The system of *varṇa* we find described (in the *Gītā*) is certainly no rigid one. The division is no division into watertight compartments.... The division was entirely vocational, in order that each might serve the best interests of the organization. If men devoted themselves to tasks for which their character and aptitude best fitted them, they would be able to give their best to the community' (Desai 102–3).

him he was wrong, particularly given the present historical context. Gandhi, however, marched to his own drum. He borrowed from nationalist readings of the *Gītā*, appropriated the text for its authority, and then, having established an odd method of 'translating', read it to suit his individual political needs. In response to Tilak's glorification of Śivāji, Gandhi offered his reading of the ideal warrior, the satyagrahi, who remains unsullied and controlled, incarnated by the *sthitaprajña* of the *Gītā* whom Gandhi claimed politics could not contaminate. The new Indian Self, embodied in the *sthitaprajña,* had nothing in common (racially and otherwise) with the Blacks and Chinese labourers Gandhi encountered in South Africa whom he depicted as wild, murderous, and given to immoral ways. More significantly, this new Indian Self had nothing in common with the Untouchables for whom Gandhi was presumably militating.

Gandhi's readings of the *Gītā* were bound to his vision of India after Independence and the future of the Untouchables insofar as they should stay within the Hindu fold and not join any Muslim voting block upon Independence. Gandhi was also intent on being the person who would 'speak for them'. This issue of 'spokespersonship' is important. It animated his battles with Babasaheb Bhimrao Ambedkar (1891–1956), Gandhi's performances at the Round Table discussions, and his hunger strikes. In all these interventions, Gandhi showed his true character. His political aim was to become the arbiter of who should and would speak for the *Harijan*. Gandhi correctly read in the *Gītā* the themes of non-attachment to the fruits of action, non-possessiveness, and non-ego centredness. But the *Gītā* does not teach any notion of trusteeship,[27] the lynch-pin concept that Gandhi would present as the justification for and the rationale with which he occluded the evil of caste. Gandhi presents the trustee as someone who has control over possessions but does not regard them as his own (Bolle 140, 144). Gandhi appropriated this concept to suit his relationship to the Untouchables. Under trusteeship, they would be kept in their debased place, controlled by caste Hindus, and remain within the Hindu fold.

[27] Gandhi defined trusteeship ingenuously from one of his old law school textbooks (*The Maxims of Equity*, by Snell, cited in Gandhi 1951: 265).

Gandhi wanted to be their trustee and spokesperson in order to control their voice and decide their fate in a free India—at roughly the status they then held. His reading of the *Gītā* positioned him to be their 'trustee', a path he chose for his personal salvation (Gandhi 1957: 265).[28] However, Gandhi's quest for 'trusteeship' and his demand for brahminical custodianship of the text would meet with considerable opposition from Ambedkar. If there was to be a trustee, Ambedkar felt (as did his followers) that it should be one of the own, and certainly not Gandhi. In Ambedkar's interpretation of the *Gītā*, he explains an alternate scenario: the Untouchables were beginning to speak for themselves without the intervention of their caste Hindu 'protectors'.

[28] This sense of trusteeship did not extend to his family. Upon receiving his revelation of trusteeship, Gandhi stopped his life insurance policy (he told one of his peons to let it lapse) because the financial well-being of his wife and children were no longer his concern.

7

Ambedkar's Counter-Revolutionary *Gītā*

Historical and Political Context

In the West, Gandhi is celebrated as the great friend and champion of the Untouchables. Those unfamiliar with Indian history see him as, perhaps, the greatest humanitarian that India has ever produced, the 'great soul' who initiated social action on behalf of those he called the *Harijans*. However, a more informed student of Indian history and literature understands that there were a number of formidable antecedents to Gandhi, such as M.G. Ranade[1] and Dayānand Saraswatī[2] who also held to a vision of Hindu *varṇa* that was originally based on merit but had declined over time to be determined by birth. As did many Indian reformers in the nineteenth century, Ranade and Dayānand also held to an image of a Vedic Golden Age, free of the excrescences that had befouled modern Hinduism (Figueira 2002, 155–19, 122–30). There was also a tradition of anti-brahmin reformers who had militated against caste, such as Chokamela,[3] the fourteenth-century Mahar (an Untouchable caste of Maharashtra) *bhakti* poet, and the seventeenth-century poet Tukārām.[4] These two mystics sang of the equality of man before God and challenged caste hierarchies (Jaffrelot 2005: 20). As befitting a devotee of

[1] Mahadev Govind Ranade (1842–1901), a Chitpavan Brahmin, was a social reformer and judge. He was a founding member of the Indian National Congress.

[2] Dayānand Saraswatī (1824–1883) was a social leader and founder of the Ārya Samāj, a reform movement.

[3] Chokamela, an Untouchable saint initiated into Bhakti spirituality by the poet-saint Namdev (1270–1350). Because of his caste, he could not enter the local temple nor even stand before its door. When he died, his bones buried near the temple were said to chant the temple's deity's name, still yearning to be allowed to visit its confines. In the twentieth century, B.R. Ambedkar visited his tomb and was also denied entry to the temple.

[4] Tukārām, an Untouchable saint known for his devotional poetry, denounced rites, rituals, sacrifices, and vows. He encouraged devotion, and thought that caste did not matter.

The Afterlives of the Bhagavad Gītā. Dorothy M. Figueira, Oxford University Press. © Dorothy M. Figueira 2023.
DOI: 10.1093/oso/9780198873488.003.0008

the mystic poet Kabir,[5] Jyotirao Phule (1827–1890) decried caste and led a nineteenth-century movement for the uplift of Untouchables and the rejection of caste (147–9). He was motivated by his mistrust of the upper castes, their control of society, and their hypocrisy. Phule was quite influential in setting up orphanages and schools for Untouchables and girls in Maharashtra, where the Mahars had become particularly active. B.R. Ambedkar follows in this rich tradition of Maharashtran Mahar social reformers.

Under the Peshwa,[6] Mahars were able to join the British Army and this affiliation afforded them a considerable degree of social mobility. For example, they could leave their villages for cities to better their opportunities. But, as noted in the last chapter, there was an unwillingness among caste Hindus to act upon the serious disabilities that Untouchables faced in India at the time. While there was a good deal of rhetoric expended, little improvement had been made in their living conditions. The fact that Untouchables continued to receive no human dignity was not really addressed. At the time in question, the clothing that Untouchables wore was regulated as well as even the colours of the garments permitted. Untouchables were not allowed to wear jewellery. They needed to sweep their footprints off the ground, by means of a broom tied to their backsides to avoid possibly polluting the feet of brahmin who might follow in the wake. They were required to hang an earthen jar from their neck to catch their spittle, lest brahmins tread on it inadvertently. They did not have access to wells and temples. In any discussion of caste, these images must remain in the forefront of our consciousness, particularly in the case of Gandhi and the Congress Party who refused to address these realities in any cogent manner.

Thanks to their exposure through the army to British institutions, the Mahars had some possibility of socialization. They also had royal patrons, such as the Maharajah of Kolhapur, who was no admirer of brahmin oppression. It was thanks to this type of patronage that Ambedkar, the future Dalit leader and framer of the Indian Constitution, was able to complete his education. In 1921, when only 2.3 per cent of the Mahars had become

[5] A fifteenth-century mystic poet and saint whose writings influence the Bhakti movement's criticism of organized religion and practices in both Hinduism and Islam.

[6] The Peshwa was the appointed Prime Minister of the Maratha Empire and de facto leader of the Maratha Confederacy in the late eighteenth century to the early nineteenth century.

literate and only 288 knew English, Ambedkar was the sole Untouchable university graduate (Jaffrelot 24). Like Gandhi, he did not know Sanskrit. Unlike Gandhi, however, his ignorance of the language was not a matter of choice. As an Untouchable, he was barred from learning it. Legal treatises such as the *Mānavadharmaśāstra* (Laws of Manu) ordained that an Untouchable who hears Sanskrit should have molten lead poured into his ears. So, whereas Gandhi had access to the *Gītā* in the original but was not interested until his Western Theosophist friends introduced him to it in the form of Arnold's English paraphrase of a translation, Ambedkar's situation was quite different. It was only later, as a student in Bonn, at the same university where the early *Gītā* translator A.W. Schlegel had been the first Sanskrit professor, that Ambedkar was able to study the language and learn it sufficiently to read texts in the original. Ambedkar adopted two approaches in his reading of the *Gītā*. He respected it, but condemned the evil of caste that it supported (Gowda 222).

Ambedkar's story is simply miraculous. Because of his initial schooling and his natural gifts of intellect, he gained admission to Elphinstone College. No other member of his caste had ever achieved this level of learning. Thanks to the support of the princely state of Baroda, he was subsequently given a scholarship to attend Columbia University in New York City beginning in 1914. He graduated two years later with a degree in economics, having submitted a thesis on the administration and finances of the East India Company. While at Columbia, Ambedkar studied public finance and taxation with Edward Seligman and pragmatism with John Dewey. Due to the stipulations of his financial aid, he was impelled to return home. He later came back to Columbia, however, to complete a MA and a Ph.D. in economics in 1917 and then onto the London School of Economics and Political Science for a doctoral work for one year. He spent 1920–3, at Grey's Inn completing a law degree. It was with this extensive training that Ambedkar analysed the issue of caste. Significantly, he did not primarily approach this topic as a victim. In 1917, he published in *The Indian Antiquary*, 'Castes of India: Their Mechanism, Genesis and Development' (Ambedkar 1979), where he claimed that Westerners who had tied caste to the issue of race were primarily reacting to their own racial attitudes. Caste had devolved as it did from the deep-seated notion of hierarchies in Indian society. Ambedkar outlined a process of what,

40 years later the sociologist M.N. Srinivas[7] would term 'Sanskritization' to describe when a lower group in a hierarchy attempts to emulate the group above it rather than seek to liberate itself.[8]

Whereas Gandhi gave the Untouchables the treacly moniker of '*Harijans*' or 'children of God', Ambedkar called them Dalits, derived from the verb *DAL* 'to split' or 'break open,' with the sense of something being ground down. The Marathi term 'Dalit' signifying 'Broken Men', ideally suited their depressed state. In *The Untouchable, Who Were They and Why They Became Untouchables*, Ambedkar made the case that Untouchability was imposed on those individuals who had left Hinduism and, in the face of brahmin persecution, refused to abandon the new faith they had adopted, Buddhism (Ambedkar 1987: 7.317). He argued that the Untouchables had a different origin from the *śūdra*s, the servants born from the feet of the primordial man in the creation myth of the *Rig Veda* (10.90). The *śūdra*s comprised the lowest *varṇa* in the hierarchy where the brahmins were first, the *kṣatriya*s second, and the *vaiśya*s third. Ambedkar was proposing an alternative Untouchable identity. He assigned to them a totally different myth of origin. Gandhi had based Untouchability on an image of an idealized Vedic Golden Age, where castes were not hierarchized. According to Gandhi, this wonderful *varṇa* system had since degenerated into the prejudice of caste. Ambedkar, in contrast, saw Untouchability as the violent response by Hinduism to the incursion of Buddhism, a religion that India had suppressed so brutally that it disappeared from the subcontinent until modern times. Ambedkar had serious reservations regarding the policies of Gandhi and the Congress Party with respect to the Untouchables.

In the early days of the quest for self-rule, neither Gandhi nor Congress focused on the plight of the Untouchables. In his book, *Hind Swaraj*, Gandhi did not even mention Untouchability. But Gandhi and Congress awoke to the Untouchable cause when it became clear that the British would be leaving India soon and plans were needed for the reallocation of power. On the other end of the caste spectrum, the idea of *swarāj* had also awakened Untouchable groups, as it brought to light new and

[7] See, in particular, his work on the Coorgs: Srinivas 1952. See also Srinivas 1956, 1966.

[8] Jaffrelot (32) sees Ambedkar as advancing this idea long before it was given its name by Srinivas.

frightening existential possibilities of how free they would be in an independent caste-bound India. The Montague Government had already begun to plan India's autonomy. Ambedkar and many in the Untouchable community knew full well how little the Congress Party and Gandhi had done or would do to improve their actual existence. Gandhi had formed his Harijan Sevak Sangh, but this party had a poor record of delivering any tangible uplift. Of the crore[9] of rupees that had been budgeted for the removal of Untouchability, only a few thousand had even been spent. After all of Gandhi's talk about the urgent need for temple entry, neither Congress nor Gandhi had even supported the Ranga-Iyer Bill of 1929, giving Untouchables the right to enter temples. They could not bring themselves to condemn Untouchability, claiming that they could do so only if the majority of Hindus were in favour of such a move (Ganaveer 1983, 50–4, cited in Gore 1993, 142–3). It was quite clear that after self-rule had been obtained, Untouchability would continue to exist. Moreover, the vast numbers of Untouchables, who had not secured the simplest rights, would not easily be able to leave the Hindu fold (Kolge 134) and maintain any livelihood to ensure their survival. The various Untouchable groups, as well as Ambedkar, were wise to the game. They were all seeking to position themselves strategically in order to garner some concessions before power changed hands. From 1927 onward, 18 Dalit organizations had been consulted by the British government's Simon Commission to weigh in on how they felt they should be represented. In 1930, the First Round Table was convened in London to discuss minority interests. Congress and Gandhi refused to attend even though the Untouchables, the Sikhs, the Muslims, the princely states, and the Hindu Mahasabha were all present. Ambedkar was a vocal and erudite participant in this Round Table discussion.

The Simon Commission came out in favour of the Untouchables receiving separate representation. This decision considerably raised the stakes for Gandhi and Congress. Already the Muslims had been given a separate electorate in the Indian Councils Act of 1909 and now there was the possibility of Untouchables receiving this same privilege. Gandhi and Congress responded to this advisory decision by the Simon Commission for separate electorates for Untouchables by claiming it

[9] The equivalent of a crore in US dollars is approximately $140,095.

was a moot ruling, since they had boycotted the First Round Table discussion. So, a Second Round Table was convened, where Gandhi spent considerable time asserting his position as spokesperson and insisting that he alone represented India. He also claimed that he alone represented the Untouchables. The cheekiness of this claim was challenged by Ambedkar. When Gandhi accused Ambedkar of having no right to speak for Untouchables, Ambedkar countered that the Dalits, in fact, supported him in his role. It was simply absurd that a privileged Bania (merchant), such as Gandhi, could claim to represent 45 million Untouchables (Roy 2016: 65). Gandhi had been so out of touch with Untouchables in general and their mobilization that when he had first met Ambedkar only a year earlier, he did not even realize that he was an Untouchable, thinking him a brahmin (Ginaveer 6, cited in Gore 132).

In their encounter at the Second Round Table, Gandhi challenged Ambedkar's knowledge of India and his right to represent his own people. After much grandstanding, posturing, and fussing over why he felt he represented all Indians, Gandhi got down to business. He adamantly opposed separate representation for Untouchables, even though he had earlier accepted it for Muslims and Sikhs. His rather weak rationale was that separate electorates would destroy Hindu unity, as if such a thing ever existed for the Untouchables. It was simply a ruse for the high castes to maintain their monopoly over all power and maintain a sizable Untouchable potential voting block in a free India. Gandhi put on quite a performance in London. Ambedkar, an able opponent, countered his arguments and composed a considerable charge sheet on how little Gandhi and Congress had actually achieved for the uplift of the Untouchables. In Ambedkar, Gandhi had found a formidable adversary.

Not only did Ambedkar and Gandhi both claim to speak for the Untouchables, each had radically different agendas. Ambedkar sought political power for the Dalits themselves (and not as a part of a Hindu block) and Gandhi held to the promise (as yet negligibly pursued) of reform and protection from above (Omvedt 170). Gandhi displayed a rather patronizing stance of paternalism toward Untouchables, denying them reserved seats, claiming that they were unnecessary, since Dalit interests would be taken care of, as always, by caste Hindus. He pretended that the Untouchables could count on their co-religionists to protect them. Gandhi also claimed that he simply could not allow separate electorates because it would divide villages, a claim to which Ambedkar countered that, due to caste, villages were already divided. Gandhi admitted that Untouchability was evil but claimed nothing could be done administratively because it was an evil that needed to be purged by Hindus themselves, spiritually. Gandhi then left the proceedings. As a parting shot, he threatened that he would resist separate electorates for Untouchables with his life. He immediately sailed back to India, stopping off in Italy on the way home to visit Mussolini, a statesman he greatly admired.

Gandhi had left the Second Round Table also claiming that he would leave it to the British Prime Minister, Ramsey MacDonald, to rule on the matter. On 26 September 1932, the MacDonald Communal Award announced separate electorates to Untouchables. Contrary to his parting statement to McDonald to abide by his decision, Gandhi's response was to undertake a vow to fast until death. This act was a brutal political move since he had promised to follow the decision of the Prime Minister during the Second Round Table. He had not really negotiated at the Round Table at all. He had primarily spent time asserting his power as India's key representative. Ambedkar noted that Gandhi had been so busy in establishing his own claim to recognition by the British as the 'dictator' of India that he forgot altogether that the important question was not with whom the settlement should be made, but what were to be the terms of that settlement (Khairmode 1987: 177, in Gore 165–6). Ambedkar had, in fact, found Gandhi unfit to negotiate (Ambedkar 1979: 1.350–1, cited in Gore 166), commenting that 'Mahātmas only raise dust' (Phadke 276, cited in Gore 139).

It was clear that Gandhi wanted the Untouchables to vote Hindu, not as partners but as poor relations (Khairmode 1987: 198, cited in Gore 1993: 166). Gandhi was forcing Ambedkar's hand, knowing that Ambedkar understood full well that if he died during his stunt of starving himself, there would be a tremendous slaughter of the Dalits by caste Hindus. As Ambedkar put it, Gandhi forced him to renounce the rights that the British Prime Minister had given to his people (Ambedkar 1945). There was, of course, great *tamāśā*[10] over the fast, with the entire country mobilizing to try and get Gandhi to reconsider and live. Even Nehru felt the fast was a diversion from the true struggle, that of Independence.

[10] A fuss, confusion, show, or performance.

Those other constituencies, who for political reasons of their own might not have lent their support to the separate electorates measure, had no problem with the Prime Minister's ruling. For example, the Marxist leader E.M.S. Namboodiripad and the Hindu chief organizer, Dr. B.S. Moonje, the President of the Hindu Mahasabha, could not fathom the fuss; they did not see separate electorates as an issue worth fighting to the death over (Kolge 171).

Nevertheless, the entire country was agitated that the Mahātma might be sacrificed out of his 'love' of Indian unity and his self-proclaimed commitment to the Untouchables. One of Gandhi's sons begged Ambedkar to save his father's life. Gandhi had successfully cast Ambedkar in the role of the enemy of Indian unity. Numerous conversations and cables circulated monitoring the great soul's failing health, until finally Ambedkar relented for the simple reason that he could not, for the sake of his people, risk Gandhi's death and the ensuing slaughter of Untouchables. The result of his capitulation was the Poona Pact. While Gandhi presented the fast as a moralistic act, it was really nothing but an act of hard bargaining (worthy of the inborn traits of Gandhi's caste, if one believes in inborn traits!), where the Mahātma was able to force his advantage over Ambedkar and other Dalit leaders (Khairmode 1987: 198, cited in Gore 167). It was a fast directed against the Untouchables by their 'avowed protector' to prevent their obtaining political power. It was truly moral blackmail with Gandhi asserting his political authority by not accepting the Communal Award. Ambedkar saw the fast as Gandhi forcing him to 'deliver my people bound hand and foot to the caste Hindus for generations to come' (Khairmode 1989: 42, cited in Gore 137). When Ambedkar lost separate electorates and the electoral advantage they would give his people and when he saw how he had lost them, he realized that caste Hindus would never afford his people any access to self-determination.

Then, after the fast, Gandhi blithely accepted reserved seats for the Untouchables, that he had previously not sanctioned and Ambedkar accepted joint elections with the provision that the Depressed Classes could stand for election in a primary. With the Poona Pact, the Untouchables lost the right to have only Untouchables choose their representatives. It was a safeguard that Ambedkar knew was necessary and indeed it was, as the Untouchables immediately learned once it was not in place to protect them. The Untouchables had to give up the second vote that gave them their choice of their candidate. Now the caste Hindus could put forward their choice of an Untouchable candidate for the Untouchable constituency (Anand 365). There was invariably some Untouchable who would follow caste Hindu and Congress interests and directives. All the Untouchables now had were the reserved seats selected by the general population, the caste Hindu majority, who had for centuries so successfully oppressed them and proven their disinterest in ameliorating the Untouchables' situation (Anand 365).

As Ambedkar would note, the goal of the Poona Pact was to outnumber Untouchable voters and prevent them from electing their own nominees (Ambedkar 1987: 9.92). It succeeded admirably in this respect. Although Untouchables did get more allocated seats, it was still a major defeat because these reserved seats were hand-picked by the upper castes. Thus, the Simon Commission which had given reserved seats to the Depressed Classes was effectively circumvented because Congress, claiming unique representation of India, had refused to participate along with everyone else who comprised India (Muslims, Sikhs, Christians, Untouchables, princely states, and the Hindu Mahasabha). Then, when they did participate in the Second Round Table, Gandhi refused to accept the decision of this meeting and subsequently forced compliance by threatening to kill himself.

Ambedkar saw Gandhi's fast for what it was, an extreme form of coercion (Anand 364). The Untouchables had to give up what Ambedkar had won for them (Anand 365).

> There was nothing noble in that fast. It was a foul and filthy act ... [It] was the worst form of coercion against a helpless people to give up the constitutional safeguards of which they had become possessed under the Prime Minister's Award and agree to live on the mercy of the Hindus. It was a vile and wicked act. How can the Untouchables regard such a man as honest and sincere? (Ambedkar 1987: 9.259)

Ambedkar could, however, take the long view, comparing the situation of the Untouchables to that of the Plebeians in Rome who could never get a Plebeian consul independent of the Patricians. So too was the situation of the Untouchables under the Poona Pact (Anand 368). The loss of the double vote was the turning point for Ambedkar (Ambedkar 1987: 9.90), particularly, in the way Gandhi had achieved his aims. It was the last straw for him in attempting to deal with Gandhi, the self-appointed 'Hindu friend' of the Untouchables.

Ambedkar on the *Gītā*

Ambedkar had originally envisioned a large work on the *Gītā* that never materialized. What we do have is Ambedkar's *Essays on the Bhagavad Gītā: Philosophic Defense of Counter Revolution* (1927).[11] Ambedkar's thesis regarding the *Gītā* was straightforward: the brahmins had lost their power to Buddhism under the Emperor Aśoka and sought to win it back. One method of retrieving their hegemony was to create an alternative scriptural source. They, therefore, produced the *Gītā* as a tool with which to fight Buddhism. They needed support for the philosophical school adhering to a Vedic conception of *dharma* and codified primarily in Jaimini's *Pūrva Mīmāṃsā,* a text proven to withstand on its own the threat posed to it by Buddhism (Ambedkar 1987: 3.363–4). The *Gītā* was the text devised to support Jaimini's vision of *dharma* and thereby combat Buddhism.

To support this thesis that the *Gītā* was written with the purpose of philosophically defending Hinduism (Ambedkar 1987: 3.363–7), Ambedkar first had to show that it was composed after Jaimini's *Pūrva-Mīmāṃsā* and after Buddhism took hold. He then had to dismantle the ancient and modern readings that sought to give the *Gītā* a universal message (3. 71–7, 357–360). In his estimation, the *Gītā* was neither universal nor a unified text. In fact, Ambedkar claimed that the *Gītā* borrowed its major themes from Buddhism (3.127–8, 369). He cited, in particular, its exposition of *śrāddha* (faith in the self), *vyavasāya* (firm determination), *samādhi* (earnest contemplation), *prajña* (knowledge), *maitrī* (kindliness), *karuṇā* (compassion) *muditā* (sympathizing joy), and *upekṣā* (unconcernedness) (3.369–71).

Ambedkar saw *varṇa* as the central theme of the *Gītā.* Its intended purpose was to protect Hinduism from the inclusion advocated by

[11] See vol. 3 of his *Writing and Speeches* (1987) as well as comments found throughout his *Writings and Speeches* (3: xi–xvii, editor's note 3:357).

Buddhism. With the *Gītā, varṇa* now became the divine law of inborn qualities (Ambedkar 1987: 3.360–1). The *Gītā* needed to promote *varṇa* because Buddhism had so effectively undermined Vedic and Brahmanical systems by instituting social equality. Under Buddhism, individuals were valued according to their merits, and not according to the *caturvarṇa*, as the *Vedas* had ordained (3.363–4). Ambedkar claimed that the function of the *Gītā* was to reinstate *varṇa*, by taking what had been presented as a creation myth in the *Rig Veda* and transforming it into divine law. In the *Gītā*, Krishna instructs that one must do one's duty as presented by one's *varṇa* and no other. He also teaches that those who worship Krishna will obtain salvation. But this devotion can only work if accompanied by the observance of the duty mandated by one's *varṇa*. A *śūdra*, no matter how devoted, will not gain salvation if he has transgressed his duty as a *śūdra*, that is, to be in service to the higher classes (3.365). So, Ambedkar viewed the *Gītā* as a particularly dangerous text, not only because it sustained the *varṇa* system, but because it invigorated it by emphasizing the caste system's divine foundation. He felt that the *Gītā* thus rendered the *varṇa* system even more cruel, inflexible, and binding (3.127), since it offered no cross-*varṇa* mobility and made no attempt to uproot its iniquity or change its severity. For Ambedkar, the *Gītā* was all about violence; it justified violence, and it certainly advocated violence against Buddhism (Ahir 162). Ambedkar wanted his readers to see the *Gītā* for what it was, a counter-revolutionary text fighting the revolution that Buddhism had successfully unleashed.

Ambedkar analysed Hinduism as a sociologist and in historical terms. He recognized that over time, the blind practices surrounding Vedic notions of *karma* had fallen into ill-repute. They had grown away from Vedic ritualism. Given the heteroclite nature of the *Gītā* as a text, Ambedkar was concerned that it could be easily manipulated, particularly with reference to *anāsakti* (desireless action) (Ambedkar 1987: 3.362–3). His fear here was that the selfishness supported by the *varṇa* system could be whitewashed by associating it with the principle of *anāsakti karma*. Moreover, if one becomes a *sthitaprajña* (as Tilak and Gandhi advised), no fault could be found with the *karmakāṇḍa* (ritual portion of the *Vedas*), since the *Gītā* defended the *karma yoga*. This was clearly not the path that Ambedkar advocated, since his aim was to obtain the rights and equality for his community that were enjoyed by caste Hindus. He saw the *Gītā* serving as a brahmin defence against the democratic and emancipating striving of the masses that Buddhism had offered his people. Ambedkar proposed therefore a radical alternative and response. He called upon his community to reject the brahminocracy (defended by the *Gītā*) and convert to Buddhism. Ambedkar firmly believed that his fellow Indians, who had been 'eulogizing' the *Gītā*, were in fact advocating nothing but transparent attempts to maintain brahminocracy.[12] In the essay 'The Rock on which is Built', Ambedkar outlined how religious sanctions that supported caste also supported the hegemony of brahmins and forestalled rebellion by denying access to knowledge (Gore 206).

As noted in the previous chapter, the *Gītā*'s statements of a theoretical or theological nature were of little import to Gandhi. He was not particularly interested in the ontological aspects of Krishna (Gandhi 1984: 32.189), *Brahman, Bhagavat, prakṛti, puruṣottama, Īśvara,* or even *bhakti.*[13] In fact, for Gandhi, *bhakti* was important only to the degree that it produced the right knowledge necessary for unveiling the true meaning of the *Gītā:* renunciation (41.95). It is important to remember that Gandhi's *Gītā* was a partial or truncated text. It consisted primarily of Chapter 2 and not even all of Chapter 2, but merely the last 19 stanzas that provided him with what he ordained was the *Gītā*'s essence—he deemed all the rest as just elaboration and explanation. Gandhi even had advised people to reject anything in the *Gītā* that gave contrary meaning to these 19 stanzas as he read them (28.316 in Jordens 94).

However, the real eccentricity of Gandhi's interpretation of the *Gītā* was that he transformed Krishna's repeated invocations to Arjuna to fight into a mandate for non-violent resistance. It was a perverse reading, by a perverse man. He presented the *Gītā* in such a way that it gave him what he politically wanted and needed. It is no wonder that the *Gītā* was the only book in Gandhi's possession at his death. The ideas he found in the *Gītā* were those that he needed: concepts he imposed on the text in order to legitimize them with its authority, as is often the case with book

[12] As Jaffrelot notes, the upper caste has shifted its dreams to success and power to the US in recent years (Jaffrelot 150) as witness by political activities aimed at the representation of India and Indians in American culture (Figueira 2021).

[13] Jordens attributed Gandhi's constantly discounting of *bhakti* to his origins in a province where the Vallabhāchārya sect, notorious for its excesses in *bhakti* rituals, was prominent (Jordens 103).

religions. Significantly, the *Gītā* also provided the textual and religiously sanctioned justification not to alter the Untouchables' situation.[14]

In his *Philosophic Defense of Counter Revolution*, Ambedkar countered Gandhi's offensive as well as other nationalist interpretations of the *Gītā*. Ambedkar highlighted and condemned the *Gītā*'s justification of caste. But Ambedkar also read the *Gītā* in support of his conversion, along with that of his people, to Buddhism. Toward this end, Ambedkar concluded that the *Gītā* respected Buddhist teaching and borrowed considerably from it. For example, Ambedkar claimed that the *Gītā*'s discussion of knowledge and ignorance (Chapter 13) derived from Buddhism, a conclusion that even the renowned *Gītā* translator K.T. Telang (1850–93)[15] advocated (Ambedkar 1987: 3.371).[16] Although he accepted the *Gītā*'s message of desireless action, Ambedkar viewed this theme as an afterthought, inserted later in the text to neutralize Buddhism (Gowda 229). He identified what he felt were the fundamental concepts in the *Gītā*'s teaching (*karma*, *dāna*,[17] *tapas*,[18] *kṣetra-kṣetrajña*[19]) and claimed they all derived from the Buddhist influence on Hinduism (Gowda 226).

Ambedkar begins his unfinished essay on the *Gītā* by saying that it is neither a book of religion nor a book of philosophy, but rather it uses philosophy to defend religion. He sees the *Gītā* as promoting several major themes. The first, expressed in 2.11–28, offers a justification for war. Since the world is perishable and unreal, why should Arjuna lament? The body and soul are not one: the body is perishable, and the soul is immortal. So, war and killing really offer no grounds for remorse (Ambedkar 1987: 3.361, cited in Kumar 2015: 155). Such is the *Gītā*'s justification for war. The second major theme that Ambedkar attributes to the *Gītā*

[14] His desire to maintain their status quo had been expressed earlier in 1920, when he had claimed that inequality would be adjusted by reincarnation (*Young India* 8 December 1920 in Gandhi 1984–: 19. 83–: 5 cited in Jaffrelot 2005: 67).

[15] Indologist and Indian judge of the Bombay High Court, whose English translation of the *Gītā* is a standard work and was published in Max Müller's *Sacred Books of the East* (vol 8) in 1882.

[16] Ambedkar also attributed Tilak's convoluted chronology for the *Gītā* to his chauvinistic inability to accept that the *Gītā* could have borrowed anything from Buddhism. The *Gītā* cannot be a debtor to Buddhism, so the Hīnayāna school of Buddhism preceded the Mahāyāna school of Buddhism, the Mahāyāna borrowed from the *Gītā*, and the original *Gītā* predates the *Mahābhārata*.

[17] *Dāna* means generosity.

[18] *Tapas* refers to the liberating action of penance.

[19] *Kṣetra* refers to the body which is material, transitory, and perishable, and *Kṣetrajña* refers to the conscious knower of the field (body, soul, physical matter).

provides the actual focus of his critique. He laments that the *Gītā*'s presentation of the *caturvarṇa* as created by God renders disciplinary obligations sacrosanct (Ambedkar 1987: 3.361). The myth of creation found in the *Puruṣasūkta* of the *Rig Veda*, where the primordial man is dismembered into the four *varṇa*s, is transformed in the *Gītā* into rules of obedience and sacrifice. Krishna gives them their sanction and Gandhi codifies them in the thematic of non-attachment (*anāsakti*) as embodied by the *sthitaprajña*. This is the crux of Ambedkar's problem with the *Gītā* and Gandhi's interpretation of it.

Like Gandhi, Ambedkar also came to the *Gītā* midstream in life. Both he and Gandhi came to it because of *varṇa*, with Gandhi supporting its vision and distinguishing it from caste, and Ambedkar identifying *varṇa* with caste and condemning it as evil. So, it is not a question in the *Gītā*, as Hegel saw it, of inactivity, quietism or (in the terminology of Humboldt) *energeia*,[20] but a matter of religious observances. Ambedkar saw the *Gītā* not as philosophy but rather as a party 'pamphlet'. He felt that by inflating the meaning of words such as *karma* and *jñāna*, patriotic Indians (like Tilak) had elevated this text to the level of a philosophical treatise, which it was not. They had imposed on the *Gītā*, just as Gandhi did, false meanings. According to Ambedkar, the *Gītā* was composed simply to support the counter-revolution against Buddhism and its serious threat to Hinduism. Buddhism had made such inroads and posed such a danger to Hinduism that the *Gītā* had to be written. According to Ambedkar. the soul of the *Gītā* (18.41–8) was the *caturvarṇa* and securing its observance (Ambedkar 1987: 3.65), by stipulating that one must not agitate (3.26) but simply do one's duty and no other. The *Gītā* preaches that there is salvation only if one does one's specific duty and acts not merely by devotion but with devotion accompanied by the observance of duty laid down by *varṇa* (3.365). Since Buddhism had rejected the *caturvarṇa*, dared to make it possible for women and *śūdra*s to become *saṃnyāsi* (renunciant mendicants), and condemned *karma* (in the form of *yajñas* or sacrifices) as violent and selfish, it needed to be delegitimized. The counter-revolutionaries had first struck back by claiming that these concepts were taught in the infallible *Vedas* and thus sacrosanct. Because Hindu dogma

[20] Ambedkar cites his reading of Humboldt on the *Gītā* in his *Literature of Brahmanism* (Ambedkar 1987: 3.246).

was authorized by the *Vedas*, it could never be challenged. When this strategy did not work, the counter-revolution came up with another form of attack. They sought to reject the Buddhist teaching of non-violence which countermanded Hinduism's belief in the *kṣatriya*'s duty to kill. The counter-revolution also needed to delegitimize Buddhism's imposition of social equality and its rejection of the boons of sacrifice.

According to Ambedkar, the initial text of the counter-revolution against Buddhism had been Jaimini's *Pūrva Mīmāṃsā*. But Buddhism had so successfully superseded Hinduism's rules and rituals that Jaimini proved to be ineffective. So, the *Gītā* was then composed to relaunch Hinduism's assault on Buddhism. It countered Buddhist compassion by asserting that Krishna's killing is not killing (a puerile defence, according to Ambedkar) and supported the *caturvarṇa* by claiming its philosophical integrity in the Sāṃkhya theory of the *guṇas,* which Ambedkar also deemed childish (Ambedkar 1987: 3.364). Ambedkar claimed that the counter-revolution against Buddhism succeeded because of the *Gītā.* In fact, he maintained that Hinduism's survival was attributable to the philosophical defence of *varṇa* offered by the *Gītā*.

As I have tried to show in this volume, the *Gītā* lent itself to a variety of often sedimented interpretations. The *Gītā* was co-opted by Indian nationalists to produce a binding ethics and mobilized in a particularly pernicious manner. Then, under Gandhi, it was transformed from a poem on violence to a treatise on non-violence. Ambedkar noted that this interpretation resulted in the 'end of criticism' once Gandhi transformed the *Gītā* into an ancient article of faith (Ambedkar 1987: 3.366, cited in Kumar 2015: 365 #96). The strength of the *Gītā*, as we indicated at the beginning of this study, had been its versatility and malleability. Ambedkar had termed it a patchwork of contingent improvisations (Kumar 2010: 401), consisting of teachings regarding *bhakti*, Sāṃkhya, and a defence of Pūrva Mīmāṃsā; there were also elements of Buddhism in it[21] and, significantly, the elevation of what had been a minor character in the epic, to the status of the Supreme God (3.377). Contrary to Tilak's claim that it was a single book of a single author, Ambedkar viewed it as

[21] He acknowledges how much Sāṃkhya philosophy can be found in the *Gītā* but also notes how derivative it is of Buddhism, particularly the *Mahāpari-nibbāṇa Sutta* (369), the *Mahāpadāna Sutta*, and the *Tevijja Sutta* (Ambedkar 1987: 3.370).

a potpourri of the ancient and the non-ancient teachings, with additions as late as the fourteenth century. As a lawyer, Ambedkar found its sanctioning of killing odd and in *Who Were the Śūdras* (preface), judged its mysticism vulgar. In fact, he came to see the *Gītā* as the most violent articulation of an oppressive religion at the centre of a corrupt and immoral system. Initially, he had thought the *Gītā* might be useful as a basis for his demand of equal rights for his people, but he quickly realized (and his encounter with Gandhi proved) how non-violence could be used as violence (Ambedkar 1979: 1.84–8, cited in Kumar 2015: 147). But Gandhi's treatment of the text effectively ruled out these other interpretations.

Ambedkar sought, therefore, to reclaim the *Gītā* from Gandhi's interpretation. He saw the text as not demanding satyagraha and not depicting an inner struggle but codifying the caste system as a form of violence and actually sanctifying it. He launched his critique against the force he saw depicted in the *Gītā*'s support of the *caturvarṇa* and the corrupt violence of this institution, as it was clothed in the *Gītā* under a veneer of mysticism. He felt that neither the nationalists nor Gandhi read the *Gītā* honestly. Gandhi had not even inherited it faithfully, as Ambedkar felt he had done from his father who taught him the epics as a child and instilled in him their degradation of *śūdras* and Untouchables. In *Buddhism and Dhamma*, Ambedkar relates how his father wanted him to understand the origins of his persecution and not have an inferiority complex. He wanted to instil in the youth a sense of revolt (Kumar 2015: 153). We need only compare Ambedkar's introduction to the text with Gandhi's exoticist and occult initiation! Who had a greater claim to a 'true Indian understanding' of the *Gītā* as a lived text—Ambedkar who learned it at his father's knee or Gandhi who needed to be introduced to it by English occultists?

In *The Hindu Social Order: Its Unique Features*, Ambedkar notes that Hindus alone have devised a social order designed by God and therefore, consecrated and made sacred.[22] This hierarchy cannot tolerate any amendment or criticism. Ambedkar comments that no other culture in the world has established such a system. What the *Gītā* teaches (4.13) is that God created innate and inborn qualities (Ambedkar 1987: 3.360, cited in Roy 2013: 64) in the *caturvarṇa*, and that this system must be

[22] See *Gītā* 3.26; 4.7–8; 4.13, and 18.41–4.

followed. One must not change one's path. The uneducated should not hope to rise (3.26, 29). In fact, Krishna will come to earth to stop the decay of the *caturvarṇa* (Ambedkar 1987b: 4.7–8).

According to the rules of *varṇa*, the *Gītā* proscribes who can sacrifice and who cannot. It also decides who can rebel, and who must do their duty and not that of another. The *Gītā* mandates that salvation cannot be gained through devotion alone but must also be based on the observance of the *caturvarṇa* system. It teaches that the *śūdra* cannot gain salvation, if he transgresses the rules of the *śūdra*. Simply, the *śūdra* must live and die in service of the higher castes (Ambedkar 1987: 3.365). For Ambedkar, the *Gītā*'s justification of the *caturvarṇa* produces a very evil alliance between the sacred and the civic. By limiting the possibilities for the underclass, the *caturvarṇa* controls souls both in this world and in the next. In short, Ambedkar saw the *Gītā* as the perfect text for containment at a time when notions of equality were being bruited about. The valorization of the *Gītā* in the period leading up to Independence made it clear to Ambedkar that there was really no potential in the present situation for a revolution of the downtrodden. The *śūdra*s and the Untouchables simply could not improve their status in the Hindu world sanctioned by the *Gītā*.

Ambedkar had thoroughly examined the nationalist interpretations of the *Gītā*. What he found so offensive in them was the ethicized religion they deduced from the *Gītā* and incorporated in popular spirituality in order to validate social and ritual behaviour. While he quoted Telang and Tilak[23] in his discussion of the *Gītā*, Ambedkar never once cited Gandhi. He either dismissed Gandhi's extensive commentary of the *Gītā* as unworthy of political national attention or saw its potential danger for his community and directed his thoughts to dismantling his argumentation (Kumar 2010: 408).

Between 1925 and 1935, when Ambedkar was still trying to keep his community within the Hindu fold, he toyed with the idea that the *Gītā* might be useful in opposing the *Vedas* and *Manu*, the main authorities whom he at the time rejected (Gore 106). But Ambedkar came to view the *Gītā* instead as a summary of *Manu*, the law book that he and his followers publicly burned. The *Gītā* philosophically and religiously justified

[23] When discussing his dating as later than Jaimini and Bādarāyaṇa, he found support in Tilak's *Gītārahasya* (2.916–22) (Ambedkar 1987: 3.366).

what *Manu* would make into law. By ratifying and condensing everything found in the *Vedas*, *Manu*, and the *smṛtis*, Ambedkar claimed that the *Gītā* sanctioned forever the violence perpetrated against his people (Ambedkar 1987: 3.81). He realized that there was really no possibility of true reform anywhere within Hinduism. At this juncture, he turned to Buddhism. It is quite possible that his projected volume on the *Gītā* never materialized because Ambedkar realized that it was as baneful a text as *Manu* and the *Vedas*, especially since its justification of caste had gained such prominence through Gandhi's convoluted reading. He perhaps realized that it was the issue of caste that absolutely had to be challenged directly. So, instead of devoting a volume to the *Gītā*, Ambedkar directed his energies to the fight over annihilation of caste. In *The Annihilation of Caste*, the work considered to be his masterpiece, Ambedkar rejected the *caturvarṇa* and its textual justification in the *Gītā*. In fact, he called for the destruction of all the holy books that legitimized caste. In this work, Ambedkar also further elaborated his thesis that Gandhi's interpretation of the *Gītā* meant the end of criticism.

The Annihilation of Caste (1936)

The Annihilation of Caste was written as the Presidential Address of the Jat-Pat-Todak Mandal, the Forum for the Break-up of Caste, a radical faction of the Ārya Samāj,[24] a reform organization that supported intermarriage and inter-caste dining. Ambedkar did not initially want to accept the invitation to present this address. He told the organizers that he did not usually take part in movements carried out by caste Hindus. But as they persisted with their invitation, he accepted. However, when Ambedkar submitted his speech to the organizers, they suggested significant revisions and asked him to delete his criticism of the *Vedas*. They also did not appreciate his critique of the 'technical side' of Hinduism.[25] Ambedkar did not make these revisions as he felt they would compromise the core of his talk. The organizers then unceremoniously disinvited him.

[24] The Ārya Samāj was a Hindu reform movement founded by Dayānand Saraswatī in 1875 promoting the authority of the *Vedas*. See Figueira 2002.

[25] See Anand 195–6, footnote #15 for contextual material on this subject.

He subsequently published the talk at his own expense, since he had already had it printed and needed to recoup the outlaid money.

Whereas in early speeches Ambedkar had consistently focused on caste disabilities, he had now become more militant. He was not asking to remove disabilities within caste structure but demanding the annihilation of caste itself. Those who had invited him to speak had focused their efforts primarily on family reform, not on Hindu societal reform. Ambedkar noted that without social reform you could not have the political reform that he felt 'cannot with impunity take precedence over social reform in the sense of reconstruction of society' (Ambedkar 1979: 1.42). Ambedkar began his address by offering a litany of recent (1936) atrocities committed against Untouchables and questioning Gandhi's silence and passive response to them. He noted that when Gandhi had on several occasions intervened, he tried to persuade aggrieved Untouchables to withdraw their complaints and not act against the caste perpetrators in response to the violence they had experienced (Ambedkar 2013: 216, footnote #14). Ambedkar responded to Gandhi's behaviour by asking whether, in an era when India was envisioning its freedom and release from colonial rule, Hindus were even fit for political power if they forbade Untouchables from access to public schools, public wells, public streets, bright and festive clothing, jewellery and ornaments or even certain foods (like clarified butter, if they could afford it)? Were Hindus even fit to govern if they attack Untouchables who dare to avail themselves of such 'privileges' (218)? He also rightly pointed out that the current reform movements did not focus on the removal of caste, but rather on matters such as child marriage and enforced widowhood, that is, issues that primarily touched caste Hindus (219). According to Ambedkar, caste had utterly destroyed public spirit, public charity, sympathy for the deserving, and charity for the needy (259). The encouragement of inter-caste dining and intermarriage was an inadequate remedy (285) in light of the actual situation of Untouchables. What was called for was the destruction of caste. One needed to deny the *śāstras* their authority, just like the Buddha and Guru Nanak had done (288), and to destroy the belief in those texts (such as the *Gītā*) that legitimized caste (287).

Ambedkar clearly took issue with the interpretation of the *Gītā* by 'reformers' such as Gandhi and Aurobindo who defended *varṇa,* by decoupling it from *jati* (caste) that they then denounced. By calling upon the *guṇa* theory, they pretended that caste was not birth-based. We have seen how the *guṇa* theory had become popular in the nationalist *Gītā* reception; it stated that the *guṇas*, or intrinsic qualities or attributes[26] alone determined *varṇa*. Ambedkar pointed out that *Gītā* 4.13, the *śloka* usually cited in support of this formulation, actually claimed that *varṇa* was determined by worth (*guṇa*) and action (*karma*), and not by birth alone as stipulated in the *Puruṣasūkta* of the *Rig Veda* (10.90). What truly mattered, however, was that the system described in the *Gītā* that the nationalist commentators found unproblematic in no way reflected the lived reality of Untouchables in India.[27]

With this reasoning, Ambedkar sought to demolish the arguments that Gandhi et al. presented to justify caste. It was not just a division of labour. It was a division of labourers! Such a division of labour was not a choice or dependent on aptitude, it was an accident of birth. Because of caste, Hinduism could not foster a unified society with a consciousness of its own. Caste was counter-productive since it hindered the development of solidarity. Society needed to be based on liberty, equality, and fraternity; caste shut down these options. So, Ambedkar concluded that caste must be annihilated and it must be done by destroying the belief in the sanctity of the *śāstras* that supported it. Ambedkar ends his address by saying that he decided to give up Hinduism and reject the *caturvarṇa* and the books, such as the *Gītā*, that legitimize it. In a moving declaration before his followers in 1935, he set in motion the vast conversion of his Dalit brethren:

> It was my misfortune to be born a Hindu. I do not have the capacity to eliminate this defect in me. However, I do have the strength to not accept the humiliating practices that I was subjected to as an Untouchable. It is within my capacity to reject the Hindu religion. I will say this publicly, that even though I was born a Hindu, I will not die a Hindu. (Cited in Roy 2013: 52)

[26] The *guṇas* are *sattva* (clarity and clearness of mind attributed to brahmins), *rajas* (passion and excitability associated with *kṣatriyas*), and *tamas* (darkness and confusion associated with śūdras).

[27] Ambedkar compared the situation of Indian minorities to the Irish situation. Ulster was intransigent to United Ireland, but the minorities were lukewarm or even negative. Ambedkar noted that the constitution makers cannot ignore the situation, just as the socialists cannot ignore economic reform or the equalization of property.

The stakes were high for the Hindu establishment, especially for Gandhi and the Congress Party. In an independent India, they did not want to lose the Untouchable voting block. Ambedkar had considerably raised the anti. So, Gandhi fought back; he inserted himself into Ambedkar's kerfuffle with the Jat-Pat-Todak Mandal. Unsolicited, Gandhi responded to Ambedkar's ungiven, yet published, speech in his journal *Harijan* on 11 July 1936.

Gandhi framed his response with an exposition of his theories on readability and translation. Because, according to Gandhi, not everything one reads in scripture is authentic, scripture needs interpretation that Gandhi claims can only be given by saints and seers since they have mystical insight making them the only true readers. Opposing Ambedkar's appeal to logic and individual conscience, Gandhi revisits the same argument that he presented in his *Gītā* analyses. Although he now acknowledges the questions that Ambedkar's indictment raised for him, he still does not address them. In short, his response to Ambedkar presents no surprises: it is evasive and patronizing; he shows his pettiness and contempt for Ambedkar. First, he mocks Ambedkar for the price he had charged for his pamphlet (Gandhi 2013: 322). It should have cost two annas and not eight. Here he is essentially telling his readers that Ambedkar's speech was worthless (Kumar 2015: 13). Then he notes that in publishing the pamphlet Dr Ambedkar shows that he was clearly a man who does not allow himself to be forgotten, accusing him thus of self-promotion. After insulting Ambedkar gratuitously on the price of the speech and his supposed vanity, Gandhi then presents his thoughts regarding who should read the *Gītā*. He claims that only those who are caste Hindus can give an authoritative interpretation of scripture (Gandhi 2013: 324). He next questions the texts that Ambedkar relied on for his interpretation, claiming them as having doubtful authority (328). He wondered whether they were even printed authorities or fragments.[28] He also questioned their authenticity and whether they said true things about untouchability and caste. What becomes immediately apparent here is that Gandhi was not going to debate the substantive issues raised by Ambedkar but chose

[28] This challenging of the existence and authority of the printed text was a strategy used also by nineteenth-century reformers. See Dayānand Saraswatī's experiences described in Figueira (2002: 105–19).

to turn the discussion around to issues of textuality, authenticity of texts, and the way in which, and by whom they are read.

Ambedkar begins his response to Gandhi's question regarding his authorities by simply stating that the texts he used to support his argument were the very texts that Tilak had used, implying that if they were good enough for the great brahmin reformer, they should be good enough for him (Ambedkar 2013: 333–56). After dismissing Gandhi's concern over the authenticity of the texts cited, Ambedkar then counters Gandhi's assertion that texts can only be understood by saints. He reminds the Mahātma that a number of saints believed that the canonical texts did not support caste and Untouchability. Besides, he notes, the ignorant masses, not knowing any better and believing what they are told, understand that the holy books enjoin the observance of caste and Untouchability. Moreover, saints are 'lamentably ineffective' as authorities. Some saints believe in caste (336) and some ignore the issue because they are concerned with the relation between man and God, not man to man (337). Besides, one does not usually go to saints when one wants to hear about the equality of man in the world, since saints are mainly concerned with the equality of all men in God's eyes.

Ambedkar's position was that religion speaks to the individual conscience, as opposed to Gandhi's privileging of certain (his and other saints') interpretations. Ambedkar noted that he accepts only interpretations of the *śāstras* given by saints who are noble and that he rejects Untouchability, asserting that the *śāstras* do not support it (Ambedkar 2013: 336). Let us keep in mind that Gandhi had earlier claimed that caste (which he rejects) has nothing to do with religion and nothing to do with *varṇa* (which he supports). In his response to Ambedkar, Gandhi had rather disingenuously maintained that all callings are noble, good, lawful, and absolutely equal in status, asserting even that the scavenger deserves the same respect as the brahmin teacher and is equal to the brahmin (Gandhi 2013: 326))! That Gandhi felt he could make such a claim truly begs incredulity, given the circumstances under which scavengers lived at the time. It is frankly insulting to socially disadvantaged Indians as well as to his reader's intelligence. Yet, Gandhi actually proposes that caste in India at this time did not denote superiority or inferiority. It just signified outlooks and modes of life. If there is a hierarchy, it cannot be blamed on the brahmins (Gandhi 1984: 22.154–5). That Gandhi proposed this argument (and did so with impunity) reflects the degree to which Hindu discourse on caste was truly disconnected from reality.

In his subsequent riposte to Gandhi, Ambedkar pointed out that, of all people, the Mahātma perhaps should not have accused him, as he did, of seeking publicity or publishing his pamphlet so as not to be forgotten. He noted that those who live in glasshouses, should not cast stones (Ambedkar 2013: 334). After duly noting how Gandhi had begun his response by insulting him, calling him mercenary, and accusing him of pathetically needing to stay in the limelight, Ambedkar then explains that he published his speech to provoke Hindus to think (333). He also notes that Gandhi completely ignored the issues he raised. So, he felt that he had to repeat these salient points. He identified them as follows:

1. Caste has ruined Hindus
2. To reorganize Hindu society according to the four *varṇa*s was impossible
3. To reorganize Hindu society on the four *varṇa*s was harmful because it degrades the masses, denies them access to knowledge and the right to bear arms
4. Society must reorganize to give liberty, equality, and fraternity
5. The sanctity of caste and *varṇa* must be destroyed
6. This destruction is to be done by discarding the texts that support caste and *varṇa*

Ambedkar recognized that Gandhi did not address any of these issues and had not answered his questions. Ambedkar noted that Gandhi had instead made several points that he would now answer.

Ambedkar countered Gandhi's assertion that a religion is judged by its best specimens and that the reform Gandhi advocated is meant to persuade the high castes Hindus to follow high standards of morality (Ambedkar 2013: 339).[29] Ambedkar responded that he was opposed to such an ideology (340), since it established a master–slave relationship (341). Ambedkar noted that Dayānand Saraswatī and the Ārya Samāj

[29] The ineffectiveness of this argument can be seen in Gandhi's own actions, as Hardiman shows (2004: 126; 348, footnote #14), when he lists how often Gandhi claimed that caste harmed no one.

saw *varṇa* according to the Vedic understanding that it was appropriate to one's natural aptitude. Ambedkar had no problem with such a definition (349), where *varṇa* is defined according to one's worth. He did, however, reject what Gandhi was claiming, that it was defined according to one's birth (350). He noted that even Gandhi personally diverged from the Vedic conception of an ancestral calling, irrespective of natural aptitudes (349). Ambedkar then denied the difference Gandhi claims exists between caste and *varṇa*. According to Ambedkar, they are both defined in practice by ancestral callings. Ambedkar then questioned why Gandhi even devised his strange interpretation. In part, he saw it as part of Gandhi's temperament and his much-vaunted simplicity. But a more damning answer was that Gandhi wanted to play the role both of a 'Mahātma' and a politician. If he opposed caste/*varṇa*, he would lose his place and power in politics. So, he came up with the idea that caste was bad, but *varṇa* was different and not bad. Ambedkar recognized the tension between Gandhi's political vision and his need for interpretive secrecy. He also recognized the people's right to the truth. Ambedkar was justifiably suspicious of Gandhi's reading of the *Gītā*.

Along with his response to Ambedkar, Gandhi had also published in *Harijan* (12 December 1935) a letter from the Secretary of the Jat-pat-Todak Mandel President, Sant Ram. This letter had sought to explain the cancellation of Ambedkar's talk (Sant Ram 2013: 329–32). The Secretary felt the need to justify his invitation to Ambedkar and ingratiatingly noted that Gandhi's philosophical differentiation between *varṇa* and caste was too subtle to be grasped by people in general (330) and dared to note that it was also impracticable because it advocated an ideal of the *varṇavyavasthā* (caste system) which justified clinging to caste and did great disservice by advocating an imaginary utility of the divisions of the *varṇas* and thus hindered reform (331).[30] Gandhi followed this letter with his reply to Sant Ram where he reiterated that the only noble interpretation of scripture is given by saints. Here too he claimed to reject untouchability and assert that the *śāstras* did not support it. He also reiterated that he believed in *varṇa* and not caste. It is interesting how Gandhi chose to

[30] One can only deduce that in publishing this letter, Gandhi sought to humiliate or alienate Ambedkar further.

insert himself so forcefully into this episode that did not concern him in any way and make himself a prime interlocutor. He simply took too much pleasure from Ambedkar's dismissal as the keynote speaker and sought the opportunity to assert his authority and co-opt the discussion, even if he had nothing new to say.

Gandhi differed from previous Hindu reformers who had sought to justify caste rather than eradicate it. Earlier reformers, such as Dayānand and even Vivekananda, advocated the Sanskritization of the lower castes, telling them to try and be like brahmins, learn Sanskrit, and be spiritual (Kolge 209). Ambedkar felt that Gandhi's tortured distinction between caste and *varṇa* allowed him to deceive himself and the people by preaching caste under the name of *varṇa*. Over the years, Gandhi's ideas concerning caste continued to be modified for the sake of exigency. Initially, Gandhi felt that caste was a useful institution if properly regulated.[31] For Gandhi, the Hindu caste system was a natural institution and it saved Hinduism from disintegration (Kolge 113). From 1920–7, caste and *varṇa* both delineated hereditary occupations for him. He had tried to merge caste into the system of the *caturvarṇa*. From 1927–32, however, he presents them as totally different concepts. Until 1927, they had been synonyms. Caste now became distinct; it was an excrescence like Untouchability.[32] Then, from 1932–45, Gandhi highlighted their differences and called for the destruction of caste.

Ambedkar's position was less strategically malleable. He felt that there could be no equality among the Hindus because the foundations of Hinduism rested on inequality and violence. There was violence in the authority that the *Gītā* placed on the *guṇas*. There was violence in the nationalist and Gandhian rhetoric on tradition. There was violence in *dharma*, especially as it was mystically condensed in the *Gītā*. Quite legitimately, Ambedkar had cause to suspect the mysticism in the *Gītā*. He reasonably saw structures of force and exclusion in it as well as in Gandhi's projection of satyagraha, non-violence and austerity onto this text (Kumar 2015: 29). Repelled by what the *Gītā* meant for his people, Ambedkar wisely turned the 'truth' of satyagraha against Gandhi by

[31] See letter to C.F. Andrews (25 May 1920), cited in Kolge 113.

[32] See the 'Brahmin-Non-Brahmin Question', cited in Kolge 140. For a summary of these attitudes, see Kolge 157 footnote #107.

claiming its counter-narrative. Ambedkar and his followers no longer wanted to be part of Hindu society (Jaffrelot 2005: 120). Concerning Gandhi, Ambedkar wrote:

> [H]e does not insist on the removal of untouchability as much as he insists on the propagation of Khaddar or the Hindu-Muslim unity. If he had he would have made the removal of Untouchability a precondition of voting in the party. Well, be that as it may, when one is spurned by everyone, even the sympathy shown by Mahātma Gandhi is of no little importance. (Cited in Jaffrelot 2005: 63)

In this quotation, we see Ambedkar's sense of humour and an appreciation of irony, traits not readily found in other readers of the *Gītā* we have examined in these pages. He recognized that Gandhi's claim that the *Gītā* spirit spoke *ahiṃsā* was not the most salient issue. Rather he saw that the strategies Gandhi put in place for reading the *Gītā* now meant that this text would never allow for the liberation of his people. But if, as Gandhi claimed, translating was no longer tied in any shape or form to the text under translation, and meaning depended on the reader's claim to lived experience, then there could be no hope for reform. In fact, Gandhi's methodology fomented textual violence meted out to his community. Such textual violence had been deployed over the centuries by traditional interpreters. Now, thanks to Gandhi's unique translation theory and practice, whatever authority the text might have retained as scripture and whatever it might say could be negated by anyone who claimed experiential authority. The caste Hindu, the godman, the great soul, the politician—the voices of whomever wielded power in a hierarchized system such as India—would certainly drown out the voice of the Dalit. Gandhi could claim that the *Gītā* spoke to *ahiṃsā*, but his strategy of translation and reading was built on an economy of violence that Ambedkar recognized all too well.

PART IV

THE WESTERN WARTIME, COUNTERCULTURAL, AND NEO-LIBERAL *GĪTĀ*

8

The Nazi *Kṣatriya* Ethos

Hauer and Himmler

> Je meurs dans la foi de la 'Bhagavad-Gītā' et du 'Zarathoustra': c'est là qu'est ma verité, mon credo.'
>
> Pierre Drieu la Rochelle, *Journal 1939–45*: 380

Introduction

The *Gītā* was a convenient source of reference in the context of global conflict. Its significance was partially due to its place in the Sanskrit epic. Otto von Bismarck (1815–98) and his ascension to power had done much to renew interest in heroic poetry and the *Gītā* became one of the texts that Germans used to formulate their understanding of the duties and privileges of a military caste (Sharpe 131). Just as it had been for Indian nationalists, so too in Germany, the *Gītā* sparked interest in the traits and behaviour that represented 'Aryan' qualities. For some German nationalists, the heroic vision that they had discovered in the *Nibelungenlied* and the *Heliand* could also be seen in the *Gītā,* the epic battle account of their 'other' ancestors (131).

As in the case of the Indian commentators, so too German translations and commentaries freely tailored the *Gītā* to polemical or ideological ends that were no less authoritative (Adluri 262–3). German Indology, however, was more interested in addressing its European peers than in grappling with issues of colonialization (266). My own initial work on the European literary reception of India touched upon the micro-level of this contact in terms of translation practices (Figueira 1989, 1990, 1991) as well as on the macro-level of exoticism (Figueira 1990, 1993, 1994, 2002).

The Afterlives of the Bhagavad Gītā. Dorothy M. Figueira, Oxford University Press. © Dorothy M. Figueira 2023.
DOI: 10.1093/oso/9780198873488.003.0009

I find it gratifying how, in the intervening years, there has been a veritable explosion in this field,[1] as scholars have focused on the degree to which German Indomania was always turned inward. In general, the Romantics had been less concerned with India itself and more focused on their own feelings (Sharpe 32). But German Indology took this exotic interest much further since they identified with the Indians as their putative ancestors. This identification fed into the German institutionalization of the science of religion (*Religionsgeschichte/Religionswissenschaft*) that had grown out of Romanticism. German Indology was also considerably influenced by German Idealism and its strains of anti-nationalism, and anti-materialism, all roots that it would share with National Socialism.

After Friedrich Schlegel had used Indian philosophy and literature to launch a broadside attack on Protestantism (Figueira 1989) and offered proof, according to Goethe, that the Catholic Church alone ensured salvation,[2] religious comparisons between Hinduism and Christianity became fairly common. But the religious polemic shifted direction entirely from F. Schlegel's alarming thesis. The *Gītā* now became a text that that could be seen as consonant with Protestant values. Whatever ethics could be read into the *Gītā* reflected virtues that could also be ascribed to Germans, such as an ideal of duty and a warrior ethos. The 'original' *Gītā* that German scholars would discover also proved to be remarkably 'Protestant' in its anti-clericism. Brahmin priests, like their Catholic counterparts, could be blamed for just about anything. Significantly, this new German narrative on the *Gītā* self-consciously rejected any whiff of quietism (Adluri and Bagshree 191). It eschewed the idea that salvation was to be found in the extinction of the Self in some pantheistic *brahman* (the reading favoured by Hegel). Rather they promoted a soteriology based on the continued existence of an active soul (*ātman*). In Cousin's reading, the warriors (*Schratrias*, in his parlance) were condemned to do battle even though it, like all else aside from 'the eternal principle', was nothing but an illusion. By the end of the nineteenth century, however, Hegel's views on Indian inertia and Cousin's understanding of action as error and illusion were no longer such desirable interpretations in

[1] See Germana (2009), McGetchin (2009), Cowen (2010), Kontje (2004), Rabault-Feuerhahn (2008), Marchand (2010). Even Sheldon Pollock (2006) has descended from the pure ether of Sanskrit studies to engage in comparative analyses, a far cry from his initial view of such work.

[2] See Struc-Oppenberg ccxxvii, cited in Adluri and Bagshree 190.

European interpretations of the *Gītā* and particularly in German translations and commentaries.

We have seen how in India the *Gītā* rationalized radical political action. Indian nationalists who had been seeking prototypes for their activities in the revolutionary movements of Italy and Ireland, soon discovered that more natural models could be found in their own history and mythology. Tilak initiated this return to native models of insurgency in his sanctification of Śivāji and the creation of popular festivals in his honour. Tilak claimed that this militancy was directly inspired by the *Gītā,* since it enabled him to resolve the problem of Śivāji killing his defenceless counterpart, Afzal Khan. To exculpate Śivāji, Tilak also claimed to be emulating the teaching of the *Gītā* and thereby encouraged others to follow suit. In *Kesari* (15 June 1897), he proclaimed that no blame could attach to killing, even of teachers and kinsmen, since such behaviour was taught in the *Gītā*. Śivāji had killed for the good of others, the *lokasaṃgraha* that Tilak inserted into and made a key feature of his translation of the *Gītā*. This chapter shifts back to Europe, specifically to Germany where nineteenth- and early twentieth-century scholars invested considerable effort in seeking to discover an 'original *Gītā*' to fit their needs. In order to draw the conclusions from the text that they desired, they claimed to analyse the text linguistically and philologically in order to strip away the accretions that had accumulated and obscured the *Urtext* that they insisted mirrored their own worldview. This process entailed rejecting large portions of the Sanskrit text as priestly distortions.

Several themes stand out in these German translations and commentaries on the *Gītā*. The poem is seen to proclaim a *kṣatriya* character that is deemed as fundamental to Indo-Aryan (alternately Indo-German) thought. This *kṣatriya* ethos of the original and authentic *Gītā* was felt to have been obscured over time by brahmin priests in favour of a more philosophical overlay. The German scholarship examined in this chapter highlights how this *kṣatriya* thematic was often infused with anti-Semitism. These German Indological translations and interpretations of the *Gītā* would subsequently fit very well with National Socialism's vision of male privilege, strength, and ruthlessness, culminating in the SS's idea of *Durchsetzungsvermögen* (commitment, enthusiasm, creative perseverance) (Poewe 141). For Nazi Germany, the *Gītā*'s pantheism confirmed one of the concerns that Nazis had with organized Christianity in general and with Catholicism in particular: a troublesome priesthood. The *Gītā* supplied the useful image of the *kṣatriya* as an alternative to the priest.

Indologists

In the essay entitled 'Deutsche Art' in a volume sent to soldiers during World War I, the German Indologist and translator of the *Gītā*, Leopold von Schroeder, wrote that the Germans were the authentic Aryans among all the Aryans; they comprised the purest, noblest, and strongest of the Aryan race.[3] It was this vision of the Germans and their connection with the ancient Aryans that may well have inspired Theodor Springmann (1880–1917) to translate the *Gītā* in the trenches of Flanders. In the introduction to his *Bhagavad-Gītā, der Gesang des Erhabenen* (1920), Springmann framed his translation to support Germany's imperial designs. He presented the German engagement in the First World War as the *Schwanengesang* of Aryan knighthood. Germany's involvement in the conflict was, as in the *Gītā*, a matter of duty (*dharma*) and action (*karma*). However, Springmann saw his war as not tied to disinterest, but rather as an expression of patriotism and the necessity of serving a cause. Springmann also brought a Hegelian vison of Indian fatalism to his rendition of the *Gītā*, no doubt fostered by the very act of translating it in the trenches. Killed in action shortly after completing his translation, Springmann died perhaps with the consolation of having performed his duty as a warrior. The focus of his translation efforts was, however, in no way unique. Early twentieth-century *Gītā* translations and commentaries emphasized the warrior ethos of the poem. They also sought to reclaim the Sanskrit text from the Theosophists who were felt to control it in the popular imagination both in India and abroad. Among these scholars who appropriated this Sanskrit text for German use, we can count Adolf Holtzmann, Jr., who formulated a pantheistic *Gītā* (1895); Richard Garbe who favoured a theistic *Gītā* (1905); Hermann Jacobi's epic *Gītā* (1918),

[3] 'Unter allen Ariern sind die Deutschen die echtesten, die am meisten arischen Arier. Den edelsten Grundzug dieser vornehmensten Völkerfamilie zeigen sie am reinsten und kräftigsten' (*Deutsche Weihnacht* 1914: 31, cited in Sharpe 131).

Hermann Oldenberg's Krishna-centric *Gītā* (1919); Rudolf Otto's trinitarian *Gītā* (1934), and Jakob Hauer's Aryan *Gītā* (1937).[4]

Following the scholarly methodology of the time, the late nineteenth- and twentieth-century Indologists set out to discover the true message of the text through a reconstruction of available recensions. Their larger project entailed the recovery of what was believed to be Aryan culture, then thought to be extant in Indo-Europeans who were in essence Indo-Germanics (Adluri and Bagchree 175). In *Die neunzehn Bücher des Mahābhārata* (1892–95), the Freiburg-based Adolf Holtzmann (1838–1914) distinguished the older *Gītā* from what he delineated as its subsequent versions. His original *Gītā* consisted of a pantheistic philosophical episode whose later accretions taught how it was pointless to fear death. In the nineteenth century, a general German fascination with the lure of death had been popular in Romanticism having found literary expression in Klopstock[5] and, more notably, in Goethe's *Werther.* So Holtzmann's claim that the *Gītā* had originally been a brief meditation on the fear of death (Adluri and Bagchree 164) and a brief battlefield encomium, would find a sympathetic reception in those Germans familiar with this literary trope. In Holtzmann's *Das Mahābhārata und seine Theile* (1895), this 'Indo-Germanic' *Gītā* was also described as rationalistic and proto-modern.

The Tübingen-based Richard Karl von Garbe (1857–1927), who produced the first direct translation of the *Gītā* by a German after Schlegel, presented an opposing view to Holtzmann. In his 1905 translation and commentary, Garbe claimed 'that the irregularities found in the *Gītā* stemmed from its composition in the second century BC as a strictly theistic tract glorifying Krishna and the pantheism of the *Upanishads*'. He speculated that this tract also was then subsequently altered by brahmins in order (most likely) to spread their duplicitous priestly agenda. In a subsequent article published in James Hastings's *Encyclopedia of Religion and Ethics* entitled 'Bhagavadgītā' (1909, vol. 2:53–58), Garbe depicts Krishna as a historical leader of a warrior tribe, a non-brahmin founder of the religion of his 'race' called the Bhagavata religion, which was a

4 For and in-depth analysis of these various translations, see Adluri and Bagchee (2014).

5 Friedrich Gottlieb Klopstock (1724–1803) a German poet who sought to move German literature away from its reliance on French models.

monotheistic and strongly ethical faith. The brahmins eventually took this religion over and added their pantheistic elements (Sharpe 11). So, in effect, Garbe accepted Holtzmann's thesis of the conflict between the *Gītā*'s pantheistic and its theistic contradictions. Unlike Humboldt and the previous generation, who might have focused on the literary aspects of the poem, Garbe viewed it primarily as a didactic work composed to disseminate specific religious and philosophical thoughts (Adluri and Bagchree 176–7). Garbe, however, agreed with Holtzmann that the *Gītā* was significantly influenced by what he identified as a primarily *kṣatriya* religion (Garbe 37). It was written by *kṣatriyas* who had played a prominent role in society and were the leaders of the people. Krishna, the warrior, had founded a monotheistic religion (27), the proof of which being that the older portions of the epic find him playing the role of the warrior and proclaimer of religious doctrines that were independent of both Vedism and Brahmanism (32). 'Krishnaism' was by nature a particularly ethical *kṣatriya* religion (32). Of the thematic triad of *bhakti*, *jñāna*, and *karma*, Garbe recognized *karma* alone as salvific (Adluri and Bagchree 199). Garbe did not focus on Holtzmann's speculations regarding the Indo-Germans. With Holtzmann and Garbe, we see a pattern clearly taking shape: The *Gītā* promotes monotheism. Any thoughts to the contrary are the distortions imposed on the text by priests. It foremost champions a warrior religion. Holtzmann and Garbe drew their conclusions by using the then prevalent methods of biblical hermeneutics which single-mindedly sought what was original in a text, what was true and authentic, and what accretions could be attributed to priestly machinations. As noted, it was a 'Protestant' reading, since it made the *Gītā* subject to the same sort of interpretation used in post-Reformation biblical scholarship.

Hermann Jacobi (1850–1937) also subjected the *Gītā* to biblical hermeneutic inquiry. While Garbe had assigned the *Gītā* to an austere, rational religion that was appropriate to ancient warriors, with Krishna as a founder of a *kṣatriya* religion (Adluri and Bagchree 209) that had been infiltrated by brahmins seeking an easy income, the Catholic Jacobi did not envision any priests (brahmins) infiltrating the *kṣatriya* religion and ruining it (211). Jacobi also discounted Holtzmann's and Garbe's separation of the theistic from the pantheistic elements in the poem; he saw rather their co-optation and exchange (208). Jacobi likewise focused on the *Gītā*'s monotheism and especially its portrayal of an incarnation which he quickly distinguished from that of Christianity. Holtzmann, Garbe, and Jacobi all agreed, however, on the general view that the *Gītā* should be studied in what they perceived as its earlier and later phases. They both accepted that Vedāntic redactors must have reworked the text. For this reason, they all embarked on a 'critical' editing process. Needless to say, this editing reflected their individual religious prejudices (215). In *Über die Einfügung* (323), Jacobi concluded that the philosophical elements of the *Gītā* were not original. In fact, the original text for Jacobi only consisted of 85 verses out of the critical edition's 700 verses (325).[6] Jacobi's considerably pared down rendition reconstructs the original as addressing heroic Indo-Germanic warriors, just as Holtzmann's version did. Following Garbe, Jacobi also focused on the monotheism existing in the worship of Krishna, an emphasis also shared by Hermann Oldenberg (1854–1920) in his 'Bemerkungen zur *Bhagavadgītā*' (321–38). As opposed to Jacobi, who saw the core of the poem to be 2.37, Oldenberg favoured 2.39 as the text's lynchpin. In Oldenberg's *Die Mahābhārata*, it was Krishna's *Siegernatur* that modern readers (male and female) found enticing (40, cited in Adluri and Bagchree 221). Oldenberg rejected Garbe's *kṣatriya*/brahmin distinction as a proto-Protestant iteration.

Rudolf Otto (1869–1937), a German philosopher and theologian (rather than an Indologist or Sanskritist), presented extracts from Chapter 11 of the *Gītā* in the appendix ('Beispiel einer numinosen Dichtung') to his best-known work, *Das Heilige* (1917).[7] All of his work on the *Gītā* would focus on its numinous quality, the key trait that Otto sought in all religions.[8] In 1933, Otto published *The Original Gītā,* where he too followed the methodology of modern biblical criticism's compositional history of the Sanskrit poem (Sharpe 153). In subsequent works, *Die Urgestalt der Bhagavadgītā* (1934) and *Lehrtraktate der Bhagavad-Gītā* (1935), Otto pursued Garbe's thesis of an early theistic *Gītā* that had been corrupted by pantheistic interpolations (Adluri and Bagchee 233).

[6] This trend was common among German scholars. Out of the 700 verses of the critical edition, Richard Garbe found 536 to be authentic and original, Hermann Oldenberg 83/700, Theodor Springmann 594/700, Rudolf Otto 144/700, and Jakob Hauer 141/700.

[7] Translated as *The Idea of the Holy* in 1923.

[8] Otto was also interested in the *Gītā*'s exposition of *bhakti*, a topic he would also examine in Otto's other major publication, *West-östliche Mystik* (1926), translated as *Mysticism: East and West*. Both this text and *The Idea of the Holy* are still important books in religious studies.

Otto discovered many such interpolations in the *Gītā*. He excised them in keeping with the German text-critical ideas of reconstructing the original core. By constructing this original *Gītā,* Otto hoped to produce a final version. He accepted Jacobi's idea that the original *Gītā* ended at 2.37. He rejected, however, Jacobi's thesis that the original *Gītā* concluded so quickly because it only set out to teach the necessity of fighting due to the soul's indestructibility and the knight's (notice the Western medieval epic terminology) code of honour. Rather, Otto felt that the original text ended at this juncture because its major theme was the experience of the numinous, the essence for Otto of religious experience according to Luther's *De Servo Arbitrio*. A devout Lutheran himself, Otto sought not only the numinous in everything (including the *Gītā*), but also an austere vision of God.

According to the German scholars noted here, the *Gītā* did not primarily teach Sāṃkhya-Yoga philosophy or *bhakti*. In fact, they believed that any real exegesis of the text was hardly necessary. The *Gītā* just needed some editing to put its central message into relief. For Otto, this message was that one had to be open to the idea of the holy as a *mysterium tremendum* (Otto 1934: 9). Otto brought a vision of the irrational as holy, personal, and incommunicative to his understanding of the *Gītā* (Adluri and Bagchee 261). All one had to do was approach the text from one's own subjective expectations and impressions, something that, since Hegel it seems, many of these interpreters and translators were doing anyway. Now we can add specialist scholars to this group. The difference with Otto was that he openly claimed (much like Gandhi) that all one had to do was experience the text from one's subjective expectations. The other German commentaries of the time still feigned objectivity.

For Otto, the *Gītā* speaks of a reformation where Krishna emerges triumphant. The lone hero, Arjuna, a warrior who has been abandoned by cultural norms and reason, is forced to turn to his personal intimation of the Divine (Adluri and Bagchree 261). We must note that Otto's vision of a warrior *Gītā,* where the hero determines his own ethics and revolt, found expression primarily between 1932 and 1936, while he was teaching at the Georg-August Universität in Göttingen. It was during the *Nazizeit*, however, that his interpretation would move from an emphasis on the mysterious and numinous to a narrower focus in the classes that he taught. In his seminars, Otto presented the *Gītā* as a text dealing with an alternative quest for salvation and compared it favourably to Christianity. The Nazi management of the university reacted favourably to this narrative. It forced students, even those who did not study religion, to attend Otto's lectures on the *Gītā* (Alles 187). Otto thus serves as a very important transition figure in the German reception of the Sanskrit poem before and during the Nazi era. He did not, however, embrace the National Socialist cause.[9] It is even possible that Otto eventually realized how his career fixation on the mystical and the numinous had contributed to the climate of irrationality (something that Carl Jung and others involved in the Ascona group of visionaries never did).[10] In any case, Otto was not a true believer, unlike his colleague the SS Indologist J. W. Hauer (1991–62).

Hauer

Jakob Wilhelm Hauer (1881–1962) was at the height of his career during the period of Nazi rule. He profited greatly from his association with the regime (Junginger 1999: 237) and became the most prominent historian of religion in National Socialist Germany. Both Otto and Hauer built a pedagogy that focused on Aryan religious thought and, especially, the *Gītā* (Alles 179). Both saw the essence of religion to be the experience and a sense of the Holy (*das Numen*). But their encounter with the numinous source of religions, while similar in some respects, differed significantly. They pursued different projects in their work in *Religionswissenschaft* (the science of religion). Otto was interested in the internal dimensions of the numinous and Hauer examined the role of race in refracting numinous experience into empirical religious forms (Alles 193). Whereas Otto sought a profound encounter in ancient Judaism, Hauer did not.

[9] Otto was not forced to comply with the system, since he had retired in 1929, and lectured as a private citizen. He fell from a tower in October 1936 and died shortly after. There was some speculation that he had jumped.

[10] Near her house on the hills overlooking Ascona and Lago Maggiore. Olga Frobe-Kapteyn, a Theosophist, set up a site for the Eranos conferences where people would convene and share research on spirituality. The area, specifically Monte Verità, had already become at the turn of the twentieth century an alternative colony for artists, philosophers, and thinkers such as Hermann Hesse, C.J. Jung, and Rudolf Steiner. With the Nazi seizure of power, Jews were excluded from Eranos gatherings. Many of the work produced there was subsequently published in the Bollingen series out of Princeton.

In fact, Germans who believed in an Indo-Germanic tradition, such as Hauer, felt that they needed to be liberated from Christianity, seen as a Judaic religion as odious as Judaism itself. There was a shared interest in comparing India and Germany, but Hauer towed the National Socialist line and Otto, although he championed the *kṣatriya* in the *Gītā,* did not. They also shared the German idea that religions arise out of experience (*Erfahrung*) (Hauer 1935: 209, 218, 231, cited in Alles 189). But as opposed to Otto, Hauer followed a tradition already in place in Schleiermacher, that sought to free Christianity from its Near Eastern Semitic form. Hauer was dedicated to reforming Christianity according to a Germanic-German spirit (Hauer 1935: 38). He also sought to uncover the *Gītā*'s Indo-Germanic essence.

Otto, in his quest for the original *Gītā* (1934b; 1935b: 24) had undercut the National Socialist worldview (Alles 188). By effecting an etymological analysis, Otto had focused on the text's various layers. Seeking to discover the numinous in Krishna's form and revelation (Otto 1934b: 23; 1935b: 120). Otto ignored what Hauer saw as essential: the role of action, duty, destiny, sacrifice, and struggle (Alles 188). Hauer acknowledged Holtzmann's heroic Indo-Germans, Garbe's reconstruction of the past, Jacobi's search for the original Aryan text, Oldenberg's focus on the combatants' ethical quandary, and even Otto's revalorization of an irrational and personal religion. Like his mentor, Garbe, Hauer also sought an Aryan *Gītā* with the aim of using it for a programme of national renewal (Adluri and Bagchee 274). He employed the methods of his predecessors, separating out the original elements from what he saw in the later Indian (i.e. not Indo-German) and Dravidian material (Adluri and Bagchee 274) in the hope of reconciling the tension in the text between contemplation, what was for him the inward part of the Indo-German soul, and the outer mandate of the *Gītā*'s call for action. According to Hauer, it was this outward urge that was needed to spur modern Germans to meet their challenges (Hauer 1934: 38). Germans needed to reconnect with their ancestors' values. Just as ancient Germans had done in the past, so too must the Germans in the 1930s adopt ancient Aryan practices in order to solve their social and political problems. Hauer came to this vision of the ancient Indo-Germans through a circuitous path and sought to apply it to the current political values of his time.

Hauer began his training as a future SS and SD scholar as a young missionary in India working for the Basel Mission Society. He had been sent to Malabar at the age of 18. He served as a school principal from 1907–11. In order to remain a missionary teacher, however, one had to be university-educated. So, the Mission sent Hauer to Oxford where he received a BA in 1914. He then returned to Germany, where he was granted a Ph.D. in 1918 and took his *Habilitation* in 1920 under Garbe. In that same year, he founded the German Faith Movement (DGB or Deutsche Glaubensbewegung). During this time, he was also interested in the anthroposophy of the esotericist and philosopher/clairvoyant Rudolf Steiner which Hauer viewed as an outgrowth of the Theosophy of Mme. Blavatsky and Annie Besant. His interest in Anthroposophy was short-lived because it included 'Jewish magic' with evolutionary theory, Greek and Egyptian hermetic traditions, the Kabbalah and, more significantly, it was tainted as 'occult'. Anthroposophy did offer Hauer, however, a vision of *Ergriffenheit* (profound emotion) and a need for the discovery of a powerful personality to grasp the living intellectual heritage of a people in order to solve its needs and valorize its ethically specific lineage. For Hauer and the National Socialists, this powerful personality would be Hitler and the valorized lineage would be that of the Indo-Germans/Aryans.

Hauer's new religion really took off in 1919 after the November Revolution, and his leaving his service to the church. With a small group that he led, the Bible Circle, Hauer entered the *Bünde* (political associations) scene that broke away from the Christian community. He then turned the Bible Circle into a new organization, the Köngerer Bund (Bund der Köngerer), of which he was the *Führer*.[11] It was essentially a mix of the Evangelical and the Free German Youth movements. He would lead this group until 1934. By rooting his organization in the German Youth Movement,[12] Hauer was able to bring together various other groups: Germanic and Nordic religions, Free thinkers and Free

[11] The various *Bünde* of the German Youth Movement placed emphasis on the personality of the leader, each group had its own *Führer* and newsletter. In general, intellectuals, like Heidegger and others who were in the habit of building student circles around them, cashed in on this German desire for a leader (Poewe 35).

[12] The first phase of the German Youth Movement (1896–1919) consisted of the Wandervogel, the Bund, and Volunteer Corps. The second phase consisted of Hauer's Köngerer Bund joining the Volunteer Corps in 1926 (Poewe 38).

Religious (Freireligiöse). So Hauer's German Faith had become a larger group; but it oversaw various new religions, ranging from versions of Hinduism to Nordic neo-paganism. It presented a vague notion of the sacred and eternal power, rather reminiscent of Otto's concept of the numinous. Religious development was not to be measured by Christian dogma, since Hauer felt that Christianity was as much a foreign faith to Germany as Islam was to India. While opposed to social Darwinism and anti-Semitic, the German Faith accepted Jesus. Founding a new religion, as Hauer had done, was not so strange for its time. Annie Besant had founded a new religious amalgamation of Christianity and Hinduism. So it was not extraordinary for Hauer to juxtapose the Indo-Aryan *Gītā* with Indo-Germanic mysticism, sagas, and literature (Hauer 39). He understood full well the then-prevalent philosophical and political interest in the regeneration of the *Volk.*[13]

Hauer's career moved along with his political ambitions. In 1922, he was *Privatdozent* of the general history of religions (*Allgemeine Religionswissenschaft*) at Tübingen (Junginger 1999: 53). He was subsequently named the Professor of Indology for a short period of time at Marburg before finally moving back to Tübingen as the Professor of Religious Studies, taking the Chair of his *Doktorvater*, Garbe. In 1934, he became a member of the National Socialist Dozenenbundes. In 1937, he joined the NSDAP and soon after became Untersturmführer in the SS (*Schutzstaffel*). That same year, he was named 'Ordenliche Professor für Indologie, Vergleichende Religioneswissenschaft und Arische Weltanschauung'. His very title showed how the institutional study of religion had moved away from religious history to ideology. History of Religion now showed a need to negate the taint of a Jewish worldview that was seen to have permeated not only Judaism but also Christianity, Marxism, Materialism, and Liberalism (Goodrich-Clarke 1998: 122, cited in Poewe and Hexham 2005: 202). In 1942, Hauer was made head of the Aryan Institut which later became the Germanisch-Deutsch Institut (Junginger 1999: 211–12).[14]

[13] Heidegger held that the *Volk* could become authentic by retrieving its roots, whether in history, literature, language, or the landscape (Poewe 5).

[14] From its inception, this Institut was a Nazi institution (Alles 184). It was made up of four divisions (Indology, comparative religion, Aryan worldview, and occultism). The Aryan worldview division dealt with the Old Germanic worldview, the later Germanic worldview, and German proverbs. The section on occultism was established at the request of Himmler.

Hauer had dreams that his vision of an Indo-Aryan religion would become the faith of the new German man, especially as it was envisioned and embodied by the SS (Poewe 18). He easily made the transition from the philological to the *völkisch* approach to religious studies. In the process of freeing Germany from the imperialism of 'Jewish' Christianity, he moulded his theories to serve the Third Reich. He joined racist blood mysticism to Indian metaphysics (Kurlander 185). However, this toxic blend, combined with Hauer's charismatic (compared to other leaders in the NSDAP) personality did not endear him to competitive and envious Nazi authorities. It was decided by management that he concentrate less on political activities and more on his scholarship, his Aryan Seminar at Tübingen, and his work as an academic spy (Kurlander 185), reporting on other scholars in the field of religion.

Hauer worked closely with Walter Wüst (1901–93), another Indologist who directed the Ahnenerbe, the Ancient Heritage organization, founded by Heinrich Himmler (1900–1945) as part of the SS to work Indo-German 'ethical' ideas into National Socialism (Poewe 7). Wűst had been appointed by Himmler to add legitimacy to the Ahnenerbe, since it had initially (thanks to Himmler) been peopled by occultists and individuals with sketchy credentials. Wüst was the Professor of Indo-German Studies in Munich[15] and took over his post in the Ahnenerbe from the 'scholar' of ancient religions and symbols, Herman Wirth, in 1938. Both Wüst and Hauer sought to use *Religionswissenschaft* to build a new Aryan belief system (Trimondi 76) and to make religious studies an instrument of what they hoped would become an Indo-Aryan Germanic religion. But Wüst and Hauer had little to do with text-based Indian philology or linguistics (Grünendahl 2008: 47, cited in Adluri 260). Their work for the Ahnenerbe was to provide information about the ancient Indians in support of Himmler's various esoteric beliefs. Once Hitler decided to crack-down on the occult elements in the party, Himmler needed to replace the charletans and hucksters he tended to favour with real scholars.[16] Wüst

[15] When researching in Munich in the early 1990s, I realized the pervasive role of Nazi ideology in Indological scholarship. Wűst's department, the Institute fűr Arische Kultur und Wissenschaft, had become the Institut fűr Indologie und Turkologie. When I was conducting research there, it still had a considerable collection of Nazi Indological scholarship.

[16] Hauer is still cited in Germany as an accepted authority. His apologist, Angelika Maliner, includes Hauer among the canonical interpreters of the *Gītā* (Maliner 2007: 25, 33, 20, cited in Adluri 201).

was thus placed at the head of the Ahnenerbe in 1936 to save it from what consisted of (and was perceived even by the Nazis as) lunatic fringe dilettantism. His predecessor, although a rabid anti-Semite, had to be replaced because he had been too virulently loud in his anti-Catholicism and believed in female seers.

Hauer would contribute to the seriousness of the Ahnenerbe by devoting his scholarship to showing Germans how their forebearers, the Indo-Aryans, accepted their destiny and acted in fulfilment of their duties (Alles 188). From 1934–58, Hauer published three almost identical versions[17] of his essay on *karmayoga* in the *Gītā*. The first iteration in 1934, which we will examine here, *Eine indo-arische Metaphysik des Kampfes und der Tat* 'validated the bellicose aims of the National Socialists in power' (Benavides 263–4). It was the task of the modern German to fulfil his heroic duty violently (Benavides 264). This was the central theme of the *Gīta* for Hauer, its core that all other translations heretofore had failed to discern. It was necessary for modern Germans to access this message, since it preserved a significant phase of their Indo-German religious history, even though it had been diluted by other influences.

Hauer's book resulted from a seminar on the *Gīta* he offered in the Winter of 1933–4 (Junginger 1999: 322), where he judged the Sanskrit text as prefiguring a full statement of National Socialist themes. The *Gītā* elucidates the fundamental Indo-Germanic motif: the necessity of acting even when one was faced with a conflict of duties. For Hauer, the *Gītā* wonderfully expressed the tension (*Spannung*) between two life poles of the Indo-Aryan populations found both in ancient India and in modern Germany: the inward path of family and the outward path of duty; the movement between duty (*Pflicht*) and honour (*Ehre*) (Hauer 4, 5, 12, 59). Acknowledging that they are in the hands of destiny and cannot escape their biology, modern Germans must learn from the *Gītā* how their ancestors, the Indo-Germans, acted through sacrifice and struggle. They must act without regard for the consequences of their actions. It is only

[17] The fifth chapter of Hauer's 1934 book on the *Gītā* appears again in *Glaubensgeschichte der Indogermanen: Das religiöse Artbild der Indogermanen und die Grundtypen indo-arischen Religion* (Stuttgart: W. Kohhammer 1937; then in 1958 as the third chapter in *Der Yoga. Ein indischer Weg zum Selbst kritische-positive Darstellung nach den indischen Quellen mit einer Übersetzung der massgeblichen Texte unbearteitete und den 2 Band erweiterte Auflage des Yoga als Heilweg* (Stuttgart: W. Kohhammer 1958).

in this way can that they become free and heroic (Hauer 6, 19, 23–4). The *Gītā* leads Germany toward this path of action,[18] a *Bundeskrieg* like the one fought in the *Mahābhārata*. The epic battle was actually a war on caste order (*Sippenordnung*). Blood remains a major cultural value for the Indo-Aryans. Like in the epic, the looming civil war in Germany required warriors to kill their relatives (4). The cause of this war or any attempt to prevent it was not at issue. The question was whether one stands before one's destiny (*Schicksal*) or capitulates. The answer given in the *Gītā* is that one must fight for honour, no matter the ensuing guilt (4). One must not be tied to ethical concerns because they hinder one's ability to act. Hauer claimed that the *Gītā* proves just how Indo-Aryans knew this truth. Life and battle are always tragic (6), but the tragic makes heroes. This realization is common to the *Gītā* and to the German faith (5). Germans had seen this dilemma before: it was a specific Indo-German problem and a tragic motif found in all the German sagas. Hauer claimed that the *Gītā* was a particularly important text for modern Germans because it specifically instructs them how to unravel the meaning of their Indo-Aryan lives. The *Gītā* teaches modern Aryans how to discover and to perform the acts required of them (5).

The movement outward places Indo-Germanic existence in conflict. The need to act beyond good and evil necessarily incurs guilt, as Arjuna feels in the beginning of the *Gītā*, when asked to commit a crime against his own blood (Hauer 4). He is told that one can only live by destroying another life (14–15). This is not a problem to be solved intellectually nor is it a problem that can be avoided. Indo-Germans cannot cease to act (5, 17). Krishna instructs Arjuna that, beyond the conflict of the warrior to fight or to love his family, he must return to the foundation of his empirical existence: honour and duty (11). It is a duty placed on him by his integration into his community as the bearer of a function and as a member of a caste with important functions.

What we have in Hauer's analysis is an interpretation of the *Gītā* from the perspective of a German generation that is fighting for a *völkisch* life

[18] Hauer concluded that the original *Gītā* probably ended at the end of Chapter 2, although the revelation of Chapter 11 was also probably part of the original. The rest of the poem that has come down to us consists of accretions describing the guilt-laden tragedy of action and the subsequent mastering of the tragedy through battle and action (Hauer 13). In this respect, Hauer agrees with Garbe regarding the length of the original text (Hauer 72, note 7).

(Hauer vi). The Aryans came from the north, the greater German realm of Scandinavia and the Baltics, and eventually made their way to South Asia, arriving in India three centuries before Christ (1). The proof of this migration can be seen in their Indo-Germanic language (Sanskrit), the Urindo-Germanic religion, and the fact that the Indo-Aryans are racially linked to Nordic Indo-Germans.[19] These Aryans differ racially from the other main *Glaubenswelt,* the Semites who include Jewish Christianity and Islam. The Near Eastern Semite is miserable, sinful, and depraved. They need to be saved from damnation by a mediator and atoner (Hauer 1935a: 232). In contrast, the Indo-Germanic strain found in Hinduism, Buddhism, and the pre-Christian Germanic faith, is in a relationship with the Divine. Indo-Germans possess an indwelling divine spark that nothing can destroy (177). The religion expounded in the *Gītā* bypasses moral prescriptions (25); it places Indo-Germans beyond good and evil. It foregrounds the role of the warrior elite as opposed to the 'womanish' Christian.

According to Hauer, the ancient Aryans followed non-violence out of a respect for life. The *Gītā* drew upon this sense of respect and pushed it to its roots. It taught that even when duty forces one to kill, one is still exhibiting non-violence, because actions do not extinguish life. The *Gītā* teaches that the frightful becomes tolerable. Guilt is not guilt, because it belongs to the temporal order and is a human necessity (Hauer 10). The *Gītā* teaches one to do one's job and in the process incur no guilt but rather fulfil one's destiny (18). Hauer drew a direct connection between the *kṣatriya* ethos and the German/Prussian military tradition. He bemoaned that the West, although entranced by Indian philosophy, had not paid proper attention to the tragic wisdom found in the first two chapters of the Sanskrit poem (13, 17). He believed that it was high time for Germans to focus on the heroic setting delineated in the *Gītā* (Sharpe 130) and act accordingly.

The *kṣatriya* must spill blood (Hauer 21) because war is holy work. Anyone who tries to restrict the sovereign will of the people (*Volk*) has no right to live anyway (Hauer 1935a: 113, cited in Alles 191). The vision of destruction portrayed in Krishna's revelation of his cosmic form should be understood as a Eucharistic act (53). Besides, killing or

[19] Hauer cites Gunther's *The Nordic Race among the Indo-Germans of Asia* (1934).

being killed is just an illusion (10). The operative analogy here is the following: German morality demands the same struggle as Arjuna's task in the *Gītā* (1935a: 120). Modern Germans too must perform their duty without questioning the results. Such behaviour makes them and their actions honourable. The *Gītā* thus becomes important because it sets down the rules for behaviour for modern Germans. It identifies the conditions that make dutiful heroic action possible (27). In order to attain the proper character and purity of will, the *Gītā* teaches Germans how to eliminate desire and maintain a proper disposition (27–33). The Yoga expounded in the Sanskrit poem is, in fact, the root of the Indo-Germanic affirmation of the world, the absolute Transcendent, the wholly Other (*dieses Ganzandersein*) (50, 68).[20] Hauer quotes Arjuna to the effect that the historical fate of the individual, including death in battle, is not the end. It is merely a minor episode in a series of births. Death becomes an *Augenblicksschicksal* (the destiny of the blink of the eye). The *Gītā* teaches Germans that death is not final. A fighter must kill, as a 'performing organ' in what is happening ('*das ausführende Organ des Geschehens im Weltlauf*') (10). Moreover, any guilt that accrues, any culpability that fate forces on us, is not eternal either, only temporary.

One can clearly see how Hauer's interpretation of this text was an easy fit for National Socialism. If death and guilt are relative or illusory (Hauer 13), then the deeds demanded by the Nazi regime of its soldiers, particularly the SS of Himmler for whom Hauer was working and translating, are justified and condoned (13). This tragic situation for the guilt-afflicted German warrior in battle was inevitable. It was important for that warrior to understand his inherited Aryan destiny and jettison any superficial Christian notions of good and evil (14). Hauer saw the *Gītā* as a text teaching the Indo-German warrior how to control his inner emotions and thoughts. The Sanskrit poem presents struggle and slaughter as the ultimate path of initiation. Struggle (*Kampf*) is, in fact, destiny (Hauer 3) and the path to heaven (11). You do not stop killing just because your opponent is a relative or relation ('*dem eigenen Blut*'). This is what the old Indo-Germans believed, and what modern Germans must accept when they fight for honour and *Reich*. It is central to the Indo-Germanic soul

[20] The liberating Indo-Germanic attitude found in the *Gītā* is the same as that found elsewhere in German thought, specifically in the work of Meister Eckhart (Hauer 47, 54).

(4). Hauer laid out a justification for doing deeds even if they are steeped in guilt (60–1). Krishna teaches 'hereditary duty' even if it is tied to some repulsive fate and guilt (61). Hauer maintained that the true German faith consisted of a line of Indo-Germanic *Führer* figures (*Führergestalten*). The Indo-Germanic worldview, originating in the ancient Aryan, flowed into National Socialism (Junginger 1999: 148, cited in Poewe 30).

Let's not forget that Hauer belonged to the SS and SD. As an academic high-ranking SS officer, he spied on colleagues, such as Martin Buber, and supplied Himmler with information of their activities.[21] In the early days of the regime, Hauer (like Heidegger) contributed to getting Jewish colleagues excluded from public and professional life. Although Hauer did not personally participate in mass murder as an Untersturmfűhrer in the SS, his vision of the *vita activa* of the Aryan warrior was central to the new German *Glaubensbewegung* as was his distinction of it from the *vita contemplativa* found in Buddhism and Yoga. Hauer's role was significant in helping his fellow Germans decide between action versus contemplation, act versus self-reflection, and war versus meditation. He believed that these conflicting choices challenged all Indo-Germans. Hauer resolved these tensions with his vision of the warrior-*yogi* (Trimondi 79). While Hauer's hands were never covered in blood, his student and the secretary of his German Faith Movement was condemned to life in prison for active participation in killing 13,000 people in the Ukraine. At his trial, Hauer's student claimed he was merely following Hauer's teaching (Hakl 146, cited in Trimondi 88). Hauer's interpretation of the *Gītā* legitimized such useful participation in the National Socialist state. He taught that if you understood the Sanskrit poem's thematic, the tragedy of life could be mastered by action and Germans could help shape the community, people, and state (*Gemeinschaft, Volk, Reich*) in line with the goals for which Germany was destined. Following their ancestors in the *Gītā*, modern Germans were compelled to conquer the Self in order to become heroic individuals (*sieghafte, heroische Menschen*) (Hauer 65).

Just as his teacher Garbe had done, Hauer produced a critical reconstruction of the Sanskrit text that tied the *Gītā*'s idea of duty to the

[21] Buber was unaware that Hauer had spied on him and sent in reports to the Nazi command in the 30s. After the war, Hauer had the supreme nerve to ask Buber for a letter of recommendation so he could get off easily during his process of denazification and Buber wrote for him a very generous letter of reference aiding him in his postwar return to teaching (Junginger 1999: 137).

contemporary situation. His product was also an amalgamation of Jacobi's epic *Gītā* and Otto's esoteric reading (Adluri and Bagchee 277). Whereas the earlier Indologists had tried to understand the epic past, Hauer sought in the *Gītā* guidance for the criminal, murderous present (277) He offered National Socialism a *Gītā* in which the heroic aspect of its 'northern blood inheritance' is based on a metaphysics of battle. Its message is to fight (Hauer 3), with action as the essence and the insight that the Indo-Germans bring to the world process. This heady brew that Hauer concocted was well received. By 1937, four years after he had been personally initiated into the SS and the SD by both Himmler and Reinhard Heydrich (1901–42),[22] Hauer was the chief Nazi Indologist teaching that, according to the *Gītā,* war is the Germans' fate (4).

It is important to stress that Hauer was not an occultist (of which there were a considerable number surrounding Himmler in the early days of the regime) and not a Romantic outsider (Trimondi 90). He really saw in Indian religion the building blocks for the creation of a new religion where he hoped to formulate a Germanic or Indo-Aryan belief system based on race.[23] He was a qualified and accepted Indologist and what he concocted was in essence a mixture of Indian philosophy and mythology with elements of National Socialist ideology to form a National Socialist *kṣatriya* religion (Trimondi 94). Hitler had decided early on not to meddle with religion. Christianity was going to be dealt with (i.e. neutralized) after the war. According to paragraph #24 of the Nazi Party programme, the National Socialist Party claimed to represent a positive Christianity without committing to doctrines of specific confessions. The government united all Protestants in a single, national-church Christianity, which led to the founding of the *Völkisch* faithlers, Young Reformers (loyal to the State but an independent church) and Deutschen Christen (rejecting the Old and New Testament but considering Jesus as a fellow Aryan) (Poewe 111). The Catholic Church, since Rome had signed the 1933 Reich Concordat, was restricted in its activity. Hauer's race-based science of religions was, therefore, useful in reinforcing elements of the National Socialist worldview. Beginning with the Köngener Bund,

[22] Reinhard Heydrich, the principal architect of the Holocaust, was chief the Reich Security Main Office.

[23] See Hauer's *Religion und Rasse* (1941) for his comparison of the Semite and Aryan.

Hauer allied with Free (non-confessional) Protestants who opposed traditional Christianity. He hoped his new religion would offer a third way, an alternative to both Catholicism and Protestantism. However, the Nazi leadership, fearing Hauer's role in the German Faith Movement, forced him to resign as its *Führer*. The movement could subsequently be taken over and become just another unthreatening appendage of the NSDAP.

Several factors contributed to sidelining the German Faith Movement in October 1934. There was no longer need for it to play a role in church politics, since Hitler by then had given up making a place for religion in the Nazi state. Also, Hauer had been neutralized by radicals in the Movement under the instigation of Heydrich (Poewe 140). Hauer would continue to propagate his German Faith, but he was not permitted to claim it as the religious soul of National Socialism (Poewe and Hexham 2005: 203). For all his racist Indo-German rhetoric, Hauer was not really a good fit institutionally. In fact, Himmler, Heydrich, and Wűst would all eventually come to oppose him. Nevertheless, Himmler took Hauer's work on the *Gītā* seriously and often consulted it (Trimondi 91).

Himmler

In *Theses Against Occultism and the Stars Down to Earth*, a series of post-World War II essays, the philosopher Theodor Adorno (1903–69) noted that the power of occultism was rooted, like Fascism, in its appeal to 'semi-erudite' individuals 'driven by the narcissistic wish to prove superior to the plain people' though incapable of carrying through the 'complicated and detached intellectual operations' necessary to reach an understanding of the natural world. Adorno goes on to say that the occult stands next to racism and anti-Semitism, providing a socio-political and scientific 'short-cut' by reducing complex problems to a handy formula. To those who felt 'excluded' from educational privileges', the occult offered the 'pleasant gratification' that they belonged 'to the minority of those who are in the know' (Adorno 424–44, cited in Kurlander 132). I would extend this theory to include a subsection of the educated classes as well.[24] Many of the Western authors described in this volume were

[24] It is a common fallacy, especially prevalent today, that only the uneducated indulge in extreme and/or fascistic belief structures. It is also true that the more brutal enforcers of Nazi

highly educated and yet they supported some very extreme and loony ideas. Their enchantment with Indian thought was the type of 'short-cut' Adorno described, or what I have termed an 'alibi' or 'elsewhere', fabricated to make them more interesting to themselves and others (Figueira 1994). The particular fascination with the *Gītā* spoke not only to this text's adaptability and accessibility, but also to the general lure of the exotic across Adorno's 'semi-erudite', the educated, and even the over-educated segments of the population.

We know that Heinrich Himmler's interest in Eastern thought and the occult was widespread and catalogued in the reading lists he kept for each year. In 1924, Himmler noted that he had read Hermann Hesse's *Damien* and *Siddharta* which presented allegories on the life of the Buddha and his teaching of austere dedication and duty. The Ferryman depicted in *Siddhartha*, teaches the value of detachment from passion. At the end of Hesse's novel, there is a description of a mystical vision when all creatures are reborn.[25] As Himmler's doctor/massage therapist Felix Kersten reports him saying, reincarnation was an Indo-Germanic tradition. In fact, Himmler himself believed that he was the reincarnation of Henry I (875–936), also known as Henry the Fowler, a Saxon king (Kersten 153).[26] Kersten also details Himmler telling him that what one does on earth does not affect the next life and that *karma* was not inexorable fate but something one could control and alter. One cannot escape what one has done on earth, but one can choose to alter one's fate in the next life (152). German belief demands no surrender to divine grace. Rather rebirth is tied to race; one is reborn 'in the clan' and 'in the same blood'.[27]

policies tended not to come from the ranks of the criminal classes, but from the educated caste; there were a large percentage of lawyers, scientists, and university professors who joined in enthusiastically in Gestapo atrocities.

[25] As Kersten noted (154), the belief in reincarnation was a popular thread running through German intellectual life, as in Goethe's remark to Charlotte von Stein, 'In some distant past you were my sister or my wife.' One thinks also of remarks on the subject by Richard Wagner, Hölderlin, and Schopenhauer.

[26] He established that the SS Ahnenerbe yearly celebrate Henry I in the Heinrichsfeiern and one of his officers composed a Henry Song (König Heinrich Marsch) in Himmler's honour (Trimondi 49).

[27] Karl August Eckhardt, a professor of Legal History, had given his book *Indische Unsterblichkeit, Germanische Glaube an die Weltverkörperung in der Sippe* (Weimar 1937) to Himmler for review (Longerich 269).

It was from his reading of Hesse that Himmler first came to appreciate the concept of *karma*, as documented in his letters and speeches (Padfield 91–2). Hesse's influence on Himmler was not something he publicized, since this author had been banned by Hitler shortly after the Nazi's ascension to power. Nevertheless, Himmler continued to believe in *karma* and reincarnation, but he needed more legitimate sources for such interests. Himmler's promotion of Hauer and his *Gītā* scholarship should be seen in this context. After all, Hauer's (and Wűst's) assignment to the Ahnenerbe had been part of a process of professionalizing that organization. What Himmler appreciated most in the *Gītā* and Hauer's interpretation of it was the image of the *kṣatriya* as a warrior caste (Padfield 2001: 91 and Poewe 130). The concept of the *ksatriya* had fascinated Himmler since the 1920s as evidenced by his booklist of 1925, where he lists Franz Haiser's *Freimauer und Gegenmauer im Kampf um der Weltherrschaft* from which he devised his understanding of the warrior caste, its *kṣatriya Moral*, and the *kṣatriya Erziehung* (Trimondi 28–30). So, even before Himmler read the *Gītā*, he was fascinated by the idea of cultivating a warrior elite. It was, therefore, a short step for Himmler to develop an interest in the Aryan ancestry of the Germans, their belief in *karma* and rebirth, and their institution of a *kṣatriya* caste. It is also not surprising that Himmler would take interest in Hauer's book on the *Gītā* when it first appeared in print in 1934. The references Himmler makes to the *Gītā* most likely come from his reading of Hauer. What he most appreciated about the *kṣatriya* was the image of the warrior's courage, ardour, endurance, and unwillingness to flee in battle, all themes Hauer repeats throughout his book. We might also keep in mind Hauer's emphasis on the *Gītā*'s justification for the killing of kinsmen. Hauer's book was published in the same year as the Night of the Long Knives, when his supervisor Himmler helped orchestrate the liquidation of Ernst Röhm (1887–1934)[28] and the elite of the SA (Trimondi 85), an instance of killing one's *eigenen Blut*, if there ever was one. Whether or not Hauer's reading of the *Gītā* was used to justify the purge of the SA in Himmler's mind is not something I hope to prove. But it is clear that use of the Sanskrit poem to sacralize terror (Kurlander 225) was entrenched in his notion of the *kṣatriya* ethos and

[28] An early member of the Nazi Party, Röhm was the commander of the Sturmabteilung (SA), the Nazi party militia.

his interpretation of the *Gītā* (Trimondi 86–9). Himmler defended his lethal decisions and the detachment he expected from the SS with words spoken by Krishna to Arjuna that Hauer had popularized (Padfield 91–3).

Himmler added to his understanding of the *Gītā* an interesting anti-clerical twist: all the Indo-Germanic *kṣatriyas* (populating the *Gītā*, *Edda*, and the *Nibelungenlied*) had been 'degraded' in an act of revenge by brahmin priests bent on eliminating 'warrior-yogis' as dangerous rivals (Trimondi 81–2, Adluri and Bagchee 69–76, 81–3, 131–2). Himmler drew parallels between the *kṣatriya* as he understood this figure from his own reading of the *Gītā* (or Hauer's interpretation of it) and visions of Germanic warriors from the *Edda* and the *Nibelungenlied*.[29] But, according to Kersten, the *Gītā* was especially loved (Kersten 1953: 189, cited in Trimondi 32). Himmler had a 'fondness' for it (152). Kersten claimed that it was one of Himmler's favourite books and that he carried the *Gītā* with him at all times (192). He 'particularly prized' the *Gītā* for its 'great Aryan qualities'. Kersten reports Himmler was often in the habit of scrolling through his vade-mecum (a notebook or aidemémoire carried at all times) to recite quotes from the *Gītā* that he had taken down, along with citations from other sources such as the *Edda*, *Ṛg Veda*, *Buddha's Sermons*, and his favourite astrological works (Trimondi 26–7; Kersten 1953: 189). But it was the *Gītā* that was especially influential in providing Himmler with his vision of the SS warrior (Kurlander 53). The archaic warriors of the Indo-Aryans developed self-control in the *Gītā*. In Himmler's *Geheimreden*, he presents them as a *Herrenvolk* that shows no Christian compassion (*Barmlichkeit*) (Trimondi 89). Here one is reminded of Hauer's depiction of Krishna teaching Arjuna that it was his 'hereditary duty' to fight even when it entailed a repulsive fate and engendered guilt (Hauer 61). Hauer claimed that, in Indo-Aryan times, this innate duty was associated with one's caste (Hauer 26). For Himmler, in modern times, the caste in question was his SS (Poewe and Hexham 2005: 206). Himmler could thus defend his lethal decisions and his call for detachment from their consequences with words spoken by Krishna to Arjuna that Hauer had disseminated. Hauer had systematically laid out

[29] The *Leselist* (reading list) can be found in the Bundesarchiv Koblenz, see booklist #235, cited in Padfield 90.

the justification for slaughter by claiming that the Aryan warrior is called to act by his fate, even if his deeds are steeped in guilt; it was his hereditary duty (*angeborene Pflicht*) to perform such acts (Padfield 91–3: 403).

Himmler had taken from Hauer's interpretation of the *Gītā* several central themes that particularly inspired him: that war was an initiation, that life and struggle were always tragic, and that war can be a mystical union with the Godhead that leads to enlightenment (Trimondi 83). Kersten relates Himmler saying:

> I admire the wisdom of those Indian religions which insisted that kings and high state officials should withdraw and meditate in a monastery for two or three months every year. One day we'll institute something on those lines.... How do you think Ribbentrop[30] or Ley[31] would take to monastic life? I would like to see Lay's face if he was offered sour milk and black bread for nourishment and the Bhagavad-Gītā to sustain his soul. (Kersten 156)

I cite the above odd conversation to show how the *Gītā* and its warrior ethos spoke to Himmler's vision of himself, his inflated sense of his spirituality in contrast to what he felt was the vanity, stupidity, indulgence, and corruption of the other Nazi high commanders. He saw himself doing his job because it was his duty. He saw himself as leading an austere life, like a holy man. He claimed to have preferred concerning himself with spiritual matters and his flower beds. He admitted that he would rather be the Minister for Religious Affairs and dedicate himself to positive achievements (Kersten 148–9). But he acknowledged that things had to be done. He told Kersten that he tried to do good, to relieve the oppressed, and to remove injustice. He admitted that he did not have the heart for all the things to be done for reasons of state. Such was the self-portrait Himmler held of himself as a spiritual esotericist. Violence was a necessary burden placed on him. It was his duty as a warrior, someone who did not actually see service in the First World War and was squeamish when he forced himself to view an extermination at Auschwitz.[32] But he fully embraced

[30] Joachim von Ribbentrop, Minster of Foreign Affairs from 1938–45.

[31] Robert Lay headed the German Labor Front from 1933–45.

[32] On another visit to Auschwitz, he brought his young daughter Gudrun along, a rather grotesque 'Take your daughter to work' day of which there is ample photo documentation.

the detachment from passion that he read in the *Gītā*. He sought to instil this detachment in the SS and cited how, like the warriors in the *Gītā*, they should be detached from sorrow, pleasure, fear, and wrath (Poewe and Hexham 2005: 206–7).

Himmler used the *Gītā* to legitimize the behaviour of the Waffen SS (combat units within the military) and the SS Totenkopfverbände (Death's Head units who administrated the concentration and extermination camps) (Trimondi 89). For Hauer and Himmler, the *Gītā* legitimized Nazi atrocities on a spiritual level (Hewitson 67). You can do what you might think is wrong for a higher cause. The SS can commit genocide. While all are expected to serve the State, only the elite can lose their soul by doing horrible things for their country. This is the 'highest ethical duty' to overcome bourgeois sentimentality (77).

The most forceful image of Himmler's appropriation of the *Gītā* appears in an episode described by Kersten. One day Himmler recited a passage to him of which he was particularly fond and often evoked. It is the memorable quote from 4.7–8:

> Sooft der Menschen Sinn für Recht und Wahrheit verschwunden ist und Ungerechtigkeit die Welt regiert, wer ich aufs Neu geboren, so will es das Gesetz. Ich trage kein Verlangen nach Gewinn.
>
> Whenever men lose respect for the law and truth, and the world is given over to injustice, I will be born anew. Such is the law. I have no desire for gain. (Kersten 152)

Himmler told Kersten that he felt this quote perfectly described Hitler; it was 'made for Hitler', who rose up out of the Germans' deepest need. When the German people had come to a dead end, Hitler was one of those brilliant figures who appeared. Goethe had appeared for the sake of art, Bismarck for the sake of the military, and Hitler for the sake of the political, cultural, and military combined. His appearance had been ordained by the *karma* of the German world. It was preordained that he should wage war against the East and install Germanness in order to save the world (Kersten 1953: 189). Hitler was an avatar who descended to earth in a time of crisis in body, mind, and soul (152); he was a figure of the greatest brilliance who had become incarnate (152).

The *Gītā* explained the appearance of Hitler as an avatar. It provided a template for what Himmler envisioned as the *kṣatriya* ethos, a fantasy he expressed as early as 18 March 1925, the founding year of the SS:

Kschatrijakaste, dass műssen wir sein. Das ist die Rettung.
Kṣatriya caste, that's what we must be. It is our rescue/salvation.[33]

Conclusion

Hauer dedicated *Eine indo-arische Metaphysik des Kampfes und der Tat* 'to the fighting race' (*das kämpfende Geschlecht*) (Hauer vi). Just as the *kṣatriya,* the German is called upon to fight. They share a common tragic fate: the door of heaven stands open to the warrior and it is wrong for them to stay at home rather than die in battle as their eternal duty demands (Hauer 1934a: 11). The *Gītā* is to be seen as a testament to one of the most important phases of the Indo-Germanic faith. The immigrant Nordic-blood Aryans who arrived in India exhibited not only spiritual sophistication but acted and struggled (1). The *Gītā* had taught them that action did not extinguish itself and the frightful was terrible. It also taught them that guilt was not eternal and unatonable. Guilt belonged to the temporal order and was part of earthly and human necessity (10).

German scholars of religion, like good German translators, were acting out Martin Luther's role in creating a new German consciousness, based on linguistic identity (Shirer 1990: 236). They shared Luther's anti-Semitism and his belief in obedience to political authority (Adluri 287). They took Luther's belief in the salvific role of translation and Hegel's method of abusing translation practices to their natural conclusions. The movement toward the Aryan Other through translation was necessary for the construction of the new Aryan Self. But the treatment of the *Gītā* need not be normative. In many instances, there was even no need to defer to experts, when appropriating the authority of the text. All one required was 'a little sophistic speculation' and 'a little armchair theorizing about "history"' (Adluri and Bagchee 264). In quite a few translations and interpretations of the *Gītā*, we witness how anyone could draw any conclusion they wanted from this text. These interpreters and translators

[33] See the Bundesarchiv Koblenz: Himmler NL 126/9, nr. 235, cited in Trimondi 27.

readily assumed the role of those very brahmins they either respected or scorned.

The *Gītā* is sometimes seen as less interesting in and of itself than as the confirmation of ideas its interpreters and translators themselves hold dear as reflections of their place in the world. The German *Gītā* translations and commentaries, in particular, are as colonizing as those of the British. The only difference was that in translating the *Gītā*, the English directed their hegemonic designs outward (toward India) and the Germans read the *Gītā* with an eye to dominating Europe (Pollack 77, cited in Adluri 2011: 253). As early as Herder, and the Romantics, through to the Nazis (and maybe even up to the current-day German bourgeois burnouts hanging out in new-age Indian ashrams), India has always existed for Germans to engage in polemical arguments about Germany and its flaws. It offers an opportunity for them to make polemical arguments regarding German identity. To cite Dietrich Bonhoeffer (1906–45),[34] who in light of his representative position in German religious circles and their belated resistance to the Nazi regime, knew from whence he spoke, German intellectuals could not accept 'that the world had come of age' and that they were like all suffering humanity and had to recognize their true situation and manage their lives in weakness and with grace (Bethge 1970: 773, cited in Poewe 1). They found this task difficult and sought an alibi, an elsewhere, in India.

[34] A German Lutheran pastor, theologian and anti-Nazi. He was a founding member of the Confessing Church. He was executed at Flossenbürg Concentration Camp for involvement in the July 20 plot against Hitler.

9

Is This What Krishna Meant?

T.S. Eliot and J. Robert Oppenheimer

The saint may renounce action, but the soldier, the citizen, the practical man generally—they should renounce, not action but its fruits. It is wrong for them to be idle, it is equally wrong to desire a reward for industry. It is wrong to shirk destroying civilization and one's kindred and friends, and equally wrong to hope for dominion afterwards. When all such hopes and desires are dead, fear dies also, and freed from all attachments the 'dweller in the body' will remain calm while the body performs its daily duty, and will be unrestrained by sin, as is the lotus leaf by the water of the tank.

E.M. Forster, 'Hymn before Action'[1]

We waited until the blast had passed, walked out of the shelter and then it was extremely solemn. We knew the world would not be the same. A few people laughed, a few people were silent. I remember the line from the Hindu scriptures; the *Bhagavad-Gītā*: Vishnu is trying to persuade the Prince that he should do his duty; and to impress him he takes on his multi-armed form and says, 'Now I am become Death, the destroyer of worlds.' I suppose we all thought that, one way or another.

J. Robert Oppenheimer[2]

[1] E.M. Forster: *A Tribute*. New Delhi: Rupa 2002: 142–4, cited in Chandan 2007: 63.
[2] Cited in Richard Rhodes, *The Making of the Atomic Bomb* 1986: 676.

The Afterlives of the Bhagavad Gītā. Dorothy M. Figueira, Oxford University Press. © Dorothy M. Figueira 2023.
DOI: 10.1093/oso/9780198873488.003.0010

Indian studies scholars have claimed that the Western reception of the *Gītā* contributed to the refusal to take India seriously (Halbfass 1988, Hulin 1979, Droit 1989). But, in the preceding pages, we have seen how the Hindu 'Song of the Lord' was taken quite seriously; it had a varied life in the West beginning with its translation into English by Charles Wilkins in 1785 and subsequent translation by A.W. Schlegel in 1823 as well as the commentaries by Wilhelm von Humboldt, G.W.F. Hegel and Victor Cousin. Embraced in the West as a text akin to the Bible of Hinduism, it influenced Ralph Waldo Emerson, and Henry David Thoreau. Quite a number of Westerners sought in the *Gītā*, models for conduct that would either inspire bravery or collide with the vision of fatalism (Figueira 1994). The *Gītā*'s call for action was never so apparent than in the readings of this emblematic Sanskrit text during the World Wars and particularly, during the Second World War, as witnessed in the preceding chapter and here in this examination of its reception by T.S. Eliot and J. Robert Oppenheimer.

T.S. Eliot

Thomas Stearns Eliot (1999–1965) shared Emerson's admiration for the *Gītā*, claiming that in his experience it was the next greatest philosophical poem after the *Divine Comedy*.[3] Eliot also shared Whitman's and Emerson's habit of sprinkling his poetry with foreign words (Figueira 2020). His most famous appropriation of Sanskrit terminology is found in *The Waste Land* (1922) which concludes with the customary formal closure found in all *Upanishads*: '*shantih, shantih, shantih.*'[4] But, earlier in the same poem, in Section V, 'What the Thunder Said', Eliot teases his readers with other Sanskrit words and sounds. He repeats the rumblings of thunder ('*Da, Da, Da*') that he borrows from the Hindu god Prajāpati and admits in another note that he had requisitioned the injunction from the *Bṛhadāraṇyaka Upanishad* 5.1: '*Datta, Davadhvam, Dāmyata.*'[5] In

[3] See the 'Dante' essay in Eliot 1932: 219.

[4] 'Peace, Peace, Peace' (line 43). Eliot explains his use of this terminology in a note.

[5] See line 432, translated from the Sanskrit as 'Give, Sympathize, Control'. Eliot directs his reader to the translation of the *Upanishads* by Paul Deussen (*Sechzig Upanishads des Veda* 1898: 489). But he may well have taken the reference from the work of his Sanskrit teacher,

these instances, one can get the sense that Eliot used Sanskrit terms much in the same ornamental manner as he quoted from Dante or Rimbaud in their original languages. Is it a form of cultural appropriation, especially since after Eliot has the Thunder God speak Sanskrit, he then has his words interpreted by Western voices (Brooker and Bentley 1990: 191)? Can we say that Eliot used Sanskrit terminology as a means of rejecting the possibility of interpretation (200), in much the same way as Hegel did? Did his evocations of India signal a willingness to engage the Other on a profound level?

One thing is certain: Eliot did not share the eclectic enthusiasm for Indian thought evinced by a number of the literati of his time. As a Director at Faber, he wanted no involvement in popular translations of the *Gītā*. He avoided W.B. Yeats's desire to promote the books of the Hindu teacher Purohit Swami (1882–1941).[6] Eliot, was too knowledgeable about Indian philosophy to engage in promoting what he considered popular commercialized visions of Hinduism. In fact, he was more informed regarding Indian philosophy than any American literary figure before and perhaps even after him, certainly more adept than the Transcendentalists. Yet, critics have not taken his involvement with Indian philosophy as seriously as they have viewed the Concord contingent's grasp of the material. English literature scholars and critics tend to see Eliot's use of Indian thought as fragmentary or, in describing it, they indulge in their own exoticism, as when Cleanth Brooks notes that *The Waste Land* contains 'the oldest and most poetical truth of the race' (Unger: 343). Eliot's use of Indian philosophical themes has even been attributed to simple psychological motivations, such as his need to check his 'drive of desire' (336). For the most part, Eliot's critics brush aside his Indian references as accidents, errors, or inconsistencies that have crept into his work.

The scholarship addressing Eliot's evocations of India is largely negative and generally dismissive (Gross 213). Conrad Aiken saw it as evidence of Eliot's overall 'decadence' (Perl and Tuck 129, n. 6). Helen

Charles Rockwell Lanman, 'Hindu Law and Custom as to Gifts', where he explains how Prajāpati taught 'Da, Da, Da dāmyata, datta, dayadhvam' (see Narayan Rao 86–7).

[6] Faber eventually published four volumes of the Swami's work. Eliot had avoided writing the introductions, avoided associating with Yeats on these projects, and refused to promote them (Sinha 44).

Gardner, who disliked Eliot's Christianity, cared even less for his allusions to Hinduism. She saw the introduction of Krishna in 'Dry Salvages' as an error that destroyed the harmony of the poem.[7] William Blisset accepted the *Four Quartets* as a Christian exposition, but found it unfortunately mixed with incompatible non-Christian themes. Philip Wheelwright dismissed Eliot's use of Indian philosophy as an awkward synthesis of Hindu ideas and Heraclitus.[8] H.H. Wagoner agreed with Gardner, especially her understanding of the *Gītā* as exhibiting an element of 'quietism' that could just as easily have also been culled from Christian thought. This last critic did not even grasp that such quietism is nowhere present in the *Gītā*. These English literature critics/professors, who have no knowledge of the *Gītā* or possess only a second-hand erroneous knowledge of it, still felt they could pass judgement on Eliot's understanding of the material (McCarthy 1952: 34).[9]

From the perspective of a comparatist, it is not so surprising that these English literature scholars would be so opinionated. It is, however, troubling the degree to which they felt fully justified in discussing Hinduism in such an uninformed manner.[10] Let me say something here that might strike some readers as outrageous, but is something I have heard voiced also by scholars in other fields in the humanities. It is the following: many English literature professors suffer from a tendency, all too prevalent in their discipline (at least in the US), of thinking that one is an expert on just about everything, because one has studied English literature, considered the acme of humanistic training. These same English literature professors who may view Comparative Literature scholars as superficial (and we are sometimes), have no problem viewing themselves as omniscient. Moreover, their expertise in pontificating on other fields does not take the form of a dialogue with other experts, that is, talking sociology with sociologists, as is the aspiration of Comparative Literature, but rather

[7] Helen Gardner, 'Four Quartets: A Commentary' in B. Rajan (1947: 69) and B. Rajan ('The Unity of the Quartets' in B. Rajan (1947: 87), cited in Srivastava (1977).

[8] Certainly, the theme of impermanence can be attributed to Heraclitus, but Eliot is actually referencing Krishna and Arjuna here, suggesting that he was talking about India and not Greece.

[9] We witnessed the same dismissal of Indian influence in the reception of Thoreau. Mark Van Doren (1916: 95) discounted India's influence on Thoreau: '[T]he total influence of Oriental philosophy upon Thoreau was neither broad nor profound.' See also more recently Robert Sattelmeyer (67–8) who was dismissive of Thoreau's interest in India which 'was relatively short-lived and led to no discernible literary results', all cited in Hodder 1993: 412, footnote 29.

[10] For more on critics, see Vimala Rao (1981).

understanding sociology enough to impress another English literature scholar. We see this same disciplinary arrogance when English literature scholars approach the foreign,[11] as in the criticism of the Indian influences on T.S. Eliot. I was quite surprised at how much has been written on India and Eliot.[12] Even a very astute scholar such as Balachandra Rajan, who happened to be of Indian origin and whom I knew to have a sophisticated knowledge of the culture, addressed Eliot's use of Indian thought as a 'maze of Oriental metaphysics' that was 'uncomfortably sinuous'. Such comments say more about the field of English literature, its role in the American/British university, and its relation to the Other than it does about Eliot. Be that as it may. It does not answer the question posed here: Did Eliot use Indian thought seriously or was his cultural appropriation merely ornamental, as quite a few English literature scholars would have us believe?

The significant difference between Eliot and the other non-specialists in Indian languages and philosophies examined in this volume was that he was quite proficient in Sanskrit. Beginning in 1911, after his return from the Sorbonne, Eliot studied Sanskrit in the Indic philology classes he took for two years with Charles Rockwell Lanman (Eliot 1934: 43–44, cited in Rao 1963: 572).[13] He had enrolled in Indic Philology 1A and 1B (elementary Sanskrit) with Lanman in his first year reading *Lanman's Reader*, Hertel's edition of the *Pañchatantra*, and the *Gītā*). Then in 1912–13, he took Indic Philology 4 and 5 (Pāli) with Lanman, reading selected dialogues of the Buddha and the sacred books of Buddhism. He also did Indic Philology 9 (Philosophical Sanskrit) with James Woods and read the *Yoga Sūtra* of Patañjali. In short, one third of his graduate classes at Harvard dealt with Asian philology and philosophy. In a letter to K.S.N. Rao, Eliot wrote of having read the *Gītā* in Sanskrit. (Rao 1970: 92, cited in Howarth 201). Eliot abandoned the study of Sanskrit, however, in the

[11] The same tendency has unfortunately been institutionalized in the American configuration of World Literature. The world, with little understanding of its languages and histories can (and should) be taught often acontextually in English translation.

[12] For an early summary of this criticism, see McCarthy (1952).

[13] Lanman had studied Sanskrit at Yale with William Dwight Whitney, who himself had studied in Tübingen under the renowned Vedic scholar Rudolf Roth. The President of Harvard, Charles Eliot, who happened to be T.S. Eliot's cousin, had brought Lanman to Harvard where he inaugurated the Harvard Oriental Series and wrote the *Sanskrit Reader*, still in use today.

spring of 1913. In lectures Eliot much later presented in Virginia, he described these studies laconically. Eliot confessed:

> Two years spent in the study of Sanskrit under Charles Lanman, and a year in the mazes of Patañjali's metaphysics under the guidance of James Woods, left me in a state of enlightened mystification. (Eliot 1934: 43–4).[14]

Eliot went on to clarify that he had concluded at the time that he would have to forget thinking and feeling as an American or a European in order to pursue these studies, something he did not care to do.[15] The bottom line is that Eliot knew his Sanskrit, had read Indian philosophy in the original (at least the *Gītā*, some *Upanishads* and Patañjali), and was far more informed than any American writer commenting on India or the *Gītā*. His knowledge of India was a direct result of his translations from the Sanskrit (along with some translating from Pāli). Having translated and annotated the *Gītā*, Eliot viewed it as different from philosophy. He felt that it addressed more worldly concerns. As Eliot observed in a 1931 essay on Pascal, even the most exalted mystics must return to the world and use reason to employ the results of their experiences in daily life. But they should do so in an informed manner. Eliot had not felt compelled, for example, to take sides during the Spanish Civil War, noting that it did not directly concern him; he was a mere observer and should reserve judgement on it. In 1937, he commented that on situations where he felt that he did not have sufficient knowledge:

> Partnerships should be held with reservation, humility and misgiving. That balance of mind which as few highly civilized individuals, such as Arjuna, the hero of the *Bhagavad Gītā*, can maintain in action, is difficult for most of us even as observers.[16]

[14] Helen Gardner would later parody this quote claiming that Eliot's poem left her as mystified as he had been by his studies of Patañjali.

[15] This statement is in no way odd, given that further study would have demanded great commitment and a shift in his ways of thinking. He felt that he was unable or unwilling to take this step. After deciding to drop Indian philosophy, Eliot bought a copy of F.H. Bradley's *Appearance and Reality* at the Harvard Coop (cited in Howarth 206).

[16] Eliot writing in the *Criterion*, cited in Ricks 252.

This generally cautious attitude would subsequently change as conflict became closer to 'highly-civilized individuals' such as himself.

Indian thought had, indeed, influenced his poetry. In a 1946 radio talk on 'The Unity of European Culture,' Eliot admitted:

> Long ago I studied the ancient Indian languages, and while I was chiefly interested at that time in philosophy, I read a little poetry too; and I know that my own poetry shows the influence of Indian thought and sensibility. (Cited in Howarth 1964: 201)

And indeed, this sensibility finds clear expression in Eliot's last poetic work, the *Four Quartets*, which were written between 1936 and 1942. This work deals extensively with desirelessness and detachment, all central themes in Indian thought and particularly central to the *Gita*. In 'Little Gidding,' Eliot wrote:

> There are three conditions which often look alike
> Yet differ completely, flourish in the same hedgerow:
> Attachment to self and to things and for persons, detachment
> From self and from things, from persons; detachment
> From self and from things and, growing
> Between them, indifference
> Which resemble the others as death resembles life,
> Being between two lives—unflowering between
> The live and the dead nettle. (1969: 195)

A similar expression of detachment can be found in the last section of the second quartet, 'East Coker,' where we learn that: 'For us, there is only the trying. The rest is not our business' (Eliot 1969: 182). This message nicely parallels the *Gītā* 2.47, where Krishna first explains detached action:

> *karmaṇyevādhikāraste mā phaleṣu kadācana*
> *mā karmaphalahetur bhūr mā te saṅgo'stv akarmaṇi*

> Certainly, you have the right to your action,
> But never the fruits of your action at any time
> You never become the cause of the fruit of your action.
> You should never be attached to not doing [your duty].

Another key theme in Indian thought, suffering, animates the second movement of the third quartet, 'Dry Salvages':

> Where is there an end of it, the Soundless wailing,
> The silent withering of autumn flowers
> Dropping their petals and remaining motionless;
> Where is there an end to the drifting wreckage,
> The prayer of the bone on the beach. (Eliot 1969: 185)

What might be seen as a Hindu understanding of suffering appears also in the third section of 'Dry Salvages' where Eliot even features the *Gītā*'s battle scene and Krishna justifying the killing of his kin to Arjuna who shrinks from battle. Krishna urges Arjuna to fulfil both his *dharma* and his appointed role in the cosmic drama. Eliot suggests that one cannot comprehend the Lord's will:

> I sometimes wonder if that is what Krishna meant—
> Among other things—or one way of putting the same thing:
> That the future is a faded song, a Royal Rose or a lavender spray... (187)

He then reiterates the central teaching of the *Gītā*—that one should act without being concerned with the fruits of one's actions: 'And do not think of the fruit of action' (188).

The Krishna and Arjuna depicted in the middle movement of 'Dry Salvages' stand for the resolute pursuit of life. They warn that whatever we are doing at this moment is what we are destined to do in eternity. Eliot asks us to consider whether we are doing what we would like to be doing in eternity and if not, amend ourselves (Howarth 205). It is significant that Eliot does not end his poem by saying 'Fare well', but rather 'Fare forward, voyagers.'

> So Krishna, as he admonished Arjuna
> On the field of battle.
> Not fare well,
> But fare forward, voyagers. (Eliot 1969: 188)

These sentiments resonate with what Krishna actually admonishes Arjuna to do:

> antakāle ca mām eva smaran muktvā kalevaram
> yaḥ prayāti sa madbhāvaṃ yāti nāsty atra saṃśayaḥ (8.5)
>
> Who at the time of death thinks of me alone, leaves the body and goes forth, he reaches My Being; there is no death.

The voyagers can be saved if they heed the advice of Krishna and only perform action without thoughts of the Self. In his advice, Eliot is essentially paraphrasing the above quote. One can die at any moment (not the immanent death facing Arjuna), so one should be intent on the highest sphere of being and thus fructify the lives of others.

Eliot is reworking several key themes present in the *Gītā*. He is not emphasizing the *Gītā*'s focus on the soul as unborn, eternal, and everlasting, nor emphasizing its theme of the world as illusion. What Eliot takes from the *Gītā* is its concept of disinterested action (*karma yoga)*—it is Arjuna's duty (*dharma*) to fight. But Eliot completes Krishna's words with an important modification—whatever one dwells on, one attains upon death (i.e. is fructified in the next life, if one is reborn). Here too, Eliot expresses the central truth of the *Gītā* 8.6–7:

> yaṃ yaṃ vāpi smaran bhāvaṃ tyajaty ante kalevaram |
> taṃ taṃ evaiti kaunteya sadā tadbhāva-bhāvitaḥ
>
> tasmāt sarveṣu kāleṣu mām anusmara yudhya ca
> mayy arpitamanobuddhir mām evaiṣyasy asaṃśayaṃ
>
> On whatever Being one is thinking at the end when one leaves the body,
> That being alone, O son of Kunti, one reaches when one constantly dwells on that Being
> Therefore, at all times, meditate on Me and fight with mind and reason fixed on Me.
> You shall doubtless come to Me.[17]

[17] Philip Wheelwright points out the almost literal translation of the *Gītā* 8.8 ('Eliot's Philosophical Themes' in Rajan 1947: 103–05, cited in McCarthy 37).

But contrary to the *Gītā*'s injunction that disinterested action leads to one's salvation (understood in the Hindu context as the release from rebirth), Eliot speaks of the fructification in the lives of others.

> At the moment which is not action or inaction
> You can receive this: 'of whatever sphere of being
> The mind of a man may be intent
> At the time of death'—that is the one action
> (And the time of death is every moment)
> Which shall fructify in the lives of others. ('Dry Salvages', lines 155–160)

In short, Eliot presents a very un-Hindu rendition of a Hindu concept. One might say he offers a compassionate (in a Christian or Buddhist sense) reading that is directed towards others. In fact, he was supplementing what we might call Hinduism's lack of a social component. Hinduism's focus on individual salvation to the detriment of a community has been seen as a weakness that distinguished it from other religions, especially those other faiths that have sought to supplant it.[18] It was this very notion of love for one's fellow humans that Eliot adds to his Hindu thematic. It is this notion of a Christian social conscience that he did not want 'to forget thinking and feeling as an American or a European' (Howarth 206). In other words, he took what he most admired in Hinduism and Christianized it (in terms of brotherly love) or rendered it Buddhist (with an emphasis placed on compassion).[19]

Near the end of 'Dry Salvages,' Eliot is questioning what concerns and what paths 'most of us', who like Arjuna are caught up in action (Fowler 1971: 414), will follow:

> And right action is freedom
> From past and future also. (Eliot 1969: 190)

Like Krishna in the *Gītā*, Eliot is encouraging detachment, as in the third section of 'Little Gidding':

[18] The social component is emphasized in the proselytizing efforts of Christianity in India as well as in Buddhism's initial success there.

[19] It is a tenet of Buddhism that there can be *Boddhisattvas*, i.e. buddhas-in-training, who forestall their own enlightenment until all sentient life reaches *nibbāna*.

> Not less of love but expanding
> Of love beyond desire, and so liberation
> From the future as well as the past. (193)

Hence, we are advised to 'fare forward', rather than 'fare well'. We are also enjoined to 'be still and wail without hope'.

To reach Little Gidding, the place embodying the state of the liberated soul, described in the quartet named after that destination,

> You would have to put off/ Sense and notion (192) . . . because in order to possess what you do not possess/ You must go by way of dispossession. (181)

'Sense and notion' can be understood here as Eliot's translation of the *Gītā*'s explication of Sāṃkhya philosophy. While one also finds a focus on self-denial and deprivation in Christian mysticism, I would hazard to suggest that it was this particular expression of these concepts, as Eliot discovered them in the *Gītā*'s code of moral conduct, that he found attractive, especially since selflessness and self-surrender (along with ardour) appear throughout the third section of 'Little Gidding', where there are numerous parallels to the *Gītā*'s description of attachment to the self and others, detachment from the self and others, and indifference.

The way of action is announced in the first section of 'Little Gidding' and the rest of this quartet reintroduces concerns found in the preceding quartets and highlights their particular significance for the tranquil, the attached, and the non-attached voyager. The second and third sections of 'Little Gidding' suggest how attached and non-attached beings may be represented and evaluated. Just as fire, water, earth, and air can never be free of action, so too are beings limited by attachment. In the fourth and final section, attraction is defined as the desire for an object. 'Higher attraction' consists of the 'drawing of this Love' for the unmoving source of unending action from which we need to be freed. It is only through an awareness of moments of intersecting life and death that the traveller with the 'drawing of this Love' (that is love unattached to endings and beginnings) becomes free and can 'fare forward'.

Indian influences are not limited to *The Waste Land* and the *Four Quartets*; they appear elsewhere in Eliot's work. In 1943. Eliot was commissioned to write a poem for *Queen Mary's Book for India* (Rao 1963: 573). His contribution, 'To Indians Who Died in Africa', was intended, as were all the contributions to the volume, to benefit the war effort.[20] The role of Eliot's poem in this anthology is quite similar to that of the *Gītā* in the *Mahābhārata*—both serve as a call to battle. Just as Arjuna is instructed to lead the Pāṇḍavas into the epic war, so too does Eliot encourage Indians to fight in the Second World War, just as they had done in the First World War.

In the *Gītā*, Krishna urged Arjuna to pursue activity without attachment to the fruits of this action. So too in his poem, Eliot sends a similar message and draws the parallel between the cosmic battle of Kurukshetra depicted in the *Gītā* and the Indians fighting in both World Wars for England. It is to be noted that at the time Eliot composed this poem, World War II had already taken a considerable toll on the Indian combatants who had been fighting for their imperial masters with little political gain. Moreover, they were in combat without the British having even consulted the Indian National Congress before declaring war on their behalf. Also, in the First World War, Britain had not bothered to poll Indian opinion. Since, in the intervening years, the English had made and broken quite a number of promises and given that the independence movement was in full swing, there were fewer Indian subjects willing to support the Second World War in the hopes of gaining concessions from the British this time around (Figueira 2013: 90). Eliot's poem is best understood in this context and in light of the Indian combatants' involvement in both World Wars. It is to be remembered that in the First World War, the role of the Indian Army was not negligible. By the time the Armistice was signed, India had provided 1,270,000 soldiers to the war effort of which 827,000 were combatants. Indians comprised one-tenth of the Empire's manpower. The Indian Army in the First World War, as in the Second, consisted mostly

[20] 'Dry Salvages' and 'To Indians who Died in Africa' were written within a year of each other. The poem was solicited by the editor Cornelia Sorabji for the war effort (Chandran 54).

of Punjabis, Muslims, and Sikhs (Omissi 1999: 2).[21] The recruits mostly stemmed from warrior castes, so Eliot's evocation of the *Mahābhārata* War to describe the modern Indian soldier is apt.

Eliot realistically portrays the morale and bravery that the Indian soldiers exhibited. As the sepoy letters from the First World War attest, the Indians were dedicated to their duty as soldiers. Unlike British soldier-poets such as Rupert Brooke who focused on the glory of battle, or Siegfried Sassoon and Wilfrid Owen who wallowed in the horror of their impending deaths, the Indian soldiers, as we can gather from their testimonies, attempted to make religious or philosophical sense out of the war (Figueira 2013: 97–100). Whether professional soldiers or hapless villagers conscripted into the Indian Army, the sepoys of the First World War exhibited in the letters they left behind a certain detachment and sangfroid in the face of destruction, Moreover, they rejected the certainties regarding battle, glory, and hallowed dust—the sentimentality and lies of wartime propaganda. Even more than the British poet-soldiers, the Indian sepoys of the First World War offered a convincing repudiation of the lies of old men, who led them into the trenches of the Ypres Salient (Figueira 2013: 101). Eliot wonderfully evoked the worldview of such soldiers when he writes in 'East Coker' (II, 76–8):

> Had they deceived us,
> Or deceived themselves, the quiet-voiced elders,
> Bequeathing us merely a receipt for deceit?

In 'To the Indians Who Died in Africa', Eliot juxtaposes the Indian soldiers fighting in Africa during the Second World War[22] to Arjuna. In both wars, the Indian soldiers fulfil the duty of their caste (as warriors) and perform without attachment to the fruits of their action. Eliot presents

[21] The British avoided recruiting from the educated classes whom they believed had been tainted by radical politics.

[22] The 2 million Indians who enlisted to fight during the Second World War comprised the biggest volunteer army that ever existed (see Geoffrey Moorhouse, *India Britannica*. London: Harvill, 1983, 242–3, cited in Chandran 58). The fourth, fifth, and tenth divisions fought in North Africa between 1939 and 1943, the fourth and fifth divisions fought in East Africa between 1940 and 1941. The fourth division smashed the Italians at Sidi Barrani and took the entire Italian army prisoner. They also led the conquest of Italian East Africa and the liberation of Abyssinia (Chandran 59).

the dilemma of the Indian soldier in terms reminiscent of the *Gītā*; where the goal of the individual warrior is salvation gained through action (3.5; 3.9).

The first half (two stanzas) of Eliot's poem present a picture of a happy old warrior whose destination should consist of returning home to his wife's cooking, sitting by his fire, and watching his grandson play. He will relate his war stories:

> A man's destination is his own village,
> His own fire, and his wife's cooking;
> To sit in front of his own door at sunset
> And see his grandson and his neighbour's grandson
> Play in the dust together.
> Scarred but secure, he has many narratives
> To repeat at the hour of conversation
> (The warm or the cool hour, according to the climate).

The last two stanzas announce that the land does not belong to anyone. Two people, two countries: one from the Punjab, the land of five rivers, and the other from the Midlands in England can share the same memories (Rao 1963: 574–5):

> Of foreign men, who fought in foreign places,
> Foreign to each other
> A man's destination is not his destiny.
> Every country is home to one man
> And exile to another. When a man dies bravely
> At one with his destiny, that soil is his.
> Let his village remember
> This was not your land, or ours: but a village in the Midlands
> Another in the Five Rivers, may have the same memories.
> Let those who go home tell the same story of you:
> Of action with a common purpose, action
> None the less fruitful if neither you nor I
> Know, until the judgment after death,
> What is the fruit of action.

In 1943, the repetition of the term 'foreign' in 'foreign men' could not but evoke the issue of foreign rule in opposition to the self-rule (*swadeshi*) demanded by the Quit India Movement. In response to such an association, Eliot asserts that the land was 'not your land, or ours.' The poem then moves from the material to the spiritual. In the beginning, a man is attached to 'his own fire, his own village, his wife's cooking, his grandson.' However, by the third stanza we find him detached from his homeland. He belongs where he bravely perishes.[23] The final stanza emphasizes the spiritual and the eternal elements. There is the exhortation to pursue action without regard to its fruits, in the manner of Krishna's advice to Arjuna and, as in the *Gītā,* the poem speaks in direct address.

In addition to the *Four Quartets* and 'To the Indians Who Died in Africa', the *Gītā's* teaching of love and non-attachment also appears in Eliot's dramatic works. In *The Cocktail Party*, Eliot presents a vision of life based on the performance of action similar to the attitude taught in the *Gītā* (Rao 1981: 195). Reilly tells Edward, Lavinia, and Celia that they all need to understand the nature of their love (self, selfish, and lovelessness).[24] He also tells Celia that her way is that of knowledge. When Celia asks Reilly to clarify what her duty is, he responds that neither way is better. The two paths presented in the *Gītā*, that of *karma* and *jñāna,* are similar to the two paths that Reilly presents to Celia. Moreover, he explains how the two paths to attain salvation are suitable to individuals according to their temperaments, similar to the *Gītā*'s teaching regarding the *guṇas*, already suggested in 'Little Gidding'. Reilly instructs his 'patients' that

[23] The Indian dead of the First World War are mourned in cemeteries throughout Belgium and France, where they were cremated and buried with full religious respect and honour. On these graves, the sepoy's name, number, name of regiment and date of death are duly noted in English. The largest and most sumptuous memorial to the Indian fallen is found at Neuve Chapelle, the site of one of their more significant engagements. The Indian Memorial at Neuve Chapelle is an impressive *lieu de mémoire*. Designed in the Indo-Saracen style, an enclosure with a 15-metre pillar resembling the pillar of Aśoka surmounted with a lotus capital, the star of India, and the imperial crown. On either side of the column are two carved tigers, guarding this temple to the dead. On the pillar itself are the written words: GOD IS ONE HIS IS THE VICTORY. This lofty sentiment is accompanied by roughly equivalent citations from the Koran written in Arabic script, from the *Sri Guru Granth Sahib* written in Gurmukhi and finally from the *Bhagavad Gītā* in devanāgarī script. The column and tigers are supported by a podium on which is carved 'INDIA 1914–19'. This monument is so spectacular; it is only surpassed by the ossuary at Verdun.

[24] Celia needs to become more universal in her love, Edward needs to change his self-love into selfless love for Lavinia, and Lavinia needs to transform her lovelessness to become responsible for Edward (Rao 1981: 196).

their duties must also conform to their position in life and be done with the proper attitude. Reilly points out to Edward and Lavinia that they are householders and that their life is as important as that of the ascetic. In other words, he presents an elaboration of the *varṇāśramadharma*,[25] as it is found in the *Gītā* and, just like the Indian interpretations of caste examined in previous chapters, Eliot also offers a justification for caste (albeit Westernized and psychologized). In the end, Reilly bids farewell to his patients with words for both a discriminating pursuit of life and its renunciation. Here, Eliot does not have him speak from the *Gītā*, but uses the words of the dying Buddha: 'Work out your salvation with diligence', a message running throughout *The Cocktail Party*.[26]

With the exception of this citation of the Buddha's last words, we would be hard pressed to see a Buddhist turn in Eliot, despite Steven Spender's comment that Eliot had almost become a Buddhist.[27] Eliot's evocation here equally shows a reliance on the *Gītā*, since in terms of ethics Hinduism and Buddhism share the same belief—that we must become emancipated from desire. Similarly, the theme of impermanence so important to Eliot and expressed in 'East Coker' and especially in 'Dry Salvages', where he writes: 'Fare forward.... You are not the same people who left that station. Or who will arrive at any terminus...', could equally well reflect his appreciation of Buddhist thought. We must remember he studied both religions and philosophies consecutively.[28] Whether we attribute themes such as *karma*, predestination, illusion, the ability to make the right choice at death to Hinduism or Buddhism, they appear throughout Eliot's dramatic work (Ghosh 1974: 131), turning up in *The Elder Statesman*, *Murder in the Cathedral*, and *The Family Reunion*.[29]

[25] Duties to be followed according to one's station in life and one's caste.

[26] This is a well-known citation from accounts of the Buddha's death that Eliot most probably took from Warren's *Buddhism in Translation* (1922: 109) that Eliot's Sanskrit teacher published in the Harvard Oriental Series. Eliot also cites Warren's anthology (still in print today and used in classrooms as source material) in 'The Fire Sermon, the third part of "The Wasteland" (Eliot 1969: 308).

[27] Spender 1976: 20, cited in Perl and Tuck 1985: 116.

[28] In 1913–14, Eliot also attended Masaharu Anesaki's class 'Schools of Religious and Philosophical Thought in Japan' which consisted of the study of Buddhism in Japan and China. Eliot thus showed a desire to study Buddhism outside India; it should also be recalled that he abandoned Sanskrit after the first year in order to study Pāli.

[29] In *The Family Reunion*, one character notes: 'O God, man, the things that are going to happen have already happened' (Eliot 1969: 317, cited in Ghosh 134).

Among the Transcendentalists, we identified two tendencies operant in their interpretations of the *Gītā*—a superficial use of Sanskrit terminology for its evocative potential and a conscious attempt to cull some religious meaning from this 'exotic' text. Eliot was far more knowledgeable in his appropriations, using the *Gītā* as an inspirational springboard for his wartime reflections on human and social responsibility. It is not without significance that Eliot chose to quote Krishna's command to fight in the middle of World War II. He was signalling the *Gītā*'s teaching that since the unchanging spirit does not dwell in the mortal body, one should continue to act and fight on the battlefield without attachment to the world. What is interesting here is not that Eliot evoked the *Gītā*, which seems to have become almost a cliché among America's artists and intellectuals, but the manner in which he appropriated it. He was telling his readers that they should not be concerned with their own fate, but rather with the good of mankind. In this sense, Eliot evoked the *Gītā*, particularly in 'Dry Salvages', in order to Christianize (and, dare I say, democratize) its message and urge the Allies to fight for the greater good of their nations and humanity: to fight the Nazis in order to preserve civilization as they knew it. It was this impulse that drew Eliot to reconnect with Hindu philosophy as he understood it from his early reading and translating of the *Gītā*. It was this same impulse that also animated the appropriation of the *Gītā* by Eliot's fellow American and fellow Harvard alumnus, J. Robert Oppenheimer, at roughly the same time.

J. Robert Oppenheimer

J. Robert Oppenheimer's (1904–67) admiration for the *Gītā* can partially be understood within the context of his upbringing. He was born into a rich New York Jewish family. His father, Julius,[30] had been a textile merchant who immigrated to the States and married a cultivated Midwestern woman who was a painter. Oppenheimer's mother was attentive to the needs of Robert and his younger brother, Frank. Handicapped with a withered hand, she sought to instil in them a certain hardiness. The Oppenheimers did not raise their sons as religious Jews. In fact, from an

[30] Oppenheimer was named after his father, the 'J' in his name. He never used his first name.

early age, Robert had been affiliated with Felix Adler's Society for Ethical Culture of which his father served on the Board of Directors. The Society for Ethical Culture rejected the transcendental aspects of religion and focused on human welfare as a basis of universal faith (Hijiya 160). It advocated that one was to assume responsibility for the direction of one's life and destiny. Adler encouraged constant self-evaluation and self-analysis. For 10 years, Oppenheimer studied at the Ethical Culture School in New York, graduating as its valedictorian. He then moved on to Harvard University, where he graduated *summa cum laude* in three years (1922–5) and first in his class with the highest grade-point average that Harvard had ever recorded. At some point in his studies, he became familiar with ancient Indian literature in English translations.[31] In fact, I.I. Rabi, who knew him as a young man and later worked with him on the Manhattan Project, would remark in 1929 that he thought Oppenheimer was more interested in the Hindu classics than he had ever been in physics.[32] He appreciated, in particular, the *Gītā* (Smith and Weiner 165). Frank Oppenheimer noted how his brother 'was really taken by the charm and the general wisdom of the *Bhagavad Gītā*', but added that he felt he had never got 'religiously involved in it'.[33] It is worth noting that Oppenheimer listed the *Gītā* along with *The Waste Land* among the 10 books that did most to shape his vocational attitude and his philosophy of life.[34] In fact, the *Gītā* gave Oppenheimer a code of belief that he would use throughout his professional life. Its teaching also afforded him a timely rationale to question and ultimately reject his upbringing in Ethical Culture.

In the 1920s, Oppenheimer was conspicuously ambitious. He was also very depressed. John Edsall, a college friend, recalled how Oppenheimer desperately wanted to make a big contribution to science. At Harvard, the distinguished physicist, Percy Bridgeman, had told him that he could not yet consider himself a physicist until he had done original work,[35]

[31] Jeffrey Wyman, interview by Charles Weiner, 28 May 1975 in *J. Robert Oppenheimer Oral History Collection,* MC 85 (transcript), Institute Archives and Special Collections, Massachusetts Institute of Technology Libraries. Cambridge, Massachusetts, cited in Hijiya 2000: 129.

[32] Rabi et al. 5, cited in Hijiya 2000: 130.

[33] Frank Oppenheimer in the film production *Day After Trinity*, cited in Hijiya 2000: 126.

[34] In addition to the *Gītā* and Eliot, he also cited Baudelaire, Bhartṛhari, Dante, Flaubert (*Éducation sentimentale*), Shakespeare's *Hamlet*, the works of the German mathematician Georg Friedrich Bernhard Riemann (1826–66) and Plato's *Theaetitus* (Hijiya 2000: 130).

[35] Interview with Weiner 16 July 1975, 14 in Oppenheimer *Oral Collection MIT*, in Hijiya 149.

and Oppenheimer fully realized how he had missed out on participating in the important breakthroughs in the field by Werner Heisenberg and others that had recently taken place. He knew full well that he needed to make his own big discoveries and that, in the field of physics, such discoveries are usually made when one is young. After graduating from Harvard, Oppenheimer went to the Cavendish Laboratory at Cambridge University to continue working in applied physics. This stint in England was calamitous. In fact, Oppenheimer became suicidal and sought treatment from psychiatrists both in Paris and in London. He was on the verge of a complete breakdown and there is some evidence that he did indeed suffer a psychotic episode at that time (Hijiya 149). Part of his problem was his failure to stand out as the most gifted applied physicist at Cambridge, an ego blow that was all the more upsetting, given his oversized ambition. His youthful training in Ethical Culture had instilled in him a sense of social burden whose ideal entailed the development of the individual's ability to change the environment and have a beneficial effect upon the world. Ethical Culture focused on the role of privileged and exceptional humans in the making of history.[36] Clearly, this philosophy contributed to his malaise. His friend, I.I. Rabi always thought that Ethical Culture had had an immobilizing effect on Oppenheimer (Bird and Sherwin 101). Rabi's wife, Helen Newmark, who had been a classmate of Oppenheimer at Ethical Culture, also commented on his conflict with its philosophy. She felt that it had soured Oppenheimer as a budding intellectual, even if it had instilled in him a profound approach to human relations.

Even so, and despite his psychological crisis and failure to flourish at Cambridge, Oppenheimer moved on to Göttingen where he completed his doctorate under Max Born in 1927. He had resolved the feelings of inadequacy he experienced at Cambridge as an applied physicist by finding his bearings as a theoretical physicist in Germany. Upon graduating, he was offered (and accepted) dual posts both at Berkeley, where he would build the Theoretical Physics department, and Cal Tech. It was at this time that, as a young professor of physics, Oppenheimer began to study Sanskrit with Arthur W. Ryder (1877–1938)[37] at Berkeley. He wrote to

[36] See Friess 122, 124, cited in Hijiya 146–7.

[37] Ryder is best known for his translations of the *Pañcatantra*, the *Bhagavad Gītā*, and Sanskrit plays.

his brother that it was 'very easy and quite marvelous' (7 October 7 1933, cited in Smith and Weiner 165). He attended Ryder's Thursday evening readings of the *Gītā*. Oppenheimer's letters to his brother also express how the *Gītā*'s teaching on detachment and renunciation could serve as a viable alternative to Adler's insistence on constant self-analysis and self-evaluation. Perhaps, Oppenheimer felt that he could replace Adler with Ryder as a more amenable guru. Oppenheimer much admired Ryder as a scholar and teacher. He had also come to view his Sanskrit teacher as a moral paragon. 'Ryder felt and thought and talked as a Stoic … a special subclass of people who have a tragic sense of life' (Thorpe 53).[38] With his reading of the *Gītā*, Oppenheimer was also perhaps adding to his life an element of spirituality that had been lacking in both Ethical Culture and his secular upbringing. It also suited his sense of his own exceptionality.

Oppenheimer's discovery of Indian philosophical thought through his study of the *Gītā* would have a tremendous influence on his future endeavours. Once Oppenheimer embraced the ethics that he found in the *Gītā,* its notion of duty, and its injunction to renounce the fruits of one's actions, he could jettison the constraints that the teaching of Ethical Culture had imposed on him. Oppenheimer preferred the *Gītā*'s laws of *karma*, destiny, and duty to Ethical Culture's stress on individual human will. Yet, in its celebration of action and engagement, Oppenheimer could also see the *Gītā* as compatible with what he did appreciate in his Ethical Culture upbringing: its mandate to succeed and produce results. Around this time, he wrote:

> I believe that through discipline, though not through discipline alone, we can achieve serenity, and a certain small but precious measure of freedom from the accidents of incarnation … and that detachment which preserves the world which it renounces. (Cited in Bird and Sherwin 100)

Oppenheimer would henceforth use the *Gītā* as a manual for regulating his life. Since the emotional crisis of 1926 at Cambridge, Oppenheimer had desperately sought equilibrium and the *Gītā* now supplied him with

[38] Neither Adler nor his father had ever elicited such praise.

it. Discipline and hard work always had worked for him in the past and with the *Gītā*, he could now raise its concept of duty to a philosophy of life.

The *Gītā* gave Oppenheimer a 'feeling for the place of ethics' and an understanding of vocation. It taught him that 'any man who does a hard thing well is automatically respectable and worthy of respect' (Thorpe 53). It is clear that Oppenheimer had found in the *Gītā* and in the behaviour he saw embodied by his teacher Ryder an ascetic ethos on which to model his own self-fashioning. In a letter to his brother, Oppenheimer wrote:

> I think that all things which evoke discipline: study and our duties to men and to the commonwealth, and war, and personal hardship, and even the need for subsistence, ought to be greeted by us with profound gratitude; for only through them can we attain to the least detachment; and only so can we know peace. (Cited in Bird and Sherwin 100)

Oppenheimer was seeking detachment from the world, yet he was still quite an intellectual snob who desired worldly fame and scientific glory. Like so many of the other exoticist *Schwärmer* (enthusiast, dreamer, sentimentalist) (Figueira 1991, 1994), Oppenheimer was also looking for an alibi in India, an elsewhere to inhabit in order to make himself more interesting to himself and others. He was also seeking some peace of mind. The *Gītā*'s concept of *dharma* combined Oppenheimer's interest in ascetic discipline with his understanding of his vocation as a scientist. What is interesting is the manner in which he used the language of the *Gītā* to express his own variation of the 'Protestant ethic' (Thorpe 53) that he had absorbed earlier from his training in Ethical Culture.

Oppenheimer felt that the *Gītā* was 'the most beautiful philosophical song existing in any known tongue'. He would always keep a copy on the bookshelf closest to his desk and had the habit of giving out Ryder's translation as gifts (Royal 64). He carried a copy of the *Gītā* in his pocket for casual consultation during his work at Los Alamos. Ryder had written in the introduction to his *Gītā* translation (1929) about the inspiration that had been found in this text by 'uncounted millions' on the road to salvation. It is clear that this was the case for his student who found in it a new ethics: the single-minded performance of personal duty. No longer focusing on Ethical Culture's humanitarianism and a quest for greatness (fruits of action), Oppenheimer now focused on the *Gītā*'s teaching regarding the execution of duty without care for the fruits of one's actions. If the *Gītā* did not free Oppenheimer from his overweening ambition for distinction, it at least soothed his frustrations at not achieving greatness for some significant discovery in theoretical physics. Although he was a man very much enmeshed in creature comforts, wealth, and a privileged lifestyle, Oppenheimer wrote in a letter to his brother (12 March 1932) how he wanted very much to free himself from the desire of things of the world (Smith and Weiner 155). The work ethic he read in the *Gītā* would guide him throughout the decade he taught in California. But at that time, Oppenheimer could not have imagined how it would subsequently be put to the test.

In 1942, despite lack of seniority, no administrative qualifications or experience, and with considerable promise yet no great discoveries under his belt (i.e. no Nobel Prize), Oppenheimer was appointed director of the laboratory for the Manhattan Project. He had greatly impressed General Leslie Groves, the head of the bomb project, with the organizational ideas he had exhibited at a conference of assembled scientists during the planning stages for the project. He had also showed an initial willingness to allow the project to be run by the military and this concession (or cluelessness) had also impressed Groves.[39] Oppenheimer's appointment surprised many. It was not only his relative lack of qualifications for the job[40] that might have disqualified him, but through a radical former fiancée, Oppenheimer, his wife,[41] and his brother had become quite active in Leftist politics. There was some speculation that he had been a Communist Party member. The 30s and 40s were not yet the time of the Red Scare of the 50s, nevertheless with his social and familial contacts, Oppenheimer perhaps had more involvement in and offered more financial support to Leftist causes than was customary, even in his cultural

[39] It was only when physicists refused to join the project if it was to be militarily run, out of concern that military bureaucracy would impede their efforts—a legitimate fear of men who had more political acumen and/or experience of the military than Oppenheimer, that he backed out of this initial stipulation.

[40] It should be noted that many other scientists were already involved in running other major laboratories for the war effort.

[41] Kitty Oppenheimer might not be seen as the ideal wife in such a situation; she was alcoholic, had contributed to Communist causes and may have been Communist, was a cousin of the Nazi Field Marshall Wilhelm Keitel, and was thrice married before her marriage to Oppenheimer. At a time when second generation Germans with ties to family back in Germany were turned down for active service in the military, she might well have been deemed a security risk.

and professional milieu. It would certainly have been deemed excessive for an appointment to such a highly sensitive position. Nevertheless, Oppenheimer was appointed to this task and became responsible for coordinating the work of 5,000 men and women. Charged with and deciding upon a location for the operation, he chose Los Alamos as its headquarters, an area he knew from summers spent there camping and horseback riding with his brother. He then went about the task of organizing and directing the project of building the Atomic Bomb with single-minded devotion and competence.

After some initial organizational glitches, Oppenheimer had the sense to seek the aid of more experienced colleagues on how to run things. There were no delays and Oppenheimer allowed no protests to impede the accomplishment of the project. The official report on the Manhattan Project cited him as the one person credited with its implementation for military purposes. The Atomic Energy Commission had judged him virtually indispensable (Hijiya 164). While at work on the project, the teachings of the *Gītā* were never far from his mind. Indeed, Oppenheimer often regaled his fellow workers at Los Alamos by citing the wisdom of the *Gītā*. He saw it as the crucial inspiration for the project's success. He explained, in a speech to the Association of Los Alamos Scientists, that it was their duty to build the bomb (Smith and Weiner 317). It was their *dharma* as scientists. In fact, this sense of duty became the key managerial tool for Oppenheimer. It allowed him to manage the work as well as any ensuing conflicts. The Manhattan Project physicist, Leo Szilard, along with 68 other scientists, had signed a petition not to drop the bomb over a city. Szilard had wanted to submit this petition to President Truman. But Oppenheimer told the physicist Edward Teller, who had come to him with the request, not to send it. He calmly stated: 'Our fate was in the hands of the best, the most conscientious men of our nation, and they had information which we did not possess' (Teller and Brown 13–4). He thus forbade circulation of the petition (Smith 1965: 155, cited in Hijiya 138). Moreover, Oppenheimer refused to advocate any target other than a city, since he believed that such a target would not intimidate the Japanese (*USAEC* 1971: 236) who would view it like a 'firecracker over the desert' (34). Furthermore, he discouraged colleagues from even discussing the consequences of the bomb, since it would distract them from creating it

(Smith and Weiner 1980: 240). Simply, he saw it as his duty to build the bomb and it was the duty of others to decide how to use it.[42]

Although happy when the test and the actual detonation over Japan were successful, Oppenheimer was otherwise detached from the fruits of his work. Just as Arjuna came to understand his duty as tied to his caste obligations as a *kṣatriya*, so too did Oppenheimer understand duty in terms of his social class (a lesson taught by Ethical Culture) and his place (as a scientist) in society. As an American citizen, he defined his duty in terms of his profession and expertise. His duty as an American physicist was to build the bomb; it was the duty of American statesmen to decide how or whether to use it (Smith and Weiner 317). 'I did my job which was the job I was supposed to do. I was not in a policymaking position at Los Alamos' (*USAEC* 1971: 236). In 'Physicists in the Contemporary World', Oppenheimer spoke about the importance of scientists doing their duty. He used here vocabulary borrowed from of the *Gītā*, (2.47; 4.20; 5.12; 12.11; 12.12; 18.2; 18.11) and emphasized especially that they should not attempt to assume responsibility for 'the fruits of their work'. Throughout the process and as the bomb neared completion, Oppenheimer continued

[42] Oppenheimer's attitude of detachment was picked up subsequently by other scientists, with varying degrees of sincerity. This stance of 'doing own's duty' was brilliantly parodied by Tom Lehrer, a MIT mathematics professor on the concert circuit in the late 1960s, in a satirical song where he sings of the 'great American know-how of scientists and their 'patriotism'. The 'American' scientist Lehrer evokes is Wernher von Braun who so easily segued from being a Nazi rocket scientist into his Cold-War usefulness to the Americans. Lehrer's song is as follows:

> Gather round while I sing you of Wernher von Braun,
> A man whose allegiance
> Is ruled by expedience.
> Call him a Nazi, he won't even frown,
> Ha, Nazi, Schmazi, says Wernher von Braun.
>
> Don't say that he's hypocritical,
> Say rather that he's apolitical.
> Once the rockets are up, who cares where they come down?
> That's not my department, says Wernher von Braun.
>
> Some have harsh words for this man of renown,
> But some think our attitude
> Should be one of gratitude,
> Like the widows and cripples in old London town,
> Who owe their large pensions to Wernher von Braun.
>
> You too may be a big hero,
> Once you've learned to count backwards to zero.
> In German oder English I know how to count down,
> Und I'm learning Chinese! says Wernher von Braun.

to cite the Sanskrit poem to his co-workers. Even at a memorial service for Roosevelt at Los Alamos after his death on 15 April 1945, Oppenheimer quoted the *Gītā*; 'Man is a creature whose substance is faith. What his faith is, he is' (*Gītā* 17.3) (Smith and Weiner 288, cited in Hijiya 130).

The extent of Oppenheimer's intense involvement with the *Gītā* as a long-term source of inspiration and a guide for living has been largely eclipsed by the quotation from the *Gītā* that he famously claimed flashed into his mind upon the detonation at Los Alamos:

> If the radiance of a thousand suns
> Were to burst into the sky,
> That would be like
> The splendor of the Mighty One. –

With a certain dramatic flair, the interviewer relating Oppenheimer's account notes:

> Yet, when the sinister and gigantic cloud rose up in the far distance, our Point Zero, he was reminded of another line from the same source:
> I am become Death, the shatterer of Worlds. (Jungt 201, cited in Hijiya 124)

Oppenheimer's *Gītā* quote solidified slowly with subsequent retellings. In *Time* magazine, the American public read:

> Oppenheimer recalls that the lines of the *Bhagavad Gītā* flashed through his mind: 'I am become death, the shatterer of worlds' ('The Eternal Apprentice', *Time,* 8 November 1948: 77).

Here too, we have an interesting instance of translation. Oppenheimer may have remembered the quote in the original Sanskrit, but what he is said to have uttered was his teacher Ryder's translation. The term in question is *kāla,* more commonly translated as 'time', but it can also signify time in a cosmic and eschatological sense. As the Princeton physicist M.V. Ramana has noted, Oppenheimer opted to translate *kāla* as 'death'. Ryder translated *Gītā* 11.32 as, 'Death am I, and my present task destruction.' Oppenheimer's adoption of Ryder's translation is totally defensible.

Other translators however, use 'time' (Wilkins, Besant, Prabhananda, S. Radhakrishnan, Eknath Easwaren, Barbara Stoller Miller). Franklin Edgerton wrote, 'Time (Death)'. Miller followed her translation with 'time grown old'. Radhakrishnan opted for 'time … grown mature'. The implication here is death, so Ryder's rendition is legitimate (Hijiya 132).

In the aftermath of the war, Oppenheimer was investigated as a potential security risk due to his poor choices in several appointments at Los Alamos, his ambiguous reporting of security risks, but primarily because of his resistance to the development of the Hydrogen Bomb—to be possibly used against the Soviets—in contrast to his willingness to develop the Atomic Bomb for use against the Japanese. His defence before the Commission was not stellar nor was the trial objective and well run. Oppenheimer was stripped of his authority and lost his security clearance. It was an unjust and humiliating ruling against someone who had so effectively served his country. Oppenheimer's 'fate' now took on a life of its own and a new hagiography was put in place. Oppenheimer was no longer viewed as the genius scientist who loved poetry and read Sanskrit. He was now seen as a victim par excellence of the Red Scare hysteria and a government that persecuted him for what they suspected was his lack of patriotism. It was no longer of any interest how he used Indian philosophy to rationalize his involvement in creating the Atomic Bomb. His persona (that he cultivated) as the slightly mystical adept of Hindu wisdom who also happened to be a scientist was replaced by the image of him as a tormented victim of the government, guilt-ridden by his contribution to the bomb. In an NBC 1965 documentary, 'The Decision to Drop the Bomb', there is a close up of Oppenheimer where he recounts his memory of moments after the blast and his now famous reference to the *Gītā*.

Much has been made of this documentary image of him. It has been interpreted as showing Oppenheimer as haunted and forlorn (Banco 2016: 143). The reality was much more prosaic. After losing his security clearance, Oppenheimer's 'exile' consisted in his becoming the Director of Princeton's Institute for Advanced Studies, not quite Ovid's banishment to the far reaches of the known world described in the *Tristia* poems. It was not a bad early forced retirement for a scientist who had never made the discoveries of a Fermi or a Heisenberg and had never produced the significant body of publications that his early promise might have foreshadowed. His directorship of Los Alamos was his legacy and, as we have seen, his love of the *Gītā* played a great role in its success.

Today, the portrait of Oppenheimer as the ultimate victim of the military industrial complex has been nurtured, supported by post-McCarthy-era scholarship and artistic production. In a recent book of criticism, Oppenheimer's comment that the bomb project was 'technically sweet' (Polenberg 46) is seen as further evidence of 'emerging from the discourse of efficiency, scientism and patriarchy' (Banco 2017: 130). But the truth is that Oppenheimer never regretted the bomb. When he visited Japan in 1960, he was asked by reporters whether he felt guilt over the bomb and replied: 'I do not regret that I had something to do with the technical success of the Atomic Bomb' (Michelmore 241 cited in Hijiya 165). He said he would do it again (Lemont 302–3) and wished he had finished the bomb sooner to drop it on the Germans for what they had done to the Jews. To the end of his days, he saw his involvement in terms reminiscent of the *Gītā*: 'I never regretted and do not regret now, having done my part of the job.' In the *New York Times* on 1 August 1965, (p. 8), he noted, 'There was uncertainty of achievement not of duty.'[43] He said on many occasions that it was his duty that mattered. After the fall of France, he felt it was necessary to do something to save Western civilization (Smith and Weiner 173). In his journal, Oppenheimer wrote, 'Krishna would approve that I am doing my work well' (Hijiya 130, cited in Rosen 85). He firmly believed (as do most historians) that it saved many American lives by speedily ending the war. He had full knowledge of the atrocities that had been committed by the Germans and were being committed by the Japanese. He hoped it would deter future wars.[44] In 1966, in the month before his death, in an argument regarding the consequences of what he termed the subsequent 'chattering', Oppenheimer clarified that the important thing was 'doing what I should.'[45]

Ethical Culture had emphasized moral action in the world aimed at improving human welfare. Oppenheimer, rebelling perhaps at his

[43] *Newsweek*, 19 July 1965: 51, both the *Times* quote and the *Newsweek* quote are cited in Hijiya 141–2.

[44] See his letter to Herbert Smith on 26 August 1945 (Smith and Weiner 297, all cited in Hijiya 128).

[45] Thomas B. Morgan, 'With Oppenheimer on an Autumn Day', *Look*, 27 December 1966: 67, cited in Hijiya 160.

upbringing, sought mystical renunciation of the world. Yet, he was also a product of his parents' German-Jewish attachment to *Bildung*. In addition to seeking the flowering of the self through aesthetic cultivation, he also sought in the *Gītā* a subjugation of the self through ascetic discipline. But this asceticism was only partial because Oppenheimer remained a worldly cosmopolitan sophisticate with his pipe and pork-pie hat gracing the cover of a scientific journal. We hear of his charm as a host, particularly with the ladies, his ability to make a perfect martini, his collection of Van Gogh, Vlaminck, and Derain paintings gracing the walls of his elegantly appointed eighteenth-century house in Princeton, complete with an artist's studio for his wife, horses and stable for his daughter, and photography studio for his son.

Oppenheimer contributed to his mythologization as the ascetic scientist. His appreciation of the *Gītā* and his frequent references to it play no small part in this portrait. Harry M. Davis in an article in the *New York Times Magazine* (18 April 1948: 57) entitled, 'The Man who Built the A-Bomb', wrote that Oppenheimer 'studied Sanskrit so that he could sip eternal truth from the bygone philosophies of India'. This article highlights Oppenheimer's mysticism; it portrays him as a genius and 'wise man' whose esoteric wisdom was as deep as his technical wizardry. Oppenheimer's appreciation of the philosophy of the *Gītā* functions here 'as an anodyne for the pangs of conscience' (Hijiya 125). For all his sincere love for the *Gītā* as a genuine source of wisdom, the Sanskrit text was also a decorative accomplishment and a wonderful means for him to display his virtuosity. In an interview on 16 November 1998, David Hawkins relates the following anecdote:

> I once was sitting in his living room before the war in Berkeley, and to the left on the bookshelf was a whole string of classics. I saw Plato and pulled down a volume, and I said, 'You know, I've just been studying this volume.' And he said, owlishly, 'I've read the Greeks, I find the Hindus deeper.' Wow! One upmanship! He had that side too. (Thorpe 54)

At the heart of Oppenheimer's scientific and intellectual identity, Hindu philosophy could function as an ornamental cultivation, offering him the opportunity to engage the world on an esoteric level while appearing to renounce it.

Like many of us, Oppenheimer sought refuge from the world in which he felt ill at ease. His friend and colleague I.I. Rabi disapproved, noting that if he 'had studied the Talmud rather than Sanskrit' it 'would have given him a greater sense of himself' (cited in Thorpe 2006: 53). The attraction of the *Gītā* was that it appeared to transcend its particular religious and cultural tradition (Thorpe 53). But, why, I ask? Here we can go back to Adler and his attempt to extract from Judaism and Christianity a universal morality. Maybe Oppenheimer was, after all, continuing Adler's universalist ideal. In this respect, he was rather not unlike other Western questers who sought solace and inspiration in the Sanskrit classic. The *Gītā* provided a guide by which privileged Westerners as gifted and entitled as Eliot and Oppenheimer could find meaning in a chaotic world, but at the same time showed that world just how cultivated and interesting they really were.

10

What Becomes of *Dharma* in a Conquered Country?

Simone Weil and Savitri Devi

> Certes, il était loin des bains chauds, le malheureux, Il n'était pas le seul. Presque toute *L'Iliade* se passe loin des bains chauds. Presque toute la vie humaine s'est toujours passée loin des bains chauds.
>
> Simone Weil, *L'Iliade*, 6

We saw how the *Gītā* translator Theodor Springmann presented German engagement in the First World War as the *Schwanengesang* of Aryan knighthood (Springmann, Introduction). As in the *Gītā,* Germany's involvement in the modern conflict was also a matter of duty (*dharma*) and action (*karma*). However, Springman did not 'do' his war in terms of disinterest, but rather as an expression of patriotism and the necessity of serving a cause. An equally bellicose German understanding of the *Gītā* appeared in print in time for the Second World War in the work of Hauer who in 1934 tied the *Gītā* to Nazi principles of blood, race, and *Heimat.* Hauer drew an equivalence between the *kṣatriya* ethos expressed in the *Gītā* and the Prussian military order. Both 'castes' are called upon to fight. In the Indian epic context, the warrior is initially unwilling to enter battle and must be reminded by Krishna of his duty. For German Indologists like Springmann and Hauer, and Americans like Eliot and Oppenheimer, it was the *Gītā* itself that reminded them of their duty by providing the vehicle by which they could conceptualize their given tasks. It would serve a similar purpose for the two French women examined in this chapter,

The Afterlives of the Bhagavad Gītā. Dorothy M. Figueira, Oxford University Press.
DOI: 10.1093/oso/9780198873488.003.0011

who also found in the Sanskrit poem a guide for their engagement with the enemy.

Simone Weil

Simone Weil (1909–43), much like J. Robert Oppenheimer, was born into a secular Jewish family and had no spiritual dogmas instilled in her from childhood. Along with her older brother, André (1909–98), she grew up in Paris with devoted parents who nurtured in both their children a love of learning and provided them with a supportive and comfortable bourgeois existence. Like his contemporary Oppenheimer, Simone's brother André prided himself on his command of Sanskrit.[1] A. Weil realized, as had Oppenheimer, that glory in his specialization depended on early success. He was so convinced of his brilliance that he chose not to sacrifice his time or possibly his life fighting for France during World War II. Claiming that mathematicians often make their greatest discoveries when young, he did not wish to lose precious years of his early career for France.[2] When repatriated back to Paris from Finland, where he had conveniently gone to avoid conscription, André Weil rather absurdly claimed that the *Gītā* gave him the justification needed for his refusal to serve his country (Pétrement 355). In his much later *Autobiography*, he wrote that the

> only right course is for each one of us to determine as best as he can his dharma, which is his alone.... Gauguin's dharma was painting. Mine ... was to devote myself to mathematics. The sin would have been to let myself be diverted from it. (A. Weil 1992: 16)

His excuse shows the extent to which he did not really understand the *Gītā*. The Hindu prohibition from killing does not apply to enemies in

[1] His command of Sanskrit was negligible according to the Indologist Charles Malamoud who on several occasions met with Weil and discussed India, Sanskrit, and Sanskrit literature (private communication with Malamoud).

[2] Although he spent his adult life and career in the US, he never took American citizenship. His stance during the war derailed any subsequent illustrious appointments or honours he hoped to receive in Paris.

war (McKenzie 61). The *Gītā* teaches that since war is unreal, it is not evil and the warrior with any ethical misgivings is persuaded to kill, just as God kills (O'Flaherty 1998: 15).

In any case, André Weil would go onto have an illustrious career at Princeton, just like Oppenheimer. Both secular Jews, both convinced of their genius, both wanting to flourish at the beginning of their respective careers, both fledging Sanskritists, one served his country admirably, the other chose not to serve at all. But they both ended their days 'exiled' in that prison for geniuses in New Jersey, Oppenheimer as the Director of the Institute where Weil worked. But it is not André Weil who concerns us here. Rather his little sister becomes the subject of our inquiry. She might have thought her brother was 'comparable to Pascal',[3] he might have outlived her by almost 60 years, but it is she who is revered the world over (justly or not) as a saint, mystic, and martyr.[4] They might have both enjoyed the same privileged family life and both thrived intellectually, but Simone took from her formative experience a great capacity for sympathy and compassion for those less fortunate. Her philosophical bent and her love of literature led her at an early age to seek to grapple with the pressing moral issues of the day. Just as for Oppenheimer, the *Gītā* would become for Simone an important guide in her life.[5] In particular, it would be instrumental in the manner for Weil in formulating her theories on force and justice.[6]

[3] His sister shared his elevated vision of his talents. Although Simone shared her brother's intellectual interests, she felt 'less of a genius' compared to him. 'The exceptional gifts of my brother, who had a childhood and youth comparable to those of Pascal, brought my own inferiority home to me. I did not mind having no visible successes, but what did grieve me was the idea of being excluded from that translucent kingdom to which only the truly great have access and wherein truth abides' (Weil 1951: 23).

[4] It must have been a burden to have a martyr, and someone deemed by many (including their father) as a saint for a baby sister. Even André's daughter felt the burden, writing in a family memoir of how difficult it was for her, a woman who liked sex, to have had Simone, a woman who disdained matters of the flesh, as her aunt. She also speaks of how it cramped her style, making it difficult to meet eligible Jewish men whose American families associated her with her aunt's perceived anti-Semitism (Weil 2009: 20).

[5] We might really want to question the role this exotic text exerted on the lives of secularized Jews and others in the West in the twentieth century. Did reading the *Gītā* in the original become a requisite reading for clever non-Indians?

[6] In this regard, see S.A. Degrâces in the presentation of vol. 1 of Weil's *Cahiers*, 'L'Inde ou le passage obligé' in that same volume (1988: vol 6, part 1: 36, 42–3), and the discussion of the *Iliad* essay.

Although a brilliant student,[7] Simone Weil did not want to be a bookish intellectual. She sought engagement in worldly pursuits, beginning with an ill-fated involvement with the Republican forces during the Spanish Civil War, where despite her poor eyesight she was issued a rifle. Attached to a unit of anarchists, Weil almost immediately injured herself by stepping into a pan of boiling water and needed to be evacuated.[8] Her parents, who protectively were across the border in France ready to intervene, came and got her. Not only was she clearly unfit for combat, but she was also incredibly naïve and idealistic to the point that she exhibited surprise and dismay at the atrocities that she witnessed committed by her fellow anarchists. This brief experience in the Spanish Civil War resulted in confirming her commitment to pacifism.

In the early days of her working life as a secondary-school teacher, Weil became involved in the workers' movement. She took numerous leaves of absence from teaching assignments at various institutions in order to work in what she saw as mind-numbing and dangerous factory jobs. She wanted to work in factories to have the joyful contact of an encounter with real life (252). In her first teaching job in Le Puy, she became deeply involved with unemployed workers who, viewing her as an employed bureaucrat, expressed no desire for her help. Her teaching suffered from such political extracurricular activities to such a degree that less than a third of her class passed their baccalaureate examination.[9] Finding her opportunities for engagement with the workers limited, Weil applied for a transfer. At a subsequent posting in Bourges, she also sought to widen her experiential horizons by entreating factory supervisors to employ her, and approaching farmers seeking to learn how to work their equipment (and breaking it on occasion, when given the chance). She lived with farmers, but refused compensation for work, since children in Indochina were hungry (Pétrement 258). She even sought employment in a mine

[7] She attended Lycée Henri IV and École Normale Supérieure (ENS), where she received the lowest grade possible to pass with her dissertation on Descartes under Brunschvicq, her advisor whom she scorned (Pétrement 66). She also scored first in the nationwide entrance exam in General Philosophy and Logic to enter ENS—with Simone de Beauvoir placed second and dozens of male students following in their wake, with Jean-Paul Sartre first among the men.

[8] In a curious parallel, while a student at Henri IV, she burned her hand in a seemingly non-accidental manner (Pétrement 39), suggesting the seeds of her later indulgence in self-mortification.

[9] The state examination that marks the end of secondary school in France.

(121). All this job searching and commitment to sharing the workers' lives took place when she was either employed teaching or on leave from her teaching assignments.

In the subsequent hagiographic accounts of her life, it is not emphasized that this factory or field work usually lasted only a few months at a time. It is one thing to be condemned, due to lack of training and educational opportunities, to such work for a lifetime and quite another to partake of it in short instalments, as someone 'slumming', so to speak, in a factory or a field, knowing full well that a civil service position awaited you after you had shared the travails of the common labourers. Weil was sincere, but she was also clearly a wilful and indulged individual who was humoured in these ventures by her family, her bourgeois sense of entitlement, and society-at-large. After the factory work, she continued this dilettante-like approach to manual labour in the fields of Ardèche and as a milkmaid, an activity she enjoyed because it called to mind Krishna and his penchant for cow-maids (Pétrement 414).[10] In these endeavours, her commitment and effectiveness replicated her involvement with the Republican forces in Spain[11] and her teaching career. Repeatedly, she worked for a bit before leaving the job or being let go due to incompetence.

However, Weil was refreshingly idealistic and non-conformist. Unlike many French Leftists, she was not attracted to Stalinism. She viewed it in the same way that she saw religious fundamentalism and as she would later see Nazism. She considered them totalitarian ideologies to which only persons in a position of uprootedness (*déracinement*) were susceptible. They were forms of enslavement. For all her ill-fated or (and some might say) frivolous attempts at engagement in the cause of the exploited and the downtrodden, she intellectually understood very well how totalitarian and fundamentalist ideologies oppressed the individual. She truly was what the modern cultural critic Andrew Ross has termed in another

[10] She badgered Father Perrin, the recipient of her *Letters to a Priest*, with whom she was in constant contact over the Church and her understanding of Catholic theology, to find her manual labour as a 'farm servant' in Ardèche. Perrin put her in contact with Gustave Thibon, a Catholic Right-wing self-taught philosopher and mystic who happened to be one of Pétain's principal speechwriters (Gray 169). Thibon would share 'vaguely anti-Semitic' jokes with Dr. Weil' (Gray 171) when her father visited her at Thibon's house.

[11] One is here reminded of Naipaul's accounts of the behaviour described in *The Return of Eva Peron and the Killings in Trinidad* (1980), where white privileged American radicals play-acted at revolution with a round-trip ticket back home.

context, an advocate for the Precariat, someone who focuses on the lives of refugees, displaced workers, and the dispossessed (Ross 2009).

Weil believed that truth could be experienced in many religions. She dabbled in Gnosticism, Stoicism, Manicheanism, Daoism, Buddhism, and Hinduism. Believing that the Johannine Gospel derived from Plato, she sought a Greek source for a Hellenized form of Christianity, a pure Christianity that she believed would be free from its Jewish heritage and any taint of Roman institutions, two traditions that she loathed (Weil 2003: paragraph 84–5).[12] She hated the Romans for their belief in having been chosen by destiny to rule the world; she hated the Jews for their belief in having been chosen by God (Weil 1956: 256). She felt that both the Old Testament and Rome had corrupted Catholicism (Weil 1965: 129). She totally rejected the Judaism of the Old Testament, seeing Yahweh as a tribal god obsessed with power and domination. She had, however, great respect for the God of the New Testament, whom she felt suffered powerlessness for a love that transcended national and racial boundaries.

While all religions, according to her teacher, the philosopher Alain,[13] were one, they were not, according to Weil, all valid, especially Judaism (Weil 1988: vol. 4, part 2.75–6). In the first volume of her *Cahiers* (Notebooks), Weil catalogues Old Testament atrocities (von de Ruhr 110). She juxtaposes them to what she sees in the Hinduism that she read into the *Gītā* (16.2–3) which she describes as emphasizing renunciation, serenity, aversion to fault-finding, sympathy for all beings, peace from greedy cravings, gentleness, modesty, and other Christian virtues (von der Ruhr 111). She felt that biblical Judaism was so inferior to Hinduism that the Old Testament should not even be deemed a sacred text (Weil 2003: 43–4). Her most violent critiques against Israel are significant for their timing. Here she was a French cradle Jew, who somehow felt in the climate leading up to and during the Second World War that it was appropriate and responsible to openly equate the religion of the Old Testament with totalitarianism (Weil 1988, vol 6, part 3: 291). Weil's decision to launch her critique of biblical Judaism when she did, points to a cluelessness or perversity that, in hindsight, is difficult to find sympathetic,

[12] See her 'Farewell Letter' to Father Perrin. See also Pétrement 456.

[13] Alain, alias Émile Auguste Chartier (1868–1951), a French philosopher, journalist, and pacifist.

as was her complete silence on the fate of the Jews in Europe at the time (Pétrement 300). In a letter to the Ministry of Public Education, she showed no solidarity with the situation of Jews in the French labour market and mocked the 'Statutory Regulation on Jews'. She took pains to deny any relation to Judaism, not in order to avoid any discrimination but rather to demonstrate her intellectual position and how she felt the word 'Jew' should be defined (Pétrement 392). The philosopher and social historian Isaiah Berlin has viewed her stance vis-à-vis Judaism and the Jews as a symptom of her self-hatred (1980: 280). The critic George Steiner termed it 'a classic Jewish self-loathing carried to a fever pitch' (1993: 4), particularly in those instances where she indulges in strident denunciations of the God of Moses and a near hysterical repugnance in what she saw as the excesses of Judaism present in modern Catholicism (Weil 2003: paragraph 14). In short, Weil's rejection of the Old Testament was exaggerated and cannot simply be ascribed to historical prejudices; it may well have also had psychological foundations (Calvert 180).

She believed that the ultimate purpose of each human is to be absorbed and possessed by God. Each person should strive towards the utmost purity in his/her life and this purity of being could only be attained through the experience of affliction (1951: 64). In *Attente de Dieu*, Weil relates three life changing religious events that seemed to confirm her beliefs. In Portugal in 1935, she saw a group of fisherwomen in procession and recognized them as engaging in a sad religion of slaves. Weil commented that she found their behaviour authentic and that she longed to be part of it. She saw in their worship a form of obedience[14] akin to that taught by Marcus Aurelius and the Stoics, an *amor fati* (love of fate), and duty to conform to divine will (1951: 24). The second experience occurred at St. Mary of the Angels in Assisi. Here, she remained for two days in the chapel and could not resist the impulse to kneel. The third religious experience occurred in 1938 while listening to Gregorian chant at the Benedictine Monastery at Solesmes. Although she had a terrible

[14] Weil had written: 'If one does something with the certainty of obeying God and without any other motive or intention than obedience, it is certain that one is obeying God. But does that mean one may do anything at all with this intent?' (1950: 258, cited in Nevin 298). One would think that if she truly believed this were the case, then the logical implication for her would be to not condemn the actions of the Hebrew patriarchs (Nevin 298). But, obviously, she did not follow this logic.

migraine, she experienced complete joy and was astonished that one could love God intensely despite affliction (1951: 26). She described this last experience as God coming down and taking possession of her (1951: 61). These experiences drew Weil to Catholicism, a faith she felt was intrinsically hers. However, she also recognized and repeatedly listed a number of issues that prevented her from joining the Church.

Primarily, she could not forgive Catholicism for its thirteenth-century suppression of the Albigensians.[15] She would revisit this crime of the Church repeatedly, comparing it to the abuses of the Roman Empire. She faulted both Rome and the Church for demanding uncritical and absolute obedience. Weil felt that the Catholic Church historically provided a model for totalitarian behaviour that would contribute to the rise of both Communism and Nazism. So, while she regularly attended mass in the Catholic Church and read the New Testament, the mystics and the liturgy, she also devoted considerable effort to excoriating Catholicism. Another difficulty Weil had with the Church was its relationship to other religions, particularly those of Egypt, India, China, and Greece (Griffiths 233). For all these various reasons, Weil felt she could not commit to Catholicism. In fact, she saw it as her vocation to remain outside the Church and not be baptized, even as she more assiduously attended mass while temporarily living in New York after fleeing occupied France. She claimed that she did so out of solidarity with those belonging to religions not accepted by Catholicism and in support of those belonging to no religion at all (1951: 32–4). As with the Republican cause, factory work, and field labour, Catholicism also offered her an opportunity, as an educated and privileged secular French Jew, to bond partially and intermittently with something she considered Other. Around the time of Weil's three religious experiences, she was exploring the theme of force and the form it took in ancient Greece. In her essay *L'Iliade ou le poème de la force* (1939), her most complete interpretation of any text and her most reworked composition, she examined this theme in some detail. This essay is of interest

[15] She was fascinated by this heretical sect which viewed the created world as evil, believed in reincarnation, and most importantly, understood the body as an obstacle to spiritual perfection (Gray 155–6). They also held that the holiest death was through self-induced starvation. She appreciated their negative assessment of the Old Testament and what she saw as their tolerance. While in Marseille, she wrote essays on the Albigensians.

for us since it foreshadows in its use of translation and its message, Weil's subsequent interpretation of the *Gītā*.

The body of Weil's essay on the *Iliad* consists of her random thoughts presented as fragmentary commentaries to certain passages of the Greek epic poem.[16] It is a disjointed text with no narrative filler and Weil's commentary often does not even reflect the quote she offers from the text. The key focus of the essay deals with the ontological status of the defeated man who supplicates his conqueror while paralysed by the immanence of force.[17] Weil emphasized those passages where the warrior is struck or about to be struck by death and is reduced to silence. She described the warrior as a suppliant, someone impersonating in advance the nothingness that is his/her fate. This person ceases to exist even before the fatal sword can strike. Force, deemed the key theme of the *Iliad*, demonstrates the pathetic debasement of all humans. It works not just on the victims but also on the conquerors (paragraph 24–32). All suffer (paragraph 33). No goodness or worth determines if one will be subject to force. It is blind destiny (*nemesis*), supervised by amoral gods in violation of measure. Force demands retribution (paragraph 34). Those who possess it, only do so fleetingly and illusorily. The operation of force can be subtle and insidious. The enemy is either reduced to a suppliant (paragraph 7–12) or experiences a form of death in life as a slave (paragraph 14–23). Those to whom fate has 'loaned' force will also perish, through their over-reliance on it. So, force affects all; it petrifies both the users and the victims (paragraph 61). Weil bases her argument in this essay on the depiction of Priam as a suppliant in his encounter with Achilles whom he approaches for the return of his dead son Hector's body. Weil arrives at her portrayal of Priam as an inert suppliant through a series of partial and

[16] This essay, initially took form in an earlier text of 1937, 'Ne recommençons pas la guerre de Troie.' Weil had studied the *Iliad* at Henri IV with Alain in 1926–7 and had read it again when she interrupted her teaching for health reasons in January 1938. *L'Iliade ou le poème de la force* was first published under a pseudonym, 'Émile Novis', in Marseille, after she had moved there with her parents after the occupation of Paris. The essay examines the similar psychological changes that force brings upon its victims and momentary possessors. According to Weil, the hero, the true subject, and the centre of the *Iliad* is force (paragraph 1). Force is the centre of all human history; it is the most beautiful and flawless of mirrors (paragraph 2).

[17] In a review of Richard Zaretsky, *The Subversive Simone Weil: A Life in Five Ideas* in the *London Review of Books*, vol. 43, no. 13 (1 July 2021), Toril Moi points out how her discussion of the *Iliad* is an interesting meditation on force. She does not address the connection of this meditation on force to the actual text of the *Iliad* (Moi 2021: 5).

faulty translations of the Greek text.[18] In terms reminiscent of Gandhi's reading of the *Gītā*, the *Iliad* is not really about a war. It does not sing the military adventures of the Greeks and the Trojans. It is actually a 'tableau de l'absence de Dieu' (Weil 1988, vol. 6, part I: 490, #55) and a portrait of the 'misère de l'homme sans Dieu' (vol. 6, part 2: 327). Even without the figure of Christ, Weil bathes the *Iliad* entirely in a Christian light (Weil 1977: 16). Her interpretation of the Greek epic was clearly informed by her involvement with Catholic spirituality. She disregarded key issues that permeate the epic and clearly did not read Homer in Homeric terms.[19] Would she approach the Sanskrit epic in a similar manner?

Weil was clearly on a quest to find a solution to her philosophical malaise. She initially sought answers in Catholicism and ancient Greece. She next approached Hinduism, a faith system that she thought might deliver what Roman Catholicism and a Christianized *Iliad* lacked.[20] And, indeed, Weil found in the *Gītā* a mystical antidote for the evil she had evinced in the mechanism of force. Hinduism, as she would understand it through her reading of the *Gītā*, offered a validation of the message first announced to her in her reading of both the New Testament and the *Iliad*. According to Weil, the *Gītā*, the *Iliad*, and the Gospels all deal with violence. They all share the pivotal moment when the decision is made to deploy brute force or deflect it (Doering 154). The advantage of Hinduism for Weil was that she could really interpret it freely, even more idiosyncratically than she had interpreted the *Iliad*. She could take from it what she wanted, since as opposed to her 'reading' of Catholicism, in her 'reading' of Hinduism, she would encounter no pesky priests[21] and

[18] In particular, she translated the meeting between Priam and Achilles as showing how in coming to his son's killer's tent the elderly man shows himself to be totally abject.

[19] George Steiner commented on how wrong she was in her reading of the epic. In the *Language and Silence* (26); He described it as a 'perverse reading'. Other critics commented on how Weil conveys no understanding of the formulaic style (Ferber 67) and seems to be blind to Homer's thematic of honour, shame, immortality, and glory. She ignores the epic's code of merit that the warrior is not only doing his job but also sustaining his renown and performing his *arête* (excellence). The essay itself was seen to present a problem and, as an interpretation, it was deemed a failure (Ferber 69). Harold Bloom viewed it as a 'strong misreading' (cited in Ferber 70), particularly in her interpretation of the encounter between Achilles and Priam. It is absurd to conclude that Priam was made into a 'thing' (Ferber 71–2).

[20] In this regard, a nice parallel (in reverse) can be seen in the case of F. Schlegel whose foray into Indian thought (*Über die Sprache und Weisheit der Indier*) catapulted him into a conversion to Catholicism.

[21] Until her death, Weil had maintained a correspondence with Father Perrin, with whom she discussed not only her thoughts on the Catholic faith, but her ruminations on religion in general.

no society of believers to thwart or contradict her interpretation. In contrast to any critique of her idiosyncratic reading of the Greek text of the *Iliad* might have engendered,[22] there were really no Western Sanskritists in the midst of World War II who had the time or energy to discuss her interpretation of the *Gītā*. She could (mis)interpret the *Gītā* with greater freedom, given the relative ignorance the French public had of this 'exotic' text compared to its general knowledge of the *Iliad* (as required reading in Greek *lycée* classes) and Catholicism.

Hinduism had fascinated Weil since her brother had studied Sanskrit at the Sorbonne in the early 1930s under the renowned French Sanskritist Sylvain Lévi. When Simone and her parents fled occupied Paris, they relocated to Marseille. There, she reconnected with René Daumel, an Indologist who had been her *khagne* mate.[23] She borrowed his books and undertook to study Sanskrit with him. With Daumel's help, she began to study the *Gītā* in the original in the Spring of 1940.[24] Just like Oppenheimer, she too fell in love with the language, writing: 'I hope never to stop loving these Sanskrit characters, which are sacred and have perhaps never served as a vehicle for anything base' (Pétrement 422, cited in Gray 167)! Unsurprisingly, just as in her reading of the *Iliad*, she felt that Krishna's teaching had a Christian sound to it. Moreover, she felt an allegiance to the truth of the *Gītā*'s message that far exceeded that of mere poetry.[25] Weil's fragmentary commentary on the *Gītā* can be found throughout her notebooks from this period. They contain selections of Sanskrit transliterations and attempts to master the *devanāgarī* script. Daumel was clearly her major source of information on Hinduism. He advised her to read René Guénon, who provided her with references to material on Indian philosophy. Unfortunately, both Daumel and Guénon had a tendency to seek facile correspondences between Hinduism and other religions. Their scholarship generally offered a series of artificial, forced, and contrived parallels between Vedic terminology and Western

[22] Among French Classicists of the time, there does not seem to be much of a response to her essay. The negative assessments I have found come mostly from comparatists and literary critics.

[23] *Khagne* is the preparatory year for the French university entrance exams.

[24] For the role of Sanskrit studies, see Degrâces in Weil 1988, vol. 6, part 1: 35–8.

[25] In *Attente de Dieu* (1951: 28), Weil wrote: 'Strange to say it was in reading those marvelous words, words with such a Christian sound, put into the mouth of the incarnation of God, that I came to feel strongly that we owe an allegiance to religious truth which is quite different from the admiration we accord to a beautiful poem; it is something far more categorical.'

philosophical and religious concepts. Combined they were, perhaps, the worst gurus for Simone Weil to have found, since their own works facilitated her predisposition to see common 'revelations'. We see this tendency throughout the *Cahiers* to juxtapose references to the *Gītā* to quotations from Heraclitus, T.E. Lawrence, Jeanne d'Arc, St John of the Cross, and numerous others. However, we cannot blame Daumel and Guénon exclusively for what we shall see as some of Weil's more extravagant analogies. Weil interpreted the *Gītā's* teaching as confirming her belief that all incarnations exemplify a potential for disinterested action and devotion to God. It was Weil's eccentricity that subsequently interprets this message as Christ sending his spirit to all those who call on Krishna at the hour of death.

For Weil, the greatest importance of the *Gītā* was its questioning of individual conduct in a war setting. Even before the war, she and her brother had discussed the *Gītā* and its advocacy of violence (Gabellieri 422). As the realities of war overtook France, Simone felt more and more guilt over her brother's disengaged political stance. So much so that at the beginning of the German offensive, the *Gītā* took on an intense topicality for her. It was, indeed, serendipitous that she was able to reconnect with Daumel, begin to study Sanskrit, and attempt to read the *Gītā* in the original at the very moment when she felt that its teaching of *dharma* could offer her a truth of the utmost importance for conducting her life (Weil 1988, vol. 6, part 2: 87). Her reading of the *Gītā* allowed her to escape from her brother's hidebound notion of non-engagement and her own ensuing reservations regarding pacifism once the hostilities had begun. She took from the *Gītā* the understanding that it was illusory to think that one can sit apart from the world and its evil actions (Nevin 296). The same pervasive nature of force that she found in the *Iliad* she now discovered in the *Gītā* and it was in the Sanskrit poem that she sought the inspiration she needed for understanding and countering force in the era of particular injustice in which she lived. The *Gītā* would be the influential text for the remainder of her life. With it, she moved from the pacifism she had espoused in the 30s to an acceptance of the use of force premised on obligation, and ultimately a movement ever upward toward the Divine.

Weil recognized that the *Gītā*'s teaching of detachment was alien to Western culture, but she did not see its foreignness as an obstacle. From the *Iliad*, Weil had discovered that the continued use of force is never desirable. Through its continued deployment, force continues to survive and thrive on itself in a spiral without end. The inevitable suppliant, whom Weil projected as a key figure in the *Iliad*, was either a dead thing or the living dead. This suppliant had to submit to force. However, with the rise of Hitler, Weil acknowledged that there were times when force demanded a response. While she believed that, since it was impossible to control the sources of action in one's nature (*guṇas*) or past deeds (*karma*), one should not adopt an erroneous perspective of action as ultimately important. Nevertheless, one must make a response and Weil's default solution was suffering. She claimed that any notions of personal responsibility arise out of our confusion regarding the individual's role as that of a sufferer. Weil read the *Gītā* as presenting a theology of suffering that she equated with the Christian mystery of the cross (Bingemer 86).

In the *Iliad*, she had sought to discover the seeds and nuances of force in order to articulate a notion of just force. The Trojan War was seen not as an aberration or a movement from order into chaos, but rather as a dramatization of existence *in extremis*, reality with intermittent 'luminous moments' of courage and love (such as the scene on the parapets of Troy between Hector and Andromache). Now in the *Gītā*, Weil also found intimations of a spiritual resolution to the dilemma of how to participate in forceful action in the course of war, while avoiding its contagion. She saw in Arjuna's teaching the combination of the duty of action and a transcendental orientation of the soul that allowed one to obey the demand of waging war without making of the war a good thing (Gabellieri 422, cited in Bingemer 81). Weil felt that her own sense of calling to fulfil her duties or responsibilities in life corresponded well to the *Gītā*'s discussion of *dharma*. It facilitated her coming to terms with the problems that she had encountered throughout her life. Most significantly, she felt that the *Gītā* permitted her to combine her early ruminations on force from her work on the *Iliad* with her new-found discovery of religious sentiment from her involvement with Catholicism. She felt the *Gītā* would enable her to carry out her duty and also love God attentively and obediently.

For Weil, the *Gītā* teaches how:

> We must die to ourselves and become defenseless to the 'fangs of life accepting emptiness as our lot in life. We must annihilate our ego

> by suffering and degradation. (Weil 1979: 21, cited in Pensakovic 2015: 393–94)

Like Oppenheimer, Weil felt that the *Gītā*'s vision of *dharma* could provide a code of behaviour she could accept. Weil saw in her own thought processes a parallel to Krishna's message to Arjuna: that he should submit to the obligation of force as to a necessity (Weil 1988, vol. 6, part 1:335). So, the *Gītā* became for Weil, just as for Oppenheimer, the master text guiding her activism. Krishna was a god she could accept and love. Even when hospitalized at the end of her life, Weil wrote cheerful letters to her parents evoking the *Gītā* and urged family and friends to see 'how it does one good the language of Krishna' (Weil 1965: 188).[26] As death approached, she refused to acknowledge God/god, because He would have been the God of the Jews or the Romans whom she loathed. Krishna provided a suitable surrogate. Up until the end, she felt it was important to distance herself from these other deities (Desgrâces 40), even when she wrote to her parents. She only spoke in her final letters of the Krishna she encountered in the *Gītā*.

But the love she evinced for Krishna had a dark side. When she had worked the fields in Ardèche, Weil welcomed her new lowly status (just as she had done earlier in her factory work), thinking that it would bring her closer to Krishna.[27] She embraced suffering, drawing an analogy between her voluntary adoption of low status and the involuntary 'estrangement' inflicted on Jews by the occupation.

> Feeling is in accord with the social order at present. If to the French people at this moment it seems good that I be among the *śūdras*, it is perhaps good that I conform myself to this. (Pétrement 422)

Comparing the French treatment of its Jews in 1941 to the Indian treatment of *śūdras* had a certain logic and veracity to it. However, exoticizing

[26] She even urges her parents when they are bored to ease their boredom by thinking of Krishna and taking comfort in him (Nevin 302).

[27] Unlike Oppenheimer, she did not believe it was her *dharma* as a philosopher to do her duty as an intellectual but, chose at all points to do the *dharma* of a labourer, either on farms or in factories, as a combatant in the Spanish Civil War, or as a parachuting nurse in combat with the Free French. Her vision of her *dharma* was at odds with her reality as a tubercular, legally blind, and physically weak person.

the French collaboration in the Nazi persecution of the Jews or even romanticizing caste was less reasonable. Passively accepting this persecution (at a safe distance en route to escaping it as a privileged refugee) is simply unacceptable. Yet, the *Gītā* was there and could be called upon to serve the important purpose of summoning Weil to 'exotic' suffering and martyrdom. She did not, however, advocate a form of meaningless suffering, rather she saw suffering in theodical knowledge (i.e. abandonment and revealing light).

Weil claimed that, contrary to what the *Gītā* says, Krishna is not an incarnation because he did not suffer[28] and incarnations require suffering and the ability to suffer. According to Weil, Christ was the only one who truly suffered, and he suffered because of his righteousness. Krishna was a mere manifestation that enlightens. But not only God, who loves man, should suffer. Man who loves God must also suffer. She felt it was more important to imitate Christ in his suffering than in his godliness. Suffering trumps goodness (Weil 2002: 87–91). She envisioned her salvation in a resignation to her present existence and renunciation of an afterlife (Weil 2002: 87).[29] Her remedy for her dis-ease with the human condition entailed a process of 'decreation' by which one sought to share in creating the world by self-abnegation and dying to oneself. Just as Christ poured himself out by emptying himself of his divinity *(kenosis)*, so too must Weil sought to empty herself of her self-attachment.

Weil sought this end by embracing affliction, suffering, and ultimately death (Weil 2002: 80–4). Affliction and suffering provide the keys to the door of wisdom. She maintained that the *Gītā* contributed to this understanding by teaching the positive lesson that one *could* make war. She felt that the *Gītā* offered her a viable response to what she saw as the comparable twin evils of Nazism and the religion of Israel. In presenting this interpretation of the *Gītā*, Weil was able to solve her dilemma with Catholicism, by assimilating Krishna to the incarnation of the Word (Weil

[28] In a *Letter to a Priest* (1942) she wrote: 'We do not know for certain that there have not been incarnations previous to that of Jesus and that of Osiris in Egypt, Krishna in India was not of that number' (Weil 2003: 19). He was, however, a manifestation of Vishnu and an enlightener.

[29] Weil could think this way because she was convinced, as she wrote in *Waiting for God*, of her natural disposition to crime (Weil 1951: 69–79); she was burdened with sadness over what she perceived as her sins, and unable to conceive the possibility of salvation through any Christian belief in the afterlife.

2003b: 19).[30] She saw a deep spiritual kinship between Krishna's utterances in the *Gītā* and Christ's words in the New Testament (von der Ruhr 107). But she acknowledged that the Hindu text taught much better than Christianity the connection between law and sin. She may well have felt the need to justify her initial decision to remain in Vichy and her reading of the *Gītā* provided a rationale when it taught that one should not adopt an erroneous perspective of action as ultimately important. The Self does not act, only Nature acts. Besides, any action demands an apprenticeship (Weil 1988, vol. 6, part 1: 330–4). This understanding of the *Gītā* enabled her to deal with the Occupation's net of complicity (Nevin 301).

The *Gītā* was also a text that helped her come to terms with the issue of force.[31] Its remedy of action without any attachment to the fruits of action became, for Weil, obedience, and self-renunciation (Weil 1950: 230). According to Weil, the *Gītā* posed the problem of how finite means can be ordered with a view toward transcendent ends; it also provided her with an acceptable response to the demand to act: the renunciation of personal will. While the *Iliad* had taught Weil the ubiquity and mercilessness of force and the Gospels revealed to her that contact with force deprived one momentarily of God, there was no such deprivation in the *Gītā* (Nevin 297). *Dharma* counterbalances force (Weil 1988, vol. 6, part 1: 297, 334). One remains thus in contact with God, since the *Gītā* teaches us how to seek good in our own acts. We can see her argument as pertaining specifically to Vichy:

> Are there certain things we can do without wanting success and others we cannot do that way? Does this criterion permit us to distinguish between our actions? It is not certain.... we can attribute some things to limited injustice, required by the social order. But how much? That's the whole question. (Cited in Nevin 289)

[30] In the Hindu trinity, she saw in Vishnu the equivalent of the Word (*Dieu manifesté*); in Brahma, she saw the Father, and in Śiva she recognized the Holy Spirit (Weil 1988, vol. 6, part 2: 328, 370, 433; see Gabellieri 427, note 221).

[31] Weil 1988, vol. 6, part 1: 297, translated in Bingemer 75: 'Contact with force, from whichever end the contact is made (sword handle or sword point) deprives one for a moment of God. Whence the *Bhagavad Gītā*. The *Bhagavad Gītā* and the Gospels complete each other.'

As noted, Weil accepted Vichy. She gave in to force but initially felt guilty and resisted it in a limited manner, particularly in her writings for *Combat* and *Cahiers du Témoignage chrétien*, both promoting Left-leaning works and virulently opposed to Vichy (Gray 175). But, it was primarily through the authority she vested in the *Gītā* that Weil found the authoritarian support she needed to justify her vision of the world, as in Weil's interpretation of the *Gītā* 4.14–21: One can only act by 'handling necessity' (vol. 6, part 1: 315).

For all her professed love of the Sanskrit language and her excitement at learning it, she seems to have mastered very little in the two and a half years she devoted to its study.[32] Initially she had considerable trouble learning the *devanāgarī* script, not being able to begin dealing with the text before she secured a transliterated version. The texts that appear in her *Cahiers* are actually not her work at all, but the translations of Émile Senart (Weil 1988, vol. 6, part 1: 250). Weil herself did not translate the passages she evokes, cites, and juxtaposes to other philosophies, authors, and even mathematical formulae. She does not compare the Sanskrit terms word for word to Senart's translation. Rather, she effects a 'reduction' between the two cultures involved. She replaces certain words in the text with Sanskrit concepts that she thinks they represent (39). She reads and cites Senart, questions the thoughts expressed in terms that reflect her own thoughts and concerns. In short, she weaves what Senart translates into her own thoughts, lightly modifying the text, grafting some of her chief concerns, such as limited human knowledge, the desire to know, obedience (i.e. all very Weilian themes) to her rewriting of Senart's translation (481, #99). These reworked translations of Senart then undergo cutting, condensation (351), and redistribution of blocks of words to make connections that establish a pre-ordained connection that Weil seeks in the text (40). Just as in her treatment of the *Iliad*, the texts tend not to match her commentary. Weil does not give literal translations. At best, she offers a very idiosyncratic interpretation (Weil 1988, vol. 6, part 2: 458). Like others studied in this volume, Weil just focuses on the topic of interest most pressing to her: that there should be no guilt associated with not acting. Her synthesis of *Gītā* 2.47–53 and 6.16–21 addresses

[32] We can chart this study from the end of December 1941 to August 1943. See Weil 1988, vol. 6, part 1: 481.

this concern. Here she translates the non-attachment to the fruits of one's actions as an injunction to reject action that is 'au-dessous de soi' (below one or beneath oneself) (Weil 1988, vol. 6, part 1: 331).

As noted, Weil's sense of entitlement was often filtered through a sense of abjection and how she sought to force this abjection onto others. In her reading of the *Gītā*, she will combine the theme of self-mortification with her newly discovered 'mystical' appreciation of Krishna as a means of addressing the dilemma of action in the time of war. Her interest in action/non-action, Krishna, and her sense of caste/entitlement are all central to her reading of the *Gītā*. They reflect her experiences as a Jew under occupation who accepts (or even welcomes) her role as a *śūdra*, her religious encounters in Assisi, Solesmes, and Portugal, and her response to Vichy. The *Cahiers*, the Sanskrit texts she copies out, and her rewriting of Senart's translations further explore these themes (*Gītā* 3.35b; 18.45–9; 18.57, cited in Weil 1988, vol. 6, part 1: 361–5). Let us look briefly at a few representative translations from Senart's *Gītā* that Weil cites and examine how she uses them to support her ideas.

The Sanskrit of *Gītā* 6.25b is as follows: 'ātmasaṃsthaṃ manaḥ kṛtvā na kiṃcid api cintayet'. This phrase can be literally translated as 'the mind fixed in the Self he should not think about anything'. Senart translated this phrase in the following manner and Weil (in brackets) made her emendations:

> Ayant obligé le [manas (mental)] à demeurer dans l'ātman [soi]; il ne faut plus penser à autre chose? Ou: [il faut], s'enfermant en soi, ne plus penser.[33]

We see that Senart took a simple statement and needlessly overtranslated it, omitting the concept of *manas* (thought, mind). Weil, in her subtle emendation places the obligation coming not from force, but from a necessary firmness of spirit, introduced by Senart by the addition of 'ou' and augmented by Weil with [il faut] (Weil 1988, vol. 6, part 1: 507, #281).

Another passage Weil cites is *Gītā* 8.12:
sarvadvārāṇi saṃyamya mano hṛdi nirudhya ca

[33] [The Self] obliged to remain in the *ātman*, it should no longer think of something else? Or (it is necessary] closed up in the Self, to no longer think.

mūrdhnyādhāyātmanaḥ prāṇam
āsthito yogadhāraṇām

Literally we might translate this verse as:

> Controlling all gates[34] and shutting up the mind in the heart
> Having placed one's breath in the head
> One is situated in yogic concentration.

Senart translates it as:

> Ayant clos toutes les portes et enfermé le mental dans le Coeur, ayant fixé son souffle dans la tête, il maintient la concentration vers l'union.[35]

Weil will translate Senart's translation as: 'Emprisonnant en soi la faculté de percevoir (/) retenant en soi le souffle vital. . . .'[36] She leaves out the bodily component (the nine gates) and omits reference to the mind (vol. 6, part 1: 351). In both these citations, there is an emphasis on the mental and a dismissal of the physical processes at work.

The focus on action or non-action pervades Weil's reading of the *Gītā*. The issue, as Weil sees it, is that Arjuna has no choice to fight or not to fight (331). But her vision of violence here does not pertain to the battlefield. As elsewhere in her work, when Weil evoked violence, it is referring to God's violence; it is existential and always perceived 'through the lens of food and eating' (Irwin 259). She writes that Arjuna can no longer 'bite on the real in the form of action' ('mordre sur le réel sous forme d'action') (259).[37] Weil's relationship with god/God as well as her inquiries into the human condition (Weil 1988, vol. 6, part 2: 439–41) are seen through eating metaphors. Amidst a discussion of Racine's *Phèdre*, the Gospel of Luke, Colette, and Heraclitus, she translates the Sanskrit term *amṛta*

34 The nine gates (orifices) of the body (eyes, nostrils, ears, mouth, penis/vagina, anus).

35 Having closed all the gates and closed the mental process in the heart, having fixed one's breath in the head, he holds concentration in order to achieve union.

36 Locking up the faculty of perception in the Self (/), holding one's vital breath . . .

37 Dans une situation donnée, certains désirs (certaines pensées) peuvent, prenant forme d'action, mordre sur le monde; d'autres ne peuvent pas, mais seulement avoir des consequences autres que leur but.

("nectar of the gods" or sometimes "immortality") as "to eat being" (manger l'être) or "to eat opinion" (manger l'opinion) (451). In the context of her discussion of Arjuna seeking good in action, Weil announces, "La nourriture est l'irréductible" (food is irreducible). In the same passage, she speaks of sacrificing her body, that she professes to love, to be consumed as food, drink, cover and fuel (439–41). This is a common theme for Weil. In *Attente de Dieu*, she wrote how God awaits her in order to eat her so that she can be changed and become Other (devenue autre) having been consumed and digested by God (Weil 1966:122, cited in Irwin 265).

It is this devouring God that she reads into the *Gītā*. In a notebook entry, alongside passages from the *Gītā*, she cites a passage from Heraclitus:

> Vivre la mort d'un être, c'est le manger. L'inverse est d'être mangé. L'homme mange Dieu et est mangé par Dieu. (Weil 1988, vol. 6, part 2: 454)[38]

It is significant that Weil highlights this quotation, actually taken from Heraclitus, in the section of the notebook that deals primarily with her interpretation of the *Gītā*. This passage is very reminiscent of Krishna's revelation to Arjuna in the *Gītā* (11.29–30):

> Just as moths enter the blazing flame to their destruction with great speed, so also the words enter with great speed your mouths, to their destruction. You lick, swallowing from all sides, all the worlds with flaming mouths. Filling with splendor all the world, Your terrible rays consume, O Vishnu.[39]

She could have just as easily attributed it to the Sanskrit poem, given how she regularly inserted the theme of eating God or being eaten by God into her readings of the *Gītā*. This thematic reflected what can only be called

[38] To live the death of being is to eat it. The reverse is to be eater. Man eats food and is eaten by God (1988, vol. 6, 2.454).

[39] Yathā pradīptaṃ jvalanaṃ pataṃgā viśanti nāśāya saṃṛddha-vegāḥ
tathaiva nāśāya viśanti lokās tavāpi vaktrāṇi saṃṛddha-vegāḥ
lelihyase grasamānaḥ samantāl lokān samagrān vadanair jvaladbhiḥ
tejobhir āpūrya jagat samagraṃ bhāsas tavogrāḥ pratapanti viṣṇo.

the issue Weil had, as an individual with an eating disorder, with the intake of food and her ultimate self-starvation. The references to eating that crop up in her discussions of the *Gītā* offer a heart-rending confession of personal, physical, and spiritual despair. They also suggest the degree to which Weil saw herself on a mission of the elect.[40]

Earlier, she had distorted the *Iliad* by ignoring passages in the text or mistranslating them. Here, she simply does not translate the words of the *Gītā* at all or simply rewrites them and juxtaposes them to other authors. Weil actually combines several strategies in her *Gītā* reception: she subtly amends Senart's translation to express her own concerns, offering little recourse to the actual text, and she throws the *Gītā* together with a variety of other works, suggesting a commonality of message and, in the process of drawing such facile and non-sensical connections, levels out meaning to universalize her own philosophy of life.

After her family had escaped from Paris through southern France, avoiding Nazi persecution and deportation, they arrived safely in the States. All Weil wanted to do was return to Europe. She devised what she termed her 'Projet d'Infirmières de première ligne', a plan to set up a group of nurses to parachute behind Nazi lines with the mission of espionage. She devoted the rest of her life trying to implement this mission.[41] She had already sought the intervention of influential friends both in the US and abroad for the project. While in the US, she had petitioned for sponsorship from the American government, asking Jacques Maritain to intercede personally on her behalf with President Roosevelt.[42] There was really no limit to Simone Weil's sense of entitlement. When, later that year, she went to London to work for the Free French, de Gaulle deemed her scheme and Weil herself 'crazy' (Pétrement 1976: 514, cited in Gray 202). She then devised another plan where she would be sent to France

[40] Irwin alludes (269) to the 'celebratory appropriation of Weil's self-expenditure by comfortable male writers' as a bit 'sinister'. I can only agree with him. One thinks particularly about T.S. Eliot, Robert Coles, Camus, and Dwight McDonald (see end of this section). The celebratory and sinister appropriation may also explain her continuing fascination in religious circles and among certain feminist authors.

[41] The Project was published in the *Écrits de Londres et dernières lettres* (Gallimard 1957: 187–95) and was reworked while she was in the US. The first version was written before the German offensive in May 1940 (Pétrement 374–5).

[42] She also importuned Admiral Leahy (the former US Ambassador to France who had been called back to Washington), the future Gaullist minister Jasques Soustelle (an old friend from ENS), Maurice Schumann (a fellow student of Alain), and the family friend and future Prime Minister of France, Pierre Mendès-France (Pétrement 1976: 476, cited in Gray 182–3).

on a special espionage mission. No one at work or among her friends and acquaintances found this idea feasible either.[43]

De Gaulle had given her a desk job. Her quest for lowly work in the past consisted of menial labour that she had herself chosen. It fit a noble and politically attractive role that she had decided to perform. But she viewed this assignment as not suitable to her extraordinary skills. For someone of her intellect and sense of self-worth, she simply could not accept such an inactive position.[44] In her last letters, she complains that no one pays attention to her ideas, just her intelligence. She wrote to her parents that she had 'deposits of pure gold' in her to be handed down and there was perhaps no one to receive them (Weil 1965: 196–7).[45] As with the other jobs, Weil did not stay long in this job either. She died shortly afterwards in a sanatorium from heart failure aggravated by pulmonary tuberculosis and self-starvation. It is said that the last word she wrote was 'nurses'. Either she was acknowledging the care she had been given or, more likely, leaving her project as a final wish to be satisfied after her martyrdom (Moi 2021: 4). The coroner's verdict was suicide (Pétrement 1976: 537), the effects of not-eating.[46]

In *The Need for Roots*, Weil defines what she saw as her duty:

> The primary social consideration for savants is purely and simply one of professional duty. Savants are people who are paid to manufacture science, they are expected to manufacture some, they feel it to be their duty to manufacture some. But that is insufficient for them as a

[43] When the Bureau Central chose to send her closest friend, Simone Dietz, to be parachuted into France, Weil was so distraught that she tried to convince Dietz to switch places with her (Gray 204). She could not understand why she had not been selected. Envious of her friend having been chosen for such a mission, Weil was thrilled when it was subsequently cancelled (Pétrement 1976: 516–17).

[44] Her own sense of entitlement, of being 'among the chosen' is ironic, since daring to feel chosen was one of the reasons she so despised the religions of the Romans and the Jews.

[45] At this point, I really wonder about genius women who are held up to us as the most gifted of our gender. Like Margaret Fuller who could not wade across 50 yards of shallow water in Long Island Sound to save herself and child from drowning, one has to wonder about Weil who needed to write to her mother in her late 20s, asking whether one had to cook bacon before eating it (Pétrement 85).

[46] If, indeed, she was anorexic, it is quite possible that she could not eat after years of not eating properly. At the end, she asked for mashed potatoes in the English sanatorium, cooked in the French way, preferable by a French cook who could be enlisted for the job (Pétrement 538). The accommodations her mother had made to satisfy her food desires were clearly seen by Weil as universal privileges that she could request of anyone anywhere.

stimulant. Professional advancement, professorships, rewards of all kinds, honors and money, receptions abroad, the esteem and admiration of colleagues, reputation, fame, titles—all that counts for a great deal. (Weil 1952: 256–7)

This vision of her duty as an intellectual was similar to that of Oppenheimer, as was her assessment of the ego constraints involved. But it is curious how someone who in her working life achieved so little and took pains to appear unambitious should have the same level of mission and grandiosity as Oppenheimer (who after all had managed the building of the Atomic Bomb that actually helped end the war). It is not by accident that they shared a similar sense of duty. They certainly shared a similar perception of their intellectual abilities. The *Gītā* is the common link. But, in the case of Weil, the belief in her exceptionalism was abetted by her parents who went to extreme lengths to enable and protect her.[47] After Simone's death, her father survived her by 12 years and her mother by 22 years. They spent that time recopying her manuscripts for posterity. They worked in the morning, broke for lunch, and continued until late in the evening. They socialized with people who came to talk about Simone with them. They devoted themselves exclusively to preserving her work (Gray 214).[48] It is thanks to them that the thousands of pages of Weil's often inchoate ramblings are available in her voluminous collected works. For someone who published so little in her lifetime, there is a considerable corpus consisting of everything she ever wrote or even doodled.

Weil's hagiography was put in place even faster than Oppenheimer's. Yet, it is indeed hard, as one reads through her collected works and especially the notebooks, which are now *soigneusement* edited and available in print, to fathom why she was taken so seriously as a philosopher in

[47] One can sympathize with a mother who feels that her child cannot cope due to physical or mental issues and tries to intercede and facilitate that child's experience in the world. But her mother was excessive in such care. She attended every teaching job placement meeting, rented and furnished apartments for her, made arrangements with roommates, landlords, and butchers to buy her the most expensive cuts of meat without her knowing it, typed her papers, and visited her regularly at all her postings. There is the account related by Pétremont describing how, on the ocean trip to America, there was one seat with a table where Weil could sit and write during the day on the top deck. Her parents took turns laying claim to this seat, when Simone needed to get up and leave it, so no one else could sit down and write. This writing table was hers and no one else deserved to use it, since her needs always came first.

[48] Gray's personal conversation with Sylvie Weil in 2000.

the late 40s that Albert Camus and T.S. Eliot would anoint her work with their introductions. Mary McCarthy quickly translated the essay on the *Iliad* and Dwight McDonald disseminated it in the States.[49] In his Preface to the English translation of *The Need for Roots*, Eliot wrote:

> We must simply expose ourselves to the personality of a woman of genius, of a kind of genius akin to that of saints. (Weil 1952: vi)

The Anglican man of letters and arbiter of what was of literary worth presents her as an original kind of Catholic mystic. Camus worshipped her so much as a formative inspiration for his own work that before his flight to Stockholm to receive the Nobel Prize in Literature, he made a pilgrimage to the Weil family's two-floor apartment overlooking the Luxembourg Garden adjacent to the Pantheon, in order to meditate in Simone's room for an hour. Once this level of veneration had begun, there was simply no stopping it. J. M Cameron noted:

> She is so attractive, her literary gifts are so stunning, her mystical vocation so evident, that it may have seemed churlish to pay too much attention to what is extravagant in her. (White 1981: 45)

The eminent Harvard psychologist Robert Coles opined: 'She also put her body on the line—a worker in three factories, a harvester on two farms.... '(White 1981: 29). More recently, intellectuals such as Susan Sontag and Judith Butler have also eulogized her. Sontag thought she exemplified the cultural heroes of our time who are both 'anti-liberal and anti-bourgeois', who are 'repetitive, obsessive, and impolite, who impress by force—not simply by their tone of personal authority and by their intellectual ardor, but by the sense of acute personal and intellectual extremity' (Sontag 1961: 58–9, cited in Gray 229).

There was, however, a counter narrative to such hagiographical assessments that looked at her thought and martyrdom in a less positive (misty-eyed, fuzzy mystical) light. Simone was high maintenance. She regularly

[49] Her work was initially launched in America by MacDonald in his anarcho-leftist journal *Politics*, for which Mary McCarthy translated the *Iliad* essay in November 1945, and later in book form in 1956.

bombarded Catholic priests in wartime, when perhaps they had more pressing duties to perform, with 30-page letters asking for interpretations of the tenets of the faith. Even her friend and admirer Gustave Thibon (1903–2001) complained how she was not detached from her own detachment (Perrin and Thibon 117). She was very demanding in her quest for abjection (Pétrement 425). She complicated the lives of those with whom she interacted. She imposed on people her self-centred vocation of self-effacement. She was inflexible in how she pursued her quest of self-immolation, the manner in which she 'mounted guard around her void still displayed a terrible preoccupation with herself' (Perrin and Thibon 116, cited in Gray 172). As her friend from ENS, Jean Cavaillès[50] told Weil, her belief that she had a special vocation with her project to parachute behind enemy lines to nurse (without any nursing experience or training whatsoever) was absurd. He pointed out to her that everyone serves where they are placed. It was not up to them to make such decisions. He had abolished the intellectual in himself and was simply a soldier. He told her she might have had a sense of exceptional nobility, but she really possessed no special vocation (Pétrement 515).

The poet Kenneth Rexroth (1905–82) was particularly critical. He felt that she killed herself for a salvation that she falsely identified with Catholicism, and he accused her of a 'captious, misinformed playing with Hinduism and comparative mythology' (Rexroth 1987: 38, cited in Gray 228). Hers was 'a sick kind of agonized frivolity'. She toyed with a 'modern mathematics of infinitudes and incommensurabilities' that he termed a 'post-Cantor—Dedekind[51] Neopythagoreanism' (Rexroth 1987: 37). Brutal, perhaps, but was he wrong? It is one thing to refuse sugar made by slave labour, but quite another to refuse to eat more than the starvation rations of occupied Paris when one is tubercular in an English sanatorium. Rexroth concluded that Weil, suffering from a moribund intellectuality and spiritual agony (38),[52] saw herself as someone who was a

[50] French philosopher and logician who specialized in the philosophy of mathematics and science. Although, like André Weil, he had a lot to give French mathematics, he chose to join the French Resistance and was captured, tortured, and executed by the Gestapo in 1944.

[51] In mathematical logic, the Cantor-Dedekind axiom states that real numbers are order-isomorphic to the linear continuum of geometry.

[52] See his review of the *Notebooks* of Weil, originally published in 'The Dialectic of Agony' (*The Nation*, January 1957, reprinted in Rexroth 1987: 35–40). Rather than seeing her as a countercultural icon, he sees her publications, particularly, *The Need for Roots*, as a 'collection of egregious nonsense surpassed only by the deranged fantasies of the chauvinist Péguy (35) who

mere actor in her own spiritual melodrama (39). Rexroth marvelled how professionals and institutions so catered to her—that hospital staff could not stop her from starving herself and that the publishing house Putnam would come out with several collections of her rambling and often inchoate journals and correspondence. He was further astonished by the reissuing of *Waiting for God*,[53] *Letter to a Priest*, *Gravity and Grace*,[54] and *The Need for Roots* throughout the 60s. He would probably be amazed to see how her work continues to be reissued today and commented on.

In an ironic turn, Weil has now even entered the canon of Holocaust Studies, with her work treated as a Holocaust testimonial, although she escaped the Holocaust, was disinterested in the fate of its victims, and never made any mention of them in her writings. The German author Ruth Kluger, begins and ends her own Holocaust memoir, *Still Alive*, with citations from Weil. Judith Butler has evoked Weil in terms of what it means to address another and experience dispossession (Dumm and Butler 2008: 102–3). In the opera *Decreation*, Anne Carson has portrayed Weil along with Sappho and the mystic Marguerite Porete. One might ask, what continuing function (as a woman, intellectual, victim, or Jew) does she serve? Is there a hidden Simone Weil in all of us that the Ruth Klugers, Susan Sontags, Anne Carsons, and the Judith Butlers believe is our common condition, and that they fear or love too much?

It was first in Greek and then in Sanskrit epic literature that Simone Weil sought guidance in dealing with force, violence, and war. Her reading of the *Iliad* did not provide her with the necessary answers. It was then that the opportunity presented itself for her to learn Sanskrit and read the *Gītā*.[55] Yet her reading of the *Gītā*, and her understanding of

presented a form of patriotism where the citizen identified corporally with the mystical body of his/her nation.' It is a weird, embarrassing relic (36) of her odd ideals. He describes her 'tortured prowlings' outside the doors of the Catholic Church like that of a starving wild animal (36). Her understanding of obedience was, according to another critic, like the suicide Gandhi presented to Buber as the proper response of Jews to their Nazi tormentors (Nevin 306).

[53] The letters to Father Perrin were edited in her posthumous book, *Waiting for God*.

[54] When she left Marseille for Morocco, she handed over twelve large notebooks of her Marseille's journals to Father Perrin. He would edit them as *Gravity and Grace* (Gray 180). In addition, Perrin and Thibon would write an account of her in *Simone Weil: As We Knew Her*.

[55] It was significant that she primarily studied the very text that her brother had read—rather the more speculative philosophical texts, such as the *Upanishads* that she could have read just as easily as the *Gītā*. In her notebooks, she primarily discusses the *Gītā*. However, she also quotes from the *Upanishads*. T.S. Eliot, (Preface to Weil's *The Need for Roots* 1952: ix) commented: 'I do not know whether she could read the *Upanishads* in Sanskrit, or if so, how great her mastery

Indian philosophical thought only partially sufficed in helping her deal with what she saw as her primary problem: discussions of *dharma* (duty) do not work in times of war. *Dharma* only works in a stable society.

> What becomes of *dharma* in a conquered country? And what are the duties toward the conqueror. Must find out. (Weil 1988, vol. 6, part 1: 336)

Weil felt that some further theophany was needed. She had recognized that the Christ of Catholicism had too much baggage—the Church, the priests, the hegemonic violence of Rome. The Hinduism of the *Gītā* had no such *impedimenta*. Its message, at least her interpretation of it, was simple: Krishna needs to come and proclaim the necessity of suffering and her human role in it (Nevin 302). Today, Weil's self-hatred aimed at her identity as a woman and a Jew evokes pity, as do her obvious psychological wounds that might have been exacerbated by the effects of *anorexia nervosa* on her body and psyche.[56] But, I cannot help also signal, when reading her in hindsight and in the tenor of her times, the arrogance that engendered the theological distortions leading to her extravagant ideas of self-mortification. It was such attitudes that marginalized her in the real world of de Gaulle yet seem to have sealed her recurring fame in academic and religious (Protestant/Anglican and Catholic)

of what is not only a very highly developed language but a way of thought, the difficulties of which only become too formidable to a European student the more diligently he applies himself to it.' Eliot was clearly talking about himself here. S. Weil's ability to read Sanskrit was quite elementary.

[56] I am frankly shocked that no one has commented on the radical change she underwent in adolescence from being a cute girl to a caricature of an unattractive, tortured woman, prone to accidents, debilitating migraines, combined with anorexia and the fetishization of suffering that eventually resulted in her suicide. Something clearly happened to this woman. I am equally surprised that her many readers have not drawn the connection regarding her decline and the speculation that it exhibits classic signs of having suffered sexual abuse. We must remember that her essay on the *Iliad* focuses on a person paralysed by the immanence of force, someone who, having suffered force 'ceases to exist' and is left to 'impersonate the nothingness of his/her fate'. Is this not Weil's testimony to some harm she might have personally suffered? It is telling that such a commentary does not exist in feminist readings, especially after her dear friend Pétrement spoke of Weil's 'obsessive terror of rape', the only crime she thought that justified capital punishment. There was also her habit of striking men who physically happened to be in her way, in the head. She told a friend that her headaches made her want to strike people on the forehead (Gray 72).

circles.[57] Obsessed as she was with the beneficial effects of suffering, it is odd that she never saw how her Jewishness placed her ideally in the role of the suffering mediator that she so desired. It is unbelievable that for someone supposedly so intelligent, she did not see that, in her immediate circumstances, the swastika superseded the cross as the emblem upon which innocence was nailed (Nevins 306) and that the story of her time was actually more terrible than what she read into the *Gītā*.

Savitri Devi

Like Simone Weil, Maximiani Portas (1905–1982) was born to comfortable middle-class parents in France (Lyons). Her Italian mother was a British citizen and her father, a Greek of French nationality. She received her education within the French system and thrived as a student. Also like Weil, she felt particularly drawn to the study of ancient religions and philosophies, with specific interest in the esoteric. As an adolescent, she had been influenced by Leconte de Lisle's (1819–94) *Poèmes barbares* (1862), a quintessential text of French exoticism. At the university, she too studied philosophy and the classics. She wrote her first doctoral dissertation on the Greek philosopher Theophilos Kaires and then completed a *doctorat d'état* on the philosophy of mathematics. After a research visit to Greece to revise her work on Kaires, she went to India in 1931 to seek out the Indo-European pagan gods whom she believed had not yet been defiled by Judaeo-Christian monotheism (Goodrich-Clarke 1998: 19–25). She found her life's mission there, drawing correspondences between Hinduism and Hitlerism. Such connections were not so bizarre as they might seem today, nor unwelcome at that time to members of the Hindu elite who admired the Third Reich's racial doctrines (Bharati 1982). Her subsequent portrayal of Hitler as the saviour of the world was not an exceptional perception among high-caste Hindu nationalists, especially

[57] I have not delved into the Jewish intellectual reception of Simone Weil. It would be interesting to compare the Jewish community's commentary on Weil to that of Edith Stein, another brilliant philosopher (assistant to Husserl) who was born a Jew but converted to Catholicism, became a Carmelite nun, and died at Auschwitz. Stein was subsequently canonized. This recognition of her sainthood was received by outrage in Jewish circles. It is interesting that Weil's anti-Semitism has not garnered much commentary in recent criticism.

when, in the early years of the war, he had prevailed over the British. It was at this time that she adopted an Indian name, Savitri Devi, an auspicious identification made up of the combined name for the avatar of the goddess of wisdom who was daughter of the sun god, and the generic Indian term for goddess.

While living in India, Devi had become involved with the Hindu Mahasabha, the Hindu nationalistic organization that followed a pro-German political policy. She supported this organization's ideas regarding Hindu nationalism. She also shared common Indian ideas regarding the Aryans that had been promulgated by Tilak, specifically in his work on the Arctic origins of the Vedas.[58] Between 1932 and 1935, Devi sojourned at Rabindranath Tagore's ashram at Shantiniketan in Bolpur (Bengal). It was economical and spiritually inspirational for her to live there, but also strained because she chaffed at the presence of émigré German Jews among the ashram's cosmopolitan community. As an ardent anti-Semite, she did not hide her loathing of them. Her behaviour, however, did not jeopardize her stay at the renowned ashram, suggesting the extent to which the Nobel Laureate's enlightened Bengali entourage tolerated Nazi anti-Semitism.

At Shantiniketan, Devi learned Hindi and Bengali. She then started teaching English and Indian history in colleges in and around Delhi. In 1936, she went to Calcutta where she worked in the Hindu Mission. Its president, Srimat Swami Satyananda, had asked her about her religious affiliation, as a point of information. She identified herself to him as an Aryan pagan and devotee of Adolf Hitler whom she felt was leading the only movement in the world where the Aryan spirit was countering Judaeo-Christianity. The Swami shared her enthusiasm for Hitler and told her that he considered Hitler's disciples as his spiritual brothers (Devi 1976: 33–5, 39, 285–7). There was clearly a meeting of the minds here. Devi then became a lecturer for the Hindu Mission and travelled throughout India in this capacity. In this environment, Devi further developed the connection she had already drawn between National Socialism and Hindu nationalism. She also started lacing her Hindu Mission lectures with references to *Mein Kampf*. As noted, Indians, on a whole, did not think disfavourably of Hitler because, in their estimation,

[58] For Indian ideas on the Aryans, see Figueira 2002.

he had valorized the superiority of their Aryan ancestors.[59] The Nazi use of the Indian symbol of the swastika was seen by Indians as a homage to their common kinship. More importantly, Hitler was seen as the enemy of the hated English; any enemy of their enemy was deemed an ally. It was not rare that Hindus would put a photo of Hitler in their family shrines at home; such representations would function as objects of devotion alongside images of personal deities. Swami Satyananda had given Savitri Devi free rein with her lectures. He told her she could talk as much as she wanted about Hitler and *Mein Kampf* in official Mission lectures. She took him at his word.

Through the Hindu Mahasabha, Devi had met Asit Krishna Mukherji (1898–1977), the pro-German brahmin publisher and editor of *The New Mercury*, a fortnightly National Socialist magazine subvented by the German Consulate in Calcutta (1935–7) until the British suppressed it. In this journal, Mukherji published laudatory articles on Hitler, the Arctic home of the Aryans, Hitler's view on all sorts of subjects, and excerpts from *Mein Kampf*. Devi married Mukherji. It was largely a marriage of convenience. On account of the lectures she had been giving through the Hindu Mission, Devi had become known to the British authorities as a problematic character. Given her Nazi sympathies, she risked detention or deportation as a foreign national. By marrying Mukherji, she became a British subject and was, therefore, less vulnerable. In fact, throughout the war, Devi and her husband were able to engage in espionage on behalf of the Germans without any consequences. They carried on seditious behaviour, while they awaited a Nazi victory (1951: 149–51, 226, cited in Goodrich-Clarke 1998: 95). Much to their surprise, the Reich was defeated. Devi nevertheless continued to support the now lost cause.

In a series of publications, Devi promoted her amalgamation of Hinduism and Nazi ideology. She identified Hitler as an avatar (Goodrich-Clarke 1998: 97), citing the *Gītā* 6.7–8 throughout her work, in volumes such as *Pilgrimage* (1958b: 7, 28, 31, 52, 173, 188–9, 261) and *The Lightning and the Sun* (1958a: 416). The latter volume, actually a panegyric to Hitler, opens by describing his incarnation (i.e. his birth in 1889), youth, and dawning mission. These accounts were all culled from

[59] Indians did not realize that Hitler had utter contempt for modern Indians. In this regard, see Figueira 1994.

Hitler's friend, August Kubizek's account of their teenage years in Linz and Vienna (1904–8). Hitler was more than just an inspiration for Devi (Devi 1958a: 215–16, 222–4). He became her obsession. In October 1945, she returned to Europe to continue proselytizing for the Nazis. She regretted not having experienced the great days of the movement and wanted to play her part in the struggle, even if only belatedly.

Devi's admiration for Hitler never waned and no harsh realities would ever diminish her faith in him. She felt tremendous guilt for having sat out the war in India, while her fellow Nazis fought to conquer the world. So, at this juncture, when the Nazis had been defeated, Devi decided it was time to serve the cause more actively. After the fall of the Reich, she made a pilgrimage to Germany in order to aid small conventicles of unrepentant Nazis, offer comfort to war criminals, and perform solitary rituals at Nazi shrines. For employment, she became the wardrobe manager for an Indian dance troupe during their European tour. In this way, she began distributing pro-Nazi propaganda in 1948 while travelling through Germany by train. Between September and December 1949, for example, she succeeded in distributing 6,000 leaflets in Western-occupied zones and in the Saarland. The handbills, graced with a swastika, exhorted Germans to be true to Hitler who was still alive and would rise up against the Allied forces. In the following five months, Devi distributed some 1,500 more leaflets before being arrested for promoting National Socialist ideas on German soil. While awaiting trial, she was sent to the British military prison at Werl. Here she looked forward to what she envisioned as her future martyrdom, since the maximum penalty for her actions was death. She noted in *Defiance* how she would go to her execution singing the 'Horst Wessel' song, giving a Nazi salute, and shouting 'Heil Hitler' (1951: 188). In lieu of martyrdom, however, she only received a sentence of three years or deportation to India. She chose imprisonment and ended up serving only six months.

During her prison sentence in 1949, Devi, just like those Indian nationalists who had been imprisoned under colonial rule, sought inspiration and solace in the *Gītā* (1951: 169, 104, 190). Even when she was confronted with Nazi atrocity exhibitions and the Nuremberg Trials, she sought to justify the criminal regime by calling upon Indian revelation as communicated to her through the *Gītā* (Devi 1958b: 243). She enlisted the *Gītā* in order to relativize truth and falsehood, wisdom and insanity.

She claimed that it had taught her how to distinguish the friends of race from inferior individuals and bastardized races. Devi clearly recognized the *Gītā*'s narrative on caste. The *Gītā* also enabled her to formulate a Manichean worldview. She was particularly impressed by its vision of the pageant of nature running its course between periodic cosmic creation and destruction. Human concerns, comforts, and rights could thus be viewed as trifling and insignificant. The *Gītā* and its calls for unattached action (*Gītā* 2.38; 2.47; 3.9; 3.25) sustained Devi in this vision (Devi 1951: 38) and taught her courage in defeat. She spent the remainder of her life trying to share with defeated Nazis and neo-Nazis what she perceived as the *Gītā*'s life-sustaining wisdom.

While in prison, she spent considerable time in her cell worshipping Hitler, often kissing a photo of him she kept with her at all times. She felt no compunction arguing with her interrogators on the innocence of the Nazis and the guilt of the Allies. There was no genocide of the Jews; they had merely died from malnourishment due to problems with supply lines during the war. Devi also used her prison stint to make important contacts with kindred spirits among the prisoners. Her new friends consisted mostly of convicted wardresses and female overseers from the Bergen-Belsen Concentration Camp, as she relates in *Gold im Schmelztiegel* (Gold in the Furnace) (1952: 129–30) the book she completed while in prison at Werl. Her best friend was Hertha Ehlert, a guard from Auschwitz whom she exonerates in *Defiance* and *Pilgrimage*. These books, in which she discussed her friendships and praised the courage of concentration camp guards, were of a devotional nature. In *Gold in the Furnace*, Devi's defence of the Nazis reached cosmic proportions when she described their role in the great wheel of creation and destruction. These volumes are still in print today, readily available, and avidly read by the neo-Nazi underground.

Savitri Devi had always, since her early youth, espoused very firm political ideas. In the First World War, she had sided with the Germans because of the Allied treatment of Greece. An unabashed racist, she evinced disgust for the French army for having mobilized Senegalese soldiers against the Germans in the Ruhr. She was both a rabid anti-Semite and anti-Zionist. In general, she disdained Christianity, individual freedom, liberality, equal opportunity, humaneness, and democracy. She exhibited religious intolerance and politicized the truths she saw articulated in ancient religious thought (1951a: 4–15).

There is no hope of 'putting things right' in such an age. It is, essentially, the age … described in the … Book of books—the *Bhagavad Gītā*—as that in which 'out of the corruption of women proceeds the confusion of castes; out of the confusion of castes, the loss of memory; out of the loss of memory the lack of understanding, and out of this, all evils'; the age in which falsehood is termed 'truth' and truth persecuted as falsehood or mocked as insanity; in which the exponents of truth, the divinely inspired leaders, the real friends of their race and of all the living—the god-like men—are defeated, and their followers humbled and their memory slandered, while the masters of lies are hailed as 'saviours'; the age in which every man and woman is in the wrong place, and the world dominated by inferior individuals, bastardized races and vicious doctrines, all part and parcel of an order of inherent ugliness far more worse than complete anarchy (1951a: 17f). Here, in *The Lightning and the Sun*, Devi also developed an evolutionary theory of men as a response to what she saw as the human bondage to time. Her ideas were fantastic on many levels. In one theory, she tried to link international 'Jewish' finance to the destructive force of the Mongol Empire.

Devi described three types of men as they appear in human time. She believed that the *Kali Yuga*,[60] the age in which we currently live, is peopled by Men of Time, active agents who are characterized by egoism, violence, and power-seeking. She saw Genghis Khan as typifying one such Man of Time. She also identified a second category, the Men Above Time, those who are described in the *Upanishads*. They were evolved enough to recognize the unity of the *ātman* with *brahman*. They are represented by the unworldly mystics, such as the Buddha and Jesus. For Devi, however, the archetypal Man above Time was the Egyptian pharaoh, Akhnaton.

Finally, there was the Man Against Time, who combined the two other types, and was represented by both the lightning and the sun (hence the title of her book). They were ruthlessly violent in order to restore the conditions of the coming *Satya Yuga*,[61] that was destined to follow the present Dark Age. Men Against Time were practical; they were ruthless

[60] The rough equivalent of the Greek mythological Age of Iron (but even worse).
[61] An epoch of Truth, roughly equivalent to the Golden Age.

in the cause of the salvation and the regeneration of the world. They were the real heroes of history; they were the builders and defenders of all new churches. They were also militant mystics. Here, Devi identified Adolf Hitler as the greatest Man Against Time that history had ever produced. She recognized him as the deity described in the *Gītā* who periodically descends to earth. Devi repeatedly evoked the *Gītā* 4.6–7 throughout her work, but it is particularly cited in *Pilgrimage*, where Hitler is presented as the figure born at the end of each cosmic cycle to restore the Golden Age (1951: 224).

Devi ascribed to Hitler the standard iconographic image. Like many others, she saw him as a lover of animals and children, a devout vegetarian, someone possessing domestic modesty and refraining from alcohol. However, Devi also exceeded this propagandistic portrait when she claimed that Hitler reflected the typical traits of a Hindu ascetic, that he was a 'yogi in spirit' (1958a: 52). Devi judged Hitler as the pre-eminent Man Against Time primarily because of his adoption of racist ideas, his anti-Semitism, his implementation of the Nuremberg Race Laws, his use of military violence, and his plan to kill all the Jews, the age-old enemies of the Aryans. When she visited the garden of Hitler's former childhood classmate's home in Leonding, she claimed to have seen *Der Führer* appear in his cosmic form, just as Krishna had appeared in the *Gītā*. Devi maintained that she in fact witnessed this manifestation of Hitler as merging into the impersonal Essence of the many-featured One, who had spoken Krishna's words to Arjuna (1958b: 28, 31). Savitri Devi believed that Hitler's philosophy was derived from the teaching of the *Gītā* (1958b: 243). She did not, however, think that his knowledge and racial theories had necessarily come from Hitler actually having read the *Gītā* himself, but rather from having 'lived' it.[62]

Devi developed her notion of the Man against Time from the Hindu idea of the *avatar*, the deity who periodically descends to earth in human, superhuman, or animal form as a mediator between God and men. Devi maintained that Hitler, like Krishna, was the *avatar* of Vishnu (1958a: 256). According to Devi, Hitler also saw himself as just such an *avatar*, as one preparing the way (Devi 1958a: 417). She cites numerous

[62] Curiously, she described this 'living of the text' in the same way that Gandhi did, although there is no evidence that she was consciously imitating the Mahātma.

reprises and uses as the motto for her book *Pilgrimage* the same passage from the *Gītā* that Himmler was reported to have cited when defining Hitler's mission:

> When justice is crushed, when evil is triumphant, then I come back. For the protection of the good, for the destruction of evil doers, for the establishment of the Reign of Righteousness, I am born again and again, age after age. (4.7–8)

Hitler was the one who had spoken in the *Gītā* and the one who had now come back. He who spoke to the German people in the Hofbräufestsaal, the Luitpold Arena, and the Reichstag was the same being who had spoken to Arjuna. He was the 'one who came back and who will come back again' (Devi 1958a: 429). She supported her claim by frequently quoting the *Gītā* with reference to Hitler.

She specifically described Hitler as the incarnation of the divine collective Self of Aryan mankind, personifying, just as Krishna had done in the *Gītā*, the warlike wisdom and territorial expansion of the hallowed race that would inaugurate a new epoch in the awakening of Aryan consciousness. Devi's message was simple: God was reborn as Hitler, an incarnation of Vishnu and the saviour of the world (1951: 503). Hitler was eternal, the one who speaks for all times the wisdom of the *Gītā* (Devi 1958a: 349). The only way in which Hitler differed from his previous incarnation as Krishna, was that he proved to be too lenient with his enemies this time around (Devi 1958a: 346). Savitri Devi viewed Hitler as a champion of old tribal principles in opposition to the degenerate capitalist and cosmopolitan world of the Allies.

Devi believed that Hitler had offered himself and the German people in sacrifice for the survival of a superior mankind and in fulfilment of the highest purpose of creation as prophesized in the *Gītā* 9.16 that she cited as the second motto of *Pilgrimage*: 'I am the Oblation, I am the Sacrifice.' She was as convinced of Hitler's extraordinary powers, as she was of her own. Devi relates how one night in London, during the Nuremberg Trials, she dreamt that she visited Hermann Göring in his cell and told him that she wished to save all the Nazis on trial but could only save one of the Nazi prisoners and that she had chosen to save him because of his kindness to animals.[63] She then noted that she felt something in her hand and gave it to him to take, telling him that he must not be killed as a criminal. She then bid him 'Heil Hitler' and vanished. The next day she overslept, (as was not her habit) and woke to learn of Göring's suicide from a cyanide capsule he had mysteriously obtained. Devi claimed that she must have astrally travelled in her subtle body in order to deliver him from an ignominious death by hanging.[64]

Just as Hitler incarnated the God of the *Gītā*, so too did the SS, like the Pāṇḍava warriors of the epic, become living expressions of the ancient Aryan wisdom of the detached violence necessary to overcome the Dark Age. Savitri Devi claimed that Nazi violence was selfless, dispassionate, and detached (1951: 298, 470), just like the violence taught in the *Gītā*. Real Nazis acted without any attachment and in the interest of shared Aryan ideals (Devi 1951: 500). SS training and racial selection guaranteed their self-mastery. In fact, according to Devi, the SS wonderfully enacted the *Gītā*'s mandate to perform action without attachment; they embodied her version of the *sthitaprajña*. The SS's violence provided Devi with living examples of the *Gītā*'s Aryan wisdom of *niṣkāma karma*. Devi interpreted their involvement in the liquidation of the Jewish ghettoes, the administration of concentration camps, the Wehrmacht attacks on the Soviet Union, the killing of Jews, and the actions led by the SS *Einsatzgruppen* as living enactments of the ancient Aryan warrior code which was described in the *Gītā* 3.19, 25 that she loved to cite: 'Perform without attachment that action which is duty, desiring nothing but the welfare of creation' (Devi 1958b: 199). In the *Gītā*'s injunction of 'taking as equal pleasure and pain, gain and loss, victory and defeat, gird thyself for battle' (2.38), Devi recognized the truth that motivated the SS *Einsatzgruppe* commander, upstanding Theosophist, and her dear friend and hero, Otto Ohlendorf, who had been condemned to death at Nuremberg.[65] She read into this Nazi war criminal's testimony the wisdom she attributed to the *Gītā*. Ohlendorf, who was responsible for the murder of some 90,000 Jewish and Soviet prisoners in the wake of

[63] She believed that Göring, as Reich Forestry Commissioner, had established conservation areas throughout Germany.

[64] See interview of November 1978, Cassette 4B, cited in Goodrich-Clarke 128.

[65] See *The Lightning and the Sun* (405f) and *Pilgrimage* (252f), cited in Goodrich-Clarke 1998: 241 #26.

the invasion of the Soviet Union, testified before the Nuremberg tribunal that '[i]n war as in peace individual life does not count. Duty alone matters' (cited in Goodrich-Clarke 164). This attitude, Savitri Devi claimed, epitomized the warlike wisdom taught in the *Gītā* (Devi 1948: 223–30; 239–47; 251–8). In *Pilgrimage*, she repeatedly evokes this *Einsatzgruppe* commander's *Gītā*-inflected vision of life (1958b: 223–30. 239–47, 251–8).

By now, you are perhaps wondering why I have spent this effort in reading the vitriolic lunacy of a figure such as Savitri Devi. Like her contemporary and compatriot, Simone Weil, she based and supported her ideas on her reading of the *Gītā* and its authority as a sacred text. At roughly the same time that Gandhi was reading into the *Gītā* a philosophy of non-violence, Devi was citing it as an apologia for extreme violence and urging M.S. Golwarkar, the leader of the Rāṣṭriya Svayaṃsevak Saṅgh (RSS),[66] to militarize along the Fascist lines that she saw prefigured in the *Gītā*. One text, two messages. Moreover, had Savitri Devi been some alienated member of the lunatic fringe circulating after the war, her attempt to justify and condone Nazi atrocities through Hindu concepts of disinterested action would merely provide a curious historical footnote.[67] The sad truth is that she was not so isolated a figure. Savitri Devi remained an active polemicist for the Nazi cause until her death in 1983 and, more tragically, her venomous ideology has not been forgotten. Her amalgamation of paganism, anti-Semitism, and esoteric Hitlerism has found a wide readership and continues to influence succeeding generations. She became, in fact, a leading light in the international neo-Nazi underground of Holocaust deniers, Hollow-Earth theorists, and Nazi UFOers. She is still published and cited today by such diverse groups as neo-pagans, skinheads, Nazi metal music fans, and neo-Fascists. Her anti-Semitic rantings and excerpts from her books grace numerous racist and occult websites. This afterlife was largely set in motion by her activities following her incarceration.

[66] The RSS is a religious–political organization that is still in existence today. It is the progenitor of the currently ruling BJP. At its inception, before World War II, it was modelled after the Hitler Jugend.

[67] If anyone doubts her continued relevance, I draw their attention to savitridevi.org and the Savitri Devi Archive, a rather extensive website, selling her publications, offering a biography of her life, selling merchandise, and soliciting contributions.

After her imprisonment, Devi travelled to France, England, and Greece continuing to write her pro-Nazi books. *Defiance,* dealing with her time in Werl and offering her admiring descriptions of her Nazi prison guard girlfriends, was published in 1950. *Gold in the Furnace*, presenting a general overview of post-war Germany from a die-hard Nazi perspective, appeared in 1952. In this volume, she relates how brave the Germans were after defeat. In order to visit her Nazi friends, Devi continued to travel in Germany in defiance of a five-year ban on such travel. She had maintained all her Nazi contacts and during these trips met other 'persecuted' Nazis and bonded with them. As noted, she made a pilgrimage in 1953 to sites associated with Hitler. As a devotee, she visited his former homes in Germany and Austria, the locales dating from the early years of the National Socialist movement in Munich and the ruins of Berchesgarten. She wrote of her mystical experiences at these sites of worship. There remained an audience for her pseudo-religious nostalgic narratives as pressure eventually lifted off former Nazis and the Cold War was gaining momentum. New political parties, such as the Deutsche Reichspartei (DRP), and the Sozialistische Reichspartei (banned in 1952) came into existence, reviving beliefs that had never actually disappeared. Denazification had not really succeeded, and former Nazis soon resurfaced and retooled themselves in new political allegiances. Savitri Devi was able to make contact with many of them, including influential Nazis, such as the Luftwaffe ace Hans-Ulrich Rudel. With introductions from him, she was launched into international die-hard Nazi networks and met with former Nazi émigrés in the Middle East and Spain, such as Goebbels's former anti-Semitic propaganda expert Johannes von Leers whom she visited for an extended stay in Cairo. He was then ensconced as head of Nasser's anti-Jewish broadcasting service. In 1961, Devi was the guest of the rather infamous Odessa operative, Otto Skorzeny, in Madrid. Skorzeny had made his reputation for having led the bold commando raid that had liberated Mussolini after the Italians spirited him away to the mountains and detained him. Skorzeny became the leader of post-war commercial and intelligence operations of German and American interests. Also, in 1961, Devi came into contact with the burgeoning British neo-Nazi movement.

Along with representatives from Nazi groups in seven countries, she met in England under the instigation of the British neo-Nazi leader,

Colin Jorden, to establish the World Union of National Socialism (WUNS) as a self-proclaimed Nazi International in August 1962. She was one of the founder-signatories of this organization which brought together various neo-Nazis groups in order to combine their forces. At this meeting, known as the Cotswold (Gloucester) camp/conference, the assembled Nazi groups drilled and did mock manoeuvres. Lincoln Rockwell, the head of the American Nazis, Savitri Devi, and some ex-SS officers can be seen in photographs watching these manoeuvres through field glasses—play-acting as commanding officers (Goodrich-Clarke 2002: 37). The Cotswold camp/conference received extensive coverage at the time in British newspapers such as *The Times* and *The Daily Telegraph* (see Goodrich-Clarke 2002: 310, #11). Through this group and her connection with British Nazis, Savitri Devi became a source of inspiration for American Nazis, especially Rockwell, who took over the WUNS and its journal. Along with its editor, William Pierce, the future author of *The Turner Diaries*, the book that inspired Timothy McVeigh's bombing in Oklahoma City in 1995, Rockwell published a condensed version of Devi's final opus, *The Lightning and the Sun*. This re-issue was a crucial step in her late-in-life publishing career. Until that time, she had only appeared in print in self-published (with her husband) Indian publications with very limited distribution. Now, she was appearing alongside Rockwell and Jorden. Eighty pages in the inaugural issue of *National Socialist World* (No. 1 Spring 1996: 13–90), cited in Goodrich-Clarke 2002: 103) were devoted to her ideas. Her work was so enthusiastically received by the Nazis and neo-Nazis that this same journal subsequently printed excerpts from *Gold in the Furnace* (*National Socialist World* No. 3 (Spring 1967: 57–71) and *Defiance* (*National Socialist World* no. 6 (Winter 1968: 64–87, cited in Goodrich-Clarke 2002: 104). These publications heralded Devi's literary debut in international neo-Nazi circles. Her work now spread beyond India, through England, France, and Germany to the US, South America, and Australia. Savitri Devi would remain influential in the neo-Nazi scene until her death.[68]

With her new-found fame and income from her publications, she retired (somehow also with a French government teaching pension). Thinking that her funds would go further in India, she returned to New

[68] Her ashes are enshrined alongside those of Rockwell in a Nazi shrine in the US.

Delhi in 1971. At this juncture, Ernst Zündel, a German–Canadian neo-Nazi publisher and Holocaust denier, contacted her there and taped hours of interviews with her. Zündel also came out with new editions of her books and effectively marketed her to an even newer audience of neo-Nazis. He publicized the re-edition of *The Lightning and the Sun* in the following manner:

> Were ancient Sanskrit laws of the universe compiled in the *Bhagavad Gītā* the secret of the Nazi's strength? Read this and find out. (Brochure cited in Goodrich-Clarke 1998: 2)

Devi was subsequently promoted by Jost Turner, a proponent of racialist Odinism and founder of the National Socialist Kindred, a group based in California in the 1980s. This association promulgated Aryo-Vedic beliefs, Norse mythology, and Hindu Tantricism. Turner had been a Vietnam veteran with sympathy for the Hippies and their notions of 'dropping out'. He was impressed by Savitri Devi and found particular inspiration in *The Lightning and the Sun*. Turner saw National Socialism as a selfless religion and believed that one must be prepared to take up arms in the spirit of the *Gītā*: 'We may be compelled by duty to harm or kill [but] it is important that our minds be kept clear of hatred, animosity and any desire for revenge' (Jost, 1995: 13, cited in Goodrich-Clarke 2002: 268).

Savitri Devi's widespread influence in the American Nazi Party, continued to grow, particularly under the leadership of Matt Koehl who had joined Lincoln Rockwell's National Socialist White People's Party (NSWPP) and rose in the ranks to succeed him as its national secretary. Koehl's text 'Resurrection', celebrating Hitler's Birthday in April 1987, cites the *Gītā* according to Savitri Devi's reading of it, Specifically, it cites her favourite quote, 'Age after age, when justice is crushed, when evil reigns supreme, I come; again am I born on Earth to save the world' (*Gītā* 6.7–8, cited in Goodrich-Clarke 2002: 17). James N. Mason, a violent Nazi who had revived the National Socialist Liberation Front (NSLF) founded in 1974, was also inspired by Devi, particularly in what he called the ZOG or the Zionist Occupation Government, a term he used to describe what he perceived as the Jewish takeover of America and the puppet regime that had been instilled to control the US government. Mason was an acolyte of the mass murderer Charles Manson, whom he regarded as the spiritual leader of his New Nazi group, the Universal Order. In *Siege*, Mason paid tribute to Hitler and Savitri Devi (Siegel, 1992: 281–322, cited in Goodrich-Clarke 2002: 19) who, because of her biocentric view of nature, had now become influential in certain New Age movements, such as Deep Ecology and New Age Paganism. More recently, the Noontide Press in California has issued Devi's *Impeachment of Man* (1991), a volume that teaches that only the strong and intelligent Aryans are fit to survive in a redeemed biocentric order.

It is certainly not my intention to draw any connection between Simone Weil and Savitri Devi beyond the obvious one: here we find two Frenchwomen who had very odd, hateful views about the Jews, were politically active at a young age, got their doctorates in philosophy, studied mathematics, and sought inspiration in the *Bhagavad Gītā* for the positions they took during the Second World War. Weil and Devi are significant because they show how this reception of the *Gītā*, although it addresses war and warriors, is not essentially gendered. Here we have an instance of two women, one considered a serious philosopher, who looked to the *Gītā* for a justification of force. They sought in the *Gītā* an apologia for their anti-Semitism, pacifism (in the case of Weil), and Nazism (in the case of Devi). They are included in this study to highlight that the *Gītā* was not exclusively a man's text. It was the exotic and esoteric potential of this Sanskrit poem that nourished their use of it for their individual grandiose visions of the world. Weil connected with the text, studied Sanskrit, used her limited knowledge of the text's language, combined with a translation by Senart and an eclectic variety of other sources, to build a thoroughly unique interpretation of the *Gītā's* message. Devi used the *Gītā* as a springboard in the creation of an exotic mythology presenting Hitler as an *avatar* of Krishna. She did not distort the letter of the text, but she constructed a fantastic reading of it, mixing elements we have seen exhibited throughout: Western esotericism, a justification of violence, nationalist rhetoric, an apologia for modern warfare, mystical revery, anti-Capitalism, etc. She pushed the *Gītā* to its extreme limits, which were illogical extensions of what other interpreters had already inflicted on the text. Devi did not mistranslate the *Gītā*. The text had already taken on a life of its own and its authority remained grounded, even as its reception history continued to accumulate odd readings. The *Gītā* was unmoored from its language and could be made to fit any number of alternative narratives, Savitri Devi's being perhaps the craziest. But Simone Weil's reading was also extreme. Their interpretations of the *Gītā* were as free as they were thanks to their precursors, among whom we can count Hegel, the Theosophists, Nazi Indologists, assorted Nazis, and various pagan occultists. The *Gītā* could really go anywhere anyone wanted to take it. And, of course, it was the darker lure of the exotic nature of this text (what was always the most attractive to Westerners) that enabled elitist and narcissistic flights of fancy. It is not just an issue of the *Gītā* itself or its malleability that accommodated such a variety of interpretations. But its flexibility was, indeed, its chief strength, along with its esoteric potential. It could satisfy the needs of idealists, men of action, seekers, contemplatives, and *farceurs*. However, it was perhaps its exotic allure that was its chief draw. The Divine spark is present in us all, but only the chosen, the born-again, the entitled, the brilliant, the self-proclaimed questers, (the unbalanced, potential extremist, and certain mystics) who can connect to this divine spark. Woe to us, those 'others', a generally uninteresting and unimaginative lot, who cannot.

11

The Beats, the Monk, and Multicultural Artists

Ginsberg, Levertov, Merton, Glass, and Adams

Introduction

Orientalism has become synonymous with exoticism. I have always maintained that they are different. Orientalism is politicized; it does not account for quixotic spiritual quests. It often discounts, as we saw in the previous chapters, the psychological, philosophical, and religious needs that occasionally motivated these questers. It does not recognize that behind the attraction for the exotic there is often the desire to make oneself interesting to oneself and to others. There is also the lure for that which ultimately cannot be grasped, the setting oneself up (consciously or unconsciously) for failure that seems to animate many forays into the exotic. Orientalism is about power; exoticism is about impotence. When we think of Orientalism/exoticism, we often think about the nineteenth-century representations. We do not think primarily of the late twentieth and early twenty-first centuries. Is there a modernist exoticism or a post-modern Orientalism?

We have seen how the *Gītā* resonates with those who experience a yearning for the esoteric, but it also speaks to the politically progressive. A prime instance can be seen in the case of the eugenicist, theosophist, and foreign-born Indian nationalist, Annie Besant (1847–1933) who was Mme. Blavatsky's successor in Britain and India. Her theosophical and nationalist leanings led her to devise an allegorical reading of the *Gītā* for political aims. According to Besant, the *Gītā* did not describe an internecine war of succession among kin but urged one to destroy the usurper who was 'oppressing the land'; it was Arjuna's duty as a warrior 'to fight

The Afterlives of the Bhagavad Gītā. Dorothy M. Figueira, Oxford University Press. © Dorothy M. Figueira 2023.
DOI: 10.1093/oso/9780198873488.003.0012

for the deliverance of his nation and restore order and peace' (Besant 1907: iv). As we have seen, this was standard Indian nationalist rhetoric of its time. But Besant added a new wrinkle; her political spiritualism tended to meld with her ideas regarding eugenics. So the souls of 'all the dead natives' go to England: where they take birth in slums, providing a population of congenital criminals and the feeble minded.'[1] Such an odd formulation evinced the racist, casteist attitudes that could coexist with Indian nationalism, especially with someone like Besant. Yet, Besant's translations and commentary on the *Gītā* (1907), as well as her other works were widely read and favourably received in both India and the West (1973: 1–2). Certainly, Besant's theosophist/eugenicist reading of the *Gītā* differed from more standard 'mystical' religious interpretations, as one found in Rudolf Otto, who as we have seen (and like other intellectuals of his time), was closer to the fringe element of the esoteric occultists than one might wish in a serious scholar.[2]

Western interest in the *Gītā*'s mysticism easily survived the two World Wars and resurfaced in post-World War II scholarship. In the next generation of scholars, R.C. Zaehner (1913–74) borrowed from Otto an interest in a mystical and theistic basis for comparing the *Gītā* to Christianity and promoted its global relevance. For Zaehner, the *Gītā* not only holds an important place as a Hindu classic (Zaehner 1957: 130), it offers an expression of devotion that is open to all (Zaehner 1966: 12). Positioned between upanishadic pantheistic monism and puranic pantheistic theism, the *Gītā* heralded a very important change in Indian religious history (Zaehner 1970: 118). It mediated between Buddhism's atheistic mysticism and Semitic 'theistic mysticism' (150) and thus provided an ideal model for interreligious dialogue. These two traits, the focus on mysticism and the importance of interfaith dialogue, would come to define the later twentieth-century reception of the *Gītā* in the West.

Queer experimenters and authors, such as Christopher Isherwood (1904–86) and Alan Ginsberg (1926–97) also discovered in the *Gītā* a text that inspired them (Copley 2006). While it would be a fascinating topic to discuss the queering of the *Gītā*, it is certainly not a conversation that would be welcome in India at this current time, with homosexuality only

[1] Annie Besant. *A Study in Karma*. Adyar: Theosophy Office. 1917: 153, cited in Bayly 12.
[2] See Appendix 2 in Otto's *The Idea of the Holy*. See also *Mysticism: East and West*.

recently decriminalized and great sensitivity exhibited by the current political regime toward Western scholars who are seen as misrepresenting sexuality in Indian thought[3] and thereby 'disrespecting' the Hindu religion. Moreover, it is a topic best left to Queer theorists, not generalists such as myself. We will, however, address the reception of the *Gītā* by a significant gay countercultural voice in Ginsberg. To a large extent, this beat poet epitomizes the politically acceptable and excessive exoticism of much of the last 60 years of American *Gītā* reception. Our examination of the countercultural readings of the *Gītā* begins with a series of 'appreciations' by Ginsberg, Denise Levertov (1923–97), and Thomas Merton (1915–68) that introduced a 1968 English translation of the *Gītā*. We will then look at two subsequent operas which use the *Gītā* in their libretti, one whose entire libretto is the *Gītā* and the other which cites the *Gītā* along with other poems from other traditions. One opera focuses on Gandhi and the other on J. Robert Oppenheimer.

The Countercultural *Gītā*

In the West, the mystical terrain had been well seeded by the scholarship of academics such as Otto and Zaehner. India had been visited by the Beatles, and Hinduism, or some simplified form of it, entered into Western popular culture as an alternative to the rottenness of its materialism and the need for social reform. It was at this juncture that Swami Prabhananda (1893–1976), the leader of the Transcendental Meditation Movement[4], and Christopher Isherwood (1904–86) collaboratively worked on an English translation of the *Gītā* for the post-World War II era. It was, however, an introductory essay to this 1944 translation by Aldous Huxley's (1894–1963) that had greater impact on the reading public of the time than the translation itself.

[3] I am thinking here primarily of Wendy Doniger (O'Flaherty) and her 'children', among whom I count myself. Fundamentalist Hindu critics have been very vocal regarding what they perceive as a sexualization of Indian mythology in her work and that of her students.

[4] The Transcendental Meditation movement was founded by Maharishi Mahesh Yogi, whose ashram in Rishikesh was visited by the Beatles in February 1968 until they became disenchanted with the yogi and the sexual advances that were allegedly made to women in their entourage.

Huxley, with his vague evocations and synthesis of East Asian thought and Greek philosophy, made this translation of the *Gītā* famous. Here, too, we have a co-optation of the text by Huxley in order to expound his 'Perennial Philosophy' as a universalist spiritual tradition that he invented and popularized (1944: 13). The *Gītā* becomes, in fact, an exemplary text of Huxley's Perennial Philosophy.[5] In his introductory comments to the translation of the text, Huxley presents himself as a foundational guru who, recognizing universal connections (Huxley 1944), joins the *Gītā* (identified here as a compendium of all Indian religious thought) together with Hebrew prophecy, the Tao Teh King (*sic*), and Platonic dialogues (Huxley 1944: 11–12). Citing the philosopher Ananda Coomaraswamy on the *Gītā*'s universal enduring value, Huxley presents the Sanskrit text as providing yet another element of his Perennial Philosophy, an amalgamation of wisdom he compiled in the company of Hollywood gurus based at the local California Vedanta Society. Inserted into Huxley's new paradigm, the *Gītā* was truly a transnational text with a message for the times.

> The *Bhagavad Gītā* is, perhaps, the most systematic scriptural statement of the Perennial Philosophy.... [for] a world at war ... it stands pointing, clearly and unmistakenly, to the only road to escape from the self-imposed necessity of self-destruction. (Huxley 1944: 23)

However, Huxley reimagined the *Gītā*'s prime injunction. He did not read the *Gītā* as instructing one to accept the necessity of killing (Sinha 2013:47), but he read it rather as a pacifist manifesto (Huxley 1944: 23). Huxley's *Gītā* offers a means to escape violence (Sinha 2013: 47). His comments, written during World War II and published before its conclusion, struck chords of sentiment similar to Gandhi's roughly contemporary pronouncements.

The next American iteration on the significance of the *Gītā* occurred in 1968, under the auspices of the International Society of Krishna Consciousness (ISKCON). Familiarly known as the Hare Krishna Movement, ISKCON was founded by the Bengali Bhaktivedanta, aka

[5] His book, *The Perennial Philosophy* (London: Chatto and Windus), was published the next year (1945).

His Divine Grace A.C. Bhaktivedanta Swami Prabhupada (1896–1977).[6] It was a religious movement that was devoted to worshipping Krishna and his consort Rādhā in an ecstatic manner. Its chief scripture was the *Bhāgavata Purāṇa*; the *Gītā* played little or no role in the movement's initial activities. However, Bhaktivedanta was a clever charismatic leader and when he brought ISKCON to the US, he decided to publish *The Bhagavad Gîtâ: As It Is*. Perhaps he sensed it was the moment for another American passivist translation, since the hostilities in the Vietnam War were escalating. In the first edition of the ISKCON translation, there is an endorsement by the aforementioned American authors: Ginsberg, Levertov, and Merton; two poets and a Roman Catholic monk. Ginsberg was a devotee, who identified as a Jewish Buddhist (as would Philip Glass, the composer we examine later in this chapter), Levertov was a poet interested in religious themes, and Merton, a Cistercian monk and accomplished author, was involved in inter-religious dialogue. While these endorsements never reappeared in any subsequent editions,[7] their existence forcefully speaks to the cultural place of the *Gītā* in 1960s' American culture.

At the time, Ginsberg was held in high esteem as an important American poet. He saw the *Gītā* as 'an ancient perfectly preserved piece of street India'. The chanting of 'Hare Krishna' was 'a universal pleasure: a tranquillity at realization of the *community* of tender hearts: a vibration which inevitably affects all men' (Ginsberg 1968: 14f, cited in Sharpe 143). What is striking about his three-page appreciation to the *Gītā* is that Ginsberg is far more interested in the fact that Swami Bhaktivedanta set up shop in a storefront on the Lower East Side of Manhattan than in elucidating the *Gītā*. Ginsberg is quite entranced that Krishna with his 'Magic Mantra' began operating locally in this 'Archetype spiritual Neighborhood', as if opening up an ISKCON office/ashram in this location, with its then cheap rents, was a truly extraordinary occurrence. Ginsberg's enthusiasm for the Hare Krishnas consisted in his own performative involvement, his staging of chanting sessions of Krishna's name

[6] Bhaktivedanta was the disciple of Krishna Chaitanya (1485–1533).

[7] These appreciations only appear in Prabhupada's abridged edition. In the unabridged version of 1972, they are omitted and replaced by a more traditional and establishment forward by Edward C. Dimock, an eminent professor of Religion and South Asian Studies at the University of Chicago.

and the mystic syllable '*om*'. He generally popularized things Indian, in the wake of the other stars of the moment, the Beatles.

Ginsberg's comments ('Swami Bhaktivedanta Chanting God's Song in America') tell us absolutely nothing about the *Gītā*. For him, its exoticism and its foreignness offered sufficient countercultural potential and cachet. In fact, it is astonishing the degree to which someone who claimed to be a prominent enthusiast of Indian religious thought was so uninformed about Hinduism, folding it into an appreciation of Pound and Blake as well as his 'understanding' of Buddhism. He subsequently visited India for almost two years (longer than many Western scholars on India and certainly much longer than the Beatles), spent considerable time discussing poetry with Bengali literati, visiting pilgrimage sites and holy men (including an audience with the Dalai Lama), experimenting with hallucinogens, annoying the Indian authorities, and generally having a pleasant countercultural neo-colonialist experience there, picking up royalty cheques from the American Express Offices, visiting the tourist sites (but, of course, doing so ironically), and being feted as the most important American poet of his generation. Before his trip to India, Ginsberg claims to have read the *Gītā,* Ramakrishna's *Table Talk*, the *Tibetan Book of the Dead*, 'lots of Buddhism', and some of Krishnamurti's translations of the *Upanishads.* On the ocean liner voyage, he claims to have read the *Passage to India* and *Kim* as well as some of the *Jātaka* tales and excerpts from the *Rāmāyaṇa.* If we are to believe that he indeed read this material, his relative ignorance of Hinduism (and Buddhism) is astonishing, given that he lived in an age when knowledge was readily available, a hundred years after Thoreau and Whitman could reasonably be confused. It is also worth noting that as an avowed Buddhist, Ginsberg did not understand how Krishna Consciousness and chanting his name were not in keeping with his adoption of Buddhism as a faith structure. For all his desire to raise his consciousness, whether through drugs, sex, or exotic spirituality, Ginsberg had a very bourgeois touristic approach to India and the *Gītā*.

Ginsberg also informs us, as did others, that we live in the *Kali Yuga*. However, this dark age meant something quite different for Ginsberg. He describes it as the 'heavy metal Age,' when the *Gītā* can only offer spiritual common sense which is 'like magic because we're ensnared in brainwash network—the mechanical conditioning of our unconditioned consciousness'. In Ginsberg's levelled-out vision of all exotic spiritualities, the *Gītā*, just like Tantricism, leads us to liberation. But he avers, one need not to be trapped in the Infinite; that would be as bad as being Buddha, that '*nirvāṇa*-junkie'. In an odd claim for an avowed Buddhist, Ginsberg asserts that he will be saved by Vishnu, or Śiva, or Buddha, or Christ, Chango, or Allah, Jaweh (*sic*), the Tao, and even Whitman. Ginsberg's understanding of the *Gītā* reveals a mishmash of very different and antithetical systems. A less generous assessment might view it as just nonsensical.

According to Ginsberg, we had the *Gītā* 'before linear media conditioned our minds.' The text is 'awesome', 'sublime', 'superior to Dante'. In the obvious acontextual vacuum in which he works, Ginsberg claims that this Hare Krishna translation of the *Gītā* presents the text for the first time to the 'Western common public'. It represents 'Hindu granny wisdom' and 'street India'. By chanting 'Hare Krishna' we can do something for a community 'of the naked and those in uniform' (1968: 14). Ginsberg was perhaps more familiar with privileged white friends from Columbia University or the counterculture who might be underclothed than with less privileged uniformed Blacks and Hispanics (without college deferments) who were then fighting in the jungles of Vietnam. In any case, he claimed that by chanting 'Hare Krishna' he 'spoke for' both groups. The American ability to quest after the exotic seems to always signal white privilege.

> It seems like Magic because we are so locked into our heads, so hung up in the metallic illusions of the *Kali Yuga* that manifestation of our natural Sacred heart desire is a rare fortune. This rare fortune (as Thoreau and Whitman our natural-hearted forefathers prophesized) is our heritage, our own truest Self, our own community of selves, our own true America. (Ginsberg 1968: 14)

Beyond the rather silly American exceptionalism of this quotation, what I find interesting here is Ginsberg's proprietary posture (not unlike what we saw in Emerson), his cultural appropriation, his co-optation of the *Gītā* as his own regardless of whether he even sought to understand it. For someone so committed to radical stances, his comments on the *Gītā* appear so colonizing and hegemonic in hindsight. Only some can partake of wisdom and truth in exotic locales, with a round-trip ticket, an audience for their commentary, and place in the establishment when they return. The counterculture was no different from the establishment in this respect, just more pretentious and self-absorbed.

In an interview given to a Bengali poet in the 1990s, Ginsberg expatiated yet again on the *Gītā*:

> In the *Bhagavad Gītā*, there is a visionary moment when Krishna shows himself with armies flowing from his mouth. That's a little bit like the high point of vision that you get in Dante's *Inferno* or some of Blake's 'Last Judgment' or other poems, and to me it seemed immediately universal.... the *Gītā* is really an universal poem, really archetypal. I had some similar visionary experiences on my own in the late forties that were related to Blake, and then in the early fifties, I had some minor experience with psychedelic drugs—peyote, mescaline, the cactus, and then in '59 lysergic acid. So I'd seen a lot of internal mandalas in my mind that reminded me of the pictures I'd seen in Tibetan Buddhism and the universal form of Krishna in the *Gītā*. So I was tuned into that kind of mythologic archetype as a real experience making it more permanent, or mastering it or getting clearer about it in my own mind.... I was interested in what that older culture still had as a living transmission of spiritual and visionary energy because in the West there didn't seem to be one. (Ganguly 2013: 156)

In contrast to Ginsberg's heightened consciousness confusion, and spiritual exceptionalism, Denise Levertov's assessment of the *Gītā* was more practical and pragmatic. In her 'Note of Appreciation' for the same Bhaktivedanta's translation, Levertov actually claims to be appalled by the religiosity of the Krishna Consciousness devotees and what she viewed as their 'alternative' fundamentalism and lack of concern to issues of war and social justice (Levertov 16f). With a certain elitist arrogance, she remarks that anyone with any sort of education has heard of the *Gītā* and may even have read it, but it is not yet part of the American cultural milieu. 'It has not been absorbed and incorporated into our lives', not because it is so alien, but rather because we have not had, until this Krishna Consciousness translation, the commentary that we have needed. Levertov sees herself as a 'syncretist', so she cannot personally believe in the *Gītā*'s 'exclusive wisdom' as its followers do. Moreover, as a proud 'political activist', she worries that the Hare Krishnas, although they share her commitment to non-violence, are too passive, particularly in their attitude to the Vietnam War and social injustice. But she concedes that they are probably kinder and more serene due to their involvement in this movement. So, for this reason, the reading of the *Gītā* can therefore be valuable, since it changes people's lives, when taken symbolically and not literally. It is a 'soul story' so it does not really matter if the reader is a fundamentalist or someone who sees it as 'yet another of mankind's metaphors of individuation and regeneration, if through it we live more fully'. For Levertov, the *Gītā* is both a calming sedative for troubled times and a mood enhancer. What is striking in both Ginsberg's and Levertov's introductory appreciations is how they both do not even attempt to illuminate the text or even respect it and its source culture enough to actually discuss it. Is there any wonder that ISKCON omitted their assessments from subsequent editions?

In the same introduction to the Bhaktivedanta's Krishna Consciousness translation, the best-selling author Thomas Merton also contributed a commentary. As uninformed as Ginsberg was, as disinterested as Levertov was, Merton shows considerably more interest in the text.[8] His contribution, significantly longer than the other two assessments, treats the *Gītā* in relation to the alternative vision of spirituality that he personally espoused.[9] Merton claimed that the *Gītā* was a treatise on the active life (Merton 1975: 348). He saw it as fusing worship, action, and contemplation. Given his vocation as a Catholic monastic, the third thematic reflected his own contemplative life and his numerous publications, rather than any specific verse that he might (and does not) cite from the *Gītā*.[10]

As a Trappist monk, Thomas Merton had been encouraged by Vatican II's invitation to dialogue with other faiths. Merton, therefore, approached the *Gītā* just as he had earlier approached the other Asian philosophies

[8] This was the only one of the three appreciations that appeared elsewhere, specifically in Merton's *Asian Journal*, and it is from this edition that I quote.

[9] I am not overly fond of Merton; there was considerable posturing in his later work; he became more and more of a 'personality' and less a creative thinker. But compared to others studied in the chapter, he is a positive genius in his reading of the *Gītā*.

[10] This introduction was one of Merton's last works and was anthologized in his *Asian Journal* posthumously. Merton died while attending an interreligious conference in Bangkok. He was accidentally electrocuted while bathing when an electric fan fell upon him.

he studied. He recognized the *Gītā*'s perennial usefulness, especially in the present age. Here Merton evokes Gandhi, of course, but also Vinoba Bhave, the founder of the Bhoodan Movement of land reform in India. Merton welcomed this Krishna Consciousness translation as a salutary reminder to the West that it lacks the inner depth of authentic metaphysical consciousness. If God in the West is dead, as the fashionable theology of the late 60s so proclaimed,[11] it is because we are overly concerned with external phenomena, and with what is objective and quantitative. With the death of God, Merton claimed, we have also the death of any moral sense and respect for life and meaning. Merton saw the *Gītā* as an antidote to the affirmation of our individual self as ultimate and supreme.

Merton read the *Gītā* in light of the ecumenical discussions of his time, contrasting, for example, the Hindu text's relationship of humankind with the Divine to Buber's I–Thou relationship with God, and noting how radically different they were. There can be no relationship to *brahman*, only what is conditioned in its various incarnations. According to Merton, part of the *Gītā's* value is its teaching that we need to live with an awareness of *līlā* (cosmic play). It also instructs us that we need an illuminated consciousness so as not to be a beast of burden. Here Merton ties the *Gītā* to existential thought, specifically Camus's *Myth of Sisyphus*. In this manner, Merton seeks to make the *Gītā* recognizable to Western Christians or Jews and the post-war (World War II, Korea, and Vietnam) issues that plague them. He also finds in the *Gītā* the same truths that he expresses throughout his many books: we must live a life that is centred on Another and we must live a life in play and in union with the Cosmic Player. We must live selflessly.

Merton does, of course, anticipate some problems with those who might read the *Gītā* as justifying violence, a point ignored by Huxley, Ginsberg, and Levertov, who all saw it as a pacifist text. He was well aware of the problem the *Gītā* posed in its endorsement of war, even if read differently by a 'few sensitive and well-meaning souls who were those individuals most likely to read it anyway' (Merton 1975: 351). He recognized that Hinduism, like other religions, espouses the concept of the Holy War

[11] I am thinking here of my former colleague Thomas J.J. Altizer whose work on the death of God (largely a rehash of Nietzsche for an American audience) earned him the cover of *Time* magazine.

and that this concept in recent years had escalated to the point where genocide had become a way of life. The idea that war is the will of God can be disastrous if not handled with extreme care. According to Merton, the *Gītā* does not justify war. It presents war as acceptable in the context of a particular kind of ancient culture in which it could be, and was, subject to all kinds of limitations. To discuss duty, Merton claims, the *Gītā* has chosen the most repellent example (war)[12] in order to bring home the message that action should be done with pure intentions and be guided by Krishna Consciousness which, he understands, imposes the strictest limitations on the use of violence.

For Merton, the *Gītā* teaches us that we should cultivate our inner spiritual consciousness. But we must realize that we are at all times in danger of falling into self-deception, narcissism, self-righteousness, and the evasion of truth—the standard temptations of all people. Already, we sense the degree to which Merton is grafting onto the *Gītā* his own spiritual exercises. The *Gītā* is clearly grounded in Merton's present. It evokes how inner feelings do, in fact, co-exist with human corruption which, he notes, were still glaringly present at the time in the haunting images of Auschwitz and recent trial of Eichmann in Jerusalem.

In what can be seen as a dig at the fuzziness of Ginsberg's reverie on the *Gītā*, Merton points out that being 'turned on' by such a text, or being 'turned off' for that matter, does not prove anything. We cannot create our own lives on our own terms because that would entail the affirmation of our individual Self as ultimate and supreme. Such behaviour is a form of self-idolatry. One wonders if Merton had had the opportunity to preview Ginsberg's contribution or whether he was just launching a general critique of the 60s (of which he too was a bit of a star and prominent quester)! He chides his counterculture readers, telling them that such behaviour is the exact opposite of Krishna Consciousness (352). He warns them that they should not surrender to a false and illusory sense of liberty (353). One can only gain transcendence by remaining open to an infinite number of unexpected possibilities. Then and only then can one fulfil the need for freedom. In this ecumenical framework, Merton compares the

[12] Merton was not spared the suffering of war. He lost his only sibling, a younger brother, in World War II. During the London blitz, he also lost a college girlfriend and her child that he had fathered.

Gītā to the Gospels—both teach us to have an awareness of an inner truth that exceeds the grasp of our own control. He warns us not to be slaves to our appetites, but to seek freedom (353).

In hindsight, it was congruent with the times that these three authors, Ginsberg, Levertov, and Merton, had been enlisted to write these appreciations to this popular ISKCON translation of the *Gītā*. Their presence here reflects the 60s' reception of India in the US, its marketing, and the Orientalism prevalent in American counterculture. Bhaktivedanta, the leader of the movement, even voiced how empty of meaning he found Ginsberg and Levertov's appreciations of the translation. But he averred that he understood that the publisher, Macmillan, felt that their endorsement would boost sales. So, he agreed with this marketing strategy and acceded to their inclusion. While Merton was not immune to the lure of the exotic or even the exotic trappings of the Hare Krishnas, he was probably more motivated to write his essay by post-Vatican II ecumenicism and a sincere interest, as a contemplative living in a monastery and writing books on spirituality and religious thought.[13] His essay on the *Gītā* is as informed as anything written by a non-specialist. Curiously, Bhaktivedanta made no public mention of Merton's contribution or its value.

Operatic Gītās

A canonical slogan in opera, 'Prima la musica e poi le parole'[14] aptly describes the use of the *Gītā* in postmodern opera. The American composer, Philip Glass (1937–) created an operatic rendering of the Sanskrit text in *Satyagraha*,[15] which premiered in 1979. Glass's opera dealt with Gandhi's development of a philosophy of non-violent civil disobedience.[16] The

[13] He was a highly prolific best-selling author. The revenue that his monastery, the Getheseme Monastery in Kentucky, received from his book sales basically kept it in good financial health, so much so that he enjoyed a privileged position in the monastery, with great allowances made for him (separate living arrangements, assistants, reduced duties) to facilitate his writing and publicity ventures.

[14] A canonical slogan for opera dating from 1786, when a burlesque of this adage by G.B. Casti (with music by Salieri) was staged opposite Mozart's *Der Schauspieldirektor* (Fink 1069).

[15] A version of my discussion of this opera appeared in Figueira 2014.

[16] This opera forms part of an operatic trilogy, preceded by an opera about science (*Einstein on the Beach*) and followed by an opera dealing with the theme of religion (*Akhnaten*). *Satyagraha* purports to deal with the theme of politics.

entire libretto consists of twenty excerpted verses from the *Gītā*. It was the task of Glass's librettist Constance DeJong to cull selections that she felt were appropriate to reflect the action depicted in the opera. The composer and his librettist chose to keep the text in Sanskrit[17] because they found its sound to be evocative (Glass 101).[18] Unfortunately, DeJong distorted the Sanskrit by subjecting it to a non-standard transliteration of the *devanāgarī* script and then further altered it with the equally non-standardized pronunciation instructions she gave to the singers. Even if one knows Sanskrit, if would be very difficult to follow this libretto as it is sung.[19]

Glass claims that he was inspired to write the opera because he was interested in Gandhi.[20] He was particularly fascinated with his early professional life in South Africa, where Gandhi developed the civil disobedience movement as a response to the discrimination Indians suffered there. However, Glass's understanding of Gandhi is not historically objective; rather it is coloured by biographical myths that were propagated both by acolytes and by Gandhi himself.[21] Glass noted that he chose to devote an opera to Gandhi because he felt Gandhi had provided the inspiration for all subsequent dissident movements. Moreover, Glass felt that Gandhi's legacy lives on, and even claimed that his mantle of effective militancy has been taken up by contemporary artists in the West. According to Glass, Gandhi's efforts were not only totally successful and revolutionary in South Africa, but his vision of satyagraha persists as an idea and reappears in all subsequent rights movements and all political activities

[17] DeJong justified her use of the *Gītā* for her libretto by claiming it was an important book for Gandhi (Glass 99), even thought, as noted, he never once cited it in his considerable writings on satyagraha.

[18] The opera is sung in Sanskrit with an occasional English (or German, French, Italian, depending on the locale of the production) summary appearing in superscript over the stage. The published libretto gives only English.

[19] DeJong claims to have culled her translation from three separate renditions: those of Sir Edwin Arnold, R.C. Zaehner, and Sri Sankaracharya. She is proud to have chosen as her source material the translations of a '[p]oet, scholar, and saint' (DeJong and Glass 39). The Sanskrit text that she provides (but does not cite) is significantly distorted by the 'phonetic Sanskrit' of the libretto. She claims that her Sanskrit was 'checked' by a scholar named Probodha (DeJong and Glass 39).

[20] Glass's fascination with India began in the 1960s when he started working with Ravi Shankar. He visited India over the next 20 years. Inspired by a newsreel that he once saw, Glass became particularly interested in Gandhi.

[21] Glass acknowledges this bias and does not pretend to present the real Gandhi but claims to offer rather an artist's vision of him (Glass 104).

ill-disposed to terrorism (Glass 9). Glass has clearly romanticized Gandhi and his political effectiveness in South Africa. He extended this vision to suggest that Gandhi continues to inspire Indians, an idea that many Indians and historians might refute.[22] Glass claims that Gandhi's life and mind have permeated nationalist movements, dissident movements, the women's movement, ecological movements et al. on a global scale (Glass 7). He also maintains that Gandhi's legacy is kept alive today by artists; hence, his stated purpose for writing the opera was to join together the many others who incarnate the spirit of Gandhi in our time (Glass 10).

Glass frames his opera on a central myth of Gandhi hagiography, namely his successful career in South Africa. According to the standard script of this myth, Gandhi, motivated by compassion for the suffering of the poor and disenfranchised, sought to rectify social injustice. As we have seen, the historical truth is a bit more nuanced. Before going to South Africa, Gandhi had no pressing problem with discrimination as codified by the Indian caste system. It was only after arriving in Africa and realizing that there was a colour bar imposed on all non-Europeans that the fight against social injustice became Gandhi's cause. Satyagraha arose as a movement only when Gandhi himself experienced more significant colour prejudice than he had experienced as a law student in England. We have seen how in India, the uplift of the Untouchables was a rather late addenda to his mission, adopted only after the nationalist movement was in full swing. Gandhi began to champion the cause of the Untouchables in part to consolidate his political control over what he feared would become their post-independence voting bloc. By keeping the Untouchables within the Hindu fold, Gandhi sought to consolidate his political control over them and co-opt their voice.

It is important to keep in mind that the discrimination experienced by the Indian professionals in South Africa was nothing compared to the horrors meted out to Untouchables in India at the time. It is also significant to note that it was only when legal safeguards did not apply to Gandhi himself as a 'son of empire' that he was moved to develop the weapons of marches, civil disobedience, passive resistance, voluntary imprisonment,

[22] See the biography by Ramachandra Guha for as a serious assessment of Gandhi's relevance. For a recent article on this topic, see Joanna Slater, 'A Hero to the World', *The Washington Post* 2 October 2019.

and public petitions. However, for all his efforts, the satyagraha movement in South Africa did not radically change the situation of Indians there. In no way did it even attempt to address the concerns of Blacks. After negotiating with the South African government (under the direction of General Smuts) and being duped by them on several occasions, Gandhi was only able to secure the promise of the repeal of the Black Act that demanded registration of Indians in South Africa. In reality, Gandhi actually achieved very little for his 20 years of militancy. He secured a never-fulfilled promise of protection for literate and financially privileged Indians already living there, and the possibility of entry for other high caste, well-educated Indians like himself—but he neither sought nor secured anything for South Africa's poor Indian labourers, nor Blacks. The myth that Gandhi 'discovered' the need for the uplift of the world's poor was a future event. Nevertheless, Glass chooses this myth as the basis for his opera.

Glass's opera opens with the battle array represented in the *Gītā*, with the two armies of cousins facing each other. Duryodhana and Arjuna appear in chariots at the centre, behind them stands Krishna, posing as Arjuna's charioteer. Gandhi is situated between the warring factions, and he begins singing Krishna's conversation with Arjuna regarding his desire not to fight his kinsmen. The translated text of the libretto provided by the librettist is as follows:

> I see them here assembled, ready to fight, seeking to please the king's sinful soul by waging war … My very being is oppressed with compassion's harmful taint. With mind perplexed concerning right and wrong. I ask you which is the better course.

DeJong claims to have culled these verses from the *Gītā* 1.23–28. They are a very generalized, truncated summary of the verses in question, ignoring the specificities of Arjuna's dilemma.

In effect, god in the form of Krishna, disappears from the text, or is rendered silent and replaced by the character of Gandhi. The libretto then jumps back and forth between truncated and summarized *Gītā* citations articulating Arjuna's (here Gandhi's) moment of doubt and weakness and Krishna's answers that are sung by a chorus made up of Europeans and Indians. At the choral climax of the scene, Gandhi speaks Krishna's words: 'Hold pleasure, pain, profit and loss, victory and defeat to be the same, then brace yourself for the fight.' DeJong culled these verses from *Gītā* 2.38. As an indication of what she does with her translation of the Sanskrit, I provide the standard Sanskrit transliteration below, followed by DeJong's phonetic rendition that she has the singers sing. The texts are sufficiently different. The Sanskrit of the texts reads:

sukhaduḥkhe same kṛtvā
lābhālabhau jayājayau
tato yuddhāya yujyasva
naivaṃ pāpam avāpsyasi

DeJong's rendition to be sung is as follows:

sŭkhudŭkhā su—mā kritva
labha -la bhau jī- a- jī- yau
tu- to jŭdha- yu yŭ-jyus- vu
nā- vum papum u- vap-syu- se. (DeJong and Glass 40)

Scene 2 takes place in 1910 on the Tolstoy Farm, an agrarian collective Gandhi founded and then jumps back in Scene 3 to 1906, when Gandhi vowed to resist the Black Act that required Indians to carry identification cards.

Act 2 moves even further back in time to 1899. It begins with Gandhi's return to Durban after a visit to India. Back in South Africa, he is accosted by ruffians and rescued by the police superintendent's wife. We then jump forward in scene 2 to 1906 and Gandhi's founding of the newspaper, *Indian Opinion*, set to *Gītā* verses[23] whose relevance to the action portrayed (as are those verses cited throughout the entire opera) is, at best, tangential. The action proper of this scene is meant to depict the printing and distribution of the paper. The final scene then jumps ahead to 1908 and the burning of the identification cards in protest of the Black Act.

[23] 'As witless fools perform their works.... so with sense freed the wise man should act, longing to bring about the welfare and coherence of the world.' DeJong culls this verse from Gita 3.25 (DeJong and Glass 54).

Act 3 moves the action even further forward to the Newcastle March of 1913. Here, the set is again the battlefield scene from the *Gītā* where Gandhi tries to persuade South African miners to join the strike against discriminatory immigration treatment.[24] The opera ends with Gandhi alone on stage, with Martin Luther King suspended in the air looking on. Glancing upward at King, Gandhi once again takes on the persona of the god when he sings Krishna words. In other words, Glass has Gandhi appear as an incarnation of God. It is interesting to note here the liberties DeJong and Glass take with the Sanskrit text. The Sanskrit of *Gītā* 4.7–8, a text we have seen often evoked in the various commentaries examined in this volume, is as follows:

> yadā yadā hi dharmasya glānir bhavati bhārata/
> abhyutthānam adharmasya tadā'tmānaṃ sṛjāmyahaṃ//
> paritrāṇāya sādūnāṃ vināśāya ca duṣkṛtām/
> dharmasaṃsthāpanārthāya saṃbhavāmi yuge yuge//

I translate these verses as:

> When indeed there is a decrease of righteousness, then I manifest myself. I come into being from age to age for the purpose of establishing righteousness for the protection of the good and the destruction of evil-doers.

Glass presents this passage at the end of the opera. In the libretto, it is translated thus:

> I have passed through many a birth and many have you. I know them all, but you do not. Unborn am I changeless is the Self of all contingent beings I am the Lord. Yet by my creative energy I consort with Nature come to be in time. For whomever the law of righteousness withers away and lawlessness arises, then do I generate myself on earth. I come into being age after age and take a visible shape to move a man with men

[24] The aim of satyagraha at this point was to fill the jails and thus burden the government. After five weeks, the government capitulated and repealed the Black Law and the accompanying Tax Law.

for the protection of good, thrusting the evil back and setting virtue on her seat again. (*Gītā* 4.5)

This rendition is clearly a case of over-translating.[25]

Any philosophical reservations one might have about the liberties taken by Glass and DeJong with the historical record and with the translation of the Sanskrit text, only occasionally projected as superscript above the stage, fade into obscurity when one views the film made from Achim Freyer's 1983 Stuttgart production of *Satyagraha*,[26] where the battlefield of the *Gītā* becomes a circus filled with absurd props, trapeze artists, and a Gandhi who holds a huge barbell that bends to the floor while he sings, tripping about under its weight. Tolstoy Farm is presented as a dystopia with rags on the floor where the actors move aimlessly, reposition ladders, and run in place to somehow depict Gandhi's vow of civil disobedience.

Freyer's Second Act opens in a bar with dwarves serving drinks from cocktail shakers and crawling menacingly after Gandhi. In the next scene from this German production, set in the newspaper office, students busily write on blackboards 'serious' words, such as *Einsamkeit, Wort, Vernunft, Ankunft, Einsicht, gemeinsam, Ausweg*, and *bewegen* while Gandhi leaps about.[27] Eventually he sits down and shows the pupils alphabet cards. Then the children begin marching about with letters on poles. They stand behind each other, moving their multiple arms like the Śiva Naṭarāja or dancing with letters folded like airplanes. The final act does not portray the Newcastle March of 1913 but rather the March to the Sea, which took place in 1930, decades after Gandhi's South African sojourn. A blue electric snowman with a dove over his head wheels in as a finale[28] and an army of zombie-like figures in slow motion advance amidst blinding red lights, Nazi-costumed guards, and police dogs. Freyer's production

[25] It is worth noting that while Himmler and Savitri Devi assigned the avatar role of Krishna to Hitler, Glass here assigns it to Gandhi, and perhaps by extension to Martin Luther King and Tolstoy. God takes very strange forms in all these readings of the text.

[26] Freyer prides himself as the last and true disciple of Brecht, as perhaps is fitting for a former East German artist, who subsequently plied his craft at the Los Angeles Opera.

[27] Curiously, Freyer's highlighting of 'serious' German terms is reminiscent of Hauer (1934a: 34), whose narrative is peppered with words such as 'Ursprung', 'Ehre', 'Pflicht' and 'Schicksal' in a similar pretentious fashion. Clearly, the philosophical element of the exotic was central for these German artists and thinkers.

[28] Another confusing aspect of the Freyer production is that he gives us three tenors who perform the role of Gandhi, one who acts, one who sings, and one who moves about the stage. Their voices and aspects differ considerably from each other, adding to the general confusion.

concludes with what can only be called an assumption scene with Gandhi covered in blood backing up a staircase to a long series of Glass's customary arpeggios. He looks rather like Jesus with the sacred heart from a distance, framed by the round stained-glass window. This self-conscious and studied spectacle fittingly closes with Gandhi's name misspelled in the credits. Even if we acknowledge that opera, as an art form, is licensed to entertain both the irrational and the hysterical, we can safely conclude that, with Freyer's production, it enters the realm of vulgarity and kitsch.

I was greatly relieved to learn that, as grotesque as Freyer's production of *Satyagraha* was, the 2011 Metropolitan Opera HD production did much to redeem Glass's opera. Here too there is no text, merely occasionally translations of several verses are projected above the stage. When those verses touch upon caste, they are truncated so as not to give the impression that there is any discussion of caste in the *Gītā*. Once again there is no attempt to bring the verses of the *Gītā* into alignment with anything happening on stage. There is, however, a very clever use of props in this production, wonderful puppetry and costuming, which play on geographically specific imagery. When Krishna appears in Act I, for example, he is wearing a blue Victorian suit. On the whole, the props and scenery are very clever, not high tech, but very effective. They are actually quite lyrical and expressive. The historical distortions are more pronounced in this version, with an emphasis on diversity where it did not historically exist. This production highlights the presence of black Africans in the South Africa setting. There is also ample presence of scavengers, distorting the issue of what population Gandhi was militating for in South Africa.[29] Rather than portraying the Indian Muslim merchant population (there are Muslims portrayed and recognized by their headgear), this version highlights the poor and tribal, thereby conflating the situation in South Africa with Gandhi's later claimed advocacy of Untouchables.

In Act 2, Scene 1 of the Met production, it is the scenery again that steals the show, with elaborate multicoloured wigs and great menacing puppets. The taunting of Gandhi on the boat nicely matches Glass's

[29] In the interviews that accompany the HD productions, the singer who performed Gandhi spoke of his preparation for the role, not reading anything Gandhi wrote or anything so arcane, but watching the Ben Kingsley's performance in the film.

repetitive arpeggios. In Scenes 2 and 3, Gandhi's work on newspapers depicting the waves' motions made by newspaper reflect the wave motion of the music. Scavengers abound and they are present in the scene where the residency passes are burnt. In case we did not understand what was happening, the second act ends with Gandhi holding up a torch.

In Act 3, Martin Luther King is projected in the rear, his presence is far greater in this version than that of Tolstoy in Act 1. King is speaking in pantomime evoked as an image against the back wall of the stage, oddly evoking Krishna's cosmic form. On other wall there are projected images of people being beaten. Swat teams descend on ropes to capture the main characters and lead them away. The final aria, with the backdrop of a twilight sky is quite effective, primarily because Reverend King continues to pantomime from his elevated pedestal. The opera concludes with the scavengers crawling about the stage. Glass clearly envisions them as representing the Untouchables Gandhi 'championed', and all the oppressed of the world, particularly perhaps the Blacks for whom King militated. I have been told by friends who have viewed this production that they found it quite beautiful and moving, and there is some truth to this assessment, if one discounts its historical accuracy and hagiography of Gandhi.[30]

I personally cannot speak for the music of Glass's opera. It was not particularly jarring, largely because his music consists, as numerous critics have noted, of simple arpeggios, repetitions, scraps of basic melody and bare scales. Glass aims to strip music of its instrumental component and scrutinize melody, harmony, and rhythm through a process of slow repetition. These concerns are partially obviated in his shift to opera, where Glass needed a less stagnant approach to harmony. Repetition is still to be found here, but it now outlines chord progressions, rather than providing a static atmosphere. One critic opined that Glass's verbal drama 'takes a back seat to surrealistic stage pageantry' (Fink 1079) and the

[30] In a subsequent 2018 BAM production by the Swedish Cirkus Cirkör, the text of the *Gītā* is explained. The programme notes claim that the texts are adaptations of the *Gītā* rather than word-by-word translations. We are assured that the spirit is preserved, but some verses are woven together. This 'work' was made by Matilda Molino Sanchez in cooperation with Indologist Mats Lindberg for Folkoperan 2018. Programme notes from 2018 BAM Swedish production by the Cirkus Cirkör attribute the translations of *Bhagavad Gītā* to Seargent (*sic*) and S. Radhakrishnan (London 1998). The Sanskrit text they say comes from Swami Swarupananda's *Srimad Bhagavad Gītā Māyāvati* (1909).

Met production certainly bears this assessment out. In my estimation, the music is far less unpleasant than the banality of the opera's message, its inchoate appropriation of the *Gītā*, its fanciful depiction of the historical record, and its pretentiousness. A particularly negative review of the Stuttgart production by Kenneth Furie encapsulates the opera's overarching thematic: Gandhi was good, oppression is bad, and there was some connection between Gandhi and Martin Luther King. This critic saw the opera as a bald instance of marketing (Kozinn 188). And, indeed, the text as culled from the *Gītā* and arranged by DeJong does seem platitudinous and prescriptive. This same critic also found the operatic scenario, a sequence of non-chronological tableaux, ineffective.[31] Another critic was more dismissive. He simply found the opera to be a travesty (Kozinn 188). In its positive celebration of Eastern thought, *Satyagraha* has been seen as an instance of 'reverse orientalism' (Lindenberger 175), seemingly more genuine because Glass had studied Indian music (176–7).[32]

As much as I would like to criticize Glass's venture, we must realize that this opera is not as radical as it might at first seem. Granted Glass takes historical material and mythologizes it, but mythologization of history is common to opera, as in the case of Bellini's *I Puritani* and Donizetti's *Anna Bolena* and *Maria Stuarta*. As a medium, opera is self-consciously a myth-making enterprise.[33] So Glass's mythologization of Gandhi's career is not without precedent. Nor are Glass's fanciful motifs in any way extraordinary. As an art form, opera deliberately and ostentatiously brackets off reality.[34] While DeJong's manipulation of the text is irksome, incomprehensible libretti are also not unknown even in languages far more understandable to the opera-going public than Sanskrit. One has only to

[31] Each act of the opera is presided over by an historical figure connected with Gandhi. In the first act, we find Tolstoy. In real life, Gandhi had never met the Russian author, but only corresponded with him a few times by letter and named the second ashram in South Africa after him. The second historical figure depicted in the opera was Gandhi's contemporary who initially sympathized with him upon his return to India, Rabindranath Tagore. Martin Luther King, Jr. presides over Act III. These individuals have only an emblematic role in the opera; they are suspended in mid-air over the action during their respective acts.

[32] Composers have, however, long sought exotic authenticity and consulted experts (Lindenberger 178, cited in Sheppard (2013: 881).

[33] I am indebted to my colleague Anne Williams for her insights into opera and literature.

[34] It was only with bel canto that opera drew away from the realm of the marvellous, mythological, and fantastic. Realism appeared on the operatic stage only with verismo.

think about the 'language' sung by Papageno and Papagena in *The Magic Flute* or the coloratura of the Queen of the Night aria.

Nearly all subjects for libretti of serious operas lay outside the everyday experience of their composers, librettists, and audiences (Everist 231). By the 1750s, Italian opera had become largely incomprehensible, with the emphasis placed on vocal display and acrobatics. That the audience of *Satyagraha* cannot understand the libretto is not an exceptional occurrence. What is interesting is that the Sanskrit verses chosen for the libretto, even if understood, do not illuminate the action. The repeal of the Black Law (Act 1, scene 3) is accompanied by the following verses attributed to Chapter 18 of the *Gītā*: 'Whoever gives up a deed because it causes pain … follows the way of darkness', and ends with similar sentiments taken from Chapter 3: 'So curse the wheel set in motion and who here fails to match his turning … lives out his life in vain.' In fact, Glass never intended for the *Gītā* libretto to be understood or even reflect the opera's plot—the *Gītā* is enlisted purely as exotic noise, not for its meaning. In the Metropolitan Opera's production, the translation of the Sanskrit also did not appear in superscript. Only occasional English summaries of the lyrics were projected. Glass's use of this sacred Sanskrit text, unmoored from any meaning within the plot of the opera, is a unique event in opera history. It directly inspired an opera by another American composer, John Adams, that also references the *Gītā* (Stein 67).

John Adams (1947–) can be seen as the father of headline opera (Everett-Green 1), particularly when one considers his *Nixon in China* (1987), *The Death of Klinghoffer* (1991), and the oratorio, *On the Transmigration of Souls* dealing with the September 11 attack on the World Trade Center for which he received a Pulitzer Prize in 2003. In *Nixon in China*, there are Orientalist elements that one might easily find in any nineteenth-century opera.[35] Adams enjoys exploiting 'Oriental' themes and settings. In *The Flowering Tree* (2006), taken from the Tamil text of that same title translated by A.K. Ramanujan, Adams vaunts his use of a 'pan-cultural flavor' (Adams 2011: 302) to a chorus text written for some reason in Spanish. The juxtaposition of foreign languages is intentionally meant to enhance

[35] One thinks how the representation of Mao and Mme. Mao draw directly from such imagery (Sheppard 2013: 274). We also find a Chinese chorus not unlike the chanting of priests in *Aida*.

the work's exoticism (Sheppard 2013: 277).[36] Peter Sellars, Adams's librettist on a number of these projects, shares the composer's penchant for 'multicultural' representations. Sellars teaches at UCLA's department of World Arts and Cultures and has studied Kabuki and Noh theatres. When he staged Bach's *Cantatas* in 2001, he incorporated Tibetan Buddhist ritual elements (Sheppard 2013: 271). Beyond the exoticism of such ventures—and I think we might reasonably suggest that postmodern opera can be as Orientalist as any earlier opera—there is also a marked political message to its avowed multiculturalism.

Sellars has claimed that the United States has 'come out as the oppressor against every popular democratizing movement in our times' (Cohen 80). Certainly, as a professor of World Culture, he must know what he is talking about. Yet, even in multicultural academic settings, this is a large claim. It suggests the degree to which modern opera outdoes its exoticist precursors (one thinks of the use of distant history in Verdi or Wagner) in its choice of relatively recent subject matter in contemporary operas. Adams himself is certainly not adverse to political statements in the operas whose subject matter he culls from contemporary history, as in the case of *The Death of Klinghoffer*, whose claim to a 'context-rich and even handed approach' to the subject matter caused a great deal of controversy.[37] This point, the issue of a 'context-rich and even-handed approach', resurfaces in the case of the Adams/Sellars co-production of *Doctor Atomic*. *Klinghoffer* had asked us to understand the killing of an elderly wheelchair-bound American Jew by Arabs for 'contextual'

[36] There is not only this play with language but use of non-musical sounds in his oratorio which was commissioned by the New York Philharmonic, the score consisted also of prerecorded city noises as well as the recitation of the victims' names (Cohen 80).

[37] This opera was composed by Adams with a libretto by the poet Alice Goodman with whom Adams had previously worked on *Nixon in China*, Adams/Goodman provoked fury in their stance of 'understanding' the terrorists who had hijacked the cruise ship, the Achille Lauro, in 1985 and murdered an elderly wheelchair-bound American Jewish passenger. The uproar caused by this opera forced Adams/Goodman to eliminate a scene where a New Jersey suburban Jewish family is mockingly depicted discussing politics around the dinner table. Goodman pulled out of *Doctor Atomic* when it was presented to her by Adams and Sellars because she found their initial concept—the good blue-eyed Jew (Oppenheimer) versus the bad, limping, and greasy-haired Jew (Teller) to be anti-Semitic. In the final version, this dynamic was toned down. She also found the refugee physicists versus the virtuous native Americans 'deeply offensive' (Fink 1080).While Adams holds to the stance that *The Death of Klinghoffer* is 'content-rich' and even-handed in its portrayal of Palestinians and Jews, one critic points out that the Chorus of Palestinian Exiles who sing in exotic melisma music and primitive drum beats, of their expulsion on 16 May 1948, fails to mention that on that very day, Israel happened to be invaded by the armies of the Arab League.

reasons, but *Doctor Atomic* asked no such contextual understanding of the bombing of Hiroshima.

Adams explained his artistic vision in the Tanner Lecture he was invited to give at Yale University (2009). Here he explained that his notion of myth, informed by the rather dated mystical and psychological theories of Joseph Campbell and Carl Jung,[38] inspires his operas, especially where he seeks to entwine myth and historical verities (Adams 2009: 52). So, in *Doctor Atomic*, the bomb is 'sprung to a mythic level' (53), since Adams had recognized the mythical potential for the story. At first, Pamela Rosenberg, the Director of the San Francisco Opera who had commissioned the piece, envisioned Oppenheimer as a Faust figure. Adams and Sellars, however, did not take to this approach. They seemed to have ascribed to a far less complex and more commonly circulated myth of the tormented Oppenheimer that, as we have seen, was already embedded in popular culture representations. What could have been an American Faust opera became 'a dissonant poem harnessed to a documentary work of experimental theatre' (Fink 1072).

As opposed to Glass's use of excerpts from the *Gītā* for his libretto, Sellars quotes from the *Gītā* in translation, along with excerpts from transcripts of wartime meetings, military orders, interviews, memoirs, and letters by participants in the Manhattan Project, weather reports, and recently unclassified documents in order to create a 'documentary-mosaic' of journalistic immediacy (Fink 1071). What Sellars terms the archival material for this 'collage' libretto (Clement 2005), is essentially assembled, not composed, and combined with the contemplative poetry that Oppenheimer loved. In this opera, we have a director moonlighting as an author (Fink 1074–5). It is hubristic for both the composer and the director/librettist to expect the audience to expect the music to carry the libretto (*prima la musica ... poi le parole*) (Fink 1090). This presupposition is seen as a weakness of the work. As one critic put it, 'a libretto is not a program note' (Adamo 2008). In a review from *Die Welt*, it was suggested that what could have been provocative, given the current relevance of nuclear power politics at the time, with Iraq and North Korea flirting with nuclear weaponry, became stale and percussion-peppered political correctness (Brug 2005).

[38] He spoke about his pilgrimage to Jung's hut in the forest in Switzerland.

Doctor Atomic premiered on the sixtieth anniversary of the bombing of Hiroshima, 1 October 2005.[39] The title derives from the *New York World Telegram* nickname given to Oppenheimer (Matthew-Waller 31). Like the appreciations penned by Ginsberg, Levertov and Merton to the Hare Krishna translation of the *Gītā*, *Doctor Atomic* shares a similar visionary Bohemian ethos of left-wing politics and attraction to Eastern thought. But Adams presents an even more self-conscious stance in his 'minimalist' or even post-minimalism atonality (Cohen 79). Even the narcissism of a Ginsberg pales in comparison to Adams's posturing when he claims to experience anxiety as a 'straight, white, middle-aged male' by even taking on a 'multicultural' creation (Adams 2011: 304, cited in Sheppard 2013: 277). Such 'sensitivity' is at odds to what the audience might experience as tone-deafness to how *Doctor Atomic* appropriates Native American terms, music, and dance. Japan appears only in the final words of the recorded woman's voice requesting water (untranslated). The Native Americans are represented in a totally exoticized form, quite anachronistic even for 1945. The Native America childcare-giver Pasqualita (Oppenheimer's wife is aided by Native American servants) and Kitty Oppenheimer represent Adams's understanding of Goethe's *ewig Weibliche*. They speak primarily in cryptic Cassandra-like Delphic utterances (2011: 286, cited in Sheppard 2013: 279). The gendered division of moral labour in the opera is simplistic. Men have power to make bombs and women exert powerlessness and feel guilt (Fink 1080).

Adams's representation of native Americans was already significantly exoticized in his source material, Muriel Rukeyser's[40] poem, the 'Dream-Singing Elegy'.[41] With the use of Rukeyer's poem, there is an issue of authenticity. Rukeyser explains that a Ghost Dance and dream singing are expressions of Native American ritual symbolism that she accessed second- or third-handedly filtered through a non-native anthropologist's interpretation.[42] The Elegy also grew out of Rukeyser's thoughts regarding

[39] My comments are based on the Santa Fe production of 2018.

[40] In a curious sidebar, Rukeyser attended the same school in New York as did Oppenheimer and his brother, Adler's Ethical Culture School, in a class a few years behind Oppenheimer.

[41] *Kenyon Review*, Winter 1944, vol. vi, no. 1 See https://www.kenyonreview.org/kr-online-issue/muriel-rukeyser-763879.

[42] She informed herself of these rituals through a paper she read by Philleo Nash, 'The Place of Revivalism in the Formation of the Intercultural Community of Klamath Reservation.' Chicago: n.p., 1937.

the Spanish Civil War. We have here an interesting case study of cultural appropriation, considerably removed from the experience of starving Native Americans, anticipating reunions with their dead, and finding hope in ecstatic dancing. The issue of cultural appropriation is only exacerbated by the Santa Fe 2018 production, where Sellars additionally staged a pre-performance Corn Dance by Native Americans, brought in presumably for local colour, to prepare the audience no doubt for the multicultural experience that awaited them. Here we once again discover something found elsewhere in Adams's work in general—an acceptable levelling out of the Other, what one critic correctly terms 'cosmological Third-Worldism' (Cohen 84), a merging of the Other, a homogenization (Cohen 81).[43] The opera has been criticized for its 'dorm-room poster' moralizing which is deemed pretentious, its ideological preachiness, and banality (Canning 2008). It is no more sophisticated than the following formula: 'Motherhood=good; nuclear weapons=bad. Hey, thanks, man!' (Fink 1075). In addition to Rukeyser's Spanish Civil War-inspired poem about starving Native Americans, the libretto also consisted of Tewa songs,[44] Baudelaire's 'La Chevulure' (sung in the love scene between the Oppenheimers), and John Donne's 'Holy Sonnet xiv', 'Batter My Heart, three person'd god', which provides the text for Oppenheimer's aria.[45] But, for our purposes, it is Adams's/Sellars's appropriation of the *Gītā* that concerns us here. We have the following lines sung by Oppenheimer that echo *Gītā* 9.19, but not as one might expect.

> I am the heat of the sun; and the heat of the fire am I also:
> Life eternal and death. I let loose the rain, or withhold it.
> Arjuna, I am the cosmos revealed, and it germ that lies hidden.

And *Gītā* 2.14:

> Feelings of heat and cold,
> Pleasure and pain

[43] The sections from Rukeyser's poem make up Kitty Oppenheimer's and Pasqualita's duet (Rukeyser 4). Kitty's aria was also based on Rukeyser's 'Easter Eve, 1945'.

[44] The Tewa were the local Indian tribe who did menial labour and childcare at Los Alamos. Pasqualita also sings a Tewa lullaby.

[45] It was the poem that inspired him to name the Los Alamos site 'Trinity'.

> Are caused by the contact of the senses
> With their objects.
> They come and they go, never lasting long.
> You must accept them.

Then there is the chorus evoking *Gītā* 11.23:

> At the sight of this, your shape stupendous,
> Full of mouths and eyes, feet, thighs and bellies,
> Terrible with fangs, O Master,
> All the worlds are fear struck, even just as I am.
> When I see you Vishnu, omnipresent,
> Shouldering the sky, in hues of rainbow,
> With your mouths agape and flame—eyes staring—
> All my peace is gone, my heart is troubled.

We know the degree to which Oppenheimer depended on the *Gītā* for inspiration. But the opera neither grasps nor portrays Oppenheimer's understanding of the text. We saw in the previous chapter how the *Gītā*'s teaching on duty motivated Oppenheimer, who fully embraced the *Gītā*'s single-minded injunction to do one's individual duty. Oppenheimer focused on his sense of caste duty as a scientist. In *Satyagraha*, Glass developed a novel message for the *Gītā*—the travails of the artist as a Gandhi-like figure of activism fighting on behalf of the world's downtrodden. Adams and Sellars continue in this vein of relativizing. However, the drawbacks of their multiculturalism—it's levelling out of the Other in a treacly display of inclusion—are all too apparent, as is their exoticism. These operatic *Gītās* as well as the individuals involved, the characters and their creators (the politically progressive Oppenheimer, Martin Luther King, Tolstoy, the neo-Buddhist Glass, or the multiculturalists Adams and Sellars) are all involved in liberatory feats. They present an exotic, feel-good *Gītā,* as an innocuous alternative worldview to Western, and particularly, American society. This *Gītā* is an artistic product marketed to a predominantly privileged white middle-class and upper-class opera-going public, where thanks to multicultural initiatives, the *Gītā* appears alongside the other exotic referent of the opera, the Native American mystic. It is certainly not 'content rich'. *Doctor Atomic* portrays Robert Oppenheimer as a lonely man in a godless world about to unleash the ultimate destruction in order to bring peace. Eager for the successful outcome at Los Alamos, the operatic Oppenheimer is depicted as anticipating remorse and doubts.[46] He is morally challenged and struggling with feelings of guilt. His concerns are contemptuously swept away by Edward Teller, who appears here as a Mephistophelean counter to Oppenheimer's tortured liberal conscience. In contrast to Oppenheimer, Teller is depicted as someone who does not realize the enormity of what he is doing (Sullivan 5). The photogenic millionaire blue-eyed American-born Jew Oppenheimer has a conscience as opposed to the dark-haired, limping, non-photogenic Hungarian Jewish immigrant Teller. The Faust myth that the commissioning director of the opera company had originally imagined as the thematic core of the initially envisioned work, is projected onto the figure of Teller.

> No amount of fiddling with politics will save our souls
> . . . I have no hope of clearing my conscience.

The opera on the whole depicts Oppenheimer as a mass of anxieties, a man who retreats in the final days before the detonation into dream-like states of erotic revery (the Baudelaire poem), spiritual abasement (Donne's sonnet), and the hubristic emulation of God (the excerpts from the *Gītā*). The operatic Oppenheimer is far removed from his historical counterpart. In fact, he is elevated to serve as the Pāṇḍava warrior, doubting whether he should engage in combat at all. The opera's portrait, as we have seen, is a distortion of Oppenheimer's actual state of mind, particularly with reference to his firm belief in the message of the *Gītā*. But a realistic depiction of the historical actors is not what Adams and Sellars sought to portray in this mythologized history.

Even more untrue to life is the depiction of Kitty Oppenheimer, who is portrayed as a bored and frustrated wife losing her husband to his work. She too is mythologized in simplistic feminist terms. The historical Kitty was a German-born privileged daughter of a prominent family, with a Nazi Field Marshall and war criminal (Wilhelm Keitel) for a cousin.

[46] Oppenheimer's aria at the end of Act II devotes a full five minutes to his doubts on the project.

Oppenheimer was her fourth husband in a string of men who were on the rise professionally. He married her after she became pregnant by him while married to someone else. She was someone who toyed with communism, but also enjoyed the good things in life, particularly the vast wealth and privilege that her marriage to Oppenheimer brought her. After Oppenheimer's death, she married for the fifth time. Having left Princeton for her second home in Barbados, she and her new husband spent their time yachting the Caribbean. She died on one of her yachts. The opera, however, presents her as a tortured victim of patriarchy. She is portrayed as a woman driven to alcoholism (she and Oppenheimer liked to drink, and he is credited with making a perfect martini) because she is the gifted, oppressed, and frustrated scientist wife whose career had to take a back seat to that of her more famous husband. The truth is that the historic Kitty took more than a decade to earn a BA in botany. She was not a female victim, as she is portrayed in the opera, who had to renounce her own work for her husband's career. To put it bluntly, her career was marrying rich men in quick succession.

However, the opera presents her not so much as a real character, but rather as a female moral consciousness of the piece. This portrayal too is misreading, since Kitty Oppenheimer desired her husband's success as much as he did, since her gracious lifestyle was also tied to it. The image of her as a woman writ large, *das ewig Weibliche*, is rather insulting to women and sexist, particularly as expressed in her Cassandra-like utterances provided by Rukeyser's poetry, itself an exoticist appropriation of what masquerades as authentic samples of Native American culture, culled by a white anthropologist, and ventriloquized by Sellars, the scholar of World Art and Culture. On that point, we might also mention the exoticist representation of the Tewa help (the historical Kitty's solidarity with the workers did not prevent her from outsourcing the care of her children to the exploited Native Americans of the area). The representation of Pasqualita as this mystical Tewa native is caricatural and racist. She was a member of an exploited underclass of servants for the Los Alamos community. She was not an exotic mystic. If anything, *she* was a female victim. But the victim portrayed and championed in Adam's/Sellars' scenario is the white woman driven to drink because she cannot fulfil herself in this male environment of scientists. We are led to believe that women were not included in the Los Alamos world[47] and were relegated to being poor baby-making machines. In short, Oppenheimer and Kitty become poetically charged abstractions and significantly, victims, entitled and tormented Whites, with whom the opera-going audience can relate. Their malaise is as attributable to the bomb's creation as it is to their existential distress. In truth, neither Oppenheimer nor his wife was crippled by the project; both wanted it to succeed, unlike their operatic counterparts.

The opera also portrays the scientists as consumed by guilt. It depicts Robert Wilson as the voice of conscience.[48] Historically, Wilson did not, as depicted, lead a consciousness-raising group.[49] In an interview 20 years later, Wilson reminisced of his glee at the detonation of the bomb (Harken). Yet, in the opera, Wilson is portrayed as the only scientist who comprehends the horror of the situation as the 'wildest nightmare of the imagination' (Sullivan 4). He too, like Oppenheimer, has been made into Arjuna at his moment of doubt—the operative theme true to the *Gītā,* but not to history.[50] The historical Szilard did call for the scientists to speak out. But, it is the operatic Wilson who sings that bombs may be effective in warfare with the caveat:

> But attacks on Japan
> cannot be justified
> until we make clear
> the terms of peace
> and give them a chance
> to surrender.

[47] This notion is historically inaccurate (Fink 1080). I may have a skewed understanding, but as a child growing up in the vicinity of the world headquarters of IBM, I had some girlfriends, whose Ph.D. mothers had worked as physicists at Los Alamos, and were now at IBM. These moms were not disenfranchised nobodies.

[48] A better choice would have been Kenneth Bainbridge, the physicist that Oppenheimer had put in charge of Trinity, the man who is reported to have said, 'Well, Oppie, now we're all sons of bitches' (cited in Kaur 74).

[49] In fact, the real Wilson was gleeful at the blast, jumping into a jeep after the detonation and racing to the crater, overtaking Enrico Fermi's jeep that had broken down on route, and 'making rude Italian gestures' to him (Harken).

[50] Truman did exactly what the character Wilson demands. On 8 May, when Germany surrendered, Truman called for the unconditional surrender of Japan and the influence of its military leaders. He said that he did not want the extermination or the enslavement of Japan (Cohen 83).

The problem here is the confusion of the opera's creators between myth and history. In numerous interviews, both Sellars and Adams make historical assumptions that evince considerable intellectual sloppiness (Cohen 82). One simply cannot mistake myth for history (Cohen 84), as satisfying as it might be for artists. The bomb was not dropped, as the opera claims, to scare Stalin. At the time, Stalin had poised 1.5 million troops on the Manchurian border. If Sellars wanted to rouse with his libretto the world's conscience to end nuclear weapons, he could have just as easily succeeded in expressing his message without distorting the historical account. Sellars also maintains that our conscience needs to be changed, because leaders now (like then) only want to wage war and do it poorly. Perhaps, the wars America has fought after World War II have been ill-conceived, even stupid and poorly waged, but I think few might say that fighting the Nazis and the Japanese in World War II was unnecessary and poorly done. Just as all Others are levelled out in the multicultural perspective, so too is history. Certainly, as Sellars claims, Hollywood depictions were 'not actually what it was like'. Well, who actually believes they were? How idiotic does Sellars think his opera-going public is? He claims to want to give us 'context-rich' depictions. But he clearly does not, at least not in his depiction of Oppenheimer, his wife, and the scientists. How 'context-rich' is a portrayal of the dropping of the Atomic Bomb on Hiroshima, with no mention of the Rape of Nanjing, Pearl Harbor, the Bataan Death March, the horrid abuse of prisoners and conquered civilians by the Japanese army, and the massive bombings of Chinese cities (Cohen 83)?

The case can be made that art need not reflect historical truth. But this argument could be better articulated if the artists themselves did not so readily celebrate their own postmodern and multicultural sensibilities to the detriment of their historical representations, especially when their collaborations prominently feature real people acting in history and overlaid with exotic/Orientalist representations (Sheppard 270). Once again, we have this odd levelling out of the world in the name of cultural awareness and celebration of other cultures. In both *Satyagraha* and *Doctor Atomic*, this levelling out is achieved by the exotic appropriation of the *Gītā* harnessed to add scriptural authority to a simplistic vision of multiculturalism, where Baghdad shares the stage with Vietnam and Los Alamos (Cohen 79). The important thing to note is that there is 'the stage' and these artists are 'staging' the Other. Native American culture is appropriated, their rituals put on display for an opera-going public to be able to wring their hands over the crimes imposed on Native Americans in crueller times. But their rituals are 'translated' by non-Native artists, such as Lucinda Childs who creates a Corn Dance as an 'evocation of the traditional Tewa ceremony' (Sheppard 2013: 280, cited in Hijaya 291–2), to be performed as entertainment in a rarefied setting and as the exotic backdrop to a postmodern opera. So too is the appropriation of the *Gītā*. Whether a ritual (Corn Dance) or a religious text (*Gītā*), what is appropriated is sacred to these Others we are supposedly celebrating here. Would this composer or librettist have dared to play with a comparable religious text, such as the Koran, as they did with the *Gītā*?

In *Doctor Atomic*, an American military leader, like Groves is portrayed as a weakling, who cannot even control his intake of chocolate. Physicists are culturally unsophisticated, spending their down time watching movies like *Beau Geste*, and thereby exposing their own colonizing tendencies by revelling in the French legionnaires fighting Bedouins. Native Americans are not portrayed as exploited menial labour but romanticized as seers and visionaries. With all its vaunted respect for the victimized Other, none of the populations depicted here seem real: they are symbolic, caricatured, and homogenized. There is, in fact, little respect for the Other evinced in this postmodern Orientalism clothed as multiculturalism. Only Natives have a healthy relationship to the physical world; all scientists despoil nature. Natives can only be mystics, speaking non-sensical and repetitive texts, just like one can find in any nineteenth-century Orientalist opera. Although the *Gītā* is evoked in this opera, the Native Americans and their rituals provide the central exotic focus.

As one critic opined, if the opera wanted to address the dilemmas facing the United States government at this critical juncture of the war, it would have behooved its creators to make the characters drawn convincingly, in 'flesh and blood', rather than as cardboard cut-ups (Matthew-Walker 32), particularly in the case of Kitty Oppenheimer.[51] Adams's and Sellar's unnuanced 'woke' politics is in the forefront of this opera; the music serves as an accompaniment (Sheppard 68) to their very slanted

[51] They even had the opportunity to revise this character after the premier but did not significantly improve her verisimilitude.

view of what constitutes the 'contextual'. Adams wrote that the audience members should 'gradually realize that they themselves are the bomb' (Cohen 81) and, I suppose, this opera should change their lives, after they leave the opera house and return to their lovely middle-class and upper-class homes. It is fitting that we conclude this study of the *Gītā*'s reception on this multicultural note. It tells us not only a good deal about the trajectory of this specific text in the non-Indian imagination, but also a good deal about the contemporary role of translation in literature as well as the politics of literary reception, multiculturalism, postcolonial theory, and exoticism today.

Conclusion

Glass's opera is performed in a language more removed from audience comprehension than most operas. The text was left in the original Sanskrit (or some deformation of it) because the composer and librettist found it evocative. Through excerpted and fragmented passages, idiosyncratic (read: incorrect) transliteration and phraseology, Glass and DeJong neither respected the text nor the language in which it was written. Let's not forget that the *Gītā* is kerygmatic, from a Hindu point of view; its appearance on an operatic stage is as inappropriate as the use of biblical narratives once were considered unacceptable. There is, however, a major difference between *Satyagraha*, Strauss's *Salome*, Saint-Saëns's *Samson and Dalila*, and Schoenberg's *Moses und Aaron*. These operas appropriated and deformed biblical stories, not a religious text itself. In Glass's exoticism, the *Gītā* is used as a colourful prop for the composer's reformulation of Gandhi's hagiography. Given its status as a sacred text, the *Gītā* adds gravitas, legitimacy, and mystical allure to an otherwise confusing and banal plot. Glass added his own personal myth—that socially conscious artists (like himself and we can assume other artists such as John Adams, Peter Sellars, Constance DeJong, and Achim Freyer) incarnate the revolutionary spirit of Gandhi in our times.

But this exotic myth-making suggests a less radical and, might I say, decadent and exclusionary interpretation. Beginning in the nineteenth century, India supplied Westerners with an alibi in the true sense of the term, an elsewhere onto which they could project their longings. People who are world-weary or have lost faith can always seek in the Indian exotic a new system of belief. They can travel farther from home than the ordinary seeker of Truth. Esoteric quests are, therefore, not egalitarian: they tend to foster elitism, such as we have seen evinced throughout this volume. It suits those for whom quotidian experience does not suffice or is not marketable, or, more generously conceived, those who seek the superordinate in order to invest their existences with greater intensity. In other words, it suits zealots and artists.

Those engaged in a Promethean flight are often attracted to the exotic precisely because of its elitist potential. When Glass and DeJong travel to India on Rockefeller money to explore spirituality in two-month instalments, are they any different from nineteenth-century seekers of the exotic, like Pierre Loti or Lafcadio Hearn?[52] The situation of Glass and his collaborator is exacerbated by the artistic climate of the late twentieth century. Gandhi's world was a much easier place in which to play the role of the truth-seeker. With *Satyagraha*, we come full circle in our study of *Gītā* translation/readings. Glass felt no need to translate the text in the libretto—it was the exotic sounds that sufficed. Some quite beautiful Sanskrit verse is reduced to exotic white noise. In both the Freyer and the Met HD productions, translated subtitles are sparse. Besides the *Gītā* verses in no way even reflect or support the action on stage.

With *Doctor Atomic*, the poetry is there, placed alongside Donne, Baudelaire, and Rukeyser. That Hindus might view this text as the word of God, not to be trifled with, is of no concern to the composer and librettist. One could ask whether the cited passages from the *Gītā* have their place in Oppenheimer's story. The answer would be affirmative since Oppenheimer himself felt that they did. But the meaning they had for him, as we noted in Chapter 9, in no way reflects the political themes that Adams/Sellars ascribe to him as a historical being. It is as if they almost believed Gandhi's reading (and Glass's rendering of it) was so true that they simply re-imposed this reading of the *Gītā* onto their own opera.

The situation with the artists discussed in these pages is exacerbated by the artistic climate of the times. In terms of respect shown to the *Gītā*

[52] Pierre Loti (1850–1923) was a French exoticist author of novels and short stories and Lafcadio Hearn (1850–1904) was an Irish author best known for his rendition of Japanese ghost stories.

and the seriousness with which the 'translators' engage the people who created it and revere it, the latter half of the twentieth century and early twenty-first century have brought us quite far away from the text that the West initially encountered in 1785. In our present day, issues of respect, appropriation and colonization are further problematized, given postmodern art's penchant for pastiche, where past signifiers are placed randomly as non-sequiturs in some new structure. These signifiers function as totemic representations of art: they connote neither meaning nor richness. Their citation need not be subtle. As evocations of past art, they reference only themselves as aesthetic structures alerting the viewer that he or she is experiencing 'art'. Paradoxically, postmodern art exists in an age that prides itself on discovering identity, respecting the Other, and valorizing other cultures. Yet, the art itself does not respect culture beyond some facile and often distorted evocation. Outrageousness and shock-value trump meaning. We began this chapter with Ginsberg's psychedelic musings and exotic chanting, and we end it with operatic untranslated/untranslatable Sanskrit white noise. With this examination of the *Gītā's* countercultural reception, we may well ask ourselves how far we have really come with our hermeneutical endeavours.

Epilogue

We have come very far. In reference to creative expression in general, the art historian Carol Armstrong has queried whether we are now 'so self-absorbed and so unwilling to undertake the effort of historical and other kinds of empathy' that we can no longer engage with earlier forms of art at all (Armstrong 87). I am also reminded of Theodor Adorno's comments regarding the appeal of the occult to 'semi-erudite' individuals who are 'driven by the narcissistic wish to prove superior to the plain people'. Cannot the same be said for the erudite who, like the semi-erudite, also seek compensation in the exotic? To what degree are both the erudite and the semi-erudite 'incapable of carrying through' the 'complicated and detached intellectual operations' necessary to reach an understanding of the world? Like the occultists that Adorno evokes, are not our more learned questers after the exotic, those who sought to 'translate' the *Gītā* in these pages, also not looking for 'a socio-political and scientific "short-cut"?' Do they not also attempt to reduce complex issues to a 'handy formula?' Do they not also seek 'pleasant gratification that they belong to the minority of those who are in the know' (Dutton 424, cited in Kurlander 132)?

We are certainly far removed from Jerome's instructions that a translation should give us a sense of 'oneness of spirit' with the Other. To what degree did the translators examined here adapt their language to that of the text? How hard did they avoid wandering off into interpretation? Some translations grappled with the text with varying degrees of faithfulness and, in some cases, sought (word-for-word) renditions. Until the 1960s, there was even some recognition of the text's scriptural status and the demands it made with regard to God's word. As Luther warned us, sacred texts require honesty and good faith. While some of the translators studied here were not too honest with the text, quite a few did seem to have the 'heart' that Luther called for as a prerequisite for translating. Among the worst offenders are those who believed less in the text and more in themselves as intellectuals or artists. Returning to Luther, we might also cite how a number of these translations and interpretations played a significant role in creating a national culture, often more negative than positive. Indians and Westerners alike all seemed to take for granted what Orientalists had taught them: one goes to India for religion and for inspiration. Throughout this volume we chart their journeys, where they sought to reduce the Other to the Same, and annex it, but also, on occasion, try to encounter it, even if their efforts might appear delusional, self-absorbed, and sometimes even genocidal. Many of their efforts follow the German Romantic translation tradition, resulting in F. Schlegel's dream of a desired potential work, the absent text that haunts its creator from outside the original but remains intrinsic to it. Some efforts call to mind Schleiermacher's idea of translation as a paraphrase, where the text remains foreign. The resultant translation or interpretation functions as an ambassador and, at times, a poor one.

All this literary production has essentially been asking the same questions. What does it mean to translate and interpret a text? How do we approach a foreign text? Should we respect its unity, or should the translator or interpreter be permitted to argue *ex hypothesi*? These same questions were asked by the general reader (Hastings), the politician (Tilak, Gandhi), the reformer (Ambedkar), the seeker (Thoreau, Weil), the artist (Eliot, Glass), the *fantasiste* (Ginsberg), and the fanatic (Savitri Devi, Himmler). Figuratively they all sought to do what the German Indologists had literally done: reduce the *Gītā* to some form where it would be free from 'accretions' and verify their own personal rendition of the text. In this respect, do they not all bear false witness? Do they not reveal that all tradition by definition is dogmatic and blind? To what degree are all translations and interpretations products of false consciousness and some form of 'priestly' machination? Are we fools to believe that modern scholarship somehow breaks this impasse and is any more critical, self-aware, and objective? It isn't. We have seen how the linguistic, philosophical, and theological scholarship examined in these pages is often sacrificed for racial or religious polemic disguised as scholarship (Adluri and Bagchree 292) and the methodology appears more 'historical' than philosophical, more deconstructive than exegetical.

We have tried to trace the *Gītā*'s commodification by philosophers, Protestant missionaries, Indologists, and artists from 1785 through the 1960s, where it became 'spiritual junk food' (Rosen 114) and 'fodder as Holy writ' (Paglia 705), up to the present. Given the text's inherited spiritual economics, ethics of work (*karma*), and promulgation of duty (*dharma*), it should come as no surprise that recently the *Gītā* has become a tool for effective business management and that it has been conscripted to teach managers how to instil a higher level of consciousness in their workers (Rarick 59). Indeed, the *Gītā* represents 'an early form of the Western theory of servant leadership' (Rarick 59). It fits nicely in the literature of 'spirituality in the workplace.'[1] The *Gītā* has much to teach fledging CEOs regarding effective leadership (Roka). It offers timeless wisdom for leaders since its message is directed at making Arjuna more effective in his work environment on the battlefield. The *Gītā*'s spirituality fosters a holistic lifestyle which benefits the community and therefore has value in the workplace (Roka). Teaching the requisite self-awareness necessary for the formation of model workers in modern offices to perform their duties more effectively, the *Gītā* is an excellent tool for corporate leadership because it promotes the value of purpose before the interests of the self. What is noteworthy here is how the *Gītā's* justification of the *varnāśramadharma*, or more specifically, the oppression of servants and Untouchables, neatly translates into corporate management and control strategies. The audience responding to the *Gītā*'s inspiration has diversified. In lieu of poets, composers, and librettists, we now have star cooks explaining to the *New York Times* how the *Gītā* informs their culinary feats.[2] Interestingly, this commentary is no less profound than the utterances of those two dedicated Buddhists, Ginsberg and Glass. Corporate managerial pundits and bad boy chefs have taken the place of philosophers and philologists. The spiritual questers of the 60s' variety, become superseded by postmodern, multicultural, or alternative gurus. The corporatized *Gītā* promotes a far more greedy (yet still puritanical) Protestant work ethic than we found in Thoreau.

I wish to conclude now with another classic American Protestant trope—the spiritual golf metaphor. Although raised a Catholic initially with the pre-Vatican-II Latin mass, I have on occasion attended

[1] See Muniapan and Satpathy for an extensive bibliography on the *Gītā* and management.
[2] David Chang, the 'bad-boy chef' behind the *Momo-Fuku* empire, claims he cannot live without the *Gītā*: 'I think about Arjuna a lot because my job seems to be always making decisions under duress. And every time I think, "Woe is me," I think about the situation he was in because if he committed to war, it would be the end of civilization.' ('David Chang Likes the Gita and "Gattaca"'. *The New York Times*, 15 March 2020: 5).

Presbyterian services with my in-laws in toney suburban Presbyterian churches where ministers speak almost exclusively in golf metaphors. These sermons are a far cry from the guilt ladled out in the Catholic Church of my youth where the priest excoriated parishioners over their presumed moral failings. I was struck by how the kindly Protestant American minister was encouraging his flock to feel good about themselves and not too guilty about their misdeeds of the previous week. He gently incited them to positive works in the coming week. Guilt and atonement, so central to Catholicism and Judaism, is often missing from mainstream American Protestantism. No congregant is too great a sinner. The minister practises homey wisdom. His message is encoded in those life lessons one learns from the diversions of white middle-class America. Morality is explored on playing fields. Here in the rural South, ministers use football metaphors. In my in-laws' churches in Michigan or Florida, it was the golf course; sometimes the vacation tour or cruise was evoked. When you think about it, golf as a religious metaphor tells us much about the state of spirituality in America today. How trivial, how dumbed down these ministers, usually from Ivy league seminaries (at least in middle-class parishes and less often in the South, where ordination can be a less regulated process), in the way they speak to their congregants! So, it came as no surprise to me to discover that if Christianity can be explicated to the average American through a golf analogy, so too can Hinduism or, at least, the religion of the *Gītā*.

In 1995, Steven Pressfield wrote the novel, *The Legend of Bagger Vance: Golf and the Game of Life* which would quickly be made into a Hollywood movie by Robert Redford, starring A-listers such as Matt Damon and Will Smith. A mysterious caddy, Bagger Vance (think: Bhagavan) divulges how one should live life through the secrets of golf. The story is set in 1931 during a 36-hole golf match with pros of the time, Bobby Jones and Walter Hagen. Also, among the players is a disturbed war hero Rannulph Junah, known as R. Junah (think Arjuna), Bagger Vance, who is 'blackish' (like '*krishna*' or dark blue), plays an instrumental role in the outcome of the match because he has the knowledge of the secret of the authentic golf swing, and the plot revolves around his instruction to R. Junah. The frame story of the novel relates how 60 years later a medical doctor, who witnessed the match as a child, shares Vance's knowledge with a discouraged medical student, so he can continue to study and succeed in life.[3]

In the course of the golf match, it becomes clear that Bagger Vance is not an ordinary mortal. In the beginning of the game, R. Junah wants to lay down his clubs just as Arjuna wants to 'lay down his weapons.' He asks what is to be gained here since he takes no pleasure in action (Pressfield 1995: 75):

> Life is action, Junah. Even choosing not to act, we act. We cannot do otherwise. Therefore, act with vigor! … Stand now, Junah, and take your place. Do honor to yourself and to your station! (*ibid.* 108) … He is told to do his duty (*ibid.* 106) … to act without attachment. (Cited in Rosen 136)

One critic has made the case that Chapter 2 of the golf novel outlines the different paths of action (*karma yoga*), knowledge (*jñāna yoga*), and devotion (*bhakti*) through Bagger Vance's instruction to R. Junah of the different paths of succeeding at golf (discipline, wisdom, love) (Rosen 136). Love is the highest path. We are not talking here of love of God or of humanity. It suffices to love the game of golf. In the novel, Bagger Vance even reveals himself in his universal form, but, as in the *Gītā*, he appears only to R. Junah. This golf-course *viśvarupa darśan*[4]occurs in Chapter 17 of the novel when Vance allows Junah to see 'the field' of true reality (2000: 195–9). Bagger Vance then tells him:

> 'Before Time was, I am. Before Form was, I am (*Ibid.* 205).'

He identifies the self with all-devouring time, just as in the *Gītā* 11.32. He likewise claims that he comes in every age to return things to balance, as in *Gītā* 4.8.[5] It is only when Junah honestly calls a penalty stroke on himself (that a less honest golfer might not have called) that Bagger Vance proclaims: 'In this hour, you have reached me (Pressfield 230).' This is how the Hindu wisdom of the *Gītā* has crystalized in popular American

[3] The frame mechanism reflects the framing of the *Gītā* in the epic. The aged medical doctor parallels the narrator, Sañjaya.

[4] See Rosen 184–6. Theophany, where Krishna reveals a vision of his universal form.

[5] Curiously, these direct allusions to the *Gītā* in the novel were omitted from the film version.

culture at the turn of the last century. It is by playing golf with discipline, wisdom, and love, by accessing the perfect swing that is in us all, one can find one's inner and authentic Self.

Both the corporate management *Gītā* and the golf *Gītā* ascribe to a self-help ethos. The message R. Junah receives from Bagger Vance is that he must transform his self-doubt into self-belief. The *Gītā* simply teaches team-playing, integrity, non-aggression. It shows us how to sacrifice our lower desires for a higher goal—exactly what is also needed in the workplace. To a certain extent, this is true. One only has to think of Oppenheimer and, horrifically, Himmler. However, to what degree do we want to trivialize the *Gītā* as corporate 'spirituality in the workplace' advocates envision, those very individuals who may actually believe more in exploiting workers than in potentializing their spiritual growth? Theosophical allegory does not look so bad when replaced with vapid feel-good motivational propaganda. We no longer encounter the *sthitaprajña* or the *satyagrahi*. In this age where we are supposedly engaging the other more seriously than previously in less enlightened times, we are confronted with Glass's and Adams's/Sellars's *Gītās* as self-administered Rorschach tests for the self-conscious, self-satisfied artist or the alternative corporate 'influencers' and leisure sports enthusiasts in need of a spiritual playbook.

I recognize that some of these authors examined here may seem out of place to specialists; they may seem lightweight and not worthy of the consideration I have given them. But they contribute what I consider the *insolites* responses to the *Gītā* that I alluded to at the beginning of this study, those texts (literary, unscholarly, intersemiotic, and sometimes downright bizarre) that stand apart from more serious interpretations of the *Gītā* examined in this volume. But it is a premise of this book that such *insolites* interpretations also contribute to the general climate in which the *Gītā* has been received. Ginsberg is not serious, yet there is no doubt in my mind that he and other countercultural commentators contributed to the postmodern and more 'seriously received' interpretation of the *Gītā* in someone like Glass. It is to be remembered that the more we move away from 'serious' or 'canonical' readings, the more idiosyncratic the *Gītā* becomes. Had it not been for the Theosophists, would Gandhi have developed his theory of translation that justified his reading of the *Gītā?* Gandhi provides an interesting case in point: it is sometimes through the *insolite* reading that the 'canonical' interpretation is formed. Eliot's and Oppenheimer's interpretations of the *Gītā* are partial and very culturally specific to their own circumstances. But, for some, they provided the only knowledge of the text in popular circulation during World War II, despite the fact that quite a number of more scholarly (and fanatically murderous) Germans were reading and interpreting the *Gītā* at the same time. In our present day, Glass's postmodern operatic *Gītā, The Legend of Bagger Vance*, and the corporate 'spirituality in the workplace' module may be the version most accessible to modern audiences. All are very 'slight' works, but it cannot be denied that they represent afterlives for the text in the West. We do not have to like it.

As we can see, translation, to borrow from Roman Jakobson and Eugene Nida, is truly a high-stakes transaction. There is the innovative movement from periphery to the centre. But we should also see it as a conservative strategy of maintaining a status quo that might be endangered. In any event, we acknowledge George Steiner's penetration, invasion, extraction, and aggression. Long after the explanatory footnotes have disappeared from the translation to be replaced by operatic programme notes, we now hold out for some experience where the translator/interpreter tries to produce some vestige of faithfulness to the original, even if it means hauling out the golf metaphors. For the sake of our well-being, let us try and ignore the damage inflicted on the *Gītā* by the lunatic fringe for 'scripturally sanctioned' criminal intent or its co-optation in some corporate spiritual training module. Let us also acknowledge that, once the ego of the translator/commentator/interpreter/artist/fanatic or HR bureaucrat has overshadowed the text, we risk engaging in a process of self-reification (common to all exotic quests), where little enlightenment can be expected.

Bibliography

Adamo, Mark. "John, Atoms." Weblog, October 14, 2005. www.markadamo.com/journal.

Adams, John. "Doctor Atomic and His Gadget." *The Tanner Lectures on Human Values*. tannerlectures.utah.edu (October 29, 2009).

Adams, John. *Hallelujah Junction: Composing an American Life*. Faber & Faber, 2011.

Adams, John, and Peter Sellars. *Doctor Atomic Libretto*. New York and London: Boosey and Hawkes. https://www.opera-arias.com/adams/doctor-atomic/libretto/.

Adisamito-Smith, Steven. "Emerson's 'Hindu Sentiments." In Tharaud, 131–64.

Adluri Vishwa P. "Pride and Prejudice: Orientalism and German Indology." *International Journal of Hindu Studies* 15, no. 3 (2011): 253–92.

Adluri, Vishwa, and Joydeep Bagchee. *The Nay Science: A History of German Indology*. Oxford: Oxford University Press, 2014.

Ahir, D.C., and K.L. Chanchreek. *Dr. B.R. Ambedkar: Buddhist Revolution and Counter-Revolution in Ancient India*. New Delhi: BR Publishing, 1996.

Allen, Gay Wilson. *Walt Whitman Handbook*. Chicago: Packard, 1946.

Alles, Gregory D. "The Science of Religions in a Fascist State: Rudolf Otto and Jakob Wilhelm Hauer during the Third Reich." *Religion* 32 (2002): 177–204.

Ambedkar, B.R. *Writings and Speeches*. Pune: Government of Maharashtra, 1987.

Ambedkar, B.R. *Annihilation of Caste: The Annotated Critical Edition*. Edited by S. Anand. Introduction by Arundhati Roy. New Delhi: Navayana, 2013.

Anand, S. "A Note on the Poona Pact." In Ambedkar, 2013: 357–76.

Ananthanathan, A.K. "The Significance of Gandhi's Interpretation of the *Gītā*." *Gandhi Marg* 13, no. 3 (1991): 303–15.

Appadurai, Arjun. "Understanding Gandhi." In *Childhood and Selfhood: Essays on Tradition, Religion and Modernity in the Psychology of Erik H. Erikson*, edited by P. Homans, 113–43. Lewisburg, PA: Bucknell University Press, 1978.

Appiah, Kwame Anthony. "Thick Translation." In Venuti, 331–43.

Arendt, Hannah. *On Violence*. New York: Harcourt, Brace and World, 1970.

Armstrong, Carol. "All-Time Favorites." *Art Forum* 49, no. 10 (Summer 2011): 87–90.

Arnold, Edwin. *The Song Celestial or Bhagavad Gītā*. Translated from the Sanskrit. London: Trűbner, 1885.

Bakker, Hans. *Gandhi and the Gītā*. Toronto: Canadian Scholars' Press, 1993.

Banco, Lindsey Michael. *The Meanings of J. Robert Oppenheimer*. Iowa: University of Iowa Press, 2016.

Banco, Lindsey Michael. "Presenting Dr. J. Robert Oppenheimer: Science, the Atomic Bomb, and Cold War Television." *Journal of Popular Film and Television* 45, no. 3 (2017): 128–38.

Bassnett, Susan, and André Lefevere, eds. *Translation, History and Culture*. London and New York: Pinter, 1990.

Bayly, Christopher A. "India, the *Bhagavad Gītā* and the World." *Modern Intellectual History* 7, no. 2 (2010): 275–94.

Benavides, Gustaus. "Irrational Experiences, Heroic Deeds and the Extraction of Surplus." In Jungerer, 2008: 263–79.

Benjamin, Walter. "The Translator's Task." Translated by Steven Rendall. In Venuti, 75–83.

Benoit, Madhi, Susan Blattės, and G.J.V. Prasad, eds. *Violets in a Crucible: Translating the Orient*. Delhi: Sage, 2021.

Bentley, Joseph, and Jewel Brooker Spears. *Modernism and the Limits of Interpretation*. Amherst: University of Massachusetts, 1990.

Berlin, Isaiah. "Benjamin Disraeli, Karl Marx and the Search for Identity." In *Against the Current: Essays in the History of Ideas*, edited by H. Hardy, 252–86. New York: Viking, 1980.

Berman, Antoine. *The Experience of the Foreign: Culture and Translation in Romantic Germany*. New York: State University of New York Press, 1992.

Berman, Antoine. "Translation and the Trials of the Foreign." In Venuti, 240–53.

Besant, Annie, trans. *The Bhagavad-gîtâ, or The Lord's Song*, Madras: GA Natesan & Company, 1907.

Besant, Annie. *Hints on the Study of the Bhagavad Gītā: Four Lectures Delivered at the Theosophical Society at Adyar, Madras*. Adyar: Theosophical Publishing House, 1973.

Bespaloff, Rachel. *On the Iliad*. Translated by Mary McCarthy. New York: Harper, 1947.

Bethge, Eberhard. *Dietrich Bonhoeffer: Theologian, Christian, Contemporary*. Translated by Eric Mosbacher and Betty Ross, Frank Clarke, William Glen-Doepel and edited by Edwin Robertson. London: Collins, 1970.

Bhabha, Homi K. *The Location of Culture*. London and New York: Routledge, 1994.

Bhaktivedanta, A.C., trans. *The Bhagavad Gîtâ: As It Is*. New York: International Society for Krishna Consciousness, 1968.

Bharati, Agehananda. "The Hindu Renaissance and its Apologetic Patterns." *Journal of Asian Studies* 29 (February 1970): 267–88.

Bharati, Agehananda. "Hindu Scholars, Germany and the Third Reich." *Update: A Quarterly Journal on New Religious Movements* 6, no. 3 (September 1982): 44–52.

Bhatt, Chetan. *Hindu Nationalism: Origins, Ideologies, and Modern Myths*. New York: Oxford University Press, 2001.

Bhave, Vinoba. *Talks on the Gītā*. London: Allen & Unwin, 1960.

Bhikhu, Parekh. *Colonialism, Tradition and Reforms: An Analysis of Gandhi's Political Discourse*. New Delhi: Sage, 1981.

Bingemer, Maria Clara L. "War, Suffering and Detachment: Reading the *Bhagavad Gītā* with Simone Weil." In *Song Divine: Christian Commentaries on the Bhagavad Gītā*, edited by Catherine Cornille, 69–89. Leuven: Peeters, 2006.

Bird, Kai, and Martin J. Sherwin. *American Prometheus: The Triumph and Tragedy of J. Robert Oppenheimer*. New York: Knopf, 2005.

Bolle, Kees W., trans. *The Bhagavad Gītā: A New Translation*. Berkeley: University of California Press, 1979.

Bolle, Kees W. "Gandhi's Interpretation of the *Bhagavad Gītā*." In *Gandhi's Significance for Today*, edited by John Hick and Lemont C. Hempel, 137–51. London: Palgrave Macmillan, 1989.

Borges, Jorge Luis. "The Translators of the Thousand and One Nights." Translated by Esther Allen. In Venuti, 92–106.

Brown, D. Mackenzie. "The Philosophy of Bal Gangadhar Tilak." *The Journal of Asian Studies* 17, no. 2 (1958): 197–206.

Brown, W. Norman. *Man in the Universe: Some Continuities in Indian Thought*. Berkeley: University of California, 1966.

Brug, Manuel. "(K)ein amerkanisher Faust: 'Doctor Atomic' John Adams and Peter Sellars in San Francisco." *Die Welt*. October 4, 2005.

Bucke, Richard M. *Cosmic Consciousness*. New York: E. P. Dutton, 1923.

Bundesarchiv, Koblenz: Himmler NL 126/9. Nr. 235.

Burkholder, Robert E., and Joel Myerson. *Critical Essays on Ralph Waldo Emerson*. Boston, Mass: G.K. Hall, 1983.

Calonne, David Stephen and Allen Ginsberg. *Conversations with Allen Ginsberg*. Jackson, MS: University Press of Mississippi, 2019.

Calvert, Timothy John. "Simone Weil: Patron Saint of Outsiders." *New Blackfriars* 81, no. 950 (2000): 177–83.

Canning, Hugh. "*Doctor Atomic*—the Sunday Times Review." *The Sunday Times*. October 19, 2008.

Carpenter, Frederic Ives. *Emerson and Asia*. New York: Haskell Books, 1968.

Carson, Anne. *Decreation: Poetry, Essays, Opera*. New York: Knopf, 2005.

Cassidy, David C. *J. Robert Oppenheimer and the American Century*. New York: Plunkett Lake Press, 2005.

Cavell, Stanley. *In Quest of the Ordinary*. Chicago: University of Chicago Press, 1998.

Cha, Yooon Sook. *Decreation and the Ethical Bind: Simone Weil and the Claim of the Other*. New York: Fordham University Press, 2017.

Chakrabarty, Dipesh, and Rochona Majumdar. "Gandhi's *Gītā* and Politics as Such." *Modern Intellectual History* 7, no. 2 (2010): 335–53.

Chandran, K. Narayana. "A Receipt for Deceit: T.S. Eliot's 'To the Indians who Died in Africa.'" *Journal of Modern Literature* 30, no. 3 (2007): 52–69.

Chandrasekharan, K.R. "Emerson's 'Brahma': An Indian Interpretation." *The New England Quarterly* 33, no. 4 (December 1960): 506–21.

Chari, V.K. *Whitman and Indian Thought*. Provo, Utah: University of Utah Press, 1959.

Chari, V.K. "Whitman Criticism in Light of Indian Poetics." In *Walt Whitman: The Centenary Essays*, edited by Folsom, 240–50. Iowa City: University of Iowa Press, 1994.

Chari, V.K. *Whitman in the Light of Vedantic Mysticism: An Interpretation*. Lincoln: University of Nebraska Press, 1964.

Chatterjee, Margaret. *Gandhi's Religious Thought*. London: MacMillan, 1983.

Chaturvedi, Vinayak. "Rethinking Knowledge with Action: V.D. Savarkar, the *Bhagavad Gītā*, and Histories of Warfare." *Modern Intellectual History* 7, no. 2 (2010): 417–35.

Chirol, Valentine. *India*. London: Ernest Benn Ltd., 1926.

Christy, A. *The Orient in American Transcendentalism: A Study of Emerson, Thoreau, and Alcott*. New York: Octagon Books, 1963.

Clements, Andrew. "*Doctor Atomic* at San Francisco Opera." *The Guardian*. October 5, 2005.

Clough, Bradley S. "Gandhi, Non-Violence and the *Bhagavad-Gītā*." In *Holy War: Violence and the Bhagavad Gītā*, edited by Steven J. Rosen, 59–80. Hampton: A Deepak Publication, 2002.

Coburn, T.B. "'Scripture' in India: Towards a Typology of the World in Hindu Life." *Journal of the American Academy of Religion* 52, no. 3 (September 1984): 435–59.

Cohen, Mitchell. "The Damnation of *Dr. Atomic*." *Dissent* 56, no. 2 (2009): 79–85.

Colebrooke, Henry Thomas. *Essays on the Religion and Philosophy of the Hindus*. London and Edinburgh: Williams and Norgate, 1815.

Coles, Robert. *Simone Weil: A Modern Pilgrimage*. Reading, MA: Addison-Wesley, 1987.

Copley, Antony. *A Spiritual Bloomsbury: Hinduism and Homosexuality in the Lives and Writings of Edward Carpenter, E.M. Forster, and Christopher Isherwood*. Lanham, MD: Lexington Books, 2006.

Copley, Antony. *Gay Writers in Search of the Divine: Hinduism and Homosexuality in the Lives and Writings of Edward Carpenter, E. M. Forster, and Christopher Isherwood*. Delhi: Yoda Press, 2006.

Cousin, Victor. *Cours de l'histoire de la philosophie*. Paris: Pichon & Didier, 1829.

Cowen, Robert. *The Indo-German Identification: Reconciling South Asian Origins and European Destinies*, 1765–1885. Rochester, NY: Camden House, 2010.

Cowley, Malcolm. "Hindu Mysticism and Whitman's 'Song of Myself'." In Walt Whitman, *Leaves of Grass* (1973): 918–26.

Crawley, Thomas Edward. *The Structure of Leaves of Grass*. Austin, Texas: University of Texas Press, 1971.

Creuzer, Friedrich. *Symbolik und Mythologie der alten Vőlker, besonders der Griechen*. Leipzig and Darmstadt: C.W. Leske, 1839–42.

Damrosch, David. 'Translations and World Literature: Love in the Metropolis'. In Venuti, 411–28.

Davis, Richard H. *The Bhagavad Gītā: A Biography*. Princeton, NJ: Princeton University Press, 2015.

DeJong, Constance, and Philip Glass. *Satyagraha. M. K. Gandhi in South Africa 1893–1911; The Historical Material and Libretto Comprising the Opera's Book*. New York: Tanam, 1983.

Derrida, Jacques. "What Is a 'Relevant' Translation?" Translated by Lawrence Venuti. In Venuti, 365–88.

Desai, Mahadev. *The Gospel of Selfless Action, or, the Gītā According to Gandhi*. Ahmedabad: Navajivan Publishing House, 1948.

Desgrâces, Alyette. "L'Inde ou le passage obligé." In Weil 1988, vol. 6, part 1: 35–52.

Detweiler, Robert. "The Over-Rated 'Over-Soul.'" In Burkholder and Myerson, 307–09.

Devi, Savitri. *Defiance*. Calcutta: A. K. Mukerji, 1951.

Devi, Savitri. *Gold in the Furnace*. Calcutta: A. K. Mukerji, 1952.

Devi, Savitri. *The Lightning and the Sun*. Calcutta: Savitri Devi Mukherji, 1958a.

Devi, Savitri. *Pilgrimage*. Calcutta: A. K. Mukerji, 1958b.

Devi, Savitri. *Impeachment of Man*. Calcutta: Savitri Devi Mukherji, 1959.

Devi, Savitri. *Souvenirs et réflexions d'une aryenne*. New Delhi: Savitri Devi Mukherjee, 1976.

Dhareshwar, Vivek. "Framing the Predicament of Indian Thought: Gandhi, the *Gītā*, and Ethical Action." *Asian Philosophy* 22, no. 3 (August 2012): 257–74.

Doering, E. Jane. *Simone Weil and the Specter of Self-Perpetuating Force*. Notre Dame, IN: University of Notre Dame Press, 2010.

Donoghue, Denis. "T.S. Eliot's Quartets: A New Reading." *Studies: An Irish Quarterly Review* 54, no. 213 (1965): 41–62.

Douglas, William, trans. *The Bhagavad Gītā*. London: Oxford University Press, 1928.

Droit, Roger-Pol. "Victor Cousin: 'La *Bhagavad Gītā* et l'ombre de Hegel.'" In *L'Inde et l'imaginaire*, edited by Catherine Weinberger-Thomas, 175–96. Paris: École des Hautes Études en Sciences Sociales, 1989.

Droit, Roger-Pol. *L'oubli de l'Inde, une amnésie philosophique*. Paris: PUF, 1989.

Dumm, Thomas, and Judith Butler. "Giving Away, Giving Over: A Conversation with Judith Butler." *The Massachusetts Review* 49 no. 1/2. (Spring-Summer 2008): 95–105.

Dutton, Denis. "Theodor Adorno on Astrology." *Philosophy and Literature* 19, no. 2 (1995): 424–44.

Eder, Milton. "A Review of Recent *Bhagavad Gītā* Studies." *Journal of South Asian Literature* 23, no. 2 (1988): 20–46.

Edgerton, Franklin, trans. *Bhagavad Gītā*. Cambridge: Harvard University Press, (1944) 1972.

Eliot, T.S. *Four Quartets*. Edited by Bernard Bergonzi. London: MacMillan, 1969.

Eliot, T.S. *The Complete Poems and Plays*. London: Faber and Faber, 1969.

Eliot, T.S. *After Strange Gods: A Primer of Modern Heresy*. New York: Harcourt, Brace, 1934.

Eliot, T.S. *Selected Essays, 1917–32*. New York: Harcourt, Brace and Co., 1932.

Emerson, Ralph Waldo. *The Letters of Ralph Waldo Emerson*. Edited by Ralph L. Rusk. 6 vols. New York: Columbia University Press, 1939.

Emerson, Ralph Waldo. *The Portable Emerson*. Edited by Mark Van Doren. New York: The Viking Press, 1946.

Emerson, Ralph Waldo. *The Genius and Character of Emerson: Lectures at the Concord School of Philosophy*. Edited by F.B. Sanborn. New York: Kennikat Press, 1971a.

Emerson, Ralph Waldo. *Collected Works*. Edited by Robert Ernest Spiller. Cambridge, MA: Harvard University Press, 1971–2013.

Emerson, Ralph Waldo. *Nature, Addresses, and Lectures*. Edited by Robert Ernest Spiller, and Alfred R Ferguson. Cambridge, MA: Harvard University Press, 1976.

Emerson, Ralph Waldo. *Emerson's "Indian Superstition": With Studies in His Poetry, Bibliography, and Early Orientalism*. Edited by Kenneth Walter Cameron. Hartford: Transcendental Books, 1977.

Emerson, Ralph Waldo. *Essays (first series)*. Edited by Alfred Riggs Ferguson and Jean Ferguson Carr. Cambridge, MA: Harvard University Press, 1987.

Emerson, Ralph Waldo. "Representative Man." In *Collected Works*. Vol 4, 1987.

Emerson, Ralph Waldo. *Journals*. Edited by E.W. Emerson and W.E. Forbes. Boston and New York: Houghton and Mifflin, 1904–1914.

Emerson, Ralph Waldo. *Indian Superstition*. Vol. 1. Hanover: Friends of the Dartmouth Library, 1954.

Emerson, Ralph Waldo. *Journals and Miscellaneous Notebooks of Ralph Waldo Emerson*. Vol. 1 1960; Vol. 9 1971; Vols. 10 and 11 1975. Edited by A.W. Plumstead,

William H. Gilman, and Ruth H. Bennett. Cambridge, MA: Harvard University Press, 1960–1982.

Emerson, Ralph Waldo. *The Early Lectures of Ralph Waldo Emerson*. Edited by Stephen E. Whicher, Robert E. Spiller, and Wallace E. Williams. 3 vols. Cambridge, MA: Harvard University Press, 1959–1972.

Emerson, Ralph Waldo. *The Topical Notebooks of Ralph Waldo Emerson*. Edited by Susan Sutton. 3 vols. Columbia, Missouri: University of Missouri Press, 1990.

Even-Zohar, Itamar. "The Position of Translated Literature within the Literary Polysystem." In Venuti, 162–67.

Everett-Green, Robert. "A Work that Could be More Explosive." (2008). https://www.theglobeandmail.com/arts/a-work-that-could-be-more-explosive/article1323566/.

Everist, Mark. "Meyerbeer's *Il crociato in Egitto*: Melodrame, Opera, Orientalism." *Cambridge Opera Journal* 8, no. 3 (1996): 215–50.

Faisal, Devji. "Morality in the Shadow of Politics." *Modern Intellectual History* 7, no. 2 (2010): 373–90.

Ferber, Michael. "Simone Weil's *Iliad*." In *Simone Weil: Interpretations of a Life*, edited by George Abbott White, 63–85. Amherst: University of Massachusetts Press, 1981.

Fernhout, Rein. "Combatting the Enemy: The Use of Scripture in Gandhi and Godse." In *Human Rights and Religious Values: An Uneasy Relationship*, edited by 'Abd Akkah Ahmad Na'im, Abdullahi A. An-Na'im, and Henry Jansen, 120–32. Grand Rapids, MI: Rodopi, 1995.

Feuerstein, G. *The Bhagavad Gītā: Its Philosophical and Cultural Setting*. Madras: Theosophical Publishing House, 1983.

Fiedler, Leslie. "Introduction." In *Waiting for God*, edited by Simone Weil, xxi–xxxiv. New York: G. P. Putnam's Sons, 1951.

Figueira, Dorothy M. "The Politics of Exoticism and Friedrich Schlegel's Metaphorical Pilgrimage to India." *Monatshefte* 81, no. 4 (1989): 425–33.

Figueira, Dorothy M. *Translating the Orient*. New York: State University of New York Press, 1991.

Figueira, Dorothy M. "Myth, Ideology and the Authority of an Absent Text." *Yearbook of Comparative and General Literature* 39 (1993): 55–61.

Figueira, Dorothy M. *The Exotic: A Decadent Quest*. New York: State University of New York Press, 1994.

Figueira, Dorothy M. "Mystical Nationalism: The *Bhagavad Gita* as a Call to Arms." In *Littérature et Culture partagée*, edited by Ibra Diene. 275–84. Dakar: Presses Universitaires de Dakar, 2007.

Figueira, Dorothy M. *Otherwise Occupied: Theories and Pedagogies of Alterity*. Albany: State University of New York Press, 2008.

Figueira, Dorothy M. "Comparative Literature: Where Have We Been, Where Are We Now, Where Are We Going?" *Working Papers*. Department of Comparative Literature, Kolkata: Jadavpur University, 2011.

Figueira, Dorothy M. "The Subaltern Can Speak: Letters from the Trenches and Across the Black Water." In *Interdisciplinary Alter-Natives in Comparative Literature*, edited by E.V. Ramakrishnan, Harish Trivedi, and Chandra Mohan, 86–106. Delhi: Sage, 2013.

Figueira, Dorothy M. "The *Bhagavad Gītā*: From German Lecture Hall to the Trenches of the First World War, From Neo-Nazi Propaganda to the Metropolitan Opera." In *Intersections, Interfaces, Interdisciplinarities: Literature and Other Arts,* edited by Gerald Gillespie and Haun Saussy, 57–70. Brussels: P.I.E. Lang, 2014.

Figueira, Dorothy M. "Translating the *Bhagavad Gita*." *Critical Practice* 21 (2014):42–54.

Figueira, Dorothy M. *Aryans, Jews, Brahmins: Theorizing Authority*, with Preface to the Indian edition. New Delhi: Navayana, 2015.

Figueira, Dorothy M. "The Translation of the *Bhagavad Gita* as a German Literary and Philosophical Event." In *Text als Ereignis: Programme-Praktiken-Wirkungen*, edited by Winfried Eckel and Uwe Lindemann, 427–38. Berlin: De Gruyter, 2017.

Figueira, Dorothy M. "The Jesuits in Asia, Ricci's Accommodation Policy, and Comparing Cultures." In *New Perspectives in the Studies of Matteo Ricci*, edited by Filippo Mignini, 49–58. Macerata: Quodlibet, 2019.

Figueira, Dorothy M. "The *Bhagavad Gītā* in American Poetry and Opera." In *Beyond Borders: The Interplay of Ancient and Modern Literatures*, edited by Valerio Massimo DeAngelis. Macerata: EUM, in press.

Fink, Robert. "After the Canon." In Greenwald, 2014: 1065–88.

Fowler, Russell T. "Krishna and the 'Still Point': A Study of the *Bhagavad-Gītā*'s Influence in Eliot's 'Four Quartets.'" *The Sewanee Review* 79, no. 3 (1971): 407–23.

Fraisse, Simone. "S. Weil, traductrice de *l'Iliade*." *Philosophie & Language* 13 (1991): 141–53.

Friedrich, Paul. *The Gītā within Walden*. Albany: State University of New York Press, 2008.

Friess, Horace L. *Felix Adler and Ethical Culture*. Edited by Fannie Weingarten. New York: Columbia University Press, 1981.

Gabellieri, Emmanuel. *Être et don: Simone Weil et la philosophie*. Vol. 57. Leuven: Peeters Publishers, 2003.

Gandhi, Mohandas Karamchand. *Young India, 1924–1926*. New York: Viking, 1927.

Gandhi, Mohandas Karamchand. *Non-Violence in Peace and War*. Ahmedabad: Navjivan Publishing House, 1942.

Gandhi, Mohandas Karamchand. *Hindu Dharma*. Ahmedabad: Navajivan, 1950.

Gandhi, Mohandas Karamchand. *An Autobiography: My Experiments with Truth*. Boston: Beacon Press, 1957.

Gandhi, Mohandas Karamchand. *The Story of My Experiments with Truth*. Allahabad: Navjivan Publishing House, 1969.

Gandhi, Mohandas Karamchand. *The Collected Works of Mahatma Gandhi*. New Delhi: Ministry of Information and Broadcasting, Publications Division, 1984–88.

Gandhi, Mohandas Karamchand. *The Moral and Political Writings of Mahatma Gandhi*. Edited by Raghavan Iyer. Delhi: Oxford University Press, 2000.

Gandhi, Mohandas Karamchand. *The Bhagavad Gītā: According to Gandhi. Text and Commentary*. Edited by John Strohmeier. Berkeley: Berkeley Hills Books, 2000.

Gandhi, Mohandas Karamchand. "A Vindication of Caste." In Ambedkar, 2013: 321–28.

Ganguly, Suranjan. "Allen Ginsberg in India: An Interview." *Ariel: A Review of International English Literature* 24, no. 4 (1993): 21–32.

Garbe, Richard. "Bhagavad-Gītā." In *Encyclopedia of Religion and Ethics,* Vol. 2, edited by James Hastings, 535–38. Edinburgh: T & T Clark, 1909.

Garbe, Richard, trans. *Die Bhagavadgîtâ. Aus dem Sanskrit űbersetzt und mit einer Einleitung űber ihre ursprungliche Gestalt, ihre Lehren und ihr Alter versehen.* Leipzig: H. Haessel, 1921.

Gardner, Helen. *Four Quartets: A Commentary.* London: Dennis Dobson, 1947.

Gardner, Helen. *The Composition of Four Quartets.* London: Oxford University Press, 1978.

Germana, Nicholas A. *The Orient of Europe: The Mythical Image of India and Competing Images of German National Identity.* Newcastle upon Tyne: Cambridge Scholars, 2009.

Ghose, Aurobindo. *Essays on the Gītā.* Calcutta: Arya Publishing House. First Series 1922, Second Series 1928.

Ghose, Aurobindo. *The Gītā: With Text, Translation and Notes.* Edited by Anilbaran Roy. Compiled from Sri Aurobindo's *Essays on the Gītā.* Pondicherry: Sri Aurobindo Ashram, 1943.

Ghose, Aurobindo. *The Doctrine of Passive Resistance.* Calcutta: Arya Publishing House, 1948.

Ghose, Aurobindo. *Essays on the Gītā.* Pondicherry: Sri Aurobindo Ashram, 1966.

Ghose, Aurobindo. *Collected Works. Birth Centenary Library.* 30 vols. Pondicherry: Aurobindo Ashram, 1970–72.

Ghose, Aurobindo. *Bande Mataram: Early Political Writings.* Vol. 1. Pondicherry: Sri Aurobindo Birth Centenary Library, 1972.

Ghose, Aurobindo. *Karmayoga: Early Political Writings.* Vol. 1. Pondicherry: Sri Aurobindo Birth Centenary Library, 1972.

Ghose, Aurobindo. *Letters on Yoga.* Birth Centenary Library. Vol. 22. Pondicherry: Aurobindo Ashram, 1972.

Ghosh, Damayanti. "Karma in a Mode of Salvation in T.S. Eliot." *Jadavpur Journal of Comparative Literature* 12 (1974): 125–35.

Ginsberg, Allen. "Appreciation." In Bhaktivedanta, 14–15.

Gipper, Helmut. "Understanding as a Process of Linguistic Approximation: The Discussion between August Wilhelm von Schlegel, S.A. Langlois, Wilhelm von Humboldt and G.W.F. Hegel on the Translation of the *Bhagavad Gītā* and the Concept of Yoga." *Studies in the History of Western Linguistics in Honor of R.H. Robbins,* edited by Theodora Bynam and F.R. Palmer, 109–28. Cambridge: Cambridge University Press, 1986.

Glass, Philip. *Music by Philip Glass.* New York: Harper and Row, 1987.

Glass, Philip. *Satyagraha* (video recording). Music by Philip Glass. Libretto by Philip Glass and Constance DeJong. Produced by Achim Freyer. Chatsworth, CA: Image Entertainment [c. 2001], 1983.

Glass, Philip, and DeJong, Constance. "Satyagraha," BAM 2018 Next Wave Festival. https://www.bam.org/opera/2018/satyagraha.

Goethe, Johann Wolfgang von. "Translations." Translated by Sharon Sloan. In Venuti, 64–6.

Goodchild, Peter. *J. Robert Oppenheimer: Shatterer of Worlds.* New York: Fromm International, 1985.

Goodman, Russell B. "East-West Philosophy in Nineteenth-Century America: Emerson and Hinduism." *Journal of the History of Ideas* 51, no. 4 (1990): 625–45.

Goodrick-Clarke, Nicholas. *Hitler's Priestess: Savitri Devi, the Hindu-Aryan Myth, and Neo-Nazism*. New York: New York University Press, 1998.

Goodrick-Clarke, Nicholas. *Black Sun: Aryan Cults, Esoteric Nazism, and the Politics of Identity*. New York: New York University Press, 2002.

Gore, Madhav S. *The Social Context of an Ideology: Ambedkar's Political and Social Thought*. New Delhi: SAGE Publications Pvt. Limited, 1993.

Goren, Leyla. *Elements of Brahmanism in the Transcendentalism of Emerson*. Edited by Kenneth Walter. Hartford, Conn: Transcendental Books, 1977.

Gosavi, P.K. *Tilak, Gandhi and the Gītā*. Bombay: Bharatiya Vidya Bhavan, 1983.

Gowda, Nagappa. *The Bhagavad-Gītā in the Nationalist Discourse*. New Delhi: Oxford University Press, 2011.

Gray, Francine du Plessix. *Simone Weil*. New York: Viking, 2001.

Gray, Gordon, and J. Robert Oppenheimer. U.S. Atomic Energy Commission. *In the Matter of J. Robert Oppenheimer: Transcript of Hearing Before Personnel Security Board*. Washington DC, April 12, 1954, Through May 6, 1954. US Government Printing Office, 1954.

Greenwald, Helen M. *The Oxford Handbook of Opera*. New York: Oxford University Press, 2014.

Griffiths, Bede. "The Enigma of Simone Weil." *Blackfriars* 34, no. 398 (1953): 232–236.

Grenadier, M.E., and K.S. Narayana Rao. "The Waste Land and the Upanishads: What Does the Thunder Say?" *Indian Literature* 14, no. 1 (March 1971): 85–98.

Gross, Harvey Seymour. *Sound and Form in Modern Poetry*. Ann Arbor: University of Michigan Press, 1964.

Grūnendahl, Reinhold "Wissenschaftsgeschichte im Schattem postorientalischer De/Konstruction." *Orientalistische Literaturzeitung* 103, no. 4–5 (2009): 457–78.

Gűnther, Hans F.K. *Rassenkunde des deutschen Volkes*. Munich: J.F. Lehmann, 1923.

Gűnther, Hans F.K. *Die Nordische Rasse bei den Indogermanen* Asiens. Munich: J.F. Lehmann, 1934.

Gupta, R.K. *The Great Encounter: A Study of Indo-American Literary and Cultural Relations*. Riverdale: Maryland Riverdale Company, 1987.

Guru, Gopal. *Humiliation: Claims and Context*. New Delhi: Oxford University Press, 2009.

Hakl, Hans Thomas. *Der verborgene Geist von Eranos-Unbekannte Begegnungen von Wissenschaft und Esoterik—Eine alternative Geistesgeschichte de 20. Jahrhunderts*. Bratten: Scientia Nova, 2001.

Halbfass, Wilhelm. *India and Europe*. Albany: State University of New York Press, 1989.

Hardiman, David. *Gandhi in His Time and Ours: The Global Legacy of His Ideas*. London: Hurst & Co., 2003.

Harding, Walter. *The Days of Henry*. New York: Alfred A. Knopf, 1965.

Harding, Walter, and Henry David Thoreau. *Thoreau's Library*. Charlottesville: University of Virginia Press, 1957.

Harris, William T. "Emerson's Orientalism." In Sanborn, 1971: 372–85.

Harvey, M.J. "The Secular as Sacred: The Religio-Political Rationalization of B. G. Tilak." *Modern Asian Studies* 20, no. 2 (1986): 321–31.

Hastings, Warren. "Advertisement" and "Letter to Nathaniel Smith." In Wilkins, A2: 5–16.

Hauer, Jakob Wilhelm. *Eine indo-arische Metaphysik des Kampfes und der Tat: Die Bhagavad Gītā in neuer Sicht mit Übersetzung*. Stuttgart: W. Kohnhammer, 1934.

Hauer, Jakob Wilhelm. *Deutsche Gottschau. Grundzüge eines Deutschen Glaubens*. Stuttgart: W. Kohnhammer, 1935a.

Hauer, Jakob Wilhelm. *Was Will die Deutsche Glaubensbewebung?* Edited by Herbert Grabert. Stuttgart: Karl Gutbrod, 1935b.

Head, Matthew. "Musicology on Safari: Orientalism and the Spectre of Postcolonial Theory." *Music Analysis* 22 (2003): 211–30.

Hecht, David K. "The Atomic Hero: Robert Oppenheimer and the Making of Scientific Icons in the Early Cold War." *Technology and Culture* 49 no. 4 (October 2008): 943–66.

Hee, Charles Chow Hoi. "A Holistic Approach to Business Management: Perspectives from the *Bhagavad Gītā*." *Singapore Management Review* 29, no. 1 (2007): 73–85.

Hegel, G.W.F. *Sämtliche Werke, Neue Kritische Ausgabe*. Edited by G. Lasson and J. Hoffmeister. Leipzig: F. Meiner, 1928.

Hegel, G.W.F. *Vorlesungen über die Geschichte der Philosophie*. Edited by J. Hoffmeister. Leipzig: F. Meiner, 1944.

Hegel, G.W.F. *Briefe von und an Hegel*. Edited by J. Hoffmeister. 4 vols. Hamburg: F. Meiner, 1954.

Hegel, G.W.F. *Vorlesungen über die Philosophie der Weltgeschichte*. Vol. I: *Die Vernünft in der Geschichte*. Edited by J. Hoffmeister. Hamburg: F. Meiner, 1955.

Hegel, G.W.F. *Vorlesungen über die Philosophie der Religion*. Edited by G. Lasson. Hamburg: F. Meiner, 1966.

Hegel, G.W.F. *Vorlesungen über die Philosophie der Weltgeschichte*. Vol. II: *Die orientalische Welt*. Edited by G. Lasson. Hamburg: F. Meiner, 1968.

Hegel, G.W.F. *Werke in Zwanzig Bänden. Theorie Werkausgabe*, Vol. 11: "*Berliner Schriften*." Edited by. E. Moldenhauer and K.M. Michel. Frankfurt: Suhrkamp, 1970.

Hendricks, George. "Whitman's Copy of the *Bhagavad-Gītā*." *Walt Whitman Quarterly Review* 5, no. 1 (1959): 12–14.

Herken, Gregg. "An Explorer in the Desert." *Science* 310, no. 5749 (2005): 284–85.

Hewiston, Justin M. "Emerson's Awakening." *The Wenshan Review of Literature and Culture* 13 (June 2, 2020): 139–49.

Hewiston, Justin M. "Peterson vs. Žižek on the Evolution of Consciousness and Happiness from Pragmatism to Sarkar's Tantra." In *Pragmatism, Spiritualism and Society: New Pathways on Consciousness, Freedom and Solidarity*, edited by A.K. Giri, 65–87. Singapore: Springer, 2021.

Hick, John, and Lamont Hempel. *Gandhi's Significance for Today*. New York: St. Martin's Press, 1989.

Hijiya, James A. "The '*Gītā*' of J. Robert Oppenheimer." *Proceedings of the American Philosophical Society* 144, no. 2 (2000): 123–67.

Hill, William Douglas Penneck, trans. *The Bhagavadgītā: Transl. from the Sanskrit with an Intr., an Argument and a Commentary*. Oxford: Oxford University Press, 1928.

Hiltebeitel, Alf. *The Ritual of Battle: Krishna in the Mahābhārata*. Albany: State University of New York Press, 1976.

Hodder, Alan D. "The Best of [the] Brahmins." *Nineteenth Century Prose* 30, nos. 1-2 (2001): 337–54.

Hodder, Alan D. "Emerson, Rammohun Roy, and the Utilitarians." *Studies in the American Renaissance* (1988): 133–48.

Hodder, Alan D. "'Ex Oriente Lux': Thoreau's Ecstasies and the Hindu Texts." *Harvard Theological Review* 86, no. 4 (1993): 403–38.

Hollander, John. *American Poetry: The Nineteenth Century*. New York: The Library of America, 1993.

Holmes, Oliver Wendall. *Ralph Waldo Emerson*. Boston: Houghton, Mifflin, 1882.

Holtzmann, Jr., Adolf. *Das Mahābhārata und Seine Theile*, 4 vols. Kiel: C.F. Haessler, 1893.

Holtzmann, Jr., Adolf. *Die Neunzehnten Bücher des Mahâbhârata*. Kiel: C.F. Haessler, 1892–95.

Howarth, Herbert. *Notes on some Figures behind T.S. Eliot*. Boston: Houghton Mifflin, 1964.

Hulin, Michel. *Hegel et l'occident*. Paris: Vrin, 1979.

Humboldt, Wilhelm von. *Wilhelm von Humboldts Gesammelte Werke*. Berlin: G Reimer, 1841.

Huxley, Aldous. *The Perennial Philosophy*. London: Chatto and Windus, 1945.

Irwin, Alec. "Devoured by God: Cannibalism, Mysticism, and Ethics in Simone Weil." *CrossCurrents* 51, no. 2 (2001): 257–72.

Ishvarakrishna. *Sāṃkhya-Kārikās*. Translated by H.T. Colebrooke. London: Valpy, 1837.

Israel, Hephzibah. "Translating the Sacred: Colonial Constructions and Postcolonial Perspectives." In *A Companion to Translation Studies*, edited by Sandra Berman and Catherine Porter, 557–69. UK: Wiley Blackwell, 2014.

Iyer, Raghavan. *The Moral and Political Thought of Gandhi*. New York: Oxford University Press, 1973.

Jackson, R. "The Construction of 'Hinduism' and its Impact on Religious Education in England and Wales." *Panorama* 8, no. 2 (1996): 86–104.

Jaffrelot, Christophe. *Analysing and Fighting Caste: Dr. Ambedkar and Untouchability*. New Delhi: Permanent Black, 2005.

Jakobson, Roman. "Linguistics and Poetics." In *Style in Language*, edited by Thomas A. Sebeok, 350–77. Cambridge, MA: MIT Press, 1960.

Jakobson, Roman. "On Linguistic Aspects of Translation." In Venuti, 126–32.

Jenson, I.M. *Manufacturing Confucianism: Chinese Traditions and Universal Civilization*. Durham: Duke University Press, 1995.

Jerome. "Letters to Pammachius." Translated by Kathleen Davis. In Venuti, 21–30.

Jones, Sir William. *The Works of Sir William Jones: With the Life of the Author by Lord Teignmouth*. 13 vols. London: John Stockdale and John Walker, 1807.

Jordens, J.T.F. "Gandhi and the *Bhagavad Gītā*." In *Modern Indian Interpreters of the Bhagavad Gītā*, edited by R.N. Minor, 88–109. Albany: State University of New York Press 1986.

Jost, T. *Purification of Body and Mind*. San Juan, CA: National Socialist Kindred, 1995.

Judge, W.Q. *Notes on the Bhagavad Gītā*. Los Angeles: The Theosophy Co., 1918.

Judge, W.Q., trans. *The Bhagavad-Gītā: The Book of Devotion*. Los Angeles: The Theosophy Co., 1928.

Junginger, Horst. *Von der philosophischen zu völkischen Religionswissenschaft*. Stuttgart: Franz Steiner, 1999.

Junginger, Horst. *The Study of Religion under the Impact of Fascism*. Leiden: Brill, 2008.

Jungk, Robert. *Brighter than a Thousand Suns: A Personal History of the Atomic Scientists*. New York: Houghton Mifflin Harcourt, 1958.

Kapila, Śruti. "A History of Violence." *Modern Intellectual History* 7, no. 2 (2010): 437–57.

Kapila, Śruti, and Faisal Devji. "The *Bhagavad Gītā* and Modern Thought: Introduction." *Modern Intellectual History* 7, no. 2 (2010): 269–73.

Kapila, Śruti, and Faisal Devji, eds. *Political Thought in Action: The Bhagavad Gītā and Modern India*. Cambridge: Cambridge University Press, 2013.

Karmakar, D.P. *Bal Gangadhar Tilak: A Study*. Bombay: Popular Prakashan, 1956.

Kaur, Raminder. "Atomic Schizophrenia: Indian Reception of the Atom Bomb Attacks in Japan, 1945." *Cultural Critique* 84 (2013): 70–100.

Kearns, Cleo McNelly. *T.S. Eliot and Indic Traditions: A Study in Poetry and Belief*. Cambridge: Cambridge University Press, 1987.

Kersten, Felix. *Totenköpf und Treue—Heinrich Himmler ohne Uniform*. Hamburg: Robert Mölich, 1953.

Kersten, Felix. *The Kersten Memoirs, 1940–45*. Introduction by H.R. Trevor-Roper. Translated by Constantine Fitzgibbon and James Oliver. New York: The Macmillan Co, 1957.

Klausen, Jimmy Casas. "Economies of Violence: The *Bhagayad Gītā* and the Fostering of Life in Gandhi's and Ghose's Anticolonial Theories." *American Political Science Review* 108, no. 1 (2014): 182–95.

Kluger, Ruth. *Still Alive: A Holocaust Girlhood Remembered*. New York: Feminist Press, 2001.

Kolge, Nishikant. *Gandhi Against Caste*. New Delhi: Oxford University Press, 2017.

Kontge, Ted. *German Orientalisms*. Ann Arbor: University of Michigan Press, 2004.

Koppedrayer, Kay. "Gandhi's Autobiography as Commentary on the *Bhagavad Gītā*." *International Journal of Hindu Studies* 6, no. 1 (April 2002): 47–73.

Kosambi, Damodar Dharmanand. *The Culture and Civilisation of Ancient India in Historical Outline*. London: Routledge and K. Paul, 1965.

Kozinn, Allan. "Glass's Satyagraha (1986)." In *Writings on Glass. Essays, Interviews, Criticism*, edited by Richard Kostelanetz, 176–88. Berkeley: University of California Press, 1997.

Kumar, Aishwary. "Ambedkar's Inheritances." *Modern Intellectual History* 7, no. 2 (2010): 391–415.

Kumar, Aishwary. *Radical Equality: Ambedkar, Gandhi, and the Risk of Democracy*. Stanford CA: Stanford University Press, 2015.

Kurlander, E. *Hitler's Monsters: A Supernatural History of the Third Reich*. New Haven: Yale University Press, 2017.

Langlois, A.S. "*Bhagavad Gītā* id est Thespesion Melos … traduit par A.G. de Schlegel." *Journal Asiatique* 4 (1824): 105–16; 236–52.

Lanman, Charles Rockwell. *Anniversary Papers in the Completion of his Twenty-fifth Year of Teaching in Harvard University*. June MCMXIII. Boston, 1913.

Larson, Gerald James. "The Song Celestial: Two Centuries of the *Bhagavad Gītā* in English." *Philosophy East and West* 31, no. 4 (1981): 513–41.

Larson, Gerald James. "The 'Bhagavad Gītā' as Cross-Cultural Process: Toward an Analysis of the Social Locations of a Religious Text." *Journal of the American Academy of Religion* 43, no. 4 (1975): 651–69.

Lefevere, André. "Mother Courage's Cucumbers: Text, System and Refraction in a Theory of Literature." *Modern Language Studies* 12, no. 4 (1982): 3–20.

Lefevere, André. *Translation, Rewriting and the Manipulation of Literary Fame*. London and New York: Routledge, 1992.

Lelyveld, Joseph. *Great Soul: Mahatma Gandhi and His Struggle with India*. New York: Alfred A. Knopf, 2011.

Lemont, Lansing. *Day of Trinity*. New York: Athenaeum, 1965.

Levertov, Denise. "A Note of Appreciation." In Bhaktivedanta, 6–17. https://vanisource.org/w/index.php?

Lindenberger, Herbert. *Opera in History: From Monteverdi to Cage*. Stanford, CA: Stanford University Press, 1998.

Ling, Trevor. *A History of Religion East and West: An Introduction and Interpretation*. New York: St. Martin's Press, 1968.

Ling, Trevor. *Karl Marx and Religion: In Europe and India*. Hong Kong: Harper & Row, 1980.

Locke, Ralph P. *Musical Exoticism: Images and Reflections*. Cambridge: Cambridge University Press, 2009.

Longerich, Peter. *Heinrich Himmler: A Life*. Translated by Jeremy Noakes and Lesley Sharpe. Oxford: Oxford University Press, 2012.

López, Alfred J. "Translating Interdisciplinarity: Reading Martí Reading Whitman." *The Comparatist* 35 (2011): 5–18.

López, Alfred J., and Robert P. Marzec. "Postcolonial Studies at the Twenty-Five Year Mark." *Modern Fiction Studies* 56, no. 4 (2010): 677–88.

Ludden, D. "Orientalist Empiricism: Transformation of Colonial Knowledge." In *Orientalism and the Postcolonial Predicament in South Asia*, edited by C.A. Breckenridge and P. van der Veer, 250–78. Philadelphia, PA: University of Pennsylvania Press, 1993.

Luther, Martin. "On Translating: An Open Letter." Translated by Charles M. Jacobs. Revised by E. Theodora Bachmann. In *Luther's Works*, Vol. 35. *Word and Sacrament I*, edited by Theodora Bachmann, 175–202. Philadelphia: Muhlenberg Press, 1960.

Lyndall, Gordon. *Eliot's New Life*. Oxford: Oxford University Press, 1987.

McCarthy, Harold E. "T.S. Eliot and Buddhism." *Philosophy East and West* 2, no. 1 (1952): 31–55.

McDonald, John W. *Walt Whitman, Philosopher Poet: Leaves of Grass by Indirection*. Jefferson, NC: McFarland, 2007.

McGetchen, Douglas T. *Indology, Indomania, and Orientalism: Ancient India's Rebirth in Modern Germany*. Madison, NJ: Fairleigh Dickinson, University Press, 2009.

McKenzie, John. *Hindu Ethics: A Historical and Critical Essay*. Oxford: Oxford University Press, 1922.

McLane, John R. *The Political Awakening in India*. Englewood Cliffs, NJ: Prentice Hall, 1970.

McLean, Andrew M. "Emerson's 'Brahma' as an Expression of Brahman." *New England Quarterly* 42, no. 1 (1969): 115–22.

McMillan, Priscilla J. *The Ruin of J. Robert Oppenheimer and the Birth of the Modern Arms Race*. New York: Viking, 2005.

Madhavan, Sandeep. "Lessons for Entrepreneurs from *Bhagavad Gītā* to Keep Their Boat Sailing in Nascent Stage." (2017) https://www.entrepreneur.com/article/302437.

Maier, Craig T. "Attentive Waiting in an Uprooted Age: Simone Weil's Response in an Age of Precarity." *Review of Communication* 13, no. 3 (2013): 225–42.

Majeed, Javed. "Gandhi, 'Truth' and Translatability." In *Modern Asian Studies* 40, no. 2 (2006): 303–32.

Majeed, Javed. *Ungoverned Imaginings: James Mill's The History of British India and Orientalism*. Oxford: Clarendon, 1992.

Maliner, Angelika. *The Bhagavad Gītā: Doctrines and Contexts*. Cambridge: Cambridge University Press, 2007.

Manthripragada, Ashwin, Emma Musanovic, and Dagmar Theison, *The Threat and Allure of the Magical; Selected Papers from the Seventeenth Annual Interdisciplinary German Studies Conference*. Berkeley, CA: Newcastle upon Tyne, England: Cambridge Scholars Publishing, 2013.

Marchand, Suzanne L. *German Orientalism in the Age of Empire, Religion, Race and Scholarship*. Cambridge: Cambridge University Press, 2010.

Mason, James N. *Siege: The Collected Writings of James Mason*, edited and introduction by Michael McJenkins (i.e., Moynihan) Denver: Storm Books, 1992.

Matthew-Waller, Robert. "*Doctor Atomic* at ENO." *Musical Opinion* 132, no. 1470 (2009): 30–3.

Maulsby, David Lee. *Emerson: His Contribution to Literature*. Tufts College, Massachusetts: Tufts College Press, 1911.

Mehta, Uday Singh. "Gandhi on Democracy, Politics and the Ethics of Everyday Life." *Modern Intellectual History* 7, no. 2 (2010): 355–71.

Mercer, Dorothy Frederica. *Leaves of Grass and the Bhagavad Gītā: A Comparative Study*. Berkeley: University of California, 1933.

Merton, Thomas. *The Asian Journal of Thomas Merton*. Vol. 394. New York: New Directions Publishing, 1975.

Merton, Thomas. "Appreciation." In Bhaktivedanta, 1968: 18–22.

Michelmore, Peter. *The Swift Years: The Robert Oppenheimer Story*. New York: Dodd, Mead, 1969.

Miller, Barbara Stoler, trans. *The Bhagavad-Gītā: Krishna's Counsel in Time of War*. New York: Bantam, 1986.

Miller, Barbara Stoler. "Why Did Thoreau Take the *Bhagavad-Gītā* to Walden Pond?" https://yogainternational.com/article/view/why-did-thoreau-take-the-bhagavd-gita-to-walden-pond.

Miller, Malcolm. "Amsterdam, Nederlands Opera: 'Doctor Atomic' and 'Wagner's Dream'." *Tempo* 61, no. 239 (2007): 45–8.

Minor, Robert Neil, ed. *Modern Indian Interpreters of the Bhagavad Gītā*. Albany: State University of New York Press, 1986.

Mitroff, Ian I., and Elizabeth A. Denton. *A Spiritual Audit of Corporate America: A Hard Look at Spirituality, Religion, and Values in the Workplace*. San Francisco, CA: Jossey-Bass, 1999.

Moi, Toril. "I Came with a Sword." Review of Robert Zaretsky, *The Subversive Simone Weil: A Life in Five Ideas*. *London Review of Books*. Vol. 43 no. 13 (July 1, 2021). https://www.lrb.co.uk/the-paper/43/n13/toril-moi/i-come-with-a-sword.

Monier-Williams, Monier. *Indian Wisdom or Examples of the Religious, Philosophical and Ethical Doctrines of the Hindus*. London: W.H. Allen & Company, 1875.

Monier-Williams, Monier. *Modern India and the Indians: A Series of Impressions, Notes and Essays*. 2nd ed. London: Trübner and Co., 1878.

Muniapan, Balakrishnan, and Biswajit Satpathy. "The 'Dharma'and 'Karma'of CSR from the *Bhagavad-Gītā*." *Journal of Human Values* 19, no. 2 (2013): 173–87.

Munshi, Surendra. "Learning Leadership: Lessons from Mahatma Gandhi." *Asian Journal of Social Science* 38, no. 1 (2010): 37–45.

Nabokov, Vladimir. "Problems on Translation: Onegin in English." In Venuti, 113–25.

Nambiar, O.K. *Whitman and Yoga*. Bangalore: Jeevan, 1967.

Nandy, Ashis. *The Intimate Enemy: Loss and Recovery of Self Under Colonialism*. New Delhi: Oxford University Press, 1983.

Nandy, Ashis. *Traditions, Tyranny, and Utopias: Essays in the Politics of Awareness*. New Delhi: Oxford University Press, 1987.

Natesan, N. Chinna, Michael J. Keeffe, and John R. Darling. "Enhancement of Global Business Practices: Lessons from the Hindu *Bhagavad Gītā*." *European Business Review* (2009): 428–43.

Nida, Eugene. "Principles of Correspondence." In Venuti, 141–55.

Nevin, Thomas R. *Simone Weil: Portrait of a Self-Hating Jew*. Chapel Hill: University of North Carolina Press, 1991.

Nietzsche, Friedrich. "Translations (1882)." Translated by Walter Kaufmann. In Venuti, 67–8.

Niranjana, Tejaswini. *Siting Translation: History, Post-Structuralism, and the Colonial Context*. Berkeley: University of California Press, 1992.

O'Flaherty, Wendy Doniger. *The Implied Spider: Politics and Theology in Myth*. New York: Columbia University Press, 1998.

Oldenberg, Hermann. "Bemerkungen zur *Bhagavad Gītā*." In *Kleine Schriften*. Vol. 2, edited by Klaus L. Janert, 149–76. Wiesbaden: Fritz Steiner, 1967.

Oldenberg, Hermann. *Das Mahâhârata: sein Inhalt, seine Entstehung, seine Form*. Göttingen: Vanderhoeck & Ruprecht, 1922.

Olender, Maurice. *The Languages of Paradise: Race, Religion, and Philology in the Nineteenth Century*. Translated by Arthur Goldhammer. Cambridge, MA and London: Harvard University Press, 1992.

Omissi, David, ed. *Indian Views of the Great War, Soldiers Letters 1914–18*. New York: St. Martin's Press, 1999.

Omvedt, Gail. *Dalits and the Democratic Revolution: Dr. Ambedkar and the Dalit Movement in Colonial India*. New Delhi: SAGE Publications India, 1994.

Oppenheimer, J. Robert. *J. Robert Oppenheimer: Oral History Collection*. Cambridge, MA: MIT Libraries, 1975.

Otto, Rudolf. *Das Heilige, űber das irrationale in der Idee des göttlichen und sein Verhältnis zum Rationale*. Gotha: Leopold Klotz, 1929.

Otto, Rudolf. *Die Urgestalt der Bhagavadgîtâ*. Tübingen: Mohr, 1934.

Otto, Rudolf. *Lehrtraktate der Bhagavadgîtâ*. Tübingen: Mohr, 1935.

Otto, Rudolf. *The Idea of the Holy: An Inquiry into the Non-Rational Factor in the Idea of the Divine and its Relation to the Rational*. Translated by John W. Harvey. New York: Oxford University Press, 1950.

Otto, Rudolf. *Mysticism East and West: A Comparative Analysis of the Nature of Mysticism*. Translated by Berthe L. Bracey and Richard C. Payne. New York: Meridian Books, 1957.

Padfield, Peter. *Himmler Reichsführer—SS*. London: Cassell and Co., 2001.

Page, Tim. "'Doctor Atomic': Unleashing Powerful Forces." *Washington Post*. October 3, 2005.

Paglia, Camille. "Cults and Cosmic Consciousness: Religious Vision in the American 1960s." *Arion: A Journal of Humanities and the Classics* 10, no. 3 (2003): 57–111.

Palshikar, Sanjay. *Evil and the Philosophy of Retribution: Modern Commentaries on the Bhagavad-Gītā*. New York: Routledge, 2014.

Penaskovic, Richard John. "Simone Weil: The Reluctant Convert." *New Blackfriars* 96, no. 1064 (2015): 391–404.

Perl, Jeffrey M., and Andrew P. Tuck. "The Hidden Advantage of Tradition: On the Significance of T.S. Eliot's Indic Studies." *Philosophy East and West* 35, no. 2 (1985): 115–31.

Perrin, Joseph-Marie, and Gustave Thibon. *Simone Weil: As We Knew Her*. London: Routledge Kegan Paul, 1953.

Pétrement, Simone. *Simone Weil: A Life*. New York: Pantheon, 1976.

Pétrement, Simone. *La vie de Simone Weil*. 2 vols. Paris: Fayard, 1973–78.

Poewe Karla. *New Religions and the Nazis*. New York: Routledge, 2006.

Poewe, Karla, and Irving Hexham. "Jakob Wilhelm Hauer's New Religion and National Socialism." *Journal of Contemporary Religion* 20, no. 2 (2005): 195–215.

Poewe, Karla, and Irving Hexham. "Surprising Mediations between German Indology and Nazism Research and the Adluri/Grünendahl Debate." *International Journal of Hindu Studies* 19, no. 3 (December 2015): 263–300.

Polenberg, Richard, ed. *In the Matter of J. Robert Oppenheimer: The Security Clearance Hearing*. Ithaca: Cornell University Press, 2002.

Poruthiyil, Prabhir Vishnu. "Using Religious Epics for Enhancing Morality: A Case for Reflective Judgments." *Economic and Political Weekly* 47, no. 45 (2012): 73–9.

Pollock, Sheldon. *The Languages of the Gods in the World of Men: Sanskrit, Culture, and Power in Premodern India*: Berkeley: University of California Press, 2006.

Pound, Ezra. "Guido's Relations." In Venuti, 83–91.

Prabhavananda, and Cristopher Isherwood, trans. *Bhagavad-Gītā: The Song of God*. Introduction by Aldous Huxley. New York: Mentor Books, 1944.

Preston, Nathaniel H. "Whitman's 'Shadowy Dwarf': A Source in Hindu Mythology." *Walt Whitman Quarterly Review* 15 no. 4 (1998): 185–87.

Preston, Nathaniel H. "Walt Whitman's Use of Indian Sources: A Reconstruction." *The Ritsummeikan Bungaku*. 627 (2012): 245–56.

Pringle, Heather. *The Master Plan: Himmler's Scholars and the Holocaust*. New York: Hyperion 2006.

Rabault-Feuerstein, Pascale. *L'archive des origines: Sanskrit, philologie, anthropologie dans l'Allemagne du XIXe siècle*. Paris: Editions du Cerf, 2008.

Rabi, I.I. *Oppenheimer*. New York: Scribners, 1969.
Rahv, Philip. "Paleface and Redskin." *The Kenyon Review* 1 no. 3 (1939): 251–6.
Raine, Craig. *T.S. Eliot*. New York: Oxford University Press, 2006.
Rajan, Balachandra, ed. *T.S. Eliot: A Study of His Writings by Several Hands*. London: Dennis Dobson, 1948.
Rajasekharaiah, Tumkur Rudraradhya. *The Roots of Whitman's Grass*. Rutherford, NJ: Fairleigh Dickinson University Press, 1970.
Ramakrishnan, Erackot Velancherry, Harish Trivedi, and Chandra Mohan, eds. *Interdisciplinary Alter-natives in Comparative Literature*. New Delhi: SAGE Publications India, 2013.
Ramana, M.V. "The Bomb of the Blue God." http://samarmagazine.org/archive/articles/36.
Ramanujan, Attipat K., Stuart H. Blackburn, and Alan Dundes. *A Flowering Tree and Other Oral Tales from India: A.K. Ramanujan;* Edited with a Preface by Stuart Blackburn and Alan Dundes. Berkeley: University of California Press, 1997.
Rao, K.S.N. "T.S. Eliot and the Bhagavad-*Gītā*." *American Quarterly* 15, no. 4 (Winter 1963): 572–8.
Rao, K.S.N. *Indian Literature*, XIV, no. 11. New Delhi: Sahitya Akademi, 1970.
Rao, Vimala. "T.S. Eliot's 'The Cocktail Party' and the 'Bhagavad-*Gītā*.' *Comparative Literature Studies* 18, no. 2 (1981): 191–8.
Rarick, Charles A., and Inge Nickerson. "Expanding Managerial Consciousness: Leadership Advice from the *Bhagavad Gītā*." In *Allied Academies International Conference. Academy of Organizational Culture, Communications and Conflict. Proceedings* 13, no. 1 (2008): 59.
Rayapati, J.P. Rao. *Early American Interest in Vedanta: Pre-Enlightenment Interest in Vedic Literature and Vedantic Philosophy*. New York: Asia Publishing House, 1973.
Reix, André. "Michel Hulin, *Hegel et l'Orient*, followed by the annotated translation of an essay by Hegel on the *Bhagavad-Gîtâ*." *Revue philosophique de Louvain* 79 no. 43 (1981): 408–9.
Rexroth, Kenneth. "The Dialectic of Agony." *The Nation* 184 (1957): 42–3.
Rexroth, Kenneth. *World Outside the Window: The Selected Essays of Kenneth Rexroth*. New York: New Directions, 1987.
Rhodes, Richard. "'I Am Become Death ...': The Agony of J. Robert Oppenheimer." *American Heritage* 28 no. 6 (1977): 70–83.
Rhodes, Richard. *The Making of the Atomic Bomb*. New York: Simon and Schuster, 1986.
Richardson, Robert D. *Emerson: The Mind on Fire*. Berkeley: University of California Press, 1995.
Ricks, Christopher. *T.S. Eliot and Prejudice*. Berkeley: University of California Press, 1988.
Ricoeur, Paul. *Freud and Philosophy: An Essay on Interpretation*. Translated by Denis Savage. New Haven, CT: Yale University Press, 1970.
Ricoeur, Paul. *Sur la traduction*. Paris: Bayard, 2004.
Ricoeur, Paul. *On Translation*. Translated by Eileen Brennan, with introduction by Richard Kearney. New York: Routledge, 2006.
Riepe, Dale. "Emerson and Indian Philosophy." *Journal of the History of Ideas* 28, no. 1 (January–March 1967): 115–22.

Robinson, Catherine A. *Interpretations of the Bhagavad-Gītā and Images of the Hindu Tradition: The Song of the Lord*. New York: Routledge, 2006.

Roka, Pujan. *Bhagavad Gītā on Effective Leadership: Timeless Wisdom for Leaders*. Indiana: iUniverse Inc., 2006.

Rosen, Steven J. "Fight or Flight: Thomas Merton and the *Bhagavad Gītā*." *Journal of Hindu-Christian Studies* 30, no. 1 (2017): 1–7.

Rosen, Steven J. *Gītā on the Green: The Mystical Tradition Behind Bagger Vance*. New York: Bloomsbury Academic Publishing, 2002.

Rosen, Steven J. *Krishna's Song: A New Look at the Bhagavad Gītā*. Westport: Praeger, 2007.

Rosenbaum, Ron. "The Opera's New Clothes. Why I Walked Out of *Doctor Atomic*." *Slate*. October 24, 2008.

Ross, Andrew. *Nice Work If You Can Get It: Life and Labor in Precarious Times*. New York: New York University Press, 2009.

Roy, Arundhati. "The Doctor and the Saint." In Ambedkar, 2013: 1–80.

Royal, Denise. *The Story of J. Robert Oppenheimer*. New York: St. Martin's Press, 1969.

Rukeyser, Muriel. "The Dream-Singing Elegy." *The Kenyon Review* 6, no. 1 (1944): 59–63. https://www.kenyonreview.Org/kr-online-issue/Muriel-rukeyser-763879/:104.

Ryder, Arthur, trans. *The Bhagavad Gītā*. Chicago: University of Chicago, 1929.

Sanborn, Frank B. "Reminiscent of Whitman." *The Conservator* 8, no. 3 (May 1897): 37–40.

Sanborn, Frank B. *The Genius and Character of Emerson*. Port Washington, NY: Kennikot, 1971.

Sanborn, Frank B. "Thoreau and Confucius." *The Nation* 90 (May 12, 1910): 481.

Sant Ram. "Varna versus Caste." In Ambedkar, 2–13: 329–32.

Sargeant, Winthrop. *The Bhagavad Gītā*. Albany: State University of New York Press, 1984.

Sarkar, Sumit, Neeladri Bhattacharya, and Dipesh Chakrabarty. *The Swadeshi Movement in Bengal, 1903–1908*. New Delhi: People's Publishing House, 1973.

Sarma, Sreekrishna. "A Short Study of the Oriental Influence upon Henry David Thoreau with Special Reference to his 'Walden.'" *Jahrbuch für Amerikastudien*. 1 (1956): 76–92.

Sartori, Andrew. "The Transfiguration of Duty in Aurobindo's *Essays on the Gītā*." *Modern Intellectual History* 7, no. 2 (2010): 319–34.

Sattelmeyer, Robert. *Thoreau's Reading: A Study of Intellectual History with Biographical Catalogue*. Princeton: Princeton University Press, 1988.

Savarkar, V.D. *The Hindu Rashtra Darshan. A Collection of the President's Speeches*. Bombay: Mahasabha Platform, 1949.

Sawhney, Simona. *The Modernity of Sanskrit*. Minneapolis: University of Minnesota Press, 2009.

Schlegel, August Wilhelm. *Bhagavad Gītā, id est Thespesion Melos sive Almi Christiae et Arjunae Colloquium de rebus divinis. Text in recensuit Adnotationes criticas et interpretationem Latinam adiccit*. Bonn: Edward Weber om Accademia Borusska Rhenau, 1823.

Schlegel, August Wilhelm. *Indische Bibliotek*. Bonn: Weber, 1826.

Schlegel, August Wilhelm. *Sämtliche Werke*. 12 vols. Edited by E. Bőcking. Leipzig: Weidmann, 1846–47.

Schlegel, Friedrich. *Dialogue on Poetry and Literary Aphorisms*. Translated by Ernst Behler and Roman Struc. University Park: Pennsylvania State University Press, 1965.

Schlegel, Friedrich. *Sämtliche Werke*. 15 vols. Vienna: I. Klang, 1846.

Schleiermacher, Friedrich. "On the Different Methods of Translating." Translated by Susan Bernofsky. In Venuti, 43–63.

Schopenhauer, Arthur. *Fragments sur l'histoire de la philosophie*. Paris: Alcan, 1912.

Sdun, Winfried. *Probleme und Theorien des Übersetzens in Deutschland vom achtzehnten bis zum zwanzigsten Jahrhundert*. Munich: Hűber, 1967.

Sebeok, T. *Style in Language*. Cambridge, MA: MIT Press.

Senart, Émile. *La Bhagavadgītā*. Paris: Éditions Bossard, 1922.

Service, Tom. "This Was the Start of a New Epoch in Human History." *The Guardian*. September 29, 2005.

Seth, Sanjay. "Gandhi's *Gītā* and Politics as Such." *Postcolonial Studies*. 91 no. 2 (June 2004): 137–50.

Seth, Sanjay. "The Critique of Renunciation: B. D. Gangadhar Tilak's 'Hindu Nationalism.'" *Postcolonial Studies* 9 no. 2 (2006): 137–50.

Sharma, Anil K., and Balvir Talwar. "Business Excellence Enshrined in Vedic (Hindu) Philosophy." *Singapore Management Review* 26, no. 1 (2004): 1–20.

Sharpe, Eric J. *The Universal Gītā: Western Images of the Bhagavadgītā; a Bicentenary Survey*. *La Salle* IL: Open Court, 1985.

Sheppard, W. Anthony. "Exoticism." In Greenwald, 797–816.

Sheppard, W. Anthony. "The Persistence of Orientalism in the Postmodern Operas of Adams and Sellars." In Walden, 267–86.

Shirer, William L. *The Rise and Fall of the Third Reich: A History of Nazi Germany*. New York: Simon and Schuster, [1960] 1990.

Sinha, Mishka. "Corrigibility, Allegory, Universality: A History of the *Gītā*'s Transnational Reception, 1785–1945." *Modern Intellectual History* 7, no. 2 (2010): 297–317.

Sinha, Mishka. "The Transnational *Gītā*." In Kapila and Devji, 2013: 25–47.

Singh, Dhananjay. "Charles Wilkins's *Bhagvat Geeta* and the Problems and Politics of Language(s) of Oriental Gods and Men." In Benoit et al, 29–41.

Skaria, Ajay. "Living by Dying: Gandhi, Satyagraha, and the Warrior." *Ethical Life in South Asia* (2010): 211–31.

Smith, Alice Kimball. *Peril and A Hope: The Scientists' Movement in America 1945–47*. Chicago: University of Chicago Press, 1965.

Smith, Alice Kimball. "Taming the Bomb: A Peril and a Hope: The Scientists' Movement in America 1945–47." *The Physics Teacher* 8, no. 4 (1970): 213.

Smith, Alice Kimball, and Charles Weiner. *Robert Oppenheimer's Letters and Recollections*. Cambridge: Harvard University Press, 1980.

Sontag, Susan. *Against Interpretation*. New York: Farrar, Strauss and Giroux, 1961.

Sontag, Susan. "The World as India." The St. Jerome Lecture on Literary Translation. www.susansontag.com/prize/onTranslation.shtml.

Spender, Stephen. *T.S. Eliot*. New York: Viking Adult, 1976.

Springmann, Theodor, trans. *Bhagavad-gītā: der Gesang des Erhabenen*. Hamburg: n.p., 1920.

Spivak, Gayatri Chakravorty. *A Critique of Postcolonial Reason: Toward a History of the Vanishing Present*. Cambridge and London: Harvard University Press, 1999.

Spivak, Gayatri Chakravorty. *The Politics of Translation*. In Venuti 320–38.

Srinivas, Mysore Narasimhachar. "A Note on Sanskritization and Westernization." *The Far Eastern Quarterly* 15, no. 4 (1956): 481–96.

Srinivas, Mysore Narasimhachar. *Social Change in Modern India*. Berkeley: University of California Press, 1966.

Srivastava, Narsingh. "The Ideas of the *Bhagavad Gītā* in Four Quartets." *Comparative Literature* 29, no. 2 (1977): 97–108.

Staal, F. *Rules Without Meaning: Rituals, Mantras and the Human Sciences*. Studies in Religion. Vol. 4. New York: Peter Lang, 1989.

Staudenmaier, Peter. "Nazi Perceptions of Esotericism: The Occult as Fascination and Menace." In Manthripragada et al., 25–57.

Stein, Robert. "Review of *Hallelujah Junction: Composing an American Life* by John Adams." *Tempo* 63, no. 248 (2009): 67–8.

Steiner, George. "The Hermeneutic Motion." In Venuti, 156–61.

Steiner, George. *Language and Silence: Essays on Language, Literature, and the Inhuman*. Canada: McClelland and Stewart Ltd., 1967.

Struc-Oppenberg, Ursula. "Einleitung." In *Kritische Friedrich Schlegel Ausgabe*, edited by Ernst Behler et al. Vol. 8: Studien zur Philosophie und Theologie, edited by Ernst Behler and Ursula Struc-Oppenberg, CLXXVII–CCXXX. Darmstadt: Wissenschaftliche Buchgesellschaft, 1975.

Sullivan, Jack. "The Met vs. the Movies: Double Take on Dr. Atomic." *American Record Guide*. (March/April), 2009: 4–5.

Teller, Edward, and Allen Brown. *The Legacy of Hiroshima*. Garden City, NJ: Doubleday, 1962.

Tharaud, Barry, ed. *Emerson for the Twenty-First Century*. Newark: University of Delaware Press, 2010.

Thomson, J. Cockburn, trans. *Bhagavad-Gitá; Or, The Sacred Lay: A Colloquy Between Krishna and Arjuna on Divine Matters. An Episode from the Mahábhárata*. Hartford: Stephen Austin, 1855.

Thoreau, Henry David. *Familiar Letters*. Edited by Frank B. Sanborn. Boston: Houghton Mifflin, 1894.

Thoreau, Henry David. *Writings*. Edited by Bradford Torrey. New York: Houghton Mifflin, 1906.

Thoreau, Henry David. *The Journal of Henry David Thoreau* (Walden edition). 14 vols. Edited by Bradford Torrey and Francis H. Allen. Boston: Houghton Mifflin, 1906.

Thoreau, Henry David. *A Week on the Concord and Merrimack Rivers*. Edited by Walter Harding. New York: Holt, Rinehart and Winston Inc., 1963.

Thoreau, Henry David. *The Writings of Henry David Thoreau*. Edited by Bradford Torrey and Francis H. Allen. 20 vols. New York: AMS Press 7 (1968): 266.

Thoreau, Henry David. *The Portable Thoreau*. Edited by Carl Bode. New York: Penguin, 1977.

Thoreau, Henry David. *A Week on the Concord and Merrimack Rivers*. Edited by Carl F. Thoreau, W. Howarth Hovde, and Elizabeth Hall Witherell. Princeton, NJ: Princeton University Press, 1980.

Thoreau, Henry David. *Walden and Other Writings*. New York: Bantam Classics, 1981.

Thoreau, Henry David. *A Week on the Concord and Merrimack Rivers: Walden or, Life in the Woods, The Maine Woods: Cape Cod*. New York: Literary Classics of the United States, 1985.

Thoreau, Henry David. *Journals*. Vols 1–8. Edited by John C. Broderick et al. Princeton, NJ: Princeton University Press, 1981–2002.

Thorpe, Charles. *Oppenheimer: The Tragic Intellect*. Chicago: University of Chicago Press, 2006.

Tilak, Bal Gangadhar, *Śrīmad Bhagavad Gītā Rahasya or Karma Yoga Śāstra*, Translated by Bhalchandra Sitaram Sukthankar. New Delhi: Asian Educational Services, 2007.

Trimondi, Victor, and Victoria. *Hitler, Buddha, Krishna: Eine unheilige Allianz vom Dritten Reich bis Heute*. Vienna: Ueberreuter, 2002.

Uberoi, Meera. *Leadership Secrets from the Mahābhārata*. London: Penguin UK, 2003.

Unger, Leonard. *T. S. Eliot: A Selected Critique*. New York: Rinehart and Co., 1948.

United States Atomic Energy Commission (USAEC). *In the Matter of J. Robert Oppenheimer. Transcript of Hearing before Personnel Board*. Washington, DC: Government Printing Office, 1954.

Vālmīki. *The Rāmāyaṇa of Vālmīki: An Epic of Ancient India*. Volume V: *Sundarakāṇḍa*. Edited by Robert P. Goldman. Introduction by Sally Sutherland Goldman. Princeton, NJ: Princeton University Press, [1984] 2017.

Van Doren, Mark. *Henry David Thoreau: A Critical Study*. Boston: Houghton Mifflin, 1916.

Van Buitenen, J.A.B. *Rāmānuja on the Bhagavad Gītā*. New Delhi: Motilal Banarsidass, 1968.

Van Buitenen, J.A.B., trans. *The Mahābhārata*. Vol 1. *The Book of Beginnings*. Chicago: University of Chicago Press, 1973.

Van Buitenen, J.A.B., trans. *The Bhagavadgītā in the Mahābhārata: Text and Translation*. Chicago: University of Chicago Press, 1981.

Varma, Vishwanath Prasad. *Modern Indian Political Thought*. Agra: Lakshmi Narain Agarwal Publications, 1971.

Venuti, Lawrence, ed. *The Translation Studies Reader*. London: Routledge, 2012.

Vivekananda, Swami. *The Complete Works of Swami Vivekananda*. Calcutta: Advaita Ashram. Vol. 1 (1994a), Vol. 2 (1995a), Vol. 3 (1995b), Vol. 4 (1985), Vol. 8 (1994b).

Viyagappa, Ignatius. *G. W.F. Hegel's Conception of Indian Philosophy*. Rome: Università Gregoriana, 1980.

Von der Ruhr, Mario. *Simone Weil: An Apprenticeship in Attention*. London: Continuum, 2006.

Walden, Joshua S., ed. *Representation in Western Music*. Cambridge: Cambridge University Press, 2013.

Ward, David. *Between Two Worlds: A Reading of T.S. Eliot's Poetry and Plays*. London: Routledge and Kegan, 1973.

Ward, Karlyn. "Batter My Heart ..." *The San Francisco Jung Institute Library Journal* 25, no. 1 (2006): 51–77.

Weber, Thomas. *On the Salt March: The Historiography of Gandhi's March to Dandi.* New Delhi: Harper Collins Publishers India, 1997.

Weil, André. *André Weil: The Apprenticeship of a Mathematician.* Translated by Jennifer Gage. Basel/Berlin: Birkhäuser Verlag, 1992.

Weil, Simone. *La source grecque.* Paris: Gallimard, 1950.

Weil, Simone. *La connaissance surnaturelle.* Paris: Gallimard, 1950.

Weil, Simone. *Waiting for God.* Translated by E. Crauford. New York: Putnam's Sons, 1951.

Weil, Simone. *The Need for Roots.* Translated by Arthur Wills, and Preface by T.S. Eliot. New York: Putnam, 1952.

Weil, Simone. *Notebooks.* Translated by Arthur Wills. New York: Putnam's Sons, 1956.

Weil, Simone. *Écrits de Londres et dernières lettres.* Paris: Gallimard, 1957.

Weil, Simone. *Seventy Letters.* Translated by Richard Ree. New York: Oxford University Press, 1965.

Weil, Simone. *Attente de Dieu.* Paris: Fayard, 1966.

Weil, Simone. *The Simone Weil Reader.* Edited by George A. Panichas. New York: McKay, 1977.

Weil, Simone. *Œuvres completes.* Edited by André E. Devaux, Florence de Lussy, Géraldi Leroy, Anne Roche, and Simone Fraisse. Paris: Gallimard, 1988.

Weil, Simone. *Gravity and Grace.* Translated by Emma Crawford and Mario von der Ruhr. London: Routledge, 2002.

Weil, Simone. *Simone Weil's The Iliad or The Poem of Force.* Edited and translated by James Holoka. New York: Peter Lang, 2003.

Weil, Simone. *Letter to a Priest.* Translated by A.F. Wills. New York: Penguin, 2003b.

Weil, Sylvie. *Chez les Weil: André et Simone.* Paris: Buchet-Chastel, 2009.

Weil, Sylvie, and Benjamin Ivry. *At Home with André and Simone Weil.* Evanston: Northwestern University Press, 2010.

White, Georg Abbott ed. *Simone Weil: Interpretation of a Life.* Amherst: University of Massachusetts Press, 1981.

Whitman, Walt. *Leaves of Grass* (Comprehensive Reader's Edition). Eds. Harold W. Blodgett and Sculley Bradley. New York: New York University Press, 1965.

Whitman, Walt. *Walt Whitman: The Centennial Essays.* Ed. Ed Folsom. Iowa City: University of Iowa Press, 1994.

Wilkins, Charles, trans. *The Bhagvat-geeta, or, Dialogues of Kreeshna and Arjoon.* London: C. Nourse, 1785.

Williams, Paul. *Race, Ethnicity and Nuclear War: Representations of Nuclear Weapons and Post-Apocalyptic Worlds.* Liverpool: Liverpool University Press, 2011.

Williams, Stanley T. "Unpublished Letters of Emerson." *The Journal of English and Germanic Philology* 26 (1923): 483–84.

Wolin, Sheldon S. *Politics and Vision: Continuity and Innovation in Western Political Thought.* Princeton, NJ: Princeton University Press, 2004.

Wolverton, Mark. *A Life in Twilight: The Final Years of J. Robert Oppenheimer.* New York: St. Martin's Press, 2008.

Zaehner, R.C. *Hinduism.* Oxford: Clarendon, 1966.

Zaehner, R.C. *Mysticism, Sacred and Profane: An Inquiry into some Varieties of Preternatural Experience.* Oxford: Clarendon, 1967.

Zaehner, R.C. trans. *The Bhagavad-Gītā: With a Commentary Based on the Original Sources*. Oxford: Oxford University Press (1969) 1973.
Zaehner, R.C. *Concordant Discord: The Interdependence of Faiths*. Oxford: Clarendon, 1970.
Zweig, Paul. *Walt Whitman; The Making of the Poet*. New York: Basic Books, 1984.

Author Biography

Dorothy M. Figueira is a Distinguished Research Professor at the University of Georgia (USA). She received her education from Vassar College (BA 1976). École Pratique en Sciences Sociales (MA 1977), Harvard University (MTS 1979) and the University of Chicago (PhD 1985). Her scholarly interests include religion and literature, translation theory, exoticism, myth theory, and travel narratives. She has served as the Editor of *The Comparatist* (2008–2011) and as Editor of *Recherche litteraire/Literary Research*. She is an Honorary President of the International Comparative Literature Association. She has held fellowships from the American Institute for Indian Studies, Fulbright, and the NEH. She has taught at Cornell University (Mellon Fellow, 1985–7), SUNY, and the University of Illinois. She been a Visiting Professor at the University of Lille (France), Jadavpur University (Kolkata, India), Indira Gandhi Open University in New Delhi (India), the University of Pune (India), the University of Tartu (Estonia) and the Jagellonian University (Poland). In 2015, she was the Matteo Ricci Scholar in Literature at the University of Macerata (Italy).

Index

For the benefit of digital users, indexed terms that span two pages (e.g., 52–53) may, on occasion, appear on only one of those pages.

Abhinavagupta 3–4
action see *karma*
Adams, John 322–33, 342
Adler, Felix 246–47, 248–49, 258
Adorno, Theodor 222–23, 337
Afzal Khan 127–28
Ahnenerbe 215–16
Aiken, Conrad 232–33
Alain (Émile-Auguste Chartier) 264–65
Albigensians 266n.15
Alfassa, Mirra 139–40
allegorical reading of religious texts 150–52, 155–58
Altizer, J.J. 310n.11
Ambedkar, B.R. 7n.19, 10, 172, 174–99
 Annihilation of Caste, The 191–99
 and *Bhagavad Gītā* 183–91
 and Untouchables 174–83
Anand, Swami 164–65
anthroposophy 213
Appiah, Kwame Anthony 23, 32
Arendt, Hannah 169–70
Armstrong, Carol 337
Arnold, Edwin 41–42, 145–46, 149, 158, 313n.19
Aryan, Aryans 139–40, 142–43, 203, 206–7, 211–12, 215–16, 217–18, 228–29, 287–88
Ārya Samāj 191–92, 196–97
Aurobindo, Sri 135–36, 137–46, 168–69, 171–72, 192–93
Auroville 139

Babri Mosque (Ayodha), demolition of 5–6
Bainbridge, Kenneth 330n.48
Bande Mataram 138–39
Bankim Chandra Chattopadhyay 116, 135–36
Barraud, Abbé J.P. 32n.4
Baudelaire, Charles 325–26, 334
Beatles 303n.4
Beauvoir, Simone de 262n.7
Benjamin, Walter 13–14, 20–21, 41, 46–47, 158–59
Berman, Antoine 17–18, 19n.7
Besant, Annie 138n.21, 149n.2, 213–14, 301–2
Bhagavad Gītā
 and *ahiṃsā* (non-violence) 164–65
 allegorical reading of 150–53, 155–58
 and American reception 8–9, 85–86, 93, 101, 103–4, 108–9, 115–16, 118–19, 304–5, 308–9
 and *anāsakti* (non-attachment) 115–16, 117–18, 119–20, 156–57, 164–65, 184–85, 186–87, 236, 275–76
 and *bhakti* (devotion) 3–4, 72–73, 122, 123–24, 125, 185
 and brahmins 37–38, 40–42, 101–2, 117–18, 183, 184–85
 and British rule 34–36, 40–42, 46–47
 and *buddhi* (reason) 131
 and Buddhism 183, 186, 187–88
 and caste (*varṇa*) 101–2, 113–14, 117–18, 135, 143, 156–57, 165–66, 183–85, 189–91
 and Christianity, comparisons with 43–45, 100, 101–2, 204–5, 207–8, 264–65
 and corporate management 338–39, 342

Bhagavad Gītā (*cont.*)
and counterculture 303–12
as cultural inspiration 32–33
and *dharma* (duty) 75, 101–2, 125–26, 131–32, 133, 142–43, 183, 216–17, 252–54
as elitist 103
English translation, first 31–32, 36, 38–39
English translations 41–42, 145–46, 149, 150–51, 153–54, 303, 304
and fatalism/passivity 61, 101–2
and footnotes 36, 37, 41
and German political appropriation 203–29, 259–60
German translations 206–8
Gujarati translation 153–54
and *guṇas* (natural qualities) 143, 165–66, 192–93, 198–99
and illusory nature of world 94, 95, 122–23
and inaction 61–62, 70–72, 77, 122–24, 142
and Indian political appropriation 5, 45–46, 113–14, 116, 127, 135–36, 139, 164, 188–89
interpretations 29–30, 97–99, 157–73, 210
and *jñāna* (knowledge/renunciation) 3–4, 119–20, 122–25
and *karma* (action) 3–4, 56–58, 71, 72–73, 74, 95–96, 102, 115–16, 118–20, 122–23, 125–26, 131–32, 135–36, 140–41, 144–45, 237, 310–11
as key to understanding Indian people 34–36
and killing of kinsmen 126, 127, 128–29, 205, 224–25
and *kṣatriya*s (warriors) 125, 135–36, 137, 140–42, 187–88, 205–6, 207–8, 218–20, 224–26, 259–60
Latin translation 21, 49, 54–55
and *lokasaṃgraha* (universal service) 131–33, 134–35, 205
and monotheism 39, 42–43, 44–45, 207–9
and mysticism 70–71
and nihilism 78
operatic renditions 312–34
original core text 209, 210, 217n.18
and quietism 65–66, 70–71, 74, 75–76
and Sāṃkhya 70, 188–89
and self-reliance 118–19
as source of all things Indian and exotic 108–9, 110–11
and *sthitaprajña* (the strong-minded) 120, 127, 134–35, 136–37, 152–53, 156–57, 171–72
translations 1–3, 29–30, 85n.1, 153–54, 163, 337–38
and violence 4–5, 45–46, 116, 125–27, 135–36, 141–42, 188–89, 198–99, 205, 216, 268–69, 270, 294–95, 310–11
Bhaktivedanta Swami Prabhupada, A.C. 304–5, 312
Bharati, Agehananda 152
Biardeau, Madeleine 1n.2
Bildung (formation) 16–17, 18–19
Bismarck, Otto von 203, 227
Blavatsky, Madame 85–86, 149n.2
Blisset, William 232–33
Bloom, Harold 268n.19
Bolle, Kees 2–3
Bonhoeffer, Dietrich 229
Bopp, Franz 76n.56
Borges, Jorge Luis 25–26
Bose, Subhas Chandra 170n.24
brahman 60–63, 92–93
Brooks, Cleanth 232
Buber, Martin 169–70, 220, 310
Buddhism 65n.40, 121–22, 128–29, 135, 177, 183–85, 186, 187–88, 217–18, 223
Buitenen, J.A.B. van 2–3, 7n.19
Burnouf, Eugène 95–96
Butler, Judith 282, 284

Cameron, J.M. 282
Campbell, Joseph 324
Camus, Albert 281–82, 310
Carson, Anne 284
caste (*varṇa*) 113–14
Ambedkar on 176–77, 183–85, 189–91
Annihiliation of Caste, The 191–99

Aurobindo on 140–41, 143, 144
Bankim on 116
Emerson on 110–11
Gandhi on 156–57, 165–66, 169–71, 177–81, 187–88, 192–93, 195–98, 199
Mahars 174–76
Thoreau on 101–2
Tilak on 133, 135
Untouchables 140–41, 156–57, 165–67, 170–71, 172, 174–83, 190, 192
Vivekananda on 117–18
Cavaillès, Jean 282–83
Chang, David 339n.2
Chapekar, Bal Krishna Hari 5n.15
Chapekar, Damodar Hari 4–5, 127
Chapekar, Vasudeo Hari 5n.15
Childs, Lucinda 331–32
Chokamela 174–75
Cholmondeley, Thomas 89n.12
Christianity 217–18
Catholicism as totalitarian 266–67
compared with *Bhagavad Gītā* 43–45, 100, 101–2, 204–5, 207–8
compared with Hinduism 34, 204–5, 264–65, 273–74
and National Socialism 221–22
tainted by Judaism 211–12, 264
tainted by Romans 264
Cirkus Cirkör 320n.30
Colebrooke, H.T. 49, 50–51, 56, 58–59, 61, 64, 65
Coles, Robert 282
Coomaraswamy, Ananda 304
Cotswold camp/conference 296–97
counterculture 303–12
Cousin, Victor 49–50, 69–76, 77, 78–79, 87–89, 204–5
Creuzer, Friedrich 67, 76n.56

Daumel, René 269–70
Davies, John 149
Davis, Harry M. 257
DeJong, Constance 312–13, 315, 333, 334
DeMan, Paul 24n.8
Derrida, Jacques 24–25
Desai, Mahadev 153–54, 156–57, 171n.26
Deussen, Paul 231–32
Deutsche Glaubensbewung (DGB) *see* German Faith Movement
Devi, Savitri 286–300
dharma (duty)
Ambedkar on 187–88
Aurobindo on 141–43
Besant on 301–2
Cousin on 71
Devi on 294–95
Hauer on 216–17, 218–20, 225–26
Nazism and 225–26, 227
Oppenheimer and 250–51, 252–54, 256, 327–28
Springmann on 206–7, 259–60
Thoreau on 101–2
Tilak on 125–26, 131–32, 133
Weil and 270, 271, 272, 272n.27, 280–81, 284–85
dhvani 55n.16
Dietz, Simone 280n.43
Dimock, Edward C. 305n.7
Dixon, Thomson 103–4
Doniger, Wendy 303n.3
Donne, John 325–26, 334
Drieu la Rochelle, Pierre 203
Dubois, Abbé Jean 76n.55
duty see *dharma*

East India Company 31, 34–35
Eckhart, Meister 219n.20
Ehlert, Hertha 290
Eliot, Charles 234n.13
Eliot, T.S. 231–46, 342–43
The Cocktail Party 244–45
Four Quartets 232–33, 236–40, 242, 245
and Simone Weil 281–82, 284–85n.55
'To Indians Who Died in Africa' 241–44
Emerson, Ralph Waldo 8–9, 85–86, 87–95, 103–4, 106, 110, 111–12
Eranos conferences 211n.10
Ethical Culture 246–48, 249, 253–54, 256–57

Even-Zohar, Itamar 23–24

Fichte, J.G. 15
Fields, James 90
Forster, E.M. 230
Freyer, Achim 318–19
Frobe-Kapteyn, Olga 211n.10
Furie, Kenneth 320–21

Gadamer, Hans-Georg 9–10, 80–81
Gandhi, M.K. 4–6, 10, 120, 145–46, 149–73, 174–75
  civil disobedience campaign 164
  fast 180–81, 182
  Gujarati translation 153–54
  interpretation of the *Bhagavad Gītā* 151–53, 155–58, 185–86, 190, 194–95, 342–43
  living the meaning of the *Bhagavad Gītā* 160, 163
  on Ambedkar 194–95
  on *bhakti* 185
  on caste 156–57, 165–66, 169–71, 177–81, 187–88, 192–93, 195–98, 199
  on Hitler 168
  on Jews 168–69
  on non-violence 155, 168–69, 185–86, 188–89
  on race 166–68, 171–72
  on trusteeship 172–73
  and *Satyagraha* (opera) 312–17
  as translator 160–63
Garbe, Richard Karl von 206–9
Gardner, Helen 232–33, 235n.14
Gaulle, Charles de 279–80
Geertz, Clifford 23
German Faith Movement 213, 221–22
Germanisch-Deutsch Institut 214
German Youth Movement 213–14
Ghose, Aurobindo *see* Aurobindo, Sri
Ginsberg, Alan 302–3, 304–12, 334–35, 342–43
Gitomer, David 7n.19
Glass, Philip 10, 312–22, 333, 334, 342
Godse, Nathuram 5–6, 145–46
Goethe, J.W. von 13–14, 15–16, 28, 69–70, 207, 223n.25, 227
Gokhale, Gopal Krishna 121n.5, 161–62
Golwarkar, M.S. 295
Goodman, Alice 323n.37
Göring, Hermann 293–94
Groves, General Leslie 251–52
Guénon, René 269–70
Guignault, J.D. 67
guṇas (natural qualities) 3n.7, 50n.10, 140–41, 143, 165–66, 192–93, 198–99

Hare Krishna Movement *see* International Society of Krishna Consciousness (ISKCON)
Harvey, Mark J. 129–30
Hastings, James 207–8
Hastings, Warren 31–37, 39, 40–42, 45, 46–47
Hauer, Jakob Wilhelm 206–7, 211–22, 224–25, 228, 259–60, 318n.27
Hawkins, David 257
Hegel, G.W.F. 9–10, 15, 41, 49–50, 55–56, 58–69, 75–79, 80, 85–86, 204–5
Heidegger, Martin 25–26, 213n.11, 214n.13, 220
Henry I (Henry the Fowler), King 223
Heraclitus 232–33, 278
Herder, J.G. von 18–19, 53–54
Hesse, Hermann 223, 224–25
Heydrich, Reinhard 220–21, 222
Hill, William Douglas 8–9
Hiltebeitel, A. 7n.19
Himmler, Heinrich 214n.14, 215–16, 219–21, 222–28, 292–93
Hinduism 217–18
  and *avatars* 292–93
  and *Bhagavad Gītā* 1–2, 44–45, 115–16, 128–29
  compared with Christianity 34, 204–5, 264–65, 273–74
  and freedom 62–63
  and individuality 62–63
  as lacking mediation of Universal with particular 62–63
  as lacking social component 239
  and self-reliance 118–19
  and tolerance 115–16
  as Western creation 1–2

Hindu Mahasabha 287
history of philosophy 60, 61, 69–70
Hitler, Adolf 168, 213, 215–16, 221–22, 227, 286–89, 291–94
Holmes, Oliver Wendell 90
Holtzmann, Adolf, Jr. 206–9
Hulin, Michel 63–64
Humboldt, Wilhelm von 16–17, 49–50, 51–58, 67, 68, 75–79, 187–88
Huxley, Aldous 303, 304

Iliad 266–68, 271
India
  ascetics 66
  and lack of dynamism 60
  nationalism 3, 4–6, 45–46, 116, 124–25, 128–29, 135–39, 145–46, 287–88
  as source of European civilization and philosophy 69–70, 87
  as source of European mythology 59–60
  and World Wars I and II 241–42, 244n.23
Indian National Congress 132–33, 177–78
Indian philosophy 48–49, 58–60, 61, 66, 69–70, 80–81, 85–86
International Society of Krishna Consciousness (ISKCON) 304–5, 308–9
Isherwood, Christopher 302–3

Jacobi, Hermann 206–7, 208–9
Jaffrelot, Christophe 177n.8, 185n.12
Jaimini 122–23, 183, 188
Jainism 121–22, 128–29, 135
Jakobson, Roman 22, 343
Jat-Pat-Todak Mandal (Forum for the Break-up of Caste) 191–92, 194
Jerome, Saint 14–15, 20
Jñānadeva 121–22, 123
Jones, Sir William 31, 37, 40–41, 48–49, 87
Jordan, Colin 296–97
Jordens, J.T.F. 185n.13
Judaism 211–12, 264–65
Judge, William Q. 150–51
Jung, Carl 210–11, 324

Kallenbach, Hermann 161n.13
karma (action) 2–3
  Ambedkar on 187–88
  Aurobindo on 140–41, 144–45
  Cousin on 71, 72–73
  Eliot on 169, 239, 240, 243
  Emerson on 93, 94
  German nationalism and 218–19
  Hastings on 46–47
  Hegel on 60–61
  Himmler and 223–25, 227
  Humboldt on 56–58
  Indian nationalism and 5–6
  Merton on 310–11
  niṣkāma karma (desireless action) 118–20, 143–44, 294–95
  Rāmānujā on 123–25
  Schlegel on 72–73
  Thoreau on 95–96
  Tilak on 122–26, 129–30, 131–32, 133, 135–36
  Vivekananda on 119–20
  Weil and 271, 273–74, 276, 277–78
Kersten, Felix 223, 225–26
King, Martin Luther 320, 321n.31
Klopstock, Friedrich Gottlieb 207
Kluger, Ruth 284
Koehl, Matt 298–99
Koestler, Arthur 5n.13
Köngener Bund 213–14, 221–22
Kosambi, D.D. 4–5
kṣatriyas (warriors) 125, 132–33, 137, 140–42, 187–88, 205–6, 207–8, 218–20, 224–26, 228, 259–60
Kubizek, August 288–89

Langlois, A.S. 49–50, 51, 55–56
Lanman, Charles Rockwell 234–35
Lassen, Christian 42n.20
Leahy, Admiral William D. 279n.42
Leers, Johannes von 296
Lehrer, Tom 253n.42
Lévi, Sylvain 269–70

Lévi-Strauss, Claude 25
language, and national character/identity 53–55
Laws of Manu see *Manu, Laws of*
Lay, Robert 226
Levertov, Denise 302–3, 304–5, 308–9
Lindberg, Mats 320n.30
Luther, Martin 14–15, 39–40, 210, 228–29, 337–38

Macaulay, Thomas Babington 33n.8
McCarthy, Mary 281–82
Macdonald, Dwight 281–82
MacDonald, Ramsay 180
McVeigh, Timothy 296–97
Madhva 3–4, 121–22
Mahābhārata 1n.2, 34–35
Maharishi Maheshi Yogi 303n.4
Maitland, Edward 151
Malamoud, Charles 260n.1
Malinar, Angelika 215n.16
Mallory, Charles 93n.16
Manhattan Project 251–53
Manson, Charles 298–99
Manu, Laws of (*Manavadharmaśāstra*) 40–41, 87n.6, 128–29, 175–76, 190–91
Maritain, Jacques 279–80
Mason, James N. 298–99
Mayo, Katherine 163–64
Mazoomdar, Protap Chunder 111–12
Mendès-France, Pierre 279n.42
Mercer, Dorothy 105
Merton, Thomas 302–3, 304–5, 309–11
Miller, Barbara Stoller 254–55
Mīmāṃsā 70n.44, 122–23, 131–32
Moi, Toni 267n.17
Molino Sanchez, Matilda 320n.30
Monier-Williams, Monier 44–45, 106
Moonje, B.S. 180–81
Mukherjee, Asit Krishna 288

Nabokov, Vladimir 21–22, 37
Namboodiripad, E.M.S. 180–81
National Socialist Kindred 298
National Socialist Liberation Front (NSLF) 298–99
National Socialist White People's Party (NSWPP) 298–99
Native Americans 325–26, 329–30, 331–32
Nazism (National Socialism) 134n.20, 203–4, 205–6, 210–12, 213, 215–17, 219–22, 227, 287–88, 289–90, 294–97, *see also* World War II
Newmark, Helen 247–48
New Mercury, The 288
Nida, Eugene 22–23, 343
Nietzsche, Friedrich 20
Night of the Long Knives 224–25
nirvāṇa 57n.22, 63
niṣkāma karma (desireless action) *see under karma* (action)
Noontide Press 298–99
nothingness 60–63, 65–66
Novalis 18–19
Nyāya-Vaiśeṣika 58–59, 70

occultism 214n.14, 215–16, 222–23
Ohlendorf, Otto 294–95
Olcott, Colonel 85–86
Oldenberg, Hermann 206–7, 208–9
operas, and the *Bhagavad Gītā* 312–33
Oppenheimer, J. Robert 230, 246–58, 324, 325, 327–28, 342–43
Oppenheimer, Kitty 251n.41, 328–30
Orientalism 9–10, 46–47, 301
Otto, Rudolf 206–7, 209–12, 301–2

Patañjali 56–57, 234–35
Phoenix Settlement 161–62, 166–67
Phule, Jotirao 174–75
Pierce, William 296–97
Plotinus 94n.17
Poona Pact 181–83
Portas, Maximiani *see* Devi, Savitri
Pound, Ezra 21
Prabhananda, Swami 303
Pressfield, Steven 340–42
Puccini, Giacomo 321n.32
Purohit Swami 232

Rabi, I.I. 246–47, 258
Radhakrishnan, S. 254–55, 320n.30

Rajan, Balachandra 233–34
Rajasekhariah, T.R. 103–4, 105
Ram, Sant 197–98
Rāmānujā 3–4, 121–22, 123–25
Ramanujan, A.K. 322–23
Ranade, M.G. 174–75
Rastriya Swayamsevak Sangh (RSS) 295
Reed, W.C. 5
re-enculturation 145–46, 152
reincarnation 223
Rexroth, Kenneth 283–84
Ribbentrop, Joachim von 226
Richard, Paul 139–40
Ricoeur, Paul 9–10, 13–14, 24–29
Rockwell, Lincoln 296–97
Röhm, Ernst 224–25
Romanticism 15, 17–18, 53–54, 59–60, 68–69, 76–77, 203–4
Rosenberg, Pamela 324
Rosenzweig, Franz 29n.13
Ross, Andrew 263–64
Roth, Rudolf 234n.13
Roy, Arundhati 166–67
Roy, Rammohun 39–40, 41–42
Rudel, Hans-Ulrich 296
Rukeyser, Muriel 325–26, 334
Ryder, Arthur W. 248–49, 250–51, 254–55

Salt Marsh 163–64
Sāṃkhya 3–4, 50–51, 56, 58–59, 63–66, 70, 78, 102, 188–89
Śaṅkara 3–4, 121–23, 126–27
Sankaracharya, Sri 313n.19
Sanskrit 35–36, 35n.11, 37, 48, 145–46, 217–18
Saraswatī, Dayānand 41–42, 174–75, 191n.24, 196–97, 198
Sarkar, Sumit 137
Sartre, Jean-Paul 262n.7
Sattelmeyer, Robert 233n.9
Satyananda, Srimat Swami 287–88
Savarkar, V.D. 4–5, 135–36, 145–46, 171–72
Schlegel, August Wilhelm 18–19, 21, 41–42, 49, 50–51, 54–56, 57, 63–64, 71, 72, 73–74, 78
Schlegel, Friedrich 17–18, 59–60, 110–11, 204–5, 268n.20, 337–38
Schleiermacher, Friedrich 19–20, 51–52, 337–38
Schopenhauer, Arthur 51–52, 76–77
Schroeder, Leopold von 206–7
Schumann, Maurice 279n.42
Sellars, Peter 322–24, 325–26, 331
Sénart, Émile 275–77
Shankar, Ravi 313n.20
Sharpe, Eric 90
Shri Śivāji Coronation Festival 128–29, 138
Śivāji 127–29, 205
Skorzeny, Otto 296
Society for Ethical Culture 246–47
Sontag, Susan 282
Sorabji, Cornelia 241n.20
Soustelle, Jacques 279n.42
Southey, Robert 87
Spender, Stephen 245
Springmann, Theodor 206–7, 259–60
Srinivas, M.N. 176–77
Stalin, Joseph 331
Stein, Edith 286n.57
Steiner, George 24–25, 264–65, 268n.19, 343
Steiner, Rudolf 213
Swarupananda, Swami 320n.30
Szilard, Leo 252–53

Tagore, Rabindranath 287, 321n.31
Telang, Kashinath Trimbak 42n.20, 186
Teller, Edward 252–53, 327–28
Theosophists 85–86, 149, 150–52, 301–2
Thibon, Gustave 263n.10, 282–83
Thomson, J.C. 41–42, 103–4
Thoreau, Henry David 85–86, 95–104, 110, 233n.9
Tieck, Ludwig 18–19
Tilak, Bal Gangadar 4–5, 120–37, 138, 186n.16, 195, 205
Tolstoy, Leo 321n.31
Tolstoy Farm 161–62
tragedy of action 216–17, 219–20, 226, 228
Transcendentalism 85–86, 88–89, 93, 97, 104, 110, 115, 303
translation 13–30
  and cultural dimension 38

translation (*cont.*)
and democratization 15
and domestic significance 13, 20
and ethics 14, 28–29, 41n.19, 159–60
and German approaches 15–20, 159
incommensurability of terminology and cultures 41, 67–68
as interpretation 85–86, 113, 159
and nationalism 15
one-to-one correspondence 51, 53–55
retaining untranslatable terms 41, 55–56
second-hand translation 160–61
Truman, Harry S. 330n.50
Tukaram 174–75
Turner, Jost 298
Turner, Samuel 76n.55

United States
and neo-Nazis 296–97, 298–99
and Protestant golf metaphors 339–42
and Sanskrit 35n.11
and World War II 251–54
Untouchables *see under* caste (*varṇa*) system
Upanishads 44–45, 89, 115–16, 117–18, 122–23, 231–32

Van Doren, Mark 233n.9
varṇa *see* caste
varṇāśrama 114n.1
Vedānta 3–4, 113–14
Vedanta Society of New York 115
Vedas 39–40, 41–42, 44–45, 115–16, 117–18
Venuti, Lawrence 14–15
violence, justification of
Aurobindo on 137, 140, 141–43, 168–69
Devi on 294–95
Indian nationalism and 4–5, 45–46, 116, 135–36
Merton on 310–11
Savarkar on 4–5, 145–46
Tilak on 124–27, 128–29, 134–36
Vivekananda, Swami 103–4, 114–15, 198

Wagoner, H.H. 232–33
warriors see *kṣatriyas*
Weil, André 260–61
Weil, Simone 259, 260–86, 299–300
Wheelwright, Philip 232–33, 238n.17
Whitman, Walt 103–9
Whitney, William Dwight 234n.13
Wilkins, Charles 9–10, 31–32, 33–35, 36, 37, 38–42, 44–45, 46, 50–51, 63n.37, 150–51
Wilson, Robert 330
Winckelmann, J.J. 17n.3
Wirth, Herman 215–16
Woods, James 234–35
World Union of National Socialism (WUNS) 296–97
World War I 206–7, 241–42, 244n.23, 259–60
World War II 8–9, 241–43, 246, 251–53, 259–60, 279–80, *see also* Nazism (National Socialism)
Wright, W.H. 114–15
Wüst, Walter 215–16, 222

Yeats, W.B. 232
Yoga (school of philosophy) 3–4, 50–51, 56–57, 218–19
yoga 58, 64
Cousin's translation 77
Hegel's translation 62, 67
Humboldt's translation 57, 75–76
Langlois's translation 51
Schlegel's translation 51, 55–56, 75
Tilak's translation 130
as untranslatable 41, 51–52, 67
Wilkins' translation 50–51, 67

Zaehner, R.C. 302, 313n.19
Zündel, Ernst 297–98

Milton Keynes UK
Ingram Content Group UK Ltd.
UKHW052302240823
427312UK00010B/87

9 780198 873488